ENCOUNTERS WITH ANCIENT EGYPT

Imhotep Today: Egyptianizing architecture

UCL
PRESS
Institute of Archaeology

Encounters with
Ancient
Egypt

Titles in the series

Imhotep Today: Egyptianizing architecture

First published in Great Britain 2003 by UCL Press,
an imprint of Cavendish Publishing Limited, The Glass House.
Wharton Street, London WC1X 9PX, United Kingdom
Telephone: + 44 (0)20 7278 8000   Facsimile: + 44 (0)20 7278 80
Email: info@uclpress.com
Website: www.uclpress.com

Published in the United States by Cavendish Publishing
c/o International Specialized Book Services,
5824 NE Hassalo Street, Portland,
Oregon 97213-3644, USA

Published in Australia by Cavendish Publishing (Australia) Pty
45 Beach Street, Coogee, NSW 2034, Australia
Telephone: + 61 (2)9664 0909   Facsimile: + 61 (2)9664 542C

British Library Cataloguing in Publication Data
Humbert, J-M.
Imhotep today – (Encounters with ancient Egypt)
1 Architecture, Egyptian 2 Architecture – Egypt
3 Egypt – History 4 Egypt – Civilization
I Title II Price, C. A.
932

Library of Congress Cataloguing in Publication Data
Data available

ISBN 1-84472-006-3

1 3 5 7 9 10 8 6 4 2

Designed and typeset by Style Photosetting, Mayfield, East Sussex
Email: style@pavilion.co.uk

Printed and bound in Great Britain

Cover illustration: The base of 'Cleopatra's Needle' (ca. 1475 BC) standing within an
Egyptianizing bronze encasement of 1878 AD, on the Thames embankment (© Jean-Marcel
Humbert).

Series Editor's Foreword

This series of eight books derives from the proceedings of a conference entitled 'Encounters with Ancient Egypt', held at the Institute of Archaeology, University College London (UCL) in December 2000. Since then, many new chapters have been especially commissioned for publication, and those papers originally provided for the conference and now selected for publication have been extensively revised and rewritten.

There are many noteworthy features of the books. One is the overall attempt to move the study of Ancient Egypt into the mainstream of recent advances in archaeological and anthropological practice and interpretation. This is a natural outcome of London University's Institute of Archaeology, one of the largest archaeology departments in the world, being the academic host. Drawing on the Institute's and other related resources within UCL, the volumes in the series reflect an extraordinary degree of collaboration between the series editor, individual volume editors, contributors and colleagues. The wide range of approaches to the study of the past, pursued in such a vibrant scholarly environment as UCL's, has encouraged the scholars writing in these volumes to consider their disciplinary interests from new perspectives. All the chapters presented here have benefited from wide-ranging discussion between experts from diverse academic disciplines, including art history, papyrology, anthropology, archaeology and Egyptology, and subsequent revision.

Egyptology has been rightly criticized for often being insular; the methodologies and conclusions of the discipline have been seen by others as having developed with little awareness of archaeologies elsewhere. The place and role of Ancient Egypt within African history, for example, has rarely been considered jointly by Egyptologists and Africanists. This collaboration provides a stimulating review of key issues and may well influence future ways of studying Egypt. Until now, questions have rarely been asked about the way Egyptians thought of their own past or about non-Egyptian peoples and places. Nor has the discipline of Egyptology explored, in any depth, the nature of its evidence, or the way contemporary cultures regarded Ancient Egypt. The books in this series address such topics.

Another exceptional feature of this series is the way that the books have been designed to interrelate with, inform and illuminate one another. Thus, the evidence of changing appropriations of Ancient Egypt over time, from the classical period to the modern Afrocentrist movement, features in several volumes. One volume explores the actual sources of knowledge about Ancient Egypt before the advent of 'scientific' archaeology, while another explores knowledge of Ancient Egypt after Napoleon Bonaparte's expeditions and the unearthing of Tutankhamun's tomb. The question asked throughout these volumes, however, is how far fascination and knowledge about Ancient Egypt have been based on sources of evidence rather than extraneous political or commercial concerns and interests.

As a result of this series, the study of Ancient Egypt will be significantly enriched and deepened. The importance of the Egypt of several thousands of years ago reaches far beyond the existence of its architectural monuments and extends to its unique role in the history of all human knowledge. Furthermore, the civilization of Ancient Egypt speaks to us with particular force in our own present and has an abiding place in the modern psyche.

As the first paragraph of this Foreword explains, the final stage of this venture began with the receipt and editing of some extensively revised, and in many cases new, chapters – some 95 in all – to be published simultaneously in eight volumes. What it does not mention is the speed with which the venture has been completed: the current UCL Press was officially launched in April 2003. That this series of books has been published to such a high standard of design, professional accuracy and attractiveness only four months later is incredible.

This alone speaks eloquently for the excellence of the staff of UCL Press – from its senior management to its typesetters and designers. Ruth Phillips (Marketing Director) stands out for her youthful and innovative marketing ideas and implementation of them, but most significant of all, at least from the Institute's perspective, is the contribution of Ruth Massey (Editor), who oversaw and supervized all details of the layout and production of the books, and also brought her critical mind to bear on the writing styles, and even the meaning, of their contents.

Individual chapter authors and academic volume editors, both from within UCL and in other institutions, added this demanding project to otherwise full workloads. Although it is somewhat invidious to single out particular individuals, Professor David O'Connor stands out as co-editor of two volumes and contributor of chapters to three despite his being based overseas. He, together with Professor John Tait – also an editor and multiple chapter author in these books – was one of the first to recognize my vision of the original conference as having the potential to inspire a uniquely important publishing project.

Within UCL's Institute of Archaeology, a long list of dedicated staff, academic, administrative and clerical, took over tasks for the Director and Kelly Vincent, his assistant as they wrestled with the preparation of this series. All of these staff, as well as several members of the student body, really deserve individual mention by name, but space does not allow this. However, the books could not have appeared without the particular support of five individuals: Lisa Daniel, who tirelessly secured copyright for over 500 images; Jo Dullaghan, who turned her hand to anything at any time to help out, from re-typing manuscripts to chasing overdue authors; Andrew Gardner, who tracked down obscure and incomplete references, and who took on the complex job of securing and producing correctly scanned images; Stuart Laidlaw, who not only miraculously produced publishable images of a pair of outdoor cats now in Holland and Jamaica, but in a number of cases created light where submitted images revealed only darkness; and Kelly Vincent, who did all of the above twice over, and more – and who is the main reason that publisher and Institute staff remained on excellent terms throughout.

Finally, a personal note, if I may. Never, ever contemplate producing eight complex, highly illustrated books within a four month period. If you *really must*, then make sure you have the above team behind you. Essentially, ensure that you have a partner such as Jane Hubert, who may well consider you to be mad but never questions the essential worth of the undertaking.

Peter Ucko
Institute of Archaeology
University College London
27 July 2003

Contents

Note: No attempt has been made to impose a standard chronology on authors; all dates before 712 BC are approximate. However, names of places, and royal and private names have been standardized.

Contributors

Margaret Marchiori Bakos is Associate Professor of History (Ancient and Brazilian) at the Pontifícia Universidade Católica do Rio Grande do Sul and Co-ordinator of the research project 'Egyptomania in Brazil' sponsored by the Brazilian Research Council (CNPq). Her publications include *Facts & Myths of Ancient Egypt* (2nd edition 2001) and 'The Significance of Wine Drinking in Love and Daily Life in Ancient Egypt' (*VI International Congress of Egyptology*, 1993). She received her PhD from the University of São Paulo.

Cathie Bryan is an independent researcher and Paris Correspondent for *Ancient Egypt* magazine. She lectures in London and Paris, and conducts private tours in Paris related to the Egyptian Revival. Her recent publications include 'Napoleon's Savants' (*Ancient Egypt, 2003*), and 'Highlights of the Egyptian Collection at the Louvre' (*Ancient Egypt, 2003*). She holds degrees in Anthropology from Hunter College and in Egyptian Archaeology from University College London, with a Business Masters from New York University.

Beverley Butler is a Lecturer in Cultural Heritage and Museum Studies at the Institute of Archaeology, University College London. Her publications include *Of Ships and Stars: a history of the National Maritime Museum, Greenwich* (1998), 'Egypt: constructed exiles of the imagination' (*Landscapes of Exile and Movement*, 2001, B. Bender and M. Winer (eds)), and *Return to Alexandria: discourses of origins and revivalism* (2001). Her current fieldwork is in Alexandria, Egypt, which also forms the basis for her recently completed PhD.

Izak Cornelius is Professor in Ancient Near Eastern Studies and Chair of the Department of Ancient Studies at the University of Stellenbosch, South Africa. Recent research projects include the iconography of the deities of Syro-Palestine, ancient studies in the digital world, and the ancient world in popular culture. His publications include: *The Iconography of the Canaanite Gods Reshef and Baal in the Late Bronze and Iron Age I Periods (c 1500–1000 BCE* (1994), and "Future of Ancient Studies in the Digital World" (*Journal of Northwest Semitic Languages*, 2000). He has carried out research in Ancient Near Eastern and Old Testament studies at several European universities, having completed his doctorate at the University of Stellenbosch.

Marie-Stéphanie Delamaire has published on 'The Ulysses Myth in the 19th Century' (*Les Dossiers d'Archéologie*, 1999), and on 'William Wetmore Story's Nubian Cleopatra' (*Cleopatra Reassessed*, 2003, S. Walker and S-A. Ashton (eds)). She is currently finishing her Diplome de Recherche at the École du Louvre in Paris.

Chris Elliott has lived in London for the last 25 years, and is currently writing a book on its extensive Egyptian connections. He worked as a Senior Producer in the leisure and reference software industry before qualifying as a teacher. He is a graduate in Communication Studies from Sheffield Hallam University, and has studied Middle and Late Egyptian hieroglyphs at City University, London.

Richard A. Fazzini is Chair of the Department of Egyptian, Classical and Ancient Middle Eastern Art of the Brooklyn Museum of Art, and Director of the museum's archaeological expedition to the temple precinct of the goddess Mut at South Karnak.

He has lectured and published extensively on ancient Egyptian art, history, archaeology, and religious iconography, with a particular focus on the Third Intermediate and Late Periods, and is the author of *Ancient Egyptian Art in the Brooklyn Museum* (1989). He has also written on Egyptomania, both independently and with Mary McKercher. He received his undergraduate and graduate degrees at the City College of New York and the Institute of Fine Arts, New York University.

Katherine Griffis-Greenberg has taught ancient Egyptian Art and History for the University of Alabama at Birmingham UAB Options/Special Studies Division, and has served as a museum consultant on museum exhibit and education issues. She is President and lead consultant for Griffis Consulting, a museum and project development consultancy. She graduated from Birmingham-Southern College, Alabama, and has a Juris Doctor in Law from the Birmingham School of Law. She has recently completed the Masters in Egyptian Archaeology at the Institute of Archaeology, University College London.

John Hamill is Director of Communications for the United Grand Lodge of England, having previously been its Librarian and Curator, and is one of today's foremost Masonic scholars and authors. He has published *The Craft: a history of English Freemasonry* (revised 1994), *World Freemasonry, an illustrated history* (1991, with R. A. Gilbert), and *Freemasonry: a celebration of the Craft* (1992). He is Editorial Director of the Grand Lodge's *MQ magazine*. He graduated from the University of London.

Colin A. Hope is Director of the Centre for Archaeology and Ancient History at Monash University in Melbourne, where he lectures on Ancient Egypt and the Near East. He has excavated in Egypt, Jordan and Syria since 1969, and currently directs excavations at Ismant el-Kharab and Mut el-Kharab in Dakhleh Oasis, Egypt. He is preparing a catalogue of Egyptian antiquities in the National Gallery of Victoria, and has written extensively on Egyptian ceramics of all periods, on the excavations in Dakhleh Oasis, and on Egyptian collections in Australia. He received his PhD from University College London.

Jean-Marcel Humbert is Conservateur Général du patrimoine and Deputy Director of the National Maritime Museum in Paris. Alongside his professional work, which has included positions in several museums such as the Louvre, the Musée de l'Armée and the Musée du Légion d'honneur, he has continued his research on 'Egyptomania', both within the Centre National de la Recherche Scientifique, as well as in many universities and museums around the world. Among his many publications are *L'Egyptomanie dans l'art occidental* (1984), *Egyptomania* (1994, with Michael Pantazzi and Christiane Ziegler) and *L'Egyptomanie à l'épreuve de l'archéologie* (ed., 1996). Apart from his many interests, ranging from Egyptology to 'Egyptomania', from museology to museography, from the military to the nautical, as well as the history of art and the history of opera, he has also been responsible for several exhibitions of 'Egyptomania'. He has a Doctorat d'Etat des lettres et sciences humaines and a Doctorat en histoire (Egyptology) from the University of Paris-Sorbonne.

Richard Lunn is an English and drama teacher in the West Country in the UK. He has long had an interest in Ancient Egypt. He taught himself to read hieroglyphs, before going on to teach them at Yeovil College in Somerset. He gained an Honours degree in English from Exeter University, followed by the Postgraduate Certificate in

Education from the University of Southampton. He has recently completed the Masters degree in Egyptian Archaeology at the Institute of Archaeology, University College London.

Mary E. McKercher is a Research Associate in the Department of Egyptian, Classical and Ancient Middle Eastern Art at the Brooklyn Museum of Art. Since 1979 she has been an archaeologist and photographer for the Brooklyn Museum's Mut expedition in South Karnak. She co-authored with Richard Fazzini the entry on 'Egyptomania' in the *Oxford Encyclopedia of Ancient Egypt* (2000).

Pierre Mollier is currently the Director of the Bibliothèque-Archives-Musée division of the French 'Grand Orient', the most ancient and important Masonic obedience of France. He has published over 30 articles on the history of ritual and symbolism in Freemasonry. He graduated from the Institut d'Études Politiques in Paris and the École Pratique des Hautes Études, University of Paris-Sorbonne.

Clifford Price worked at the Building Research Establishment until 1983, when he was appointed Head of the Ancient Monuments Laboratory, English Heritage. In 1990 he moved to the Institute of Archaeology, University College London, where he is Professor of Archaeological Conservation. His primary research interest is in the conservation of historic buildings and archaeological sites. He has published two books on the conservation of stone, and is on the Editorial Boards of *Reviews in Conservation* and *Journal of Cultural Heritage*. He has advised on the conservation of stone monuments in many parts of the world, including the Osireion at Abydos, Egypt. He received his PhD in Natural Sciences from the University of Cambridge.

Gloria Rosati is a Researcher of Egyptology at the Dipartimento di Scienze dell'Antichità, University of Florence, where she also teaches Egyptology. Her research interests include the Middle Kingdom and particularly the funerary stelae of that period. Recently, she studied and published some hieroglyphic and hieratic papyri from Tebtynis, dating from the Roman period: *Papiri geroglifici e ieratici da Tebtynis* (1998). She has also worked on a sarcophagus of Amenemhet-seneb in Florence, and is now compiling a catalogue of the Middle Kingdom stelae in the Turin Museum. She graduated from the University of Florence.

Alex Werner has been Deputy Head of the Later London History and Collections Department at the Museum of London since 1992. With responsibilities for the Museum's extensive social and working history collections, he was lead curator of the permanent World City Gallery (2001) and the London Bodies temporary exhibition (1998). His publications include *Whitefriars Glass: James Powell & Sons of London* (1995, with W. Evans and C. Ross), *Dockland Life: a pictorial history of London's Docks 1860-2000* (2000, with C. Ellmers), and *London's Riverscape Lost and Found* (2000, with C. Ellmers). He graduated from the University of York and received a diploma in Museum and Art Galleries studies from the University of Manchester.

Helen Whitehouse is Curator of the Egyptian Collections in the Ashmolean Museum, Oxford; her long-standing interest in the western interpretation of ancient Egyptian culture began with a doctoral thesis on Roman Nilotica. Among her publications on the subject is an overview contributed to the Scribner/Macmillan *Civilizations of the Ancient Near East* (1995). Her current research on painting and drawing in Roman Egypt embraces fieldwork in Dakhleh Oasis, as well as the study of illustrated papyri, and recent publications include *The Paper Museum of Cassiano dal Pozzo: ancient mosaics and wallpaintings* (2001). She received her D Phil from the University of Oxford.

List of Figures

COLOUR SECTION

CHAPTER 1

INTRODUCTION: AN ARCHITECTURE BETWEEN DREAM AND MEANING

Clifford Price and Jean-Marcel Humbert

This book is about the use in architecture of designs from Ancient Egypt: so called 'Egyptianizing' architecture. The authors of the various chapters demonstrate that Egyptianizing buildings and monuments have been constructed in many parts of the world, over many centuries. Cavetto cornices, torus mouldings, battered walls, sphinxes, pyramids, obelisks and numerous other features have been used to decorate structures that range from suspension bridges to zoos, from cinemas to reservoirs, and from prisons to museums. These designs have contributed to the creation of an exotic cultural image, and they can convey a range of powerful connotations, open to numerous interpretations. This may explain why the phenomenon of 'Egyptomania' has lasted so long (Rice and MacDonald 2003). Here, we use the term 'Egyptomania' for any kind of approach to anything ancient Egyptian, and 'Egyptian Revival' and 'Egyptianizing' for the use of styles originally from Ancient Egypt (and see below). 'Egyptophiles' are those who are enthusiastic about the subject of Ancient Egypt, and one might wish to coin the term 'Egyptopaths' (in preference to 'Egyptomaniacs') for those who are completely crazy about anything and everything to do with Ancient Egypt!

Visitors throughout history – be they ancient Romans, travellers, missionaries, soldiers of Bonaparte's campaign, or our own contemporaries – have all regarded *in situ* Egyptian architecture with astonishment. The colossal scale of the pyramids and the temples (Werner, Chapter 5; Whitehouse, Chapter 3), the originality of design, the mystery of the hieroglyphs and the exoticism of the sphinxes and zoomorphic gods are all features which have been claimed to characterize and distinguish Ancient Egypt from other civilizations. This has resulted in an enduring fascination with Ancient Egypt that is very much alive today (Jeffreys 2003: 15–16; MacDonald and Rice 2003), and which continues to influence the imagination of architects, designers and those who commission them.

Egyptomania takes many shapes; sometimes it is the shapes themselves (notably pyramids and obelisks) that are considered to be the very essence of an ancient Egyptian identity; sometimes the Egyptian hallmark is manifested in other self-contained structures such as tombs and garden ornaments that draw heavily on Egyptian designs; sometimes decorative elements in supposed Egyptian style are 'bolted on' to non-Egyptian functioning structures; on some occasions entire buildings may be modelled on structures that derive from Ancient Egypt; whilst less permanent structures may be built for exhibitions and for theme parks.

This is not the first book on Egyptomania in architecture. There are several renowned accounts (Curl 1994; Humbert 1989; Humbert *et al.* 1994), but we hope that the present work will prompt the reader to address some of the questions and problems that Egyptomania presents, and that have not, perhaps, been sufficiently addressed before. How, for example, can one determine whether a particular feature is truly derived from Ancient Egypt? And why have Egyptian features been adopted in so many parts of the world, when other cultures have not been adopted in the same way? The book also considers the triggers that have led to the adoption of ancient Egyptian elements into different, relatively recent circumstances. It does not provide all the answers, but we hope that, at least, it does clarify some of the questions.

Manifestations of Egyptomania

Pyramids and obelisks

Both the pyramid (Humbert, Chapter 2) and the obelisk (Hassan 2003a) are less obviously meaningful by their shapes than might first be imagined. For the ancient Greeks the term for the former was a variety of cake, and for the latter a roasting skewer (Harrison 2003). Nevertheless, both have been adopted repeatedly, in designs ranging from monumental architecture to contemporary art, and they are still often seen today. Pyramids, in particular, never cease to be present in cemeteries, appearing in a wide range of sizes and materials. Even during the last 30 years, further testaments to their popularity have been built around the world, such as the entrance to the Louvre in Paris (Humbert, Chapter 2: Figure 2:7), a hotel-casino in Las Vegas (Fazzini and McKercher, Chapter 8: Figures 8:14, 8:15), and pyramid houses, shops and offices in Memphis, Tennessee (Fazzini and McKercher, Chapter 8: Figure 8:13). Clearly, a relationship of some kind has been established between a 'new' and an 'ancient' Egypt. In the USA, this may have continued the early 19th century American need to define new symbols representative of the country (Carrott 1978: 49–50): thus, the river Mississippi became the 'American Nile', with modern incarnations of Memphis, Cairo, Karnak and Thebes all bordering its banks. Perhaps a continuing search for roots, particularly for ancient ones, has been responsible for the pyramid (as well as other objects of Egyptomania) being adopted for the private residence. A striking example is the domestic complex built for the American Jim Onan near Chicago in the 1980s (Fazzini and McKercher, Chapter 8: Figures 8:9, 8:10, 8:11 col. pls.); it is reported (Humbert 1989: 90–91, 120–121) that, much to the amusement of the owner, the structures prompted considerable public interest!

An intriguing question in itself is why the pyramid has become so firmly, and often exclusively, attached to Ancient Egypt in the recent and modern, popular (and, for that matter, Egyptomanic) mind.[1] The Pyramid shape – pyramids – are also to be found in use in ancient Mexico, so why are pyramids not equally associated with Mexico? It is certainly not because the public are aware that diffusionist theories have been rejected by almost all professional archaeologists (Champion 2003: 140–145; Medina-González 2003). Why, then, should Ancient Egypt have a monopoly on the pyramid? The pyramid is, after all, one of the simplest three-dimensional shapes, and it must surely have been known since humankind's very earliest attempts at design. What alternatives are there? A cube, perhaps? But this would require three times the volume of building materials. A sphere? Impossible, with traditional construction techniques. A regular tetrahedron? But this cannot be built so readily with regular blocks of stone, and the square plan of the pyramid lends itself also to the construction of internal chambers.[2] There is little wonder, therefore, that Ancient Egypt seized upon the pyramidal form, and that other cultures have done the same – without necessarily mimicking Egypt.

Similar arguments may be applied to the obelisk, for it is difficult to imagine what other shape might be adopted to create a tall structure with modest use of both natural and human resources. A column with circular cross section, certainly, although the architect Liégeon argued in 1800: "I believe that a column can be regarded only as forming part of a monument, and not as a monument in itself; whereas an obelisk by itself is a monument, since it has never formed part of any other monument" (Archives Nationales, Paris: F/13 630). Almost anything other than an obelisk or a column would be too flimsy or too 'fancy'. Little seems to be understood (even less than with the pyramid) regarding the popular and extensive spread of copies and pastiches of obelisks, despite the fact that there are an enormous quantity and variety of them worldwide (from Australia – Hope, Chapter 9, to Brazil – Bakos, Chapter 13).[3] What does seem certain (Hassan 2003a: 27, 35–36) is that the (partially, at least, assumed) original significance(s) of obelisks for Ancient Egyptians – some kind of connection with the sun, and its giving substance to the sun's rays – was completely ignored once they entered the wider European context. Indeed, in this wider context, from having usually been one of a pair in Ancient Egypt, the obelisk is usually erected alone.

Since the ancient Roman and later diaspora of the obelisk, it has been argued that a solitary obelisk attracts attention and adds originality to an environment. But obelisks have not always served as monuments: they have also functioned as ornamentation on other monuments, such as fountains (Hassan 2003a: Figure 2:25), bridges (Figure 1:1; Whitehouse, Chapter 4: Figure 4:15), tombs, cenotaphs and war memorials; quite frequently they have been used to commemorate an event or a personality. Both as memorials and commemorations, obelisks have served political and social roles in a variety of contexts. For example, they have acted as a dedication to a specific person, such as Chancellor d'Aguesseau in Paris, ca. 1753 (Humbert 1974: fig. 6); to commemorate a technological landmark, such as the 'Canal du Centre' in Chalon-sur-Saône, central France, 1788; and to mark a historical occasion, such as the 1590 battle of Ivry-la-Bataille in Eure, France, 1802; or a notable political event, such as the 'Column of the Jews' in Nice (1826, destroyed in 1863). However, such uses of obelisks as commemorative devices did not automatically exclude perceptions of either charm or a certain esotericism:

> Set in the forest of Crécy, this obelisk occupies the centre of crossroads where three intersecting roads converge. This almost gives the crossroads the aspect of a six-pointed star. However, this star, or Seal of Solomon, is formed of the two triangles of water and fire that are joined at the tops: the symbol of the alchemist's work. This is why, according to Fulcanelli, the obelisk shows our planet subject to 'the combined forces of water and fire', when the end of civilization comes.
>
> (Charpentier 1980: 136)

Figure 1:1   Egyptian bridge, 1828 (restored in 2002), Minturno, Italy (© Jean-Marcel Humbert).

One common denominator in all these contexts, it appears, is that obelisks, whether in a wood or in a city, were adopted to be seen from afar, to attract attention. They can perhaps be taken as the expression of an architectural act designed to be a point of convergence for both eyes and ideas, linking together important events or personalities with significant places.

It is not only 'obelisk-significance' that has changed and developed since ancient Egyptian times, but also the modes of construction employed to create them (even if they have often maintained an ancient Egyptian height and volume). None of the modern interpretations are monoliths, and most frequently they consist of stone blocks that are either rendered or left exposed. They have also been constructed from materials such as concrete, or even bricks.

The 18th century witnessed an important innovation with regard to obelisks, namely their presence as park decoration, which became such a tradition that no 'self-respecting' Anglo-Chinese garden would have been considered complete without one. Typically they were combined with pyramids, Japanese bridges, Chinese pagodas and Gothic ruins, all of which are usually taken today as having represented a desire for exoticism and nostalgia. Several are still visible, dating from the early 18th century (such as the one installed by William Kent in Chiswick House Park in 1736 (Jekyll and Hussey 1927: 146, 149; Wilson 1984: 193–194)) through the 19th century (e.g. the suburban Pallavicini villa park in Pegli, Genoa (Calvi and Ghigino 1999: 39); Rosati, Chapter 12), and they remain popular to this day. Some of such modern examples are gigantic, such as those at Bunker Hill in Boston (68 m high), Washington (169 m; Carrott 1978: 139–141; Fazzini and McKercher, Chapter 8: Figure 8:2), and Buenos Aires (67 m). These are equipped with internal staircases, observation platforms and even lifts.

However, the most important single message deriving from the study of the obelisk that must be appreciated in the context of this book is about changing perceptions of material culture. Such perceptions may alter depending on the nature of the audience as well as the particular historical and political contexts of the occasion. Such differing perceptions may even take on nationalistic glosses. For some people, and perhaps for some nationalities, the obelisk can give an instant reminder of Ancient Egypt. Archaeological artefact and curiosity – even when copied – it became to the French one of the symbols of Bonaparte's expedition, and from the reign of Louis-Philippe it celebrated the fusion of the Egyptian myth with that of the triumphant 'Napoleonic' period. By contrast, there are probably few English people who would associate the war-memorial obelisk on the village green with Ancient Egypt.

In the chapters of this volume the obelisk receives the following epithets: "giving substance to the sun's rays", "the expression of an architectural act designed to be a point of convergence for both eyes and ideas, linking together important events or personalities with significant places", "an instant reminder of Ancient Egypt", a symbol of "justice and truth" (this Introduction); a symbol of "American expansionism", of "liberty enlightening the world", and of "phallus-father, unifying god, military victor, masonic warrior for freedom" (Fazzini and McKercher, Chapter 8); a pointer to both Imperial Rome and to Catholicism, and an indicator of "the rescue of (Egypt's) past from oblivion by Napoleon and indirectly by Champollion", of "the role of France in safeguarding antiquities for 'world heritage'", and of the "association between Napoleon and a pharaoh famed for his military conquests and empire building" (Bryan, Chapter 10); "symbols of (Australia's) gold or other mineral output", "symbols of victory" and of "cultural achievement and aspiration" (Hope, Chapter 9). These many symbolic roles – where they have been correctly identified – are in addition to the obelisk's perhaps less contentious functions as location marker, decoration, commemorative monument or funerary monument.

Thus the obelisks created during the last four centuries have addressed multiple cultural and social needs. Sometimes they have concealed important and original meaning beneath a somewhat banal and repetitive surface; on other occasions, they appear to have been selected simply on grounds of tradition and geometrical efficacy. The very sites chosen to exhibit obelisks are the best sign of their success: in the centre of public places, parks and gardens, and always in a privileged location.

Tombs and funerary monuments

Manifestations of Egyptomania have spread to an extraordinary number of cemeteries throughout the world. Only sometimes do the reasons seem self-evidently clear: the individual who is buried or commemorated in the cemetery may have had very strong links with Egypt during his/her lifetime. Bryan (Chapter 10) cites numerous examples. On other occasions, the reason is less evident, and 'interpretations' have had to make allusions to an assumed human commonality of concern with an afterlife. This is then somehow brought into a derivative relationship with Ancient Egyptians, who are characterized as having concentrated more effort into death and the hope of an afterlife than any other peoples. Such a view recognizes that an assurance of having a correct interment constituted one of the four supreme graces to which all Egyptians aspired. The Egyptian, remarked a Greek, puts more heart into preparing his eternal house than setting up a home (Yoyotte 1959: 288).

Apparently based on such perceptions, many have argued that ancient Egyptian architecture embodies a message of eternity: its grandeur and imposing aspect, its solidity and its durability, all seem appropriate to the job of sending the deceased off to the Kingdom of the Dead. Such perceptions stress that although the belief systems and construction methods of Egyptianizing designers have obviously differed widely from those of Ancient Egypt, the important common denominator is the making of due provision for the afterlife and leaving behind a tangible reminder of 'oneself'. The choice of a funerary obelisk shape is explained – albeit only at a very general level – with reference, for example, to its "stern and severe proportions [which] seem to speak of eternal duration" (Gallier 1836: 381).

The first explicit links between Egyptomania and the Christian realm of death took place in churches. There, funerary monuments quickly consecrated an assimilation of ancient beliefs about an afterlife, by promising the deceased, consciously or not, a happy continuation of life, such as the Ancient Egyptians believed in. Sphinxes could also be used in this sense, decorating the tomb of Guillaume de Bellay (Marquet 1983: 22–23) in 1557, followed in 1563 by the funerary column of the heart of François II (Erlande-Brandenburg 1976: fig. 16); however, from the 17th century onwards it was the obelisk and the pyramid which were the forms most commonly adopted for funerary monuments.

Other Egyptianizing funerary forms that are frequently found include 'chapels' (characterized by their entrance which is often framed by columns and topped by a pediment) and mastabas, which resemble a pylon with a door and perhaps windows, but without any non-Egyptian decoration. Both have a small space in their interior, which allows visitors to enter. These give the impression of being little houses built for the afterlife, and their designs are noticeable for their inventiveness. Further forms include pylons with battered walls and cavetto cornice, stelae, hypogeums, naos shrines (for example, the tomb of Joseph Fourier in Père-Lachaise cemetery, Paris – Bryan, Chapter 10), columns and capitals, winged disks, floral and faunal decoration (notably torus moulding), and (rarely) figures with Egyptian hairstyles and clothes. Such forms were not always restricted to tombs and monuments themselves, but could sometimes also be seen as part of cemetery gateways (e.g. in France (Figure 1:2) – in Italy (Figure 1:3) – in the UK (Elliott *et al.*, Chapter 6) – and in the USA (Fazzini and McKercher, Chapter 8)).

Most published discussions of this subject have failed to consider the extent to which structures and forms must be similar to their putative 'inspirations' before they can, or should, be recognized as their 'derivatives'. Clearly, the forms taken by post-ancient Egyptianizing tombs are very different from those of ancient ones. Externally, with the exception of pyramids – although these are rather small – the former appear inventive, even overly-spectacular, creations. Internally, there are usually no painted decorations describing the life aspired to in the hereafter; and seldom are there sarcophagae or mummies, despite the extremes to which some passionate tomb builders go (Humbert 2001: 165).

Figure 1:2 The entrance to the cemetery of Terre Cabade, Toulouse, France, designed by Urbain Vitry, 1840 (© Jean-Marcel Humbert).

Figure 1:3 The entrance to the cemetery at Alberobello, Italy, designed by Antonio Curri, 1882–1905 (© Jean-Marcel Humbert).

Applied decoration

There are many examples of Egyptomania in the form of applied decoration. France provides three notable examples from the beginning of the 19th century: the façade of the Biteaux house in the rue des Trois-Frères (Humbert 1998a: 101) which is decorated with mummies and sphinxes, the Hotel Beauharnais which includes a neo-Egyptian porch built in 1806–1807 (Humbert 1998a: 98–102; Bryan, Chapter 10), and the 34 Egyptian heads – capped with Nemes – which frame the windows of a house built in Louviers in 1812 (Humbert 1988a: 55). Such appliqué works are independent of the architectural style upon which they are superimposed.

Blocks of flats – no doubt on account of their high visibility – are among those whose Egyptianizing decoration are often most striking. One of the most famous of these is the 'Place du Caire' in Paris, in which the shops were designed to copy a Cairo *souk*. Built by the architect Berthier, and decorated in 1828 with three monumental Hathor-like heads created by the sculptor G-J. Garraud (Figure 1:4; Garraud 1887: 27, 107; Humbert 1998a: 147–153), the heads were surmounted by a characteristic décor ('copied' from *Description* 1809–1828), and the applied frieze depicts chained prisoners with pharaoh in his chariot.

Built in Chicago in 1923, the Reebie storage and removals firm not only reveals the impact that the discovery of Tutankhamun's tomb had on architecture and decorative arts in the United States, but it also introduces the subject of the use of hieroglyphs within Egyptomania. Constructed by Charles S. Kingsley, it was decorated by Fritz Albert with a vast display of polychrome terracottas. Decorative motifs included several full-length statues of Ramesses II (Figure 1:5 col. pl.), representations of the goddess Hathor, winged beetles and hieroglyphic friezes. The colours – pink, coral, fawn, indigo and light green – and golden disks with blue wings and green snakes, appear to shine as brightly today as when they were first created. The influences of 'Art Déco' are clear in the use of many of the symbols – particularly floral designs – while hieroglyphs overtly proclaim the function of the building: "I offer protection to your furniture" (Gordon and Nerenberg 1979–1980).

Figure 1:4   One of three Egyptian heads on the Egyptian flat in the Place du Caire, Paris, designed by G-J. Garraud, 1828 (© Guillemette Andreu).

Legible non-ancient hieroglyphs have also been used in Freemasonry. From the mid-19th century onwards, Masonic lodges increasingly displayed outdoors what had, until then, remained hidden indoors (Hamill and Mollier, Chapter 11). For example, a Masonic lodge was built in 1860 in Boston, England, with a design resembling a pylon. The entrance porch was supported by two palmiform columns, covered with hieroglyphs. The top – following perhaps in the footsteps of the elephant house of the Antwerp zoo (see below) – was engraved with a readable hieroglyphic inscription: "In the Twenty-third year of the Reign of Her Majesty the Royal Daughter Victoria, Lady Most Gracious, this Building was Erected" (Curl 1994: 196).

Such use of hieroglyphs raises important theoretical points that need further consideration. It has to be presumed that very few recent observers of monumentalizing architecture and its associated decorative and other features are able to read the ancient Egyptian script, or its modern counterpart. Yet the current use of hieroglyphs in, for example, the Harrods store (as reported in Elliott *et al.*, Chapter 6) challenges several assumptions commonly made about the nature of 'authenticity'. The urge to make the modern use of the ancient Egyptian script 'accurate' (to the extent and degree that it could have been understood by the ancients)[4] is not necessitated by a wish to have the observer recognize the modern artefact as deriving from the ancient Egyptian. The mere presence of a 'hieroglyphic-looking' script should be sufficient to accomplish this aim; in such a situation, the hieroglyphic marks act as signs (rather than symbols) giving out the same primary message – that a representation or object derives from, or is at least related to, Ancient Egypt. Of course, such an overriding message still allows plenty of secondary flexibility: beyond a general allusion to Ancient Egypt, reference may be to the Egypt of any era, to coded messages, to remote civilizations, or even to the observer's own feelings of ignorance or lack of initiation.

These facts draw attention to the undoubted existence of 'Egyptomania' already in the ancient world; then, as now, the 'exported' stone vessel with hieroglyphic inscription was almost certainly not legible to the vast majority of ancient Near Easterners (and others) who received and probably treasured such products, but their (non-legible) written inscriptions identified them precisely as derived from Egypt (Bevan 2003: 58–59; Sparks 2003: 39–40, 43, 46). The reading of today's hieroglyphic inscriptions must therefore be accepted as a conceit, a message about the elite nature of at least some aspects of Egyptomania. Full comprehension is – as it was in ancient Egyptian times also – a matter of social standing and of a supposed cultural sophistication.

Apart from anything else, these examples have drawn attention to the very significant point that 'Egyptomanic practice' existed already in antiquity. Egyptian designs were repeatedly copied and adapted throughout the Near Eastern and Mediterranean worlds. Few areas of art were untouched; although it is often remarked that it was particularly in architecture and architectural ornamentation that the most astonishing adaptations and uses of Egyptian themes occurred, it is often forgotten that Egyptianizing elements were widespread also in other contexts. Thus, for example, Assyrian palaces housed Egyptianizing ivories, and their walls may have been decorated with frescoes influenced by Egypt (Kaelin 1999).

Perhaps we would do well not to undervalue such ancient Egyptianizing activities and perhaps we should recognize them too as 'Egyptomania' (Maehler 2003), thus reserving the term 'Egyptian Revival' for the Egyptomania of the past 200 to 400 years.[5]

Entire structures

A few recent buildings were designed to be unequivocally in an Egyptian style, and they were often highly conspicuous. In general, their design relies on temple architecture, and uses columns and capitals to alleviate the heavy forms of pylons. In 1805, architect James Randall (1806: pl. xxiv) designed a manor to be built in England in the Egyptian style which "will, I hope, evince it has beauties not inapplicable to this climate, when combined with taste and judgment". The exterior of the house, entirely covered with pseudo-hieroglyphs, was to reproduce all the various Egyptian orders; the pylon was to contain windows, and the central colonnade (which was lowered) was to be used as a terrace. The architect also recommended that the interiors should be decorated and furnished in the same style. Unfortunately it was never built. It was therefore the 'Egyptian Hall' in London, built in 1811 and demolished in 1904 (Medina-González 2003: 109–111; Werner, Chapter 5: Figure 5:3), which was the first building to be built entirely in an Egyptian style.

Between 1889 and 1911, two painters – Virginie Demont-Breton and Adrien Demont – had an Egyptian manor built in Wissant, northern France. The 'Typhonium', as it became known (Bourrut-Lacouture 1990), constitutes an impressive testament to the continued influence of Egyptian architecture on the artistic world (Figure 1:6). Fazzini and McKercher (Chapter 8) describe several private houses in the United States that are built entirely in an Egyptian style. There are also other examples in Europe, with one particularly interesting one in Nice, France (Figure 1:7). Exceptionally, the style has been employed in Australia (Hope, Chapter 9), for example in the brilliant contemporary business architecture at 530 Collins Street in Melbourne.

Figure 1:6   The 'Typhonium' designed in Wissant, Pas-de-Calais, France, by two painters, Virginie Demont-Breton and Adrien Demont (© Jean-Marcel Humbert).

It is only over the past few years that material culture studies have come to recognize the way in which different contexts of use and changes in the 'housing' of objects may alter the very nature of the objects themselves; similarly, changes in such contexts alter the observers' perceptions of an object's 'meaning' or 'significance' (Ucko 2001). Material culture objects are nowadays considered to have – or at least to deserve – their own biographical histories (Gosden and Marshall 1999). The Egyptomania literature has by and large ignored the effects of the difference in environment and situation between Ancient Egypt and the locations of recent pseudo-Egyptian monuments. This feature of modern 'reconstructions' – namely that they often 'reappear' in locations very different from their original contexts – has only been remarked upon when reviewing reactions to architectural innovations (see below). Meanwhile, the two black cats of the Carreras building in London (Elliott *et al.*, Chapter 6: Figures 6:2–6:4; Rice and MacDonald 2003: 8–11) have now been parted: "one now stands[6] outside [Carreras'] Basildon plant [in Essex] ... [, while] the other basks in the sunshine outside the factory of Carreras of Jamaica Ltd at Spanishtown leading a life not too far removed from that of the original domestic black cat" (Carreras 1976) (Figures 1:8, 1:9).

Clearly, it is necessary in the study of Egyptomania to assume as a matter of course that the nature of an Egyptianizing monument can never be 'read' as if it were an ancient construct (however 'accurately' legible its hieroglyphic inscriptions); the 'modern' observer will never be able to perceive the monument in exactly the same way as a member of a past society. This is, of course, just as 'true' for contemporary Egyptian 'Egyptomania' (Butler, Chapter 15; Haikal 2003) as it is for Egyptianizing monuments and activities located elsewhere in the world.

If the perceived meaning of an object may be seen to change according to where it is housed, how it has been curated, or how it is displayed in a museum show-case, the perceived meaning of an Egyptianizing edifice or representation must inevitably change when it is located far from a hot Nile-fed 'landscape'. Landscapes are cultural constructs at least as much as physical reality (Layton and Ucko 1999), and the snow-covered sphinx (Whitehouse, Chapter 4) must have an impact on the viewer that is quite different from that of sphinxes standing out in the Egyptian heat. Indeed, it may be necessary to assume that the snow-based Egyptian monument within a Russian urban context may be morphologically identical to others in Ancient Egypt (i.e. actual ancient objects transported elsewhere for whatever reasons), or morphologically similar to those of the ancient world (i.e. those constructed recently, and especially to be located outside Egypt, and termed

Figure 1:7 Egyptian house in Nice, France, on the Promenade des Anglais, built ca. 1925 (© Jean-Marcel Humbert).

Figure 1:8   One of a pair of black cat statues originally located in Central London, now outside the Tabacofina-Vander Elst Museum, Antwerp, Holland (© Werner Arts). Height of cat 2.53 m.

Figure 1:9   The other black cat statue originally located in Central London, now (2003) outside the Carreras Factory, Spanishtown, Jamaica (© Dorrick Gray).

'Egyptianizing'), but they will have quite different significances (Figure 1:10). No studies exist of the reasons why tourists buy miniature sphinxes in Russia, but they will undoubtedly have little to do with ancient Egyptian concerns (Whitehouse, Chapter 4: Figures 4:6, 4:7). Indeed, a recent (January 2003) exhibition in London, "Winter in St Petersburg", "to celebrate the 300th anniversary of St Petersburg highlights sphinxes in the snow in 'presenting' the city in various artistic approaches – real, imaginative, mystical and 'absolute'".

Egyptomania offers countless valuable examples of similarity of morphology that do not necessarily equate with continuity of 'meaning'. The Russian case alone offers several different contemporaneous perceptions of, for example, 'sphinx': from the snow-covered static and 'monumental' to the portable pocket-sized 'souvenir'. Each will be seen differently by the observer according to whether he or she is in Russia or a visitor returned back home; the 'nature' of the depiction will alter as stories are recounted about the snowy surroundings, and they will almost certainly differ if the tales are accompanied by photographs (Walker 2003).

Even without snow, the symbolism of the sphinx is itself both bewildering and instructive (Curran 2003: 109, 119, 125; Champion 2003: 163–164). The Theban sphinx of Greek legend is probably derived from Phoenician sources, and representations of sphinxes have been found in Assyria and Babylonia. The question remains as to why the 'sphinx' is nowadays so readily associated with Egypt. Is it simply that we *want* to associate it with that particular ancient civilization (for some unknown reason), that we inevitably call to mind the Great Sphinx at Giza, or that we were instructed at

Figure 1:10   Praslov's daughter making use of a sphinx in a way presumably never imagined by the Ancient Egyptians! (1975, © S. Praslov.)

school that sphinxes derived from Egypt? After all, there are presumably few members of the public well enough educated in 'matters sphinx' only to accept those depicted with Nemes headdress as Egyptian, and 'Nemes-less' as non-Egyptian. And why is it that, in ascribing a variety of current, new symbolic meanings to the sphinx phenomenon (Haikal 2003: 134), we appear to have ignored the change of sexual ascription to the sphinx that occurred between Egyptian and classical times? The sphinx of Ancient Egypt was invariably male, and Bryan (Chapter 10) recounts how the male sphinx re-asserted itself in Paris after Bonaparte's Egyptian campaign.

The development of Egyptomania in context

The history of Egyptomania has often been recounted (Carrott 1978; Curl 1982, 1994; Conner 1983; Leclant 1985; Humbert 1987, 1989, 1996b, 1998a, b; Humbert, Pantazzi and Ziegler 1994). Although instances of Egyptomania can be traced right back to Ancient Egypt, it is likely that they were less intensive than the great surge of Egyptian Revival which has taken place in the past 200 to 400 years. Many authors, including several in this volume, have drawn attention to particular events that fuelled the phenomenon; those that are usually highlighted are Bonaparte's campaign in Egypt (1798–1801) and the subsequent publication of the *Description* (1809–1828), Champollion's breakthrough in the decipherment of hieroglyphs (1822), the opening of the Suez Canal (1869), and the discovery of the tomb of Tutankhamun (1922).

Delamaire (Chapter 7) has also drawn attention to the role played by World Exhibitions, whilst others (Hope, Chapter 9; Werner, Chapter 5) have stressed the impetus of museum collections on the development of public interest in, and knowledge about, Ancient Egypt. Each of these occasions, it is correctly observed, sees the creation of new objects, works, and buildings that try to associate the contemporary stylistic heritage with that of Egyptian antiquity. Nonetheless, whilst there is evidently a correlation in some instances, it would be naive to assume that all spurts of Egyptomania can be associated with a particular event. First, we have already referred to examples of the spread of things 'ancient Egyptian' to other parts of the ancient world, and these, by definition, were obviously not triggered by any modern events. Second, several chapters in this volume document the spread, and sometimes copying, of Egyptian objects (and buildings) in widespread areas of the world that had no direct contact with the above mentioned historical events. For example, in several countries including Russia (Whitehouse, Chapter 4), knowledge about Ancient Egypt derived not from Egypt itself and events which took place there, but via travel to Rome. Hamill and Mollier (Chapter 11) state categorically that the discovery of Tutankhamun's tomb "had no impact whatsoever on Masonic design or architecture".

In previous reviews, there is one trigger that appears not to have been given sufficient attention: the role of the individual. The acts of 'Egyptophile' individuals shine out from several chapters of this book: Denon in France (Bryan, Chapter 10), Van der Lingen in South Africa (Cornelius, Chapter 14), Barry in Australia (Hope, Chapter 9), Belzoni and other Freemasons in Brazil and in England (Bakos, Chapter 13; Hamill and Mollier, Chapter 11; Werner, Chapter 5). Other individuals have been the driving force behind the Egyptianizing of individual structures, regardless of external triggers. It could be argued that just a handful of individuals are responsible for much of the Egyptianizing architecture that is to be seen in some non-European areas of the world today.

However, before the contexts of development can be further discussed and assessed in any serious way, it is necessary to explore the contentious methodological point of how 'close' to an original a copy must be to qualify as a replication of an ancient Egyptian design or construction. This is not merely a question of academic definitions, removed from any reality, but a matter of identification and recognition in the world around us. Consider the 'Egyptian House' in Penzance, England (Figure 1:11 col. pl.). Restored in 1973, the building illustrates a number of Egyptianizing features (Figure 1:12 col. pl.): cavetto cornice, torus moulding, pylon form, and so on – and it has rediscovered the bright colours that had originally attracted the public to the historical and geological museum it housed. This, perhaps, is an easy case. After all, the name tells us that there is some connection with Egypt, and the architecture is certainly very different from that of every other house in Penzance. But take another case: a staircase in the Anatomy building of University College London (UCL) (Figure 1:13). The iron balusters incorporate a distinctive design, apparently echoed in the stonework of the building's façade. This example raises some interesting points of detail as well as some of general concern.

There can be no doubt that the building itself was an Egyptianizing construct, and little doubt about the intended ancient Egyptian design of the balusters. We know about its context since it was UCL's Anatomy Professor, Sir Grafton Elliot Smith, who

Figure 1:13   Alleged Egyptianizing balusters in the staircase of the 1930s University College London Anatomy building, Gower Street, London (© Stuart Laidlaw).

was awarded a large grant from the Rockefeller Foundation in 1919 for a new anatomy building (Young 1973). Elliot Smith was the 'extreme diffusionist' who saw all important cultural innovations as having derived from Ancient Egypt (Champion 2003: 127–132). The Professor of Architecture entrusted with the new building was instructed by UCL to consult with Elliot Smith (UCL Minutes, Richard Furter, pers. comm.). So far we are dealing with events and views that can be supported by direct documentary evidence. Now hearsay (Michael Day, pers. comm.) and secondary evidence take over, to recount that it was Elliot Smith who insisted on the design of the building's façade and the internal stairwell bearing ancient Egyptian designs, and that:

> Because of his interest in Egyptology, the architect, who I understand was a Professor Simpson, took an Egyptian model for his building. I wonder how many of you walking down Gower Street have ever noticed this. There is a lot of decoration, all with Egyptian motifs and looking at one entrance it might almost be the doorway of a tomb. Inside there are pillars on the landing and the staircase. I expect many of you have had your hands on the stair rail and never noticed that it had Egyptian motifs too.
>
> (Young 1973: 107)

In other words, the alleged ancient Egyptian inspiration appears to have been largely forgotten until participants in an Elliot Smith memorial conference were reminded of it. Nevertheless, there seems no doubt that both in the 1930s and again in 1972 (when Young spoke the above words), the façade and the fan-shaped baluster designs and pillars were acceptably identified as ancient Egyptian in inspiration and derivation. Not so today, however, when both items are classified as "the most Egyptian-free building I have ever seen – quite astonishingly Egypt-free for a 1930s building. Every single detail in it is derived from ancient Greek art" (Stephen Quirke, pers. comm.). So in 2003, classical – not Egyptian (or even Egypto-classical) – in derivation!

This cautionary story should warn us against assuming that ascriptions of derivations are always reliable, or that such identifications remain static. On the contrary, nowadays it is clear that such interpretations change over time. Indeed, Tanner (2003: 127–132) has documented the difficulties in reliably determining which "formal details of the monumental Doric temple" can be determined as ancient features originally derived from Ancient Egypt, which were adapted and adopted from there by the Classical World, and which were "indigenous Greek". "Doric columns like Egyptian columns have sixteen flutes and they share similar proportions." Clearly it may be no easy matter to decide on the 'authentic' nature of an 'Egyptianizing' design, and great caution is therefore necessary in ascribing origins and originating causes of Egyptomania.

Perhaps the best example of the problems of authenticity is provided by hieroglyphics. As seen above, several authors in this book refer to the use of Egyptian hieroglyphs to spell out a contemporary message: a message that could not possibly have been written in Ancient Egypt, since the people to whom the message refers were not to be born for several thousand years. Nevertheless, the hieroglyphs themselves can be considered 'authentic' in the sense, and to the degree, that they could have been read by somebody in Ancient Egypt.

Clearly, the situation is complex; even when an object on 'display' to the public is an original ancient Egyptian construct, this cannot of itself be thought of as

'Egyptianizing'. There is nothing Egyptianizing about the Luxor obelisk in the Place de la Concorde in Paris (Hassan 2003a: Figure 2:39), for example. The ancient obelisk was re-erected on a pedestal that depicted its transport and re-erection, but no Egyptian designs were incorporated into the pedestal or its immediate surroundings despite many proposals to do so. Cleopatra's Needle in London (Hassan 2003a: Figure 2:5), on the other hand, whilst also an ancient obelisk, was set on a base with designs derived from Ancient Egypt (see cover illustration), with flanking bronze sphinxes and nearby benches incorporating features of camels and sphinxes. The added ornament is Egyptianizing; the obelisk itself is 'merely' Egyptian.

The presence of hieroglyphic-looking marks (even if invented, and not interpretable) may render an object 'authentic' to the (ignorant) observer. Similarly, to many casual observers it is the very Egyptianizing designs of the bronze sphinx or sculpted bench that may confer 'authenticity' on the obelisk itself; so it may be the 'modern' designs that confer the accolade of 'genuine' or 'real' on the 'ancient' object or depiction. The use of hieroglyphs can add to this. Nor is it any longer clear today what exactly constitutes 'authenticity' – certainly not public awareness or enjoyment of an artefact – since there is good reason to believe that casts can often take the place of the 'original'. Humbert *et al.* (1994: 356) quote the public reaction to copies of original artefacts, on display at the 1867 Universal Exhibition in Paris:

> One never tires of looking at these wonderful stelae. They are authentic because they were cast directly from the monuments themselves and coloured under the watchful supervision of Mariette Bey[7] by an historical painter.

Although it is probably true that such appreciation of 'copies' (casts or not) no longer applies today, the point to be realized is that concepts and standards of acceptability are also not static, so that what may be considered acceptable (or even 'authentic') at one time may be considered *ultra vires* at another.

Rosati (Chapter 12) refers to copies of Egyptian lions in Florence on the ramp to the Campidoglio in Rome, reproducing even the minutest details, such as a small hole on the mouth. But the lions in Rome did not have this hole originally – it is the outlet of a small water pipe that was added in the 16th century when the lions were turned into fountains! Any clear distinction between 'authentic' and 'copy' becomes more and more difficult to demonstrate or sustain.

The demand for accuracy and detail is a complex matter, not least in the context of Egyptomania. If it is accepted that at least a significant part of Egyptomania is to do with enjoyment of its exuberance, its acceptance of the flight of fancy, and its sheer fun, then it may appear amazing that accuracy and 'authenticity' of copied depiction should continue to have any place when the contexts of depiction – a flight of escalators, a cinema, an elephant house in a zoo – could themselves self evidently have nothing to do with Ancient Egypt.

Egyptianizing symbolism

Many of the contributors to this volume refer to the symbolism of Egyptian designs. Indeed, earlier in this Introduction we ourselves referred to the symbolism of obelisks. Firth (1973: 15) stated that "the essence of symbolism lies in the recognition of one thing as standing for (re-presenting) another, the relation between them being that of concrete to abstract, particular to general". The word 'recognition' is crucial: the observer must be aware of, and thus be able to recognize, the relationship between the concrete symbol and the abstract concept that it stands for, or else the symbolism is lost. The same is true of a sign, except that in the case of a sign the observer is explicitly told what the sign represents. A red traffic light, for example, means 'stop', as set out in national and international traffic codes. The symbolism of the colour red, on the other hand, may be less well defined, as shown by Fougasse and McCullough (1935: 45) in their light-hearted introduction to the new-fangled practice of motoring:

1	Why is a red light used for danger?
Answer:	Because a bright colour that cannot be confused with anything else is essential.
2	Why is a red light used for advertising restaurants, cinemas, drinks, shops, pills and everything else?
Answer:	See above.

We might parody this by asking why, if a sphinx may stand for the concepts of protection and safety (Bryan, Chapter 10), it was also used in Ancient Egypt for kingship (Khafra), deity (Horemakhet), the owner of a department store (Elliott *et al.*, Chapter 6), or can even be found on the sign-board for a brothel (boulevard Edgar-Quinet, Paris). This is all very well provided that everybody understands and knows the 'code'. But symbols do not necessarily mean the same to all observers (e.g. in South Africa – Cornelius, Chapter 14). Later in this chapter, we show how the might of Egyptian architecture may frighten the villain whilst reassuring the upright citizen. Symbolism, like beauty, could be said to vary according to the eye of the beholder.

Here indeed we may be confronting another of the weaknesses of the current literature on Egyptomania. There is little to suggest that there has been adequate consideration of the target of the Egyptianizing message. There often appears to be an underlying assumption that the symbolism of Egyptomania is universally understood (Rice and MacDonald 2003). Yet who has not been baffled on occasions by an advertisement that seems completely meaningless, and that obliges one to assume that the significance must be more apparent to those of a different age or social group. It must similarly be assumed that some Egyptianizing designs are aimed at the initiated, the *cognoscenti*, whilst others are intended for a broader audience. Thus, Hope (Chapter 9), Hamill and Mollier (Chapter 11) and Rosati (Chapter 12) describe Egyptianizing decoration and ornament that have particular significance only to Freemasons, whilst Werner (Chapter 5) and Delamaire (Chapter 7) describe exhibitions which aimed to attract millions of ordinary people. And what should one conclude about the intended audience of a recent Chinese postage stamp issue (Figure 1:14 col. pl.) which in October 2001 included one stamp depicting Tutankhamun's golden mask? To the future historian of Egyptomania, this might be taken as further evidence of the worldwide impact of the 1920s famous tomb discovery. In fact, the stamp refers to collaboration in trade between modern China and modern Egypt (Wang Tao, pers. comm.).

Another of the interesting features of the study of Egyptomania has already been alluded to above, namely the necessity to assume different interpretations of symbolism and meaning as the Egyptianizing motifs have had their contexts changed. This has been partially recognized, at least in discussions of the success or otherwise of Egyptianizing activity, as advertising. As Leigh Hunt (1861: 43; Beevers 1983: 84) said:

> Egyptian architecture will do nowhere but in Egypt. There, its cold and gloomy ponderosity ('weight' is too pretty a word) befits the hot, burning atmosphere and shifting sands. But in such a climate as this, it is worth nothing but an uncouth assembly. The absurdity, however, renders it a good advertisement. There is no missing its great lumpish face as you go along. It gives a blow to the mind, like a heavy practical joke.

But such a recognition still leaves countless questions to be answered regarding the way that we can ever attempt to 'know' what symbolic weighting was intended by the artist/commissioner concerned. The potential pitfalls are huge, as evidenced by the initial decoration of a Homebase store with Egyptianizing designs, and their subsequent destruction (Elliott *et al.*, Chapter 6: 115–116). Originally a development project, the Egyptianizing theme was one among several suggested by the developer, Ian Pollard, and selected by a special committee set up by Sainsbury's. Pollard perceived the chosen Egyptian focus as symbolizing longevity and the forward progression of human creativity. At the same time the overall concept was to provide a highly decorative milieu for potential shoppers at what was to be a Sainsbury's

Homebase store. The sale of the building to Sainsbury's had been concluded with the Egyptian element overtly to the fore – indeed, special marketing strategies had been developed, involving touristic flights to the Nile and its sights/sites. After it had been completed, and indeed its entrance furnished with a sculpted sphinx, this conceptual architectural and design 'dream' was shattered on the instruction of Sainsbury's Chairman, Sir John (now Lord) Sainsbury, who had the decorated pillars pulled down and the carved sphinx removed. However, what do still remain are a few entrance pillars (Elliott *et al.*, Chapter 6: Figure 6:11) and a frieze of Egyptian relief carvings of gods and their symbols (Elliott *et al.*, Chapter 6: Figure 6:12 col. pl.). What also is there to be seen by the observant viewer is the 'DIY'-inspired joke of the alteration of the original ankh sign carried by Seth to depict a power drill in its place (Figure 1:15; Richard Kindersley, Ian Pollard, pers. comms.). Additionally, it is alleged

Figure 1:15   Homebase building: Carved power drill in the hands of the god Seth (© Richard Kindersley).

that the hieroglyphic inscriptions received a last-minute addition in the form of a response to the Chairman's actions – of course, transformation of previously created representations to fit current needs by re-inscription had already occurred in Ancient Egypt (Wildung 2003)!

Conclusions

It is extraordinary that Egyptomania has gripped so many cultures around the world, over such a long period of time. It is still not understood why Egypt, in particular, has attracted so much attention. There is an undeniable fascination with Ancient Egypt's zoomorphic deities, its startling use of polychromy and the colossal scale of its monuments (Whitehouse, Chapter 3), but other ancient cultures also have the ability to inspire awe and wonder. What is weird about Egyptomania is that it has spread to so many areas where function has no part to play: zoos, escalators, cinemas, suspension bridges, do-it-yourself stores, war memorials.

Nevertheless, it is true that there are some instances of Egyptomania where the link to Egypt is clear. Hamill and Mollier (Chapter 11), for example, establish the reasons behind Freemasonry's widespread adoption of Egyptian designs. It is understandable, too, that the veterans of Bonaparte's Egyptian campaign should be buried in Egyptianizing tombs (Bryan, Chapter 10). But there are many instances where the link is not self-evident, and where it may be easy to fall into the trap of applying one's own assumptions and interpretations, regardless of the evidence.

Hopefully, not everything needs to be thought of as contentious in the interpretation and understanding of Egyptianizing activities. Thus, there is no reason to doubt some of the more conventional views of the functions of Egyptomania. These include an educational function, often linked to recreational enjoyment. Egypt has often been regarded as a land of wisdom, knowledge and culture (Ucko and Champion 2003), and the supposed nature of the Alexandria library, for example, is still referred to today with respect and admiration (Butler, Chapter 15). Thus, it is hardly surprising to find an Egyptianizing style often to the fore in designs and decorations of museums, libraries and schools.

A link to recreation can be most easily observed in the presentation of some zoos. One of the most beautiful is preserved in Antwerp (Figure 1:16 col. pl.), where the elephant house was designed in the shape of an Egyptian temple. Fortunately preserved, and remarkably restored in 1988, it shows the extraordinary polychromy that such a building inspired. Based on the temples of Philae, and built by Charles Servais in 1855–1856, it is painted on both the inside and outside. Floor mosaics resemble Egyptian flora, and above the entrance, a dedication translated into hieroglyphs recalls: "In the year of the Lord 1856, under His Majesty the King, sun and life of Belgium, son of the sun, Leopold I, this house was made to delight Antwerp and to educate its inhabitants" (*Monumenten en Landschappen* 1988; Zoo d'Anvers 1988). The pedagogic goal was copied by other zoos (the flamingo house in Hamburg and the ostrich house in Berlin) and was the inspiration for the pavilions of several World Fairs. More recently, as recalled by Fazzini and McKercher (Chapter 8), other zoos, particularly in the United States (Memphis, Detroit), have appropriated this concept. World Fairs were both the initiators and the heirs of this pedagogic concept.

Egyptianizing exhibits, museums and World Fairs gave rise to even more didactic and recreational uses: leisure, fun or theme parks,[8] where Egyptianizing motifs were fully in evidence. For example, 'The Crypt of the Pharaohs' in Paris' Luna Park (Bryan, Chapter 10: Figure 10:9) had the appearance of a true film set: beside the counter, a small sphinx attracted the visitor towards a monumental pylon that leant against an artificial rock. Topped by two obelisks, it also included a staircase bordered by smaller sphinxes that led to a monumental sphinx, and it was entirely decorated with scenes inspired by Ancient Egypt and painted in bright colours (Humbert 1998a: 142–143). Other impressive examples exist in France (Walibi Schtroumpf at Metz and Walibi Rhône-Alpes at Chambery) and Spain (e.g. at Benidorm (Humbert, Chapter 2: Figure 2:10 col. pl.)). And movie theatres became modern 'palaces of dreams' for Egyptomania (e.g. Sid Grauman's Egyptian Theatre in Hollywood), a medium which continues today.

Another area in which Egyptomania has undoubtedly been used, and continues so to do, is in advertising and propaganda. As has already been noted, advertising was occasionally expressed in hieroglyphic messages – despite the fact that only very few could be expected to be able to understand them. It appears that the advertising messages were sometimes even less self-evident.

Charles B. Cooper constructed a building in Philadelphia in 1847 (Carrott 1978: 71, 102), the Egyptianizing decorations of which were made of cast iron. This supposedly referred to the owners' trade, whilst attracting the attention of customers to the product's solidity and longevity – assumed by some commentators to be symbolized by Egyptian architecture. The architectural decoration of some pharmacies similarly refers to medicine and to ancient Egyptian beliefs. The period between 1820 and 1850 appears to be marked by the appearance of such dual meanings and advertisements. Some of today's advertising is at least as ambiguous as earlier examples (Schnitzler 2003). Unfortunately, we still await in-depth analysis of how such advertising motifs, drawn from a supposed ancient Egyptian repertoire and iconography, are identified and selected by advertisers.

At a presumably rather superficial level of analysis, it has often been assumed that the occasional use of Egyptianizing architecture for suspension bridges and railways was to allay concerns over innovative structures or alarming inventions. In these cases, Egyptian art was seemingly utilized to reassure people by its reputation for, once again, solidity and longevity. These intentions can seldom be found stated overtly by designers or architects and it is difficult to 'prove' them, although the presence of Egyptianizing decoration suggests that the pylons and columns were not adopted for structural reasons alone.

It is also often postulated that reassurance against fear may also have been behind the association between Egyptianizing architecture and railway stations. But here, once again, it is difficult to find hard evidence to demonstrate any deliberate intention that travellers, apprehensive of the new mode of transport, would be reassured by the ancient, massive and solid architecture, or that their attention was to be diverted away from fear by the surprise novelty of a station's architecture. In 1836, and for the first time, an English architect, William J. Short, proposed an Egyptian-style station. In his presentation, Short based his choice on the aesthetic aspect, beauty, elegance and grandeur of Egyptian architecture, without neglecting the economic benefits of simple forms and the absence of ornate decoration (Carrott 1978: 122, 164, 193). Reassurance against fear received no mention.

Whilst it is possible that the solidity and durability of Egyptian architecture might give reassurance, its awesome might, its deities and its bizarre creatures – half human, half animal – could, it is often assumed, equally inspire fear. This has been suggested as the motive behind the use of Egyptianizing designs for many prisons and court houses. James Elmes, an English architect, conceived an Egyptian-style law court and prison which would, according to him, represent immortality, sacred solemnity and undeniable grandeur (Honour 1955: 244). The concept – on both an intellectual and architectural level – was popular throughout the 19th century, in particular in the United States, where police stations too were designed to frighten gangsters yet reassure the respectable middle-class.

Whatever the ongoing unknowns about Egyptomania and its Egyptianizing architecture, there can be no doubt of its efficacy in creating an impression. This is in part revealed by its success in gaining an extensive presence within cemeteries and the other localities reviewed above, but also, sometimes, by the overt opposition to its overall architectural features. For example, architect A. C. Busby (1808: 11; Beevers 1983: 83) deplored the Egyptian style:

> Of all the vanities which a sickly fashion has produced, the Egyptian style in Modern Architecture appears the most absurd: a style which, for domestic buildings, borders on the monstrous. Its massy members and barbarous ornaments are a reproach to the taste of its admirers; and the travels of Denon have produced more evil than the elegance of the engravings and splendour of his publication can be allowed to have compensated.

And, much later, the National War Memorial project proposed by Sir Franck Baines in London (1920) was denounced as:

> Dreadful ... Of all the styles suited to London, the Egyptian is the most unfit and alien; and the bigger it might be, the more vulgar it would be. It is heavy, passive, sulky; it is the style of a caste-ridden people; it requires the sunlight and the desert; it would show the dirt; it proclaims complete indifference to the hard estate of the poor.

> (*The Builder*, 23 July 1920: 93; Curl 1994: 210)

A more recent example, in France, is the glass pyramid in the courtyard of the Louvre (Humbert, Chapter 2). Its construction was controversial, and even at its opening it seemed incongruous to some observers. However, much of the initial opposition to the pyramid is now forgotten (Humbert 1998a: 190–191); it has become part of the Parisian 'landscape' and a recent English guidebook describes it as "popular" and "a star feature" (Gray 1997: 122, 123).

Such occasional criticism should not lead us to believe that architectural Egyptomania was badly received by everyone. The opposite is true. The taste for all things Egyptian appears anchored in western culture, and Egypt still appears omnipresent in the collective subconscious (Rice and MacDonald 2003). Egyptian architecture is the architecture of dreams, of imagination, of the exotic, and of a yearning for another time, another place. At the same time, it always appears to be expressing something more, and its presence certainly conveys very diverse ideas. As is shown throughout this volume, Egyptianizing architecture is not a matter of simple and meaningless copying. It carries complex meanings, translating ideals that are supposedly inspired by Ancient Egypt, albeit sometimes mixing esotericism and Freemasonry. Furthermore, its capacity to integrate art from all periods highlights its power. Since the 16th century, Egypt has never ceased to inspire western architects and, with time, it has significantly broadened its influence throughout the world.

Excitingly, the Egyptianizing process has not stopped: nor can it conceivably be classified as static, its manifestations being continuously modified and 're-created' through opera (Humbert 2003), film (Lupton 2003; Serafy 2003) and now television (Schadla-Hall and Morris 2003). Sometimes this ongoing process may seem quite preposterous – such as the proposal to "refurbish" ancient Egyptian obelisks scattered around the world by "refurnishing them with golden pyramidions to make them symbols of a unifying internationality" (Rupert Hillinger, pers. comm., 27/12/2000). But not preposterous at all is the Unesco effort regarding Alexandria, which Butler (Chapter 15) describes as the concept of Ancient Egypt being returned to modern Egypt. She sees the international activity "as an emancipatory force within Egypt itself ... encouraging a more subtle history of Egypt's encounter with the 'other'". We are thus encouraged to rejoice that the architecture of Ancient Egypt is far from being dead.

Notes

1   This may indeed be a relatively recent 'attachment', for there is some evidence (Matthews and Roemer 2003: 18) that when, in 10 BC, Caius Cestius had a tomb erected for him by his heirs in the shape of a pyramid, this may have had more to do with the representation of the 'exotic', rather than any intention of being seen to be buried as a pharaoh.

2   It does, nonetheless, seem surprising that there has been so little monumental use of the regular tetrahedron. Many authors have written of the purity and simplicity of the pyramid, with its four triangular sides and square base. It could be argued that the regular tetrahedron, comprising only four equilateral triangles, has at least as strong a claim to simplicity and symmetry.

3   Sometimes obelisks may serve as fountains, especially in the south of France and in Italy; sometimes they serve purely as decoration on churches (for example, the exceptional Dessau-Waldersee bell-tower in Germany (Alex and Kluge 1994: 59)) and bridges; or they may be used to furnish tombs and cemeteries (Henry [1852]: folder). Others can be found on classical façades and are thus once again in pairs, though often at a distance from each other. Others – halfway between obelisk and pyramid – were used as landmarks, such as the one built in Montmartre in 1736, and used to fix the Paris meridian.

World War I gave rise to an international generation of highly diverse commemorative obelisks (Coombs 1983: 18, 40, 44, 48, 59, 60, 91, 94, 96, 97, 103, 110, 124, 142, 149, 153), often lower and more massive than previous examples, and this concept was maintained after World War II.

4   As is the case with the title pages of each chapter in all the books in this present series.

5   The terms 'Egyptian Revival' and 'Egyptomania' are often used as synonyms (e.g. Assmann 1997: 17–19; Curl 1994; cf. Brier 1993; Hornung 1994; Humbert et al. 1994; Iversen 1993; Morenz 1968; Pevsner and Lang 1968; Staehelin and Jaeger 1997; Whitehouse 1995), but there have also been suggestions that one should be more specific. Hornung (1994: 1–2) uses the term '*Ägyptenrezepion*' but excludes matters such as films and advertisements. In a later study Hornung (1997: 333) is even more critical and reacts against what he calls a confusion of terminology; he makes a clear distinction between the 'Egyptian Revival' – the continuing use of Egyptian motifs in art and architecture, and in literature, music and religion – and the more popular 'Egyptomania', which is part of what he terms the

'periphery' as manifested in the enthusiasm for things Egyptian after the discovery of the tomb of Tutankhamun. He adds '*Ägyptosophie*' to designate the tradition of esoteric wisdom as represented by Hermes Trismegistus and its modern developments. Humbert (1989: 10–12, 1994: 21) also warns against the indiscriminate use of the term 'Egyptomania'. Brier (1993: 41), on the other hand, uses the term 'Egyptomania' to include everything which reflects the universal fascination with Egypt, including those in ancient times.

6   Carreras' Basildon factory no longer exists (March 2003); the black cat is now in Antwerp, Holland (Figure 1:8).

7   The French Egyptologist Auguste Mariette (1821–1881) was the first to have the idea of setting up an 'Egyptian park' at the 1867 Paris Universal Exhibition. This space comprised four buildings, one of which was an ancient temple preceded by an alley of sphinxes and a triumphal entrance (Humbert 1998a: 124–132, 2002: 289–309). Mariette also designed an Egyptian house for the 1878 Universal Exhibition (Humbert 1988a: 132–133). After his death, the concept he had pioneered was continued and, in 1889, as part of the 'Histoire de l'habitation' retrospective, a small temple adjoined the 'Old Cairo street' not far away from the modern Egyptian house designed by Charles Garnier (Humbert 1988a: 133–139).

8   The oldest theme park to be decorated in an Egyptian style was created in Paris. It was in 1818 that the 'Egyptian Promenades' opened. Their principal attraction was the 'Egyptian mountains' which were inspired by the Russian roller coasters that were popular at the time. The entrance porch to the ride was covered by a cavetto cornice and a winged disk. The main building was an attempt to reconstruct an Egyptian house, the interior of which included a "vast Egyptian-style lounge" (Humbert *et al.* 1994: 321–322). It was demolished in 1825 during the construction of the present rue du Delta.

Acknowledgments

We are grateful to Professor Izak Cornelius for the analysis of terms as presented in n. 5, above, and to Professor Michael Day for the reference to J. Z. Young's account of the features of UCL's Anatomy building. Much of our information concerning Homebase derives from conversations between the Series Editor and Richard Kindersley and Ian Pollard, to whom we are very grateful.

CHAPTER 2

THE EGYPTIANIZING PYRAMID FROM THE 18th TO THE 20th CENTURY[1]

Jean-Marcel Humbert
(translated by Daniel Antoine and Lawrence Stewart Owens)

"From the top of these pyramids, forty centuries look down upon you ..." Whether or not Bonaparte really uttered these words on the Giza plateau, the pyramids have aroused admiration and have fascinated travellers throughout history. Dominique Vivant Denon too was struck by their enormous size and purity of form when he first saw them at the beginning of Bonaparte's Egyptian campaign. In his works (Denon [1802] 1990), he describes better than anyone the impact they had:

> My soul was moved by the great spectacle of these great objects; I regretted seeing the night extend its veils over an image that dominates both eyes and imagination ... The precision of the pyramids' construction, the inalterability of their form and construction, and their immense dimensions, cannot be admired sufficiently. One could say that these gigantic monuments are the last link between the colossi of art and those of nature.

A perfect shape with unusual powers

Egyptian pyramids are certainly one of the most perfect and extraordinary shapes ever created by humans (Schadla-Hall and Morris 2003). The Giza examples are truly exceptional in terms of their enormous size – which makes them visible even from the moon! For five centuries, pyramids have influenced not only visitors to Egypt, but also those who have never seen them for themselves but have heard of them or seen poor reproductions (Humbert 1997b: 32–33). Bossuet (1681 quoted in Kérisel 1991: 8), whilst emphasizing the ostentation of Egyptian pyramids, admired their solidity, regularity, simplicity and 'ordered' yet bold design. Hegel (quoted in Kérisel 1991: 7) regarded the pyramid as being the building *par excellence*, the balanced form that "offers us, in all its simplicity, the very image of symbolic art itself". In 1931, Alain (quoted in Kérisel 1991: 9) also wondered if the pyramid was not "the secret model for every single building, or the inevitable outcome or aim of architectural form".

Despite this, however, the pyramid has always remained an incomprehensible concept for much of the general public: why build such spectacular structures? What became of the rulers who were buried there? How many men were sacrificed in order to build both accurately and quickly? These and many other questions have been posed, including whether or not the pyramids were made of artificial stone, were flown from another planet, are oriented in order to supply them with supernatural power, are home to supernatural forces, or – of course – they conceal fabulous treasures.

Confusion of shape

Because most people know about the Egyptian pyramids by hearsay or through representations rather than by personal experience, they might be said to be more dream than reality. Until the 18th century, engravings of the pyramids were highly inaccurate and seldom displayed their correct proportions (e.g. Fischer von Erlach's (1721: fig. 11) pointed structures). Moreover, and until Bonaparte's campaign, the pyramid was mainly known from a first century AD Roman copy, the pyramid of Caius Cestius,[2] in Rome. This tomb – far more modest in dimensions than its Egyptian ancestors – had a distinctive tall, slim shape (Figure 2:1 col. pl.), and became the primary model for all the pyramids built in the west between the 18th and 19th centuries. For example, Piranesi (see Werner Chapter 5; Whitehouse Chapters 3 and 4, all this volume) used it in his decorations for the 'Café des Anglais', Piazza di Spagna in Rome (1760), Hubert Robert (Whitehouse Chapter 3, this volume; Humbert *et al.*

1994: nos. 26, 82–83) in his 'Ronde de Jeunes Filles autour d'un Obélisque' (1798), and Jean-Michel Moreau le Jeune (Humbert *et al.* 1994: nos. 74, 148) in his 'Funérailles d'une Reine d'Egypte' (1793). The majority of 'Grand Tour' artists passed on the pyramid's characteristic form, with the result that there was confusion between Egyptian and Roman pyramids, and it was the Roman form – albeit while retaining the Egyptian emotional association – that was to experience both rejuvenation and universal applause.

Indeed the pyramids built by S. Bridgeman (1739) in Stowe, by Charles Cameron at Tsarskoye Selo (between 1770 and 1780; Whitehouse Chapter 3, this volume; Lemus 1984: ill. 133; Gladkova *et al.* 1961: 126), by Schwarzkopf in the avenue of the tombs in the Wilhelmshöhe Park close to Kassel (1775) (Figure 2:2), by Carmontelle (Carrogis 1779: 9–10) at Monceau (Paris, 1779) and Potsdam, 1791 (Baltrusaitis 1967: 52–54) were

Figure 2:2   The pyramid in the Wilhelmshöhe Park, Kassel, designed by August Daniel Schwarzkopf ca. 1775 (© Jean-Marcel Humbert).

all still using the same Roman model. It was only many years later that smaller and more pointed pyramids (based on the private tomb pyramids of Deir el-Medina of the nineteenth and twentieth Dynasties, or the Meroe pyramids of the Sudan (Fuller 2003: Figure 11:2; Wildung 2003: 74–75) became known to both artists and the general public.

The Egyptianizing pyramid: an attempt at a typology

The pyramid occupies a unique place in the field of 'Egyptomania'. Egyptianizing pyramids differ in dimensions, purpose, and appearance from those of their great ancestors.

Many types of Egyptianizing pyramids exist, varying in shape (according to period), dimensions, whether hollow or filled, with or without doors. Variety can be found also in their coatings and colours, decoration (inscriptions, hieroglyphs), and even whether they were intended as monuments, factories, ice-houses (Martin 1997), tombs, or Masonic displays. Unlike the obelisk or the sphinx, the pyramid is the most difficult of all the ancient Egyptian art creations to replicate or adapt and, for this reason, pyramids tended to be created in significantly reduced size.

Of course, although still keeping to Cestius' proportions, there are exceptions; for example, that of Alexandre Brongniart – built in the Maupertuis Park around 1775 – is much bigger than its contemporaries. Furthermore, it is distinctive in having one of its sides converted into an entrance, with the opening constructed from four Doric columns surmounted by a flattened arch (Anon. 1977: nos. 225A–E, 136, ill. p. 12; Anon. 1986: nos. 357, 363, 364 and 366). Other examples of more faithful copies of the Giza pyramids (albeit in reduced dimensions) appeared in paintings from the mid-19th century onwards, intended to evoke the magic of Ancient Egypt (e.g. Sir John Poynter's 'Israel in Egypt', 1867 – Rice and MacDonald 2003: Figure 1:2 col. pl.). In short, the hundreds of Egyptian-inspired pyramids which have been built throughout the world attest to the extent to which a revival can become both multiple and complex by impacting on fields as diverse as architecture, beliefs and social phenomena.

Garden pyramids: from exoticism to esotericism

The first manifestations of 'Pyramidomania' occurred within 'Anglo-Chinese' gardens, an early 18th century English fashion consisting of objects spread across a cleverly 'domesticated' landscape. Such constructions – notable exponents of which included William Kent, Charles Bridgeman and Alexander Pope – did not rely solely upon Egypt for their inspiration. As Baltrusaitis (1957: 99) points out: "it is the wild paradise that England has rediscovered under Milton (*Paradise Lost* 1667–1674) and which it has returned to its parks." Nature was bent to accommodate an idealized vision of the world. Lakes, hills, paths and vegetation all served to emphasize microcosms in which Japanese bridges, Chinese pagodas, Gothic ruins, obelisks, various tombs, and – of course – pyramids, were built. These landscapes and architectural installations were immensely successful in England and they subsequently spread rapidly across Europe (Laborde 1808: 135; Rosati Chapter 12, this volume). Not everyone agreed. Thus, Delille (1782, quoted in Baltrusaitis 1957: 108):

> Banish from gardens all these confused clusters
> Buildings of all sorts, lavished by fashion,
> Obelisks, rotunda, kiosks and pagodas,
> These Roman, Greek, Arab, Chinese buildings,
> Architectural chaos without aim and without choice
> Whose fruitful profusion barrenly
> Confines in a garden the four corners of the World ...

Such opposition was unsuccessful, and the garden pyramids continued their popularity[3] as primarily decorative elements, even though they were sometimes described as "pharaoh tombs".[4]

Egyptianizing pyramids proved to be most inspirational in the field of esotericism (Humbert 2001: 181–200). For instance, around 1775, in the gardens of Maupertuis, Alexandre Brongniart built a "fake ruin of a step pyramid equipped with a primitive Doric entrance covered by a cracked pediment (decorated with motifs closely associated with the horns and moon crescent of Isis, and thus presumed to be Egyptian, whereas the pediment is unknown in traditional architecture until the 1st century AD)" (Anon. 1986: no. 367). "This entrance leads to a cave under the pyramid, the design of which was inspired by the passages and arched underpasses described in *Sethos* (1731) by Abbot Jean Terrasson. Similar sources of inspiration can be found in Jean-Jacques Lequeu's temple of Wisdom" (Humbert 1989: 41).

Although the Potsdam pyramid (Figure 2:3) was created as an ice-house and was "built in 1791–1792 according to Carl Gotthard Langhans' plans, forming – within the

Figure 2:3   The ice-house pyramid in the New Gardens in Potsdam, Germany, designed by Karl Gotthard Langhans, 1791–1792 (© Jean-Marcel Humbert).

design of the New Gardens – an architectonic counterweight for the Marble palace which corresponds, on the opposite side, to the façade of the kitchens" (Streidt and Frahm 1996: 115), its association with initiatory rites of passage is clear. The door, topped by cabalistic signs, and enormous hieroglyphic friezes contribute to creating an atmosphere which is intended to be both mysterious and elitist.

That the pyramid became a symbol favoured by Freemasonry at the beginning of the 19th century is not surprising (Humbert *et al.* 1994: nos. 177–178, 300). In fact, since 1773, close to 100 architects or students of the Academy had been members of the Parisian Masonic lodge of the 'Grand Orient de France' (Hamill and Mollier Chapter 11, this volume).[5]

The pyramid of Monceau (Figure 2:4) became a place of meditation, its period descriptions (1779) confirming its esoteric and Masonic role. As Carmontelle (1779: 9–10) describes it:

> The principal pyramidal tomb is Egyptian. The inside is decorated with eight granite columns buried to one-third of their height, with Egyptian head capitals supporting a bronze entablature. Both to the right and to the left, there is an ancient black marble tomb; straight ahead and facing the door, there is a niche that contains an ancient green marble basin; in the basin, a figure of a woman, sitting on her heels, is pressing her breasts from which water falls. This figure is Egyptian, made from the most beautiful black stone, with the hairstyle consisting of a headband and silver strips. In the corners there are four niches, each containing bronze incense burners. The entrance is closed by a grille and two Egyptian caryatids make up the side posts of the door, each carrying the ancient green marble serving as lintel.

Figure 2:4   The Monceau pyramid in Paris, designed by Carmontelle, 1779 (© Jean-Marcel Humbert).

This period – which was instrumental in the development of Freemasonry – saw the creation in 1784 of Count Cagliostro's Parisian 'Mother Lodge for the Adaptation of High Egyptian Masonry' in the rue de la Sourdière in Paris, in which the Count had constructed a 'temple of Isis' and where he himself served as a Grand Master (Baltrusaitis 1985: 46; Rebold 1851: 147; Thory 1815: 305). His role within mysticism only ceased with his arrest in Rome in 1789 (Baltrusaitis 1967: 58; Durliat 1974: 30–41). The close links connecting Isis with Freemasonry – which officially drew its strength from ancient Egyptian sources – ensured that the goddess became part of mainstream 'Egyptomania' (Humbert 1997a: 626–655; Hamill and Mollier Chapter 11, this volume).

At the beginning of the 19th century – in order to complement such esoteric concepts – it was suggested that pyramids should be used to house conference rooms and in particular Masonic lodges, and Egyptian-inspired lodges multiplied.[6] The 'Sovereign Pyramid', created in Toulouse in 1806, contained "the altar, dedicated to God-Humanity-Truth ... positioned before figures of Isis and Osiris. Two sphinxes guard the door ... Hieroglyphs, carefully copied from ancient Egyptian engravings, contribute to the decoration" (Caillet 1959: 22–57; Durliat 1974: 30–41). Egyptian-like costumes for the initiates were envisaged and carefully described. The large pyramid that Prince Hermann von Pückler-Muskau had built in his Branitz Park (Germany) was part of this esoteric movement (Figure 2:5).

Figure 2:5   Pyramid built for Prince Hermann von Pückler-Muskau in his Branitz Park (Germany), mid-19th century (© Jean-Marcel Humbert).

The monuments of the Revolution

The French Revolution chose to reuse aspects of Egyptian antiquity for propaganda purposes. One might have thought that the Revolutionists would condemn the absolutism of pharaoh and would have destroyed it, as they had the symbols of royalty and feudality. However, in practice, it proved to be a utopian concept of Ancient Egypt as 'Antique Guarantor' of an idealistic purity that triumphed. The pyramid became a central theme in a multitude of projects imagined by visionary architects. They were even used in factory designs, and at Chaux, Claude-Nicolas Ledoux proposed a forging mill and a woodcutter's house and workshop including pyramids (Anon. 1968: nos. 80 and 91). It is hardly surprising, therefore, to see that the pyramid also became a major symbol in several large-scale popular gatherings where, as a very temporary structure, it nevertheless conjured up the 'epic' nature of Ancient Egypt. The Champ-de-Mars was partially redecorated for the commemoration of the third anniversary of the storming of the Bastille on 14 July 1792. The central podium, which had been installed for the 'Feast of the Federation' two years earlier, was retained, but a tall pyramid made of wood and fabric was added halfway between the podium and the military school. Its significance remains rather obscure: perhaps it represented the symbol of immortality referred to during the ceremony (which preceded the 'final' abolition of feudal rights on 25 August 1792). It was certainly intended to add to the monumental and decorative atmosphere of this solemn occasion.

Another temporary Egyptianizing pyramid, designed by architect Bernard Poyet, was constructed for the 25 August 1792 ceremony honouring those who had died on 10 August. Jean-Georges Wille (1857: 357–358) gave an account of the ceremony:

> I saw the construction of a large blackish pyramid at the Tuileries, with inscriptions on the four faces; it was positioned in the large round basin opposite the principal door of the castle, and commemorated those who lost their lives whilst attacking the castle on the 10th August. A few days earlier, an obelisk was positioned in its place, at the entrance of the large alley; however, it was regarded as being too thin and without effect, and was at once destroyed. The ceremony, which was very military and lugubrious, took place on the 25th, towards nightfall, but I almost did not see it as the number of spectators was too much for me; I left and returned quietly to my home.

Certain authors also noted: "the black serge pyramid built in the basin of the Tuileries with the inscription: Silence, they rest" (Renouvier 1863: 419). A notice (quoted in Drumont 1879) posted in the streets invited the Parisians to gather:

> Citizens, a national ceremony will be celebrated on Sunday, in honour of our brothers who died whilst fighting for liberty. The representatives of the people will deposit civic wreaths at the foot of the pyramid, which will be built at the Tuileries. May each citizen attend this majestic festival with their oak or flower garland, with their wreath, to deposit it – at the end of the ceremony – at the base of the monument raised to the glory of the heroes who helped us to overcome the tyrants!

The choice of a pyramidal shape for this albeit temporary monument – which was nonetheless intended to be commemorative – was based on its volume, considered to have great visual and emotional impact.

Funerary monuments

Under various guises the pyramid was to rediscover its ancient funerary role; it invaded cemeteries as both mausolea and as tombs (e.g. Bryan Chapter 10; Cornelius Chapter 14; Hope Chapter 9; Rosati Chapter 12, all this volume). The 1684 mausoleum of Turenne in the Saint-Denis basilica consisted of a mural pyramid (subsequently transferred in 1800 to the dome of the Église des Invalides, where it can still be seen), which was one of the first French examples of a funerary art style that subsequently had a long and widespread success.[7]

In these types of monuments the pyramid had not yet rediscovered its original three-dimensional form, which finally reappeared thanks to visionary architects such as Etienne-Louis Boullée, whose projects included pyramid-shaped cenotaphs around 1780–1785 (Humbert *et al.* 1994: nos. 78–80, 151–153). In 1778, Léon Dufourny (Bandiera 1983: 25–32) proposed a cenotaph for Henri IV consisting of an imposing pyramid of which the entrances would be colonnaded, surmounted by a triangular pediment. All these would have been framed by two long galleries intersected at regular intervals with small decorative obelisks. In 1785, Pierre-François-Léonard Fontaine (Anon. 1968: nos. 146–147, 232–233) imagined a "sepulchral monument for the sovereigns of a great empire" derived from that of Boullée. A large central pyramid was surrounded by obelisks and a fence, which linked a series of smaller pyramids, the large pyramid including a vast internal cupola. In 1801, Pierre Giraud wanted to construct a sepulchral monument in the gardens of the Champs-Elysées – "a pyramid surmounted by an ancient tripod carrying a radiant sphere, through which these sacred words would be read: 'Respect the Spirits'". Its author (quoted in Christ 1970: 84–85) presented it as an ensemble "unique of its kind, more majestic than all those Egypt glorifies itself as possessing".

From the beginning of the 19th century, pyramids were widely utilized as tombs, particularly in the Père-Lachaise cemetery in Paris. The trend of using Egyptianizing decorations continued with the designs for Napoleon's tomb. Ingres (in Issartel 1990: 129) – then the Director of the French School in Rome – considered the possibility of a gigantic monument:

> ... an immense Egyptian-like pyramid, which would not have fitted under the dome of Les Invalides, but would undoubtedly have looked admirable on the top of a hill – at the end of Champ-de-Mars for example. The pyramid would have been a superposition of floors, crowned by the statue of the Emperor; all around the steps would have been statues representing the resounding victories of the Empire.

Another project in the mid-19th century, by architect Lacugne, concerned the possibility of constructing an imposing pyramid "on the model of that of Memphis", to contain the sarcophagus of Emperor Napoleon I (Issartel 1990: 140). Another (1853) suggestion was that "a standing statue of king Menes who erected the pyramid of Memphis would be on the platform, to the left of that of Napoleon III, to whom we will owe the pyramid of Paris".

A certain number of not dissimilar projects in other countries were carried out, and are still visible today, such as the 1794 mausoleum at Blickling Hall, Norfolk, of the Count and Countess of Buckinghamshire, by Joseph Bonomi Senior (Figure 2:6). In 1823, in Karlsruhe, a pyramid-mausoleum by Friedrich Weinbrenner (Figure 2:7) housed the tomb of the city's founder, Prince Karl Wilhelm, margrave of Bade-Durlach.

Figure 2:6   The 1794 Mausoleum at Blickling Hall, Norfolk, designed by Joseph Bonomi Snr (© Dean Sully).

Figure 2:7   Pyramidal mausoleum of Prince Karl Wilhelm at Karlsruhe, Germany, designed by Friedrich Weinbrenner, 1823 (© Jean-Marcel Humbert).

During this same period, the pyramid invaded cemeteries. As testified by the large number of recent examples in all shapes and dimensions, its appeal continues today. These include those of cemeteries in Chicago, Milan and Recanati (where the tenor Beniamino Gigli is buried – one of the greatest Radames of the century in Verdi's *Aida* – Humbert 2003). The non-elite cemetery pyramids often have nothing to do with Ancient Egypt; for example, the pyramid in the cemitério dos Prazeres in Lisbon, crowned by the Virgin and a cross.

Commemorative monuments

Pyramids offer large surfaces suitable for long inscriptions, and, as such, they lend themselves to serve as memorials (e.g. Maréchal's 1790 design for the 'Philosophy and Patriotism Vanquishes all Prejudice' project). They were readily used to honour personalities directly linked with Egypt, such as the late 18th century monument to General Desaix that was planned to take the form of a pyramid at the edge of a lake (Humbert 1998c: 219–232, 1999: 88–89). The pyramid was often considered particularly appropriate to commemorate Egyptologists such as Mariette Pasha, whose monument in Boulogne-sur-Mer (unveiled 16 July 1882) was topped by a statue by Alfred Jacquemart: the Egyptologist with his hand resting on an Egyptian head (Figure 2:8). In Granger's (unveiled 17 September 1899) monument to François Chabas at Chalon-sur-Saône, a very small pyramid and a sphinx accompany an 'Egyptian-style' massif decorated with ankhs and hieroglyphic texts, which supports a bust of the Egyptologist. Elsewhere in the world (Cornelius Chapter 14, this volume) pyramids were used to commemorate others, not only Egyptologists, but there are also frequent examples of pyramids commemorating notable events unconnected with Egyptology (e.g. the Nîmes World War II resistance martyrs, built around 1955).

Contemporary pyramids

The claimed purity of line and sobriety of shape of a pyramid predisposed it for acceptance in contemporary art (but see Chapter 1), and since the 1970s, the erstwhile residence of the dead has become that of the living. During this period the pyramid gave its name to several real estate operations, and to one entire area in Paris. Large-scale operations have followed since then, such as 'La Grande Motte' (1964–1984) where architect Jean Balladur has created several pyramidal shaped buildings offering maximum exposure to the sun. The operation was launched using an advertising campaign where one programme was called 'Khéops', another 'The European Pyramid', and even the transformers were shaped as pyramids.

The genre has found new vigour. At the beginning of the 1980s, Jim Onan, a rich American entrepreneur, had an 18 m high, 24-carat gold-plated pyramid built in Wadsworth (Illinois) (Fazzini and McKercher Chapter 8: Figures 8:9, 8:10, 8:11 col. pls., this volume; Humbert 1989: 90). Lit by numerous windows, this curious country house is reached by an alley of sphinxes and is surrounded by three smaller pyramids, a sacred lake and a multitude of statues. Being in the private domain, this kind of construction provoked little controversy. This is not so when public buildings become caught up with political forces confronting one another. Such was the "battle of the

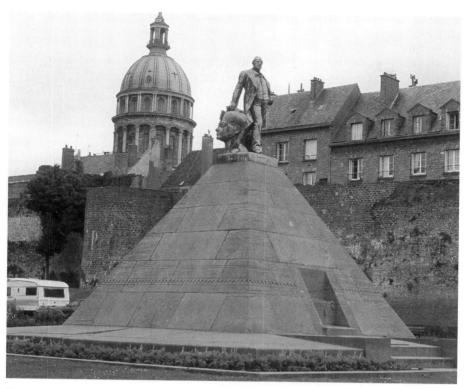

Figure 2:8   Commemorative pyramid erected in 1882 in Boulogne, France, in honour of the renowned Egyptologist Mariette Pasha, designed by Alfred Jacquemart (© Jean-Marcel Humbert).

Louvre pyramid" (1984–1989), which became so fiercely acrimonious that the project was nearly dropped. The architectural claims were particularly fascinating (Figure 2:9).[8]

> Positioned in the middle of water features which will give it life by mingling their reflections with those of the sky and the clouds, the pyramid was selected because – of all possible forms – it is the one that least devours space: it is one which, at its height, represents the most mobile surface with regards to a moving observer, and which symbolically offers the most resonance. The solution suggested by I. M. Pei incorporates both elegance and ability; at no moment does it aim to clash architecturally with the palace: nothing evokes competition or contradiction with the original builders. It is a monument made with modern materials, that collides more with nature – water, sky, clouds and light – than with the surrounding architecture.
>
> (Anon. 1985: 2)

For Claude Parent (1985: 2), the symbolic content of the pyramid is:

> ... associated [with] the notion of density, the value of secrecy, its precise boundaries, the confrontation of pure geometrical form and of nature. One cannot escape this esoteric message that no generation has dared to contradict or question ... One should thus admit that architect Pei – even though he uses tradition and history to defend the

Figure 2:9   The Louvre pyramid, 1989, designed by Ieoh Ming Pei (© Jean-Marcel Humbert).

presentation of his work – employs for his own ends a symbolic digression of the shape. Such symbolic inversion appears on all levels of architectural intervention: opacity contrasts with alleged transparency. Mass opposes lightness, while the full is replaced by the hollow. The base is replaced by a crater, which stops the continuum and makes the base – the fifth face of the pyramid that is so important in its symbolic significance – disappear. The hierarchy of spaces disappears ... The pyramid, once deprived of its symbolic contents, its esoteric load, its mass and the relation of its fifth face with the ground, is no more than a modernistic object among many others.

What is particularly interesting about this example is that its Sino-American architect, Ieoh Ming Pei, has always refused to acknowledge any Egyptian affiliation with his pyramid. Instead he stresses use of transparency, its interior vacuum and its absence of mass. However, Parisians – as well as most of the world – immediately recognize it as a pyramid and give it Egyptian, rather than esoteric, meaning (see Chapter 1) – even though it is on an axis that was purposely designed to connect the Louvre to the Grande Arche de la Défense.

The last few years have seen the creation of two other gigantic pyramids, in the United States. The first was built in Memphis, Tennessee (1990–1991) and houses offices and a museum inside a pyramid 60 per cent as large as that of Kheops. The second – the Luxor Hotel-Casino built in Las Vegas in 1992–1993 (Fazzini and McKercher Chapter 8: Figure 8:14, this volume; Humbert 1998b: figs. 86–89 and 130–133) – is fronted by an obelisk and a monumental sphinx, and has already undergone several modifications and enlargements. Less gigantic examples include two American restaurants: the Pyramid Supper Club by Earl Furgeson (1961) in Beaver Dam (Wisconsin) (Humbert 1998b: 30–31), and the 1990s Hard Rock Cafe housed under a 70 ft pyramid conceived by the Zakaspace group, in Myrtle Beach (South Carolina) (Pagler 1997: 110–113).

Nowadays, 'Pyramidomania' has entered the world of money, patrons and financial institutions. Its effectiveness as an advertising tool is such that it is often used by clubs, such as Ilie Nastase's sporting complex 'The Pyramids' (Port Marly, close to Paris), or for stores in almost all parts of the world (e.g. close to Niagara Falls, at the exit of Prague, close to Dessau and near Verona). Its potential seems far from exhausted. As a symbol of indestructibility, the pyramid has been hijacked by advertising and used as a logo for a multitude of companies worldwide, mostly related to the construction industry (and see MacDonald and Rice 2003). The Saint-Gobain glassmaking company also chose the pyramid form to store its archives in Blois: by using glass with solar heating, it has created a variation on the theme of an Egyptian tomb, perpetuating the memory of the company (Woldman 1983: 72). The uses show infinite variety, and include greenhouses (e.g. in Edmonton, Canada and Sydney, Australia) and aquaria (e.g. Madrid Zoo, in Spain, 1995), a sporting pavilion for the United Arab Republic at Osaka Universal Exhibition in Japan (1970), and large theme parks (e.g. 'Pharaoh's Lost Kingdom Adventure' in Redlands, California, USA, 1996, and Terra Mítica near Benidorm in Spain, 2000) (Figure 2:10 col. pl.).

Finally, pyramids are even found on top of skyscrapers (e.g. in Montreal). Contemporary techniques allow for ever greater creative flexibility: inverted pyramids that balance on their point (e.g. at Créteil, Head Office of Pernod, designed by Jean Willerval, 1974 (Figure 2:11; Bratislava, Slovak broadcasting building, and in the underground Carrousel shopping mall in the Louvre, Paris, by Ieoh Ming Pei, 1993). Creativity is also the hallmark of some contemporary works incorporating pyramidal elements. Thus, Gerard Chamaillou's floating pyramid or 'Hâpitrône' (1985), which combines a throne, a pyramid and a ship, is 12 m high (Humbert 1989a: 89). And there are many other examples (e.g. the 1971 Barnett Newman 'Broken obelisk'; Pierre Baey's 1985 pyramid cut into four; and Jacques Leclercq's 1992 large pyramids or "strange movements of the Kheops shapes", made from compacted straw, steel structure and fibre optics.

Over time, many pyramids have decreased in size, thus enabling the pyramid to slip into our close environment by transforming itself into works of art or everyday furniture – such as the pyramidal bed designed by Fabio Fabbi around 1890 (Humbert 1989a: 141), or the pyramidal desk designed by Philippe Starck in 1986 for President Mitterrand. But it has also become a mainstay of opera and films (see Humbert 2003; Serafy 2003) and, in novels and comic strips, the pyramid represents an ideal setting for adventures with highly evocative titles (see Schadla-Hall and Morris 2003). But perhaps the most intriguing of new pyramidal accomplishments is that devised by cartoonist Bilal, who – under the control of ancient Egyptian gods – even succeeded in making a pyramid fly ...

Conclusions

A perfect shape into which multiple symbolic content can be slipped, the pyramid appears also to carry an underlying esoteric message, which seems to have been

38   Jean-Marcel Humbert

Figure 2:11   The 'inverted' pyramid built for the Pernod Society at Créteil, France, designed by Jean Willerval, 1974 (© Jean-Marcel Humbert).

recognized and understood by all (Rice and MacDonald 2003). Whatever its final use, it has always enjoyed immense popularity. Making use of its exceptional evocative powers, the pyramid – like all other 'Egyptomania' – has always adapted to the fashions of the moment, to give it the best chance of success. Egyptian pyramids refer to dreams more than to reality, they take their shape according to artistic creations or specific orders. Their power to inspire has not only remained intact for some 5,000 years, but the myths and the symbols – which have long been attached to it – have been enriched by quantities of new associations accumulated over time. Over three centuries a new generation of pyramids has been created which – although no longer having anything to do with those of antiquity – nevertheless maintains a strong affiliation to, and an exemplary link between, Ancient Egypt and the imagination of our contemporaries.

Notes

1   Some of the material in this chapter was first presented in the "Revivals" section of the 30th International Congress on the History of Art, held in London in September 2000.
2   Magistrate Caius Cestius, who died 12 BC, had a pyramid with marble cover built in Rome, next to the Saint-Peter gate. The characteristic shape of this pyramid (37 m high, 30 m wide at the base) has often been copied since the 16th century.
3   Examples can be found at Ancy-le-Franc (France), the Catherine Park in Tsarskoye Selo (by Vasily Neyelov and Charles Cameron, Russia), Wilhelmshöhe (near Kassel, Germany), Branitz (Germany), Wespelaar (Belgium), Caserte (Italy), Villa Il Pavone (Sienna, Italy), and Wilhelmsbad in Hanau (Germany) (Figure 2:12), which makes one think of Jean-Jacques Rousseau's tomb which was built on an island in the centre of a lake, thus celebrating the Arcadian myth.
4   It could be argued, however, that the ubiquitous presence of pyramids in parks reflects more than meaningless structures. Their external appearance and their Egyptian

connection could be seen as linking them – even if subconsciously – to tombs and the idea of death (and see the pyramid by William Kent in Stowe Park, 1736).

5   They included architects Boullée, Ledoux, Chalgrin, Brongniart, De Wailly, Peyre, Petit-Radel, Poyet, Victor Louis; the sculptors Pajou and Clodion; painters Saint-Aubin, Greuze, Hubert Robert, Joseph Vernet, Boilly, Regnault and Fragonard.

6   E.g. the 'Ordre sacré des Sophisiens', 'Rite des parfaits initiés d'Egypte', 'Rite de Misraïm', 'Rite de Memphis', or 'l'Ordre d'Alexandre Du Mège', 'les Amis du Désert', with its mother-lodge – 'Souveraine Pyramide' – in Toulouse.

7   Several examples were derived from this prototype, such as the mausoleum of bishop Armand de Montmorin, built by Michel-Angel Slodtz in 1747 (Saint-Maurice cathedral of Vienne, France), the tomb of Philippe V and Elisabeth Farnèse (chapel of the royal palace of Granja de San Ildefonso, around 1748), the tomb of Titian by Antonio Canova, 1795, and the cenotaph of archduchess Marie-Christine (d. 1798) by Canova in 1805 (Church of the Augustins, Vienna, Austria). This last example is 5 m tall, and is constructed from Carrara marble, surmounted by a medallion bearing a portrait of the deceased; Virtue, Happiness and Charity are depicted advancing towards the tomb.

8   A vigorous press campaign, led essentially by *Le Figaro*, tried to ruin the project. Cf. for instance in *Le Figaro* 'Louvre: la bataille de la pyramide', no. 12 262, 3 February 1984: 1, 27; 8 February 1984: 23; *Figaro magazine*, 2 February 1985: 56–57, review of the "anti-pyramid" book by Sébastien Loste, Antoine Schnapper and Bruno Foucart : *Paris mystifié – la grande illusion du grand Louvre*, Paris, 1985; the *Gazette des Beaux-Arts* regularly reported about the affair's growth in its 'Chronique des Arts', from no. 1383 April 1984 till no. 1404 January 1986; *Connaissance des Arts* published a regular column from no. 385 (March 1984) till no. 398 (April 1985), as well as *Beaux-Arts Magazine*, far more tactful (nos. 17, October 1984, 26, July–August 1985 and 28, October 1985). And architect Pei was renamed 'Le pharaon du Louvre' by *Télérama*, no. 1912, 3 September 1986 ...

Acknowledgments

I am grateful to Didier Avond for his patient and fruitful hunting for European pyramids and to Daniel Acosta, Departmento de Prensa, Comunicación Terra Mítica, Parque Temático de Benidorm, Spain.

Figure 2:12   Pyramid on the island of the Staatspark of Wilhelmsbad in Hanau, designed by Franz Ludwig von Canerin, 1784 (© Jean-Marcel Humbert).

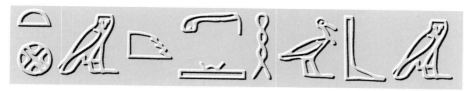

CHAPTER 3

ARCHAEOLOGY WEDDED TO ART: EGYPTIAN ARCHITECTURE IN 19th CENTURY PAINTING

Helen Whitehouse

An oil sketch by Jean-Léon Gérôme recently acquired by the Ashmolean Museum (Figure 3:1) shows the temple of Luxor as many 19th century visitors would have first viewed it – from the river, the long axial structure steadily diminishing in height from its entrance pylon through its columned sanctuaries (Whiteley 2001). When Gérôme first saw it in 1857, one of the two obelisks at the front had already been taken to Paris (the tip of the other is just visible in his painting), but the rest of the temple was still untouched, encumbered around and within by mud-brick houses (Hassan 2003a: Figure 2:8). The sketch is a charming study in soft grey-blues and sandy-browns, the great monument silhouetted against a pearly sky and shimmering in reflection on the water. But Gérôme, the most successful Salon artist of his day, was the creator of dramatic canvases; his first visit to Egypt supplied him with the reference material and inspiration for a new direction in his work, and North Africa was to be a major source of subject-matter for the rest of his career. The Luxor riverbank reappeared in a typically striking composition in which the ancient ruins served as the backdrop to a scene from the life of modern Egypt – a life full of colour, mystery, cruelty, and sometimes overt sensuality, too, according to the version presented to an eager European public by Gérôme and his fellow practitioners of the orientalist genre. In 'The Prisoner' (exhibited at the Salon of 1861; Nantes, Musée des Beaux Arts), temple and riverbank shimmer behind a sombre boat in which a manacled and prostrate felon is being rowed to the east bank under the stern gaze of an official with a stave, and the mockery of a guard playing the *oud* (Ackermann 2000: 48–49, 54, 248–249, nos. 134–135).

Gérôme's 'The Prisoner' is typical of one category of 19th century painting in which pharaonic architecture is combined with the life of contemporary Egypt – here with a narrative purpose and to atmospheric effect. Gérôme deftly plays on the viewer's sensibilities to create a frisson of fear, and to suggest a completely foreign ambience, to which the ruins make their contribution, testifying that this ancient land has always been culturally different. Other paintings by Gérôme's contemporaries observed both ancient and modern in a more detached spirit of record – John Frederick Lewis' 'Edfu, Upper Egypt' (exhibited at the Royal Academy in 1861; Tate Britain) presents an axial view of the temple of Horus in its half-buried state, with the foreground occupied by a camel train at rest, the beasts and their riders seated at the

Figure 3:1   J-L. Gérôme, 'View of the Nile at Luxor', 1857, oil on canvas (Ashmolean Museum, Oxford).

level of the column capitals of the outer court of the temple (De Meulenaere *et al.* 1992: 78–79). The eye can roam with pleasure over the informative detailing of saddle-bags and harness, intricate leatherwork, turbans, textiles, the reliefs on the temple pylon, and the drift of sand against its columns. In either category of painting, the artist presents a composite image of Egypt which meets the expectations and experience of the western visitor. Vivant Denon, arriving in 1798 at the age of 51 with Bonaparte's expedition, as eager to see the mosques, *hammams* and dancing-girls as to record the ruined monuments of the pharaohs, typifies the complex interest which Egypt held for outsiders, in which the temporal and cultural separation of pharaonic, hellenistic, and Islamic was often blurred.

A third category of 19th century painting in which the representation of ancient Egyptian architecture figured large was the historical recreation, in which scenes from Egyptian history, the Egyptian episodes in the Old Testament, or the imagined daily life of the Egyptians, were re-enacted against massive backdrops of monumental (and often inappropriate) architecture, based – usually with pedantic accuracy – on the surviving temples of the Nile Valley: the monuments of New Kingdom Thebes and the Ptolemaic foundations of Dendera, Edfu, Esna, and Philae, much the same sequence of sites that the modern Nile traveller encounters (El Daly 2003a). Although there was nothing intrinsically new in this recreative aim (the few famous names – notably Cleopatra VII, Joseph, and Moses – had long been accorded this kind of treatment in western art), the concern for authenticity, the wealth of archaeological detail, and the often didactic purpose, were all new. The heyday of this genre, the second half of the 19th century, coincided with the growth of Egyptian archaeology and tourism in the Nile Valley; it was also the period at which the material prosperity of industrialized Europe and America, the manufacturing of consumer goods in any desired historical style, and the improvement of public taste, were celebrated and promulgated at successive international exhibitions where Egypt, ancient and modern, was also on display (Çelik 1992; Delamaire Chapter 7, this volume). Sometimes these recreative canvases, so heavy with informative detail, seem designed to reassure the viewer that the Ancient Egyptians, too, lived and consumed like the exhibition visitor, who could acquire metalwork, jewellery or furniture akin to what they saw in the pictures, or a sculpted version of Cleopatra or Pharaoh's Daughter whose stories were re-enacted in the paintings in the shade of hypostyle halls and towering porticoes. Often functioning as a sub-section of the orientalist genre – many of the leading painters produced works in both modes – history painting could share the same exotic licence which permitted a degree of sex and sadism not to be found in European history subjects.[1]

In fabricating the architectural background to these scenes, artists could work from a substantial body of reference material. The records published by Denon (1802 and other editions and translations), and subsequently in much greater detail by his colleagues in the *Description* (1809–1828) provided the first informative stimulus for artists to incorporate extensive images of ancient Egyptian architecture into their work. Most importantly, the *Description* (1809–1828) showed the way by including magnificent recreative visions of the monuments, in which the scientific draftsmanship of the French Expedition's architects and engineers was brought to life, with priests pacing in the columned shade of the temples of Edfu, Philae and Karnak, or pensively contemplating the reliefs in the Memnonion, and with processions winding through the southern gateway of Karnak or the hypostyle hall of Dendera (*Description*, Antiquités vols. I (1809), pls. 18, 61; III (1812), pl. 42; II (1812), pl. 37; III , pl. 31; IV (1817), pl. 30). For the most extravagant recreation (Figure 3:2), the records of the expedition did not suffice – the detachment of soldiers observed by priests from the northern gateway at Dendera marches along the causeway of a marina-like landscape created with details from the late hellenistic Nile mosaic of Palestrina (Walker 2003: Figures 11:5, 11:6, 11:7 col. pls.).

Like the more realistic views showing the half-buried ruins of the same monuments with the small figures of the *savants* dotted around, these grandiose recreations with their minuscule Egyptian inhabitants confirmed what was already established in 18th century writing on the architecture of Ancient Egypt – that it was on a scale more vast than that of any other civilization. At the turn of the 18th and 19th centuries, Louis-François Cassas (1798) had already potently combined this grandiosity with his first-hand observation of Egyptian monuments in a series of

Figure 3:2   'Denderah (Tentyris): élévation perspective de la porte du nord', drawn by G-A. Chabrol and E. Jomard (*Description* 1809–1828, IV: pl. 6).

paintings (engraved for his *Voyage Pittoresque*) which were influential on other artists and stage designers in the early decades of the 19th century (Figure 3:3) (Gilet 1989). This vastness was to become a keynote in the depiction of pharaonic architecture in painting, stage sets, and panoramas of the first half of the 19th century, celebrated in its own right – Egyptian landscape and architecture were peculiarly well suited to the medium of diorama and panorama (Altick 1978: 182, 206, 209, 422–423, 474) – or dwarfing the human actors who often appeared literally in its shade. In apocalyptic compositions such as J. M. W. Turner's painting 'The Fifth Plague of Egypt' (exhibited in 1800; Indianapolis Museum of Art; Conner 1983: 75, 81), the mezzotints of John Martin ('The Daughter of Pharaoh Finding Moses', 'The Seventh Plague of Egypt' (Werner Chapter 5: Figure 5:9, this volume), 'The Destroying Angel'; Campbell 1992: 138, 140, 102, 157), and David Roberts' 'The Israelites Leaving Egypt' (exhibited in 1829: City Museum and Art Gallery, Birmingham; Werner Chapter 5: Figure 5:10, this volume; Champion 2003; Pantazzi 1994d), Egyptian architecture itself becomes almost the protagonist, viewed in the sweeping perspectives with which Claude Lorrain had mythologized classical architecture. Roberts painted his version of "That Grand although simple style of architecture the Egyptian ..." before ever setting foot in Egypt (Guiterman and Llewellyn 1986: 72–73, 76–77, 112 no. 114); his travels there in 1838–1839, from which he returned with brimming sketchbooks, were to change the style of his own representations of pharaonic architecture, create a vogue for topographical paintings of Egypt, and set the example of direct visual experience for later artists (Guiterman and Llewellyn 1986: 69–85).

The perception of massive scale sometimes carried with it a negative judgment of the qualities of Egyptian architecture – generally in comparison with the achievement of the Greeks in developing a rational and harmonious system of proportions and orders, thus continuing the old aesthetic battle in which Piranesi had been such a pugnacious defender of the Egyptians in the 18th century (Piranesi 1769; Rosati Chapter 12, Werner Chapter 5, both this volume). Interestingly, to at least one viewer in the earlier 19th century, the scale and superficial features of Egyptian architecture (and that of other 'oriental' cultures) seemed to provide a visual analogy for the new industrial landscape (which, ironically, from the mid-century onwards began to use Egyptianizing designs). As he toured the midlands of England in 1826, Karl Friedrich Schinkel saw 'obelisks' and 'pyramids' everywhere in the stark and unfamiliar vistas of factories and smoke-stacks: for this artist and architect with the classical ruins of Italy in his mind's eye, "the towns of this industrial region [the Potteries] have a queer Indo-Egyptian appearance because of the numerous factories" (Ettlinger 1945: 133).

Despite a lingering prejudice in favour of the Greeks, in the 19th century teaching of architectural history Egypt was placed at the beginning of an evolutionary sequence of human building history. The documentation provided by the French publications, and subsequently the work of the Franco-Tuscan and Prussian expeditions and individual scholars (Lepsius 1849–1859; Rosellini 1832–1844; Wilkinson 1837), was absorbed and utilized in this didactic endeavour. 'The Professor's Dream' by C. R. Cockerell, exhibited at the Royal Academy Summer Exhibition in 1849, presented a synopsis of world architecture in four ascending levels, of which Egypt was the first, represented by the temples of Abu Simbel, Karnak and Edfu, the Theban colossi of Memnon, and the Giza sphinx. The painting (London, Royal Academy) was a distillation at approximately half-size of the 4.2 x 3 m 'visual

Figure 3:3 L-F. Cassas, 'Temples égyptiens avec tous les genres d'accessoires dont on pourrait supposer que la magnificence égyptienne décorait ces grands monuments', engraving (Cassas 1798, I: pl. 60).

aid' with which Professor Cockerell illustrated his lectures on architecture at the Academy from 1841 onwards (Watkin 1974: 105–132). Summaries of his lectures appeared in *The Builder* from 1843 onwards, and this universal approach, in which the Egyptian achievement was given an unprejudiced assessment, was to be echoed in the teaching of architecture by the comparative method later in the century. More romantically, the American painter Thomas Cole envisaged the New York architect Ithiel Town, himself a practitioner of neoclassical, and later, neo-Gothic, designs, in 'The Architect's Dream' (1840; Toledo Museum of Art), slumbering at the foreground of a historical perspective of architecture. It moves through the fuliginous Gothic of the north via the gleaming creations of the Greeks to arrive at the rosy dawn of the Egyptian pyramids (Parry 1988: 244–248). In their different ways, both Cockerell's and Cole's pictures confirm the status of Egyptian architecture in the mid-19th century, and the validity of its presence in both teaching and art.

The archaeological publications of the 19th century which fed intellectual and creative interest in Ancient Egypt were the beneficiaries of the generous record of its material civilization left by pharaonic Egypt. This was by no means typical of other cultures of the ancient world, and this imbalance is reflected in the disproportionately great interest in Egypt, whose firm and strongly-coloured image has continued to prevail to the present day (and see MacDonald and Rice 2003); but it also made Egypt a fruitful source which could serve for other, less well-preserved, areas when a visual image was needed. The ubiquitous pyramids had enlivened eastern landscapes in western art from the Middle Ages onwards, and continued to do so into the 19th century (Humbert Chapter 2, this volume). Most of John Martin's non-Egyptian biblical scenes include pyramids; but with the genesis of Egyptology, a wider range of objects and buildings began to appear in unexpected contexts. In his painting of 'The Death of Sardanapalus' (Paris, Musée du Louvre), exhibited at the Salon of 1828, Eugène Delacroix utilized not only the appropriate Persian motifs but also Indian, Islamic, Classical, and Egyptian (Pomarède 1998). In his orgasmic vision of the last moments of an oriental despot, the treasure heaped amidst the carnage at the foot of the Persian king's bed includes golden elaborations of Canopic jars and a sistrum; the soldier about to dispatch a concubine at the top right of the picture wears headgear that is a free adaptation of the Egyptian royal Nemes, while the king's cup and flagon rest on a painted shrine with a winged-disk cornice. Delacroix's eclectic use of antiquity reflects the kind of pan-orientalism so noticeable in the 18th century, when Egypt was ranked amongst other Middle and Far Eastern cultures, but it also displays a kind of artistic pragmatism with which the painter would have been familiar from his early training: at the age of 17 he had joined the atelier of Pierre-Narcisse Guérin, whose historical canvases include two versions of an episode from Vergil's *Aeneid*, where the Trojan hero, resting at Carthage, recounts to Dido the misfortunes of Troy (Figure 3:4); no visual reference for Carthage being available, Guérin places Aeneas and the queen outside a portico whose columns are supported by Egyptian papyrus capitals, probably based on those of the temple of Esna as seen in Denon's (1802: pl. 59.9) publication.

Such discreet borrowing to fill out a lacunose archaeological record was not typical of the recreative canvases that were to follow later in the 19th century, when awesome visions of various ancient Near Eastern cultures were advanced with imaginative confidence and the gradually increasing support of archaeological

Figure 3:4 P-N. Guérin, 'Enée et Didon', 1815 (Musée des Beaux Arts, Bordeaux; another version, shown at the Salon of 1817, is in the Louvre).

information (McCall 1998: 189–199). For Egypt, the recreative endeavour was from the beginning firmly underpinned by the considerable volume of published information available, which could be verified by the consumers of such art, themselves familiar with the relevant publications, and often possessed of first-hand knowledge of the monuments in Egypt as well as the contents of museum collections nearer to home. Background research and fidelity to the sources were perceived as desirable attributes of history painting: Edward Poynter's vast 'Israel in Egypt' (London, Guildhall Art Gallery; Rice and MacDonald 2003: Figure 1:2 col. pl.; Werner Chapter 5, this volume) was greeted with enthusiasm by the press in 1867 for these very virtues. This extraordinarily elaborate picture had its origin in 1862 in a sketching-club subject, 'Work' (Conner 1985: 113); appropriately, commentators on the finished painting perceived that a lot of work had gone into it. The *Illustrated London News* (11 May 1867: 478) was pleased to see the young Poynter giving "every evidence of having fully profited by recent Egyptological research ... a typical example of the successful application of the modern principle of wedding archaeology to art". In stage-managing this union, Poynter conflated features of the temples of Thebes, Edfu, and Philae, backed by the Great Pyramid at Giza and the limestone cliffs of Thebes, to serve as the cinemascope-like background to the enforced labours of the Israelites, who haul a granite lion modelled on one of the 'Prudhoe' pair in the British Museum (Conner 1985: 113–114). The earnest studiousness which marked this kind of transfer of surviving ancient art and architecture into colourful recreation was pinpointed by Poynter's contemporary Frederic Leighton, who, viewing the tomb paintings in the Valley of the Kings, dutifully found them "of high interest from an ethnographic point of view ..." but mischievously added, "Poynter would have a fit over them" (Barrington 1906: 145). Leighton confined his own recreative efforts to his classical subjects – his few works with Egyptian or biblical reference are figure paintings with minimal background detail – but he produced some wonderfully atmospheric sketches of Egyptian landscape and monuments on a Nile cruise of 1868 (Jones *et al.* 1996: 152–155). Poynter eventually turned his early interest in Egyptian subjects to the benefit of archaeology, by becoming Secretary of the new Committee (later Society) for the Preservation of the Monuments of Ancient Egypt in 1888, when there was growing concern at the deterioration of the pharaonic legacy in the face of government indifference (Drower 1982: 29). Leighton also became involved in the following year.

For many artists, following in the footsteps of Roberts, direct experience of Egypt and the compilation there of sketches and reference material to feed their creations was an essential element in their production – Gérôme, for instance, visited the country seven times between 1857 and 1880 (Ackerman 2000: 42–44). Some even took up residence in Egypt – Lewis, consummate painter of oriental interiors, lived in Cairo for 10 years from 1841 onwards (Lewis 1978: 37–42; Llewellyn 1985), and Théodore Frère, whose evocative landscapes combined pharaonic ruins and genre scenes, had a studio there (Fine Art Society 1978: 43). Occasionally the artist was eyewitness to the nascent activity of archaeology (Figure 3:5 col. pl.). For most, the experience was probably more valuable for the opportunity to observe the unique quality of the light, and the very particular landscape of the Nile Valley, than for the detailed recording of the pharaonic monuments, for which they could draw on extensive reference material – increasingly, from the mid-19th century, photographic. Occasionally, however, an artist worked directly from the ancient monuments with a more systematic compilatory purpose: Owen Jones, Superintendent of Works for the Great Exhibition of 1850 and creator, with Joseph Bonomi, of the Egyptian Court at the Crystal Palace, travelled in Egypt with Jules Goury in 1833, compiling the detailed drawings of architecture and ornament which would feed the re-creations at Sydenham of parts of the temples of Thebes, Abu Simbel, Dendera and Philae (Jones and Bonomi 1854; Werner Chapter 5, this volume). Excerpted into the coloured plates of column capitals, ceiling patterns and stylized plant forms in Jones' *Grammar of Ornament* (1856: 22–25, pls. iv–xi), they provided generations of artists and designers with material that was carefully observed from Egyptian sources.

Precise observation did not, however, depend on autopsy in Egypt: Lawrence Alma-Tadema, one of the foremost producers of scenes from pharaonic life with the most detailed architectural backgrounds and furnishings (Werner Chapter 5: Figure 5:11, this volume), painted all but one of his 26 Egyptian pictures without first-hand knowledge of the land of Egypt. As was the case with his even more prolific output of classical scenes, he used a meticulous visual reference system based on personal study in museums, as well as publications and photographs (Pohlmann 1997; Raaven 1980). At the end of the 1880s, like Poynter and Leighton, he joined the campaign for the preservation of Egyptian monuments, but when he finally reached Egypt in 1902, as a member of Sir John Aird's party at the inauguration of the first Aswan Dam, he did not like the country; the picture he subsequently painted, 'The Finding of Moses' (1904; subsequently bought by Aird), seems if anything less Egyptian than all his previous academic compilations (Swanson 1990: 88, 267, 475, no. 410). So scrupulously academic were they that several were engraved for the illustrations to Georg Ebers' popular introduction to Ancient Egypt (Ebers with Birch 1887), together with the work of other history painters rich in 'authentic' detail, amongst them Ernst Weidenbach, who copied the Beni Hasan tomb paintings for the Egyptologist Heinrich Brugsch, and subsequently decorated the Egyptian galleries of the Kunsthistorisches Museum in Vienna in this style (Seipel 1998: 6). Apart from the outdoor 'Finding of Moses', Alma-Tadema's Egyptian standing at his doorway (Figure 3:6) is rare amongst his works in attempting a credible Egyptian domestic setting, and also moving a little way into the open air. The concentration on massy interiors in his work perhaps reflects his conscious lack of first-hand knowledge of the larger Egyptian environment, but also derives from a lacuna in the archaeological record which was common to all: as in Edwin Long's equally detailed works with their sentimental portrayal of domestic situations (Quick 1970), Alma-Tadema's Egyptians feast, dance, and mourn their dead mostly in the context of monumental temple architecture, with additional decorative features from tombs. The record of built Egypt was firmly grounded in this area, by reason of its substantial preservation by contrast with the almost total lack of a record for domestic settings.

Amongst the few artists who could move imaginatively out from this restricted record, perhaps the most persuasive is J. J. A. Lecomte du Noüy, who painted with equal panache the louche interior scenes of the triptych 'Rhamsès dans son harem' (1885–1886, private collection; De Meulenaere *et al.* 1992: 92–93) and the sweeping vista of ancient Thebes, where Pharaoh lounges, malign and moody, atop his palace roof, with the bodies of the emissaries who have failed to find Tahoser, reluctant object of his love, sprawled bleeding on the terrace below (Figure 3:7) (Jullian 1977: 66). The night-time cityscape over which he broods is composed largely of temple pylons and

Figure 3:6   Sir Lawrence Alma-Tadema, 'A Citizen of Memphis', engraved from the painting of 1865 for Georg Ebers (1887), 'Egypt'.

Figure 3:7   J. A. Lecomte du Noüy, 'Les Porteurs de mauvaises nouvelles', 1872 (Tunis; J. Seznec archive).

Figure 3:8   G. Doré, 'Moïse devant Pharaon', engraving (Doré 1866).

colonnaded halls, with something very like the island of Philae bisecting the Nile, with the dark cliffs of the western bank rising behind it; but despite these inapposite features, Lecomte du Noüy gives us more sense of a credible inhabited world than do most of his contemporaries. The origin of these interior and exterior scenes in Théophile Gautier's *Roman de la Momie* (1858), the storyline and details of which the artist followed closely, doubtless gave them a liveliness beyond the bare scenarios which accompanied most other recreative canvases of this kind. Lecomte de Noüy had first-hand experience of Egypt. Following the advice of Gérôme, his teacher, he travelled there in the mid-1860s (Montgailhard 1906: 16) and the fluent sensuality of his other, orientalist, pictures can also be seen at work in these pharaonic recreations. He returned to Gautier's novel later in his career with 'Tristesse de Pharaon', exhibited at the Salon of 1901 (Montgailhard 1906: 139 and pl. following 96).

The *coup de théâtre* of Gautier's novel is the revelation that Poëri, object of Tahoser's love, is Moses, about to lead the captive Hebrews out of Ramesside Egypt. The Egyptian episodes in the stories of Joseph and Moses figured frequently amongst the chosen subjects for history paintings with a pharaonic milieu, and it was this Old Testament connection which brought such scenes to a much wider public in illustrated bibles and popular magazines. Appearing thus in the rather stark black-and-white medium of woodcuts and engravings, these pictures seem more than ever burdened with archaeological detail, their protagonists overshadowed by the oppressive scale of buildings which often form an improbable context for the action. In Gustave Doré's realization of Exodus 7:10 (Figure 3:8), Aaron has cast down his rod before Pharaoh in a court derived from the hypostyle hall of the temple of Hathor at Dendera, with the screen walls of the façade becoming a kind of balcony from which Pharaoh and his servants observe the miraculous serpent into which the rod has been transformed (Humbert 1989: 260–261). In England, the Dalziel brothers commissioned paintings of Old Testament subjects from various artists in order to transform them into wood-engraving for an illustrated Bible (Dalziel and Dalziel 1880): seven out of 12 pictures painted by Poynter between 1861 and 1864 presented episodes of the Joseph and Moses stories in elaborate pharaonic architectural settings which sometimes echoed elements subsequently seen in 'Israel in Egypt', and one of the Dalziel family, Thomas, contributed two of the plagues of Egypt in similar, if less elaborate, style. At the time, biblical associations were a potent factor in attempts to raise funds for the earliest fieldwork in Egypt (Drower 1982: 9), and the mental pictures generated by these images perhaps helped in this endeavour. Equally, they served to validate this kind of architectural recreation as the appropriate *mise-en-scène* when the 20th century film industry directed its attention to biblical epics: the paintings of John Martin, with their thrilling scale, were especially influential (Feaver 1974: 211–213; Serafy 2003).

Stripped of their colours and reduced to the leaner form of woodcuts and engravings, Egyptianizing recreations as they appeared in bibles, illustrated magazines and popular handbooks seem more than ever to deserve the patronizing criticisms levelled at them by some of their less enthusiastic contemporary commentators: "five o'clock tea antiquity" indeed, in the words of James Whistler, responding to Alma-Tadema's 'Finding of Moses' (Swanson 1977: 29). From the privileged position of her Luxor home – Henry Salt's old house built into the ruins of the temple, towards the left of Gérôme's sketch of the monument (Figure 3:1) – Lucie

Duff Gordon (Gordon with Ross and Searight 1983: 140) could smugly write in 1864, "Fancy pictures of Eastern things are hopelessly absurd, and fancy poems too. I have got hold of a stray copy of Victor Hugo's 'Orientales', and I think I never laughed more in my life". Her remark was prompted by the mirth of an Arab friend at seeing a published engraving of William Hilton's 'Rebecca at the Well' (1833: Tate Britain): "Why did he not paint a well in England with girls like English peasants?", inquired Sheikh Yussuf. Why indeed; yet the image of Ancient Egypt promulgated in bible pictures and the illustrated papers through the medium of history paintings probably supplied more people with their ideas of Egyptian architecture than any purely academic source, just as the cinema has definitively shaped more recent concepts of built Egypt. With the news that the archaeologist Brian Fagan was proposing to excavate the set for Cecil B. DeMille's 1923 film of *The Ten Commandments* from the sands of California (*The Times*, 10 April 1985), the encounter between archaeology and art seemed to have come full circle.

Note

1   The genre of Egyptian history painting has been well served by publications in recent years: in addition to monographic treatments of particular artists or the genre itself, there are also useful discussions within surveys of orientalism or 'Egyptomania'. A general overview with lavish illustrations and short biographies of many of the leading practitioners is provided by De Meulenaere *et al.* 1992. For more concise selections, see Clayton 1982: 177–181; Humbert 1989: 237–270. A useful view of Egyptianizing paintings within the wider context of orientalism is provided by: Fine Art Society 1978, 1980; Jullian 1977. Many of the monographs of individual artists cited in the references for this chapter include a *catalogue raisonné* or complete list of their works.

CHAPTER 4

EGYPT IN THE SNOW[1]

Helen Whitehouse

The traveller who leaves St Petersburg in winter by the southbound road meets
Egyptian sphinxes (Figure 4:1) in the snow at Pulkovo, where the road branches. They
sit guarding Thomas de Thomon's neoclassical fountain (Whitehouse 1996: fig. 1),
built in 1809 to water the imperial carriage horses on their way to the great complex of
palaces and parks at Tsarskoye Selo (Petrov *et al.* 1969: 420–421, fig. 4), and they are the
harbingers of other Egyptian images to come in that great creation of Tsarist Russia;
indeed, an Egyptianizing *tempietto* figured amongst other fountain designs for
Pulkovo by Andrei Nikiforovich Voronikhin (Grimm 1963: 76, fig. 157, no. 150).

Figure 4:1
Pulkovo
fountain, on
the road
from St
Petersburg
to Tsarskoye
Selo (©
Nikolai
Praslov).

Perhaps the most surprising of these Egyptian images at Tsarskoye Selo is the entrance gate where the St Petersburg road enters the park on the north-west side (Figure 4:2; Humbert *et al.* 1994: 189, fig. 313). Designed by the Scottish architect Adam Menelas for Tsar Nicholas I, it was constructed between 1827 and 1830 (Lemus 1984: pls. 164–165; for an 1829 drawing by Menelas, see Bardowskaja and Schwarina 1982: 66, no. 21, fig. 38). The massive pylonesque towers of brick, faced with cast-iron plate reliefs (Whitehouse 1996: figs. 4, 5; Figure 4:3) by the sculptor Vassily Demut-Malinovsky, show clearly the influence of the illustrations in the *Description de l'Égypte* (*Description* 1809–1828). The gateway is one of a number of oriental creations in the parks of Tsarskoye Selo, and one that is typical of its period – comparable, for instance, to Luigi Canina's Egyptian portico (Whitehouse 1996: fig. 6) added to the Borghese Gardens in Rome at exactly the same period.[2] It also exemplifies the more archaeological approach which is manifest everywhere in Egyptianizing designs of the 1820s, thanks to the publications generated by the French expedition.

The creation of the Tsarskoye Selo gate falls within a period when there was quite a strong Russian interest in the burgeoning academic discipline of Egyptology, and particularly in the decipherment of hieroglyphs. Russian scholars corresponded with Champollion (Dewachter 1993),[3] and just before work began on the gate, the collection of antiquities formed in Egypt by C. O. Castiglione had been acquired by the Russian Academy of Sciences (Berlev 1991: 23; Piotrovsky *et al.* 1974: 5–6). In 1832, a few years after the gate's completion, a pair of Egyptian sphinxes from the mortuary temple of Amenophis III at Thebes was placed on the Neva embankment in St Petersburg (Figure 4:4 col. pl., Figure 4:5; Porter and Moss 1972: 453–454). The site – the landing stage beside the Academy of Arts – was chosen by Nicholas I himself, the setting was designed by the Academy's Professor of Architecture, Konstantin Thon,

Figure 4:2   Egyptian entrance to the Alexandra Park at Tsarskoye Selo, 1827–1830, designed by Adam Menelas (© Nikolai Praslov).

and the sphinxes came to number among the most familiar landmarks of the city, down to the present day when miniatures of them are sold as tourist souvenirs (Figure 4:6), and their image is firmly lodged in art and imagination (Figure 4:7). They also set a fashion for sphinxes on other embankments (Figures 4:8, 4:9, 4:10). Yet the entrance of real Egyptian antiquities into the urban landscape of St Petersburg paradoxically marks the end of the phase in which Egyptian motifs were fashionable in the design of interiors and gardens in Russia, a terminus which coincides with the waning of the fashion elsewhere.

In Russia the Egyptian style largely predates a marked interest in or engagement with Egypt, and its roots must be seen to lie in Italy, for many of its decorative sources as well as some of its executants, and especially in France, for the impetus given by the *retour d'Égypte* there. In its Russian manifestations, the

Figure 4:3   Detail of entrance gate in 4:2 (© Nikolai Praslov).

Figure 4:5   One of the Amenophis III sphinxes today (see Figure 4:4 col. pl. for a 19th century painting of the same location; © Nikolai Praslov).

vogue for *Égyptienneries* is thus, to some extent, an indication of the capacity of the Egyptian style to flourish as a decorative form, independent of the archaeological exploration of Egypt. Despite this remoteness, however, the quality and range of Russian creations in the Egyptian style make the phenomenon particularly interesting, and the visual presence of Egypt imprinted so strongly in a remote culture may be one reason why Egyptian imagery subsequently plays a striking role in Russian literature. A fundamental collection of the Russian material was published some years ago by Katsnelson (1976), and many individual works have appeared in books on Russian architecture and the

Figure 4:6   Tourist souvenir sphinx (length 72 mm) (© Helen Whitehouse).

Figure 4:7   'Christmas in St Petersburg' by Alexander Bazarin (b. 1963) used in 2002 as a card to support the relief of hardship and suffering in Russia (courtesy of L. and A. Gallery).

decorative arts, but a comprehensive synthesis remains to be made, and would require a thorough investigation of Russian collections and archives.

Like most great parks of the later 18th century, the gardens of Catherine the Great's palace at Tsarskoye Selo were embellished with a pyramid (Figure 4:11), constructed during the period in the 1770s and 1780s when the Scottish architect Charles Cameron was in charge of building works there, and Vasily Neyelov laid out the landscape garden with the assistance of Catherine's English gardener, Mr Bush (Lemus 1984: pl. 133). As one of an array of orientalizing buildings and artful ruins, it was typical for a garden of that period, yet atypical in its function – instead of being an emblematic monument or a practical ice-house, it was the resting place for three of Catherine's favourite dogs, including

Figure 4:8   Sphinxes by the sculptor Mikhail Shemyakin (b. 1943) on the Robespierre embankment (© Nikolai Praslov).

Figure 4:9   Sphinxes on the Sverdlovsk embankment (© Nikolai Praslov).

Figure 4:10   Detail of one of the sphinxes in 4:9 (© Nikolai Praslov).

Figure 4:11   Pyramid in the grounds of Catherine the Great's Palace at Tsarskoye Selo (© Nikolai Praslov).

her beloved English whippet, 'Sir Tom Anderson'. The park contained also that other quintessential Egyptian monument, the obelisk (Figure 4:12), in this case designed by Antonio Rinaldi and raised in honour of General Piotr Rumiantsev's victory of 1770 over the Turks at Kagul (Lemus 1984: 171, pl. 123; for a drawing of 1825–1826 see Bardowskaja and Schwarina 1982: 67, no. 26, fig. 34). It was to be followed in 1799 by the Rumiantsev obelisk erected in St Petersburg to the design of Vincenzo Brenna, originally sited on the Champ de Mars, but moved in 1820 to Rumiantsev Square (Petrov and Bulgakov 1976: 306–307).[4]

In the 1790s lions modelled on the familiar Egyptian lions of Rome (Roullet 1972: 130–132, nos. 271–272, 273–274) began to appear in the repertoire of garden statues and architectural ornaments in Russia, and continued to be popular over the next few decades.[5] Among later examples are the lions (Figure 4:13),

Figure 4:12   Obelisk at Tsarskoye Selo (1770), commemorating victory over the Turks at Kagul (© Nikolai Praslov).

modelled on the Capitoline pair, on either side of the entrance porch to the
Oussatchev-Naïdenov house at 53, Ul. Tchkalova (old Sadovoye Koltso), in Moscow
(architects: D. Gilardi and A. Grigoryev; Ilyin and Aleksandrov 1975: 110–111, pl. 319).
An original variant of the Acqua Felice sculptures marks the balustrades of the
Kuzminki Park (Tikhomirov 1955: figs. 240–241, 243). The form of these lions and the
circumstances of their creation typify two aspects of the Egyptian style in Russia: it
was heavily reliant on the decorative repertoire of the second half of the 18th century,
and it was often the work of émigré Italian and French architects and designers
working in conjunction with serf architects and craftsmen (for the Italians, see Lo
Gatto 1943, 1993).

   An early example of the Egyptian style in interiors is provided by the house at
Ostankino (now absorbed into greater Moscow), built and decorated for Count
Nikolai Sheremetev through the 1790s by Giacomo Quarenghi and others, and
finished in 1801. Each doorway in the suite of state rooms is surmounted by a pair of
gilt sphinxes, but the Egyptian detail is most pronounced in the Blue Room, where the
entablature of the doorway is supported by figures in the familiar shape of the
Egyptian Antinous (cf. Roullet 1972: 86, no. 98), transformed here by their execution
in blue-grey marble consonant with the cool blue décor (Semionova 1981: pls. 24, 28–
29, 33, 35). The sense is of a modest Egyptian intrusion into a classical scheme, but a
more pervasive Egyptian influence can be seen at the great imperial palace of
Pavlovsk, built for Catherine the Great's son Paul by Cameron and Brenna, but with
the interior décor modified after a disastrous fire in 1803 (Massie 1990). The design of
the celebrated Egyptian vestibule by Voronikhin dates to this modification (Flit *et al.*
1993: 103–104; Massie 1990: 71, figs. between 268–269; Whitehouse 1996: fig. 17): the
original statues of the 12 months were replaced with Egyptian figures by the sculptor
Ivan Prokofievich Prokofiev. The theme is taken up in the fresco by Giovanni Scotti in

Figure 4:13   Lions in the entrance porch of 53 Ul. Tchkalova, Moscow (© Valentin Arkatov).

the adjoining stairwell, where a peaceful park landscape is framed by pilasters with palm-capitals; a pair of statues sitting in relaxed pose at the left recall Clodion's charming terracotta *Égyptiennes* with their corkscrew-curl hairstyles and headcloths (Humbert *et al.* 1994: 128–129, nos. 53–54), and the latter detail is echoed on the figures of the otherwise classical frieze which the pilasters support (Flit *et al.* 1993: 105). The bronzed sculptures are by contrast rather severe, backed against the walls with their arms held rigidly at their sides, static copies of the canonical types of Egyptian sculpture in Italian collections, the ensemble giving the impression that the visitor has just walked into a Roman sculpture gallery of the 18th century. In the antechamber there are two further statues, one an Antinous figure, the other a copy of a statue in the Vatican Museum (Roullet 1972: 116, no. 205).

Voronikhin was also the designer of some of the furniture at Pavlovsk, which includes a pair of striking consoles supported by carved and gilded figures reminiscent of inscribed shabtis (Chenevière 1988: 189, pl. 195). The design is a more systematically Egyptian elaboration of the type of furniture with sphinx monopod legs already familiar in Russia in the 1790s and undoubtedly imported from France (cf. Humbert *et al.* 1994: 285, no. 166), where it was already prominent in pre-Napoleonic neoclassicism; there are several other Russian examples (e.g. Chenevière 1988: 88, pl. 69, 152–153; pl. 149, 168; pl. 168, 188; pl. 194, and unpublished pieces in the Hermitage). Though the origins of the style may be French, when created by Russian craftsmen in light-coloured native woods such as birch and poplar, such furniture takes on new aspects of colour and contrast, as well as, on occasions, a certain naiveté (e.g. Sokolova and Orlova 1973: figs. 134, 137).

As he seems to have been a key figure in the creation and diffusion of the Egyptian style in Russia, certain aspects of Voronikhin's career are of significance (Chenevière 1988: 148–177; Flit *et al.* 1993: 61–62; Grimm 1963). The protégé (and almost certainly the natural son) of Count Alexander Stroganov, he travelled in Europe from 1786 to 1790 with his patron's legitimate son and heir Paul and his French tutor, and would have been exposed to the currents of contemporary design which included important forerunners of the Napoleonic Egyptian style. His patron's influence also determined many of the fields in which he worked: as President of the Academy of Arts in 1800, Stroganov took a particular interest in the development of the stone-polishing factories established after the discovery in the later 18th century of deposits of semi-precious stones in the Urals and the Altai mountains (Chenevière 1988: 259–281). Voronikhin's work as a designer for the new industry doubtless accounts for the Egyptian elements which appear in some of the bronze mounts applied to the opulent hard stone vases from the imperial factory at Ekaterinburg (Sverdlovsk). A striking example is the pair of quartz vases borne by bronze Egyptians (Chenevière 1988: fig. 299; Whitehouse 1996: fig. 13), for which there is a drawing by Voronikhin dating to 1809 (Alexeieva *et al.* 1993: 198; Grimm 1963: 114, 165, no. 471). They are the massive sisters of the jauntier male figures who function as the fruit-stands designed for the Sèvres Egyptian dinner services after Denon's (1802) illustrations (Humbert *et al.* 1994: 226–227, no. 117). The first service, given to Tsar Alexander I by Napoleon, arrived in St Petersburg at the end of 1807, so the Ekaterinburg design bears a direct chronological relationship to this event; despite this topicality, however, it looks back to earlier sources in the detailing of the granite bases with chunky gilt hieroglyphs and miniature Capitoline lions. In other designs, too, the Ekaterinburg vases hark back to the 18th century Egyptianizing style – a pair of languid Antinous-like figures resting against the sides of an agate-jasper vase dated to 1805 (Sokolova and Orlova 1973: pl. 36; Whitehouse 1996: fig. 14) are clearly influenced by one of the vases (Whitehouse 1996: fig. 15) published by the Abbé de Saint-Non in 1763 after a drawing by Hubert Robert (Cayeux 1964: 333, no. 50). Voronikhin's Egyptianizing work may have extended into the second decade of the century at the Golitsyn estate at Kuzminki, south of Moscow, though the Egyptian pavilion in the grounds is perhaps the work of his collaborator there, Domenico Gilardi, who also executed Egyptian frescoes in the Orangery (Tikhomirov 1955: figs. 234, 244).

The fashion for Egypt in interior decoration seems to have lasted until about 1830 in Russia, without deviating significantly from its 18th century roots. The substantial redecoration after a fire in 1820 of the Golitsyn palace at Arkhangelskoye, by then the property of Prince Nicolai Yusupov, included an Egyptian décor for the state dining room which, it has been suggested, reflects the Masonic interests of the architect in charge of the restoration, Yevgraf Tiurin (Rapoport *et al.* 1984: 143, pls. 50–51). Whatever the motive, the scheme is an interesting blend of two 18th century sources, Piranesi (see Werner Chapter 5, this volume; Whitehouse Chapter 3, this volume) and Robert (Humbert Chapter 2, this volume), the latter represented elsewhere in the palace by a number of his paintings. Distinctly reminiscent of Piranesi's Egyptian designs are the heavy masonry forms, but their massy effect is here reduced by the charming pastel colours and the intrusion of the Robert-like landscape with ruins. The same Piranesi-like effect may be seen, on a more domestic scale, in the frescoes of the entrance hall (Figure 4:14) of the Verstovsky house in Moscow, of the same decade (Ilyin and Aleksandrov 1975: pl. 317).

As we have already seen with Menelas' gateway for Tsarskoye Selo, the style of Egyptian creations was changing in the 1820s with the accessibility of new archaeo-logical information, and it was also begin-ning to be directed to some unexpected purposes. In common with several other places in the 1820s and 1830s, St Petersburg acquired its 'Egyptian Bridge', that strange marriage of Egyptian forms to the wonders of 19th century technology: the penultimate bridge over the Fontanka canal, built in 1826, was a chain bridge (Figure 4:15) de-signed by the engineers P. S. Kristianovich and G. Traitteur, suspended between iron pylons and decorated at either end with sphinxes by the sculptor Piotr Sokolov, then usefully bearing lamps on their extraordi-nary extended Nemes-headdresses.[6] After its collapse in 1905, the old bridge was re-placed by another with a steel frame. Only the sphinxes remained, and to reinforce the Egyptian theme, two pairs of small cast iron

Figure 4:14   Entrance hall of the Verstovsky house, Moscow, 1820–1830 (© Jean-Marcel Humbert).

Figure 4:15   'Egyptian Bridge' over the Fontanka canal at St Petersburg, print of 1834 (Ashmolean Museum, Oxford).

Figure 4:16   Detail of the 'Egyptian Bridge' in St Petersburg today (© Nikolai Praslov).

obelisks were added (Humbert *et al.* 1994: 315, 323 n. 1; Figure 4:16); there are also two copies of the Fontanka bridge sphinxes on the Bolshoya Evka embankment (Figure 4:17). Possibly also of the 1820s are the Egyptians who labour to support the oriel windows of no. 8 Naberezhnaya Dvortsovaya in St Petersburg (Figure 4:18; Whitehouse 1996: fig. 20), a house with a complex history, originally designed by Francesco Rastrelli in the 18th century, but remodelled twice in the 19th (Petrov *et al.* 1969: 482; Vityazeva and Kirikov 1986: 104). This addition may date to the alterations apparently carried out by Luigi Rusca, who also worked extensively at Pavlovsk between 1820 and 1830, although the date is problematic: the figures are in the tradition of much earlier Egyptian telamones, derived ultimately from the pair of granite figures of Antinous from Tivoli (Roullet 1972: 87, nos. 101–102), but they also echo the popularity of classical atlantes and caryatids in Petersburg architecture, a fashion particularly strong in the mid-19th century.[7]

With the chain bridge and the arrival of the sphinxes on the Neva embankment six years later, we seem to be virtually at the end of the Egyptian vogue in Russia. The style does not seem to have enjoyed the substantial revival seen elsewhere in the second half of the 19th century, under the impetus of the construction of the Suez Canal. The rash of 'post-Tutankhamun' constructions of the 1920s and 1930s elsewhere seems to have been only faintly experienced in Russia; in St Petersburg, a striking block of flats at 23, Ul. Kalyaeeva (today 23, Ul. Zakharevskaya), with figures of pharaohs flanking the doors, as well as a façade decorated with Egyptian motifs which continue into the passages and the inside courtyard, seemingly predates 'Tutmania' (Figures 4:19, 4:20; Whitehouse 1996: figs. 21–24).

Figure 4:17   Sphinxes on the Bolshoya Evka embankment of 'Stone Island' (© Nikolai Praslov).

Despite maintaining a constant academic interest and producing some notable Egyptologists, Russia did not become a major force in Egyptian archaeology, nor did she accumulate a vast national collection of Egyptian antiquities (Berlev and Hodjash 1998): the efforts of private collectors were more significant in this respect.[8] Perhaps the absence of these factors, and the remoteness of Egypt, separated physically and mentally by the vast tracts of Russia's own orient, may explain why some of the later developments of the Egyptian style which can be observed in Europe and America seem not to have impinged on Russia. Russian ballet was to dip into Egypt, as into many other exotic areas, for subject matter: Théophile Gautier's *Roman de la momie* (1858) in particular (Whitehouse 1996: fig. 27) provided the inspiration for several creations,[9] and on occasion Egyptianizing stage designs of great imaginative quality appeared, as in Leon Bakst's work (Humbert *et al.* 1994:

Figure 4:18 Egyptian figure on the façade of 8, Naberezhnaya Dvortsovaya, St Petersburg (© Nikolai Praslov).

Figure 4:19 Façade of 23, Ul. Kalyaeeva, St Petersburg, ca. 1910–1920 (© Nikolai Praslov).

447, no. 303) for the original 1909 production of Fokine's *Cléopâtre*, a ballet
freely adapted from Pushkin's *Egyptian
Nights*, or Sonia and Robert Delaunay's
designs for the 1918 revival in London
(Sotheby and Co. 1972: 18, pl. 1Xa, 80–
81, pl. XXXV, no. 75). Apart from such
specifically theatrical creations, Russian
art does not seem to have shared the
penchant for Egyptian historical subjects manifest in 19th century painting
in western Europe and America, possibly because the history and geographical diversity of Russia provided
sufficient material for its painters.[10]

Figure 4:20   Detail of entrance and portico of
23, Ul. Kalyaeeva (© Nikolai Praslov).

The sight of *Aegyptiaca* in the snow
is indeed a strange one, and the strongly
alien presence of such images in the
frosty light of winter or the white nights
of summer may be one reason why the
Egyptian style in Russia makes an
impression which is disproportionately
strong in relation to its relatively
confined appearance there. Another
potent factor may be its connection with
the great flowering of the imperial Russian style in St Petersburg and Moscow in the
early decades of the 19th century. It is perhaps in part because of the strength of this
image and its cultural associations that the concept of Egypt is explored more
frequently and in more various ways in Russian literature than in any other. Many of
the themes and metaphors employed are familiar from the western mental construct
of Ancient Egypt, as shaped by classical tradition and located firmly in the sphere of
'opposite' oriental cultures – a negative view of Egypt as the quintessence of what is
ancient and dead, the paradigm of an oppressive and despotic society, the antipole to
western thought and culture. But in the work of Russian writers of very different
periods, these negatives take on a new and personal relevance, since they are invoked
with direct reference to Russia itself. Pushkin's unfinished story *Egyptian Nights* is set
in the decadent Alexandrian court of Cleopatra, as characterized in Roman literature;
during the long period of its evolution from the poem *Cleopatra* (1824) to the story of
1835, Pushkin seems to have carried in mind the image of an Egypt, not only
hellenistic but also pharaonic, which he saw echoed by contemporary society (O'Bell
1984: 56–68, 125). In his eyes, the uncongenial occupants of an aristocratic St
Petersburg drawing-room might be "mute, motionless mummies which remind me
of the Egyptian tombs ...", chillingly repellent because "nothing European occupies
their thoughts" (a fragment of 1830 quoted in O'Bell 1984: 58). At the period at which
he wrote this, Pushkin was acquainted with representatives of contemporary
Egyptology, in the persons of I. A. Gulyanov, and Champollion's Russian
correspondent A. N. Olyenin (O'Bell 1984: 66), yet his negative view seems firmly

anchored in the 18th century vision of Egypt, just as was the style of the kind of 'Egyptian' furniture and décor that he might have seen in those St Petersburg salons (see O'Bell 1984: 64–65 on the character of the parallel drawn between Russia and Egypt in the 18th century).

In a very different era of Russian history, Osip Mandelshtam drew upon the image of Egypt, and also Assyria, as societies which paralleled that into which he perceived Stalinist Russia was evolving in the early 1920s. Reviewing the cultural bias of the two preceding centuries in his critical essay 'The Nineteenth Century', he saw that "our century has begun under the sign of great intolerance, exclusiveness, and conscious noncomprehension of other worlds. The heavy blood of extremely distant, monumental cultures, perhaps of Egypt and Assyria, flows in the veins of our century" (trans. in Harris 1991: 143). In its senseless pursuit of the monumental at the expense of the individual, contemporary Russia was for Mandelshtam locked into one of the "epochs which maintain that man is insignificant", as when "Egyptians and Egyptian builders treat the human mass as building material in abundant supply ..." (Harris 1991: 181; from 'Humanism and the Present' 1923). But Egypt also serves as a more generalized image of the past and of futility in Mandelshtam's writing. In his story 'The Egyptian Stamp', published in 1928 but set retrospectively in 1917, the year of revolution, the imagery of Ancient Egypt runs like an *ostinato* through the text, evoked not only in the distant spectre of pyramids and the mummified recipients of animal worship, but also in the palpable and immediate Egyptian images of St Petersburg itself (West 1980: 60–61): the Theban sphinxes opposite the University on the Neva embankment, the chain bridge which "never so much as smelled Egypt" over the shabby Fontanka (trans. in Brown 1967: 149–189, and see also 32–57). The stamp of the title is a modern Egyptian postage stamp, a thing of no value, and it figures among the insults flung at the weak hero Parnok, who timorously clings to a remembered clutter of past things, his "dear Egypt of objects"; the culture of the pyramid builders is also the metaphor for utter futility.

A potent and more positive Egyptian theme for some of Mandelshtam's literary contemporaries was the idea of mystic Egypt, particularly as purveyed in the Neoplatonic and esoteric writings of late antiquity. In the 19th century this occult tradition had provided a rich vein of material for alternative cults and philosophies everywhere, including a notable example with Russian roots: in the early stages of the Theosophy movement, Helena Petrovna Blavatsky drew extensively upon the tradition for her 'bible', *Isis Unveiled* (1878), and the Egyptian members of the movement's invisible 'Brotherhood of Masters'.[11] Theosophy and related mystic ideologies were to figure among the major influences on the work of the Russian Symbolists, in which Egypt, and especially the image of the sphinx in both its Egyptian and classical manifestations, form an important strand. Many of these writers had first-hand experience of Egypt, notably Andrei Bely, who travelled there in 1911 and recorded his reactions in notes published the following year (Bely 1912a, b, c; Schmidt 1986: 69–142). Typically, it was a place of mystic revelation for Bely: he gazed into the eyes of the Sphinx at Giza for a half hour, and – like many symbolist writers – found that its expression changed (letter from Bely to Blok, in Schmidt 1986: 283). But he also registered strongly an alien quality which he used as a parallel for the contemporary culture of Tsarist Russia in its terminal stages. In the ambiguous coda to his novel *Petersburg*, published in three parts 1913–1914 but set in the strife-torn year

of 1905, the novel's central character, Nikolai Apollonovich Ableukhov, failed
parricide and revolutionary, retreats to an Egyptian exile which seems to represent a
kind of limbo from which he will be regenerated into new and innocent life (for
various interpretations, see Elsworth 1983: 83–111; Nivat 1967; Woronzoff 1990). This
is the landscape of death, in which he abandons the study of Kant and becomes an
Egyptologist, writing a monograph, 'On the Letter of Dauphsekhrut' (the text now
known as 'The Satire of the Trades'), but it also represents the summation of failure;
in the shadow of the decaying head of the Sphinx, he sees himself at the apex of his
own pyramidal culture destined to crash into ruins. As befits the novel's title, St
Petersburg itself is almost a character in the book, present in the strong and oppressive
images which Bely reads in its neoclassical architecture; but in focusing upon his
actual experience of Egypt, he does not draw upon that strange antithesis posed by the
presence of Egyptian relics and symbols in the north that is explored in other
Symbolist writing. It forms the basis of Vyacheslav Ivanov's poem *Sfinksy nad Nevoi*
(Sphinxes beside the Neva), where the mystery of the granite statues of the Neva
embankment, brought from Thebes "into the captivity of polar marvels", is seen to be
heightened by their alien surroundings (Ivanov 1911, I: 135). With the descent of
Bely's anti-hero into Egyptology, we move towards the intrusion into Russian
literature of Egyptian imagery drawn more directly from pharaonic sources, a trend
exemplified in Velimir Khlebnikov's (1968, II, iv: 47–69; trans. in Khlebnikov 1985: 85–
104) short narrative *Ka*, a fantastic kaleidoscope of time and perceptions, in which the
narrator uses the device of the Egyptian *ka* "the soul's shadow, its double, its envoy to
the world some snoring gentleman dreams of ...", to travel backwards and forwards
in time, dipping into the Egypt of Amenophis IV, and moving forward to the year
2222. Underlying Khlebnikov's futurist text is a more old-fashioned fascination with
the orient (see Mirsky 1975: esp. 26–31), and an intoxication with words, the play on
words, and the power of their sound – Egyptian names are strewn through the text,
and Amenophis' soul, migrated into an ape, moves from hymn-like speech to
monkey-babble. Khlebnikov's literary exploitation of Egypt is a far cry from Pushkin's
evocation of a decadent, non-western culture echoed by Russian society of his own
time, yet he himself saw in it a parallel – "I struck a harmonious note to 'Egyptian
Nights'", he wrote, "the attraction of the snowstorm of the North to the Nile and its
tropical heat" (O'Bell 1984: 126–127) – and in this definition we may perhaps read the
motive behind many of those creations which brought Egypt into the alien territory of
Tsarist Russia.

Notes

1   This chapter is a revised version of a paper published in French (Whitehouse 1996). The
     editors have inserted some cross-references to other chapters in books within the series,
     and have supplied some new illustrations.
2   Already in the time of Nicholas' brother, Alexander I (ruled 1801–1825), Jakub Kubicki
     had designed an Egyptian temple for the grounds of the Belvedere Palace in Warsaw
     (Dmochowski 1956: 389–390; Kwiatowski 1986: 29–30, 32, fig. 33, col. pl. 42).
3   An even earlier – but isolated – interest is witnessed by the copies of inscriptions on the
     Egyptian obelisk in Istanbul (Hassan 2003a: Figures 2:13, 2:14; Iversen 1972: 9–33, esp. figs.
     6–9) filed in the archives of Tsar Alexis I Mikhailovich, who ruled from 1645 to 1676
     (Waugh 1977).
4   Earlier examples included the (no longer extant) alley of obelisks leading to the triumphal
     arch in Moscow (Ilyin and Aleksandrov 1975: 27), and the obelisk commemorating the

foundation of Pavlovsk Palace outside St Petersburg in 1777 (Flit *et al.* 1993: 185, 221), as well as smaller obelisks dating to the 1780s (Petrov 1969: 296–297).

5   For instance, at Arkhangelskoye, two pairs of lions (unfortunately currently boarded up, 2003) flanked the entrance on the west side of the palace, which was designed in Paris in 1780 by Charles de Guerne; they may date to the landscaping of the palace grounds, begun in 1799 by Giacomo Trombara (Rapoport *et al.* 1984: 20, pls. 9–10). Another pair of lions guard the entrance to the La Valle house, at 4, Nab. Krasnogo Flota, in St Petersburg (architects: Voronikhin and Thomon, 1790–1800; Petrov *et al.* 1969: 71–72, fig. 1).

6   The Director of Kristianovich and Traitteur's department, P-D. Bazaine, planned an even larger Egyptian bridge on the Neva at the level of Vasilevsky Island, but this was never realized (Pantazzi 1994e).

7   The best-known examples are the imposing sculptures of the entrance portico to the Hermitage by Alexander Ivanovich Terebeniev (1812–1859), following a design of Leo von Klenze (1784–1864), executed in 1849. See also those of the Demidov house, 43, Ul. Gertsena (1840–1850), and of the Yussupov palace, 42, Liteenye Prospekt (Petrov *et al.* 1969: 333–335, figs. 1, 3, 340–341, fig. 1).

8   Vladimir Semionovich Golenischev (1856–1947) – orientalist and collector – made the first of numerous trips to Egypt in 1879. By the early 1900s, his collection of objects and papyri numbered some 8000; the collection is now in the Moscow Museum of Fine Arts (S. Hodjash, pers. comm.; Dawson and Uphill 1995: 170). For other private collections, see Berlev 1991: 23–28.

9   M. Petipa's ballet after Gautier's novel, *The Pharaoh's Daughter*, created at the Bolshoi in 1862, was greatly modified for its 1905 revival, where the dancers were shown in profile in the style of Egyptian reliefs (Money 1982: 58–62). After having triumphed in the role of Princess Bint-Anta in this ballet, Anna Pavlova performed *The Egyptian Mummy* ('The Egyptian Ballet'), where she "scrupulously imitated the attitudes learnt from close study of Egyptian papyri and stelae" (Hyden 1931: 165–166). She danced *The Egyptian Mummy* in Cairo in 1923. *The Pharaoh's Daughter* was revived at the Bolshoi in May 2000.

10 Egyptian antiquities have nonetheless attracted the attention of several Russian painters. Vasily D. Polenov (1844–1927), an influential teacher, put together a small collection as part of the 'museum' in his studio (Polenov 1982: 36–37, 170). Martiros Sarian (1880–1972), who visited Egypt in 1911 (Sarian 1976: 138–168), sometimes depicted Egyptian objects in his paintings, notably in his portrait of the poet Charents, where a mummy mask appears in the background (Sarian 1976: 159).

11 The Egyptian component was removed when Mme Blavatsky turned her attention to India in 1878 (Washington 1993: 46–58). Theosophy, banned in Russia until 1908, subsequently became very popular. Egypt also figured in the later, but not fundamentally dissimilar, ideology of G. I. Gurdjieff (Washington 1993: 174), and a recent manifestation of its continuing mystique may also be noted: a *heka*-sceptre figured amongst the regalia of the so-called Maria Devi Khristos (M. Tsvygun), 'messiah' of the 'White Brotherhood' cult which waited for the end of the world in Kiev in November 1993.

Acknowledgments

In writing my original paper (Whitehouse 1996), I was aware of having entered a domain in which I am no expert, and I was grateful for the help of many colleagues: L. Haskell, D. Howells and the staff of the Slavonic section of the Taylor Institution in Oxford, the late A. Kennett, E. Martin, S. Taylor, and the staff of the Britain-Russia Centre in London. W. and G. Vogelsang provided the occasion for a memorable visit to St Petersburg in 1988, during which O. Neverov guided me through the Hermitage. I owe especial thanks to J. C. Baines, who was the first to draw my attention to the Egyptian elements in the work of Mandelshtam, and generously supplied translations and references for other Russian literature, too; C. Cooke, who advised on the problematic history of 8, Naberezhnaya Dvortsovaya; and R. Fazzini, who provided information on 23, Ul. Kalyaeeva.

We are indebted to Jean Galard, Chief of the Service Culturel of the Louvre Museum, for permission to include the updated version of Whitehouse 1996 here.

Figure 1:5   Polychrome terracotta of a full length statue of Ramesses II, designed by Fritz Albert; on Reebie's storage and removals company building in Chicago, MA, built by C-S. Kingsley, 1923 (© Jean-Marcel Humbert).

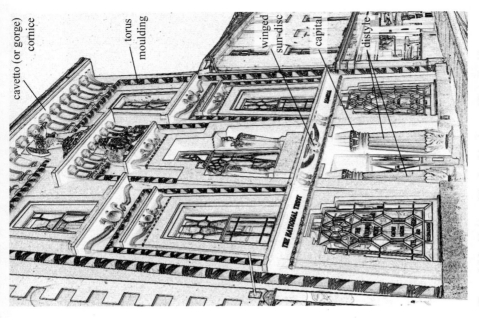

cavetto (or gorge) cornice

torus moulding

winged sun-disc

capital

distyle

THE NATIONAL TRUST

Figure 1:12 Main architectural features of Egyptianizing buildings. The battered (i.e. sloping) mouldings give the impression of a pylon tower.

THE NATIONAL TRUST

Figure 1:11 The Egyptian House in Penzance, built in 1836 by John Lavin to house a geological collection (© Jean-Marcel Humbert).

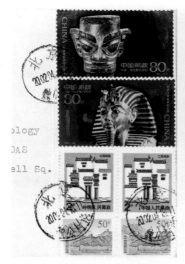

Figure 1:16   Elephant House of Antwerp Zoo designed in the shape of an Egyptian temple from Philae, built by Charles Servais 1855–1856. Note the legible hieroglyphs specifying the king under whose reign the zoo was built "to delight Antwerp and to educate its inhabitants" (© Jean-Marcel Humbert).

Figure 1:14   Chinese special stamp issue of October 2001, including Tutankhamun's gold mask (© Stuart Laidlaw).

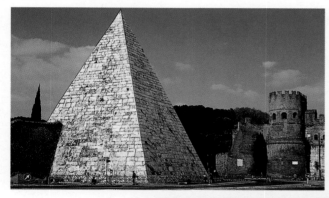

Figure 2:1   The Caius Cestius pyramid tomb in Rome (© Jean-Marcel Humbert).

Figure 2:10   The temple and obelisk at the entrance to the Terra Mítica Theme Park, Benidorm, Spain, 2001(© Jean-Marcel Humbert).

Figure 3:5 Thomas Seddon, 'Excavations at the Sphinx', watercolour, 1856 (Ashmolean Museum, Oxford).

Figure 4:4 Maxime Vorobyov's 1835 painting, 'The Neva Embankment by the Academy of Arts', St Petersburg, Russian Museum; see Figure 4:5 for a photograph of the sphinx today (© Jean-Marcel Humbert).

Figure 6:1   Arcadia Works building of Carerras Ltd, Mornington Crescent, London (© Katherine Griffis-Greenberg).

Figure 6:6   Hoover Building, Perivale, West London (© Katherine Griffis-Greenberg).

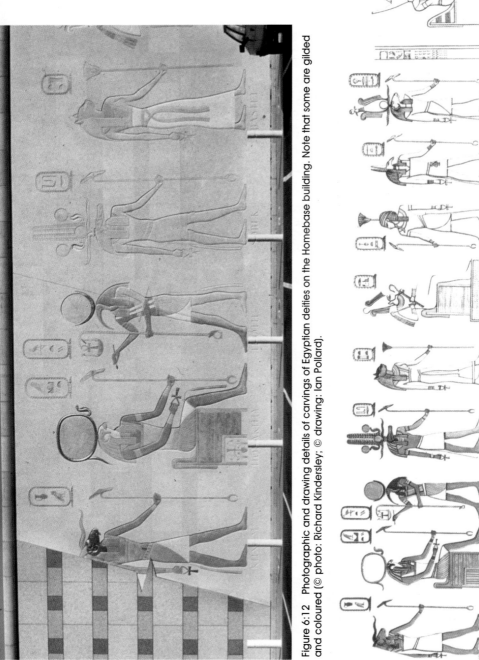

Figure 6:12   Photographic and drawing details of carvings of Egyptian deities on the Homebase building. Note that some are gilded and coloured (© photo: Richard Kindersley; © drawing: Ian Pollard).

Figure 6:7 Front entrance doorway, Hoover Building (© Katherine Griffis-Greenberg).

Figure 6:9 Carlton Cinema, Islington, London (© Chris Elliott).

Figure 6:17 Huge stained glass rendering, in Harrods, of a scene based on an ancient wall relief currently in the British Museum (© Katherine Griffis-Greenberg).

Figures 6:19–6:21   Ceremony to celebrate the opening of the Egyptian Halls in Harrods (© William Mitchell).

Figure 8:9   Jim Onan's private house in Wadsworth, Illinois, 1977 (© Roberta L. Stadler).

Figure 8:10   Detail of the entrance to Figure 8:9, showing sphinxes and pyramid-shaped house (© Roberta L. Stadler).

Figure 8:11   Detail of Figure 8:10 (© Roberta L. Stadler).

Figure 8:12   Pythian Temple, New York (© Renan Pollès).

Figure 11:2   Removal of Ramesses II's sculptured bust from the Ramesseum, Thebes (nineteenth Dynasty) (British Museum).

Figure 11:3   Ramesses II's bust pictured in Figure 11:2, now on display in the British Museum (British Museum EA19).

Figure 11:6 Chapter Room (1901–1902) of the Supreme Grand Royal Arch Chapter of Scotland, Queen Street, Edinburgh.

Figure 11:8   Grand Temple, rue de Laeken, Brussels, Belgium.

Figure 13:1   Oil painting by Leandro Joaquim (1789) of the 'Fountain of the Pyramid' in Rio de Janeiro (Museu Histórico Nacional do Rio de Janeiro).

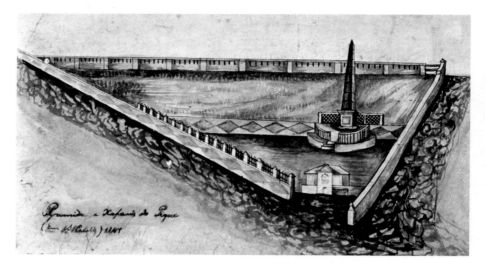

Figure 13:3   Watercolour by Miguel Dutra (1847) of 'Pyramids and Fountain of the Piques' (Museu Paulista, São Paulo).

Figure 13:5   Egyptian Room; Fernando Schlatter, ca. 1922 (Public Library, Porto Alegre).

Figure 13:8   Front door of the main entrance to the Rosicrucian Temple, Vittoria, showing the cartouche of Tuthmosis III (© Fernanda C. Pereira).

Figure 13:9   One side of the Sphinx Alley of the Rosicrucian Temple, São Paulo (© Jean-Marcel Humbert).

Figure 15:1   A model showing the Bibliotecha Alexandrina's "cosmopolitan" design (Unesco).

Figure 15:5   Detail of a new mosaic showing the founding of the city by Alexander the Great (© Beverley Butler).

Figure 15:6   Posters of Mecca and the Spice Girls sold side by side in downtown Alexandria (© Beverley Butler).

CHAPTER 5

EGYPT IN LONDON – PUBLIC AND PRIVATE DISPLAYS IN THE 19th CENTURY METROPOLIS

Alex Werner

... Every thing now must be Egyptian: the ladies wear crocodile ornaments, and you sit upon a sphinx in a room hung round with mummies, and with the long black lean-armed long-nosed hieroglyphical men, who are enough to make the children afraid to go to bed.

(Southey 1807: letter LXXI)

Displays of Ancient Egypt were a prominent feature of the 19th century metropolis (Curl 1994). Only a few visual reminders remain of them today in London, such as the modern sphinxes guarding the upper terraces to what was once the immense exhibition building at Crystal Palace in south London. This was a period when knowledge about Ancient Egypt was increasing through discovery, recording and study. Collectors and museums acquired and displayed Egyptian artefacts. Exhibition organizers, architects and artists were all involved in presenting and communicating this new evidence to an eager and excited public. There was something about Ancient Egypt that appealed to the popular imagination, an attraction that still remains today (Price and Humbert Chapter 1, this volume; MacDonald and Rice 2003).

Before the 19th century, Londoners had only a limited exposure to Ancient Egypt, its monuments and culture. As the Near East did not form part of the Grand Tour, it was left to more intrepid travellers to explore the region. For collectors who amassed cabinets of curiosities, Egyptian mummies were one of the most prized exhibits. Gradually, during the course of the 18th century, illustrated works (e.g. Montfaucon 1719; Piranesi 1769; Whitehouse Chapters 3 and 4, this volume) began to disseminate the architecture and artefacts of Ancient Egypt to a wider audience. Although the most comprehensive works were produced in France and Italy, there were books published in London that described and illustrated Egypt and its antiquities (Pococke 1,743–1,745). The British Museum displayed a few curiosities such as a mummy coffin from Saqqarah that had been bequeathed to it in 1755 by Colonel William Lethieullier. It was not long before London-based designers and architects were inspired to introduce Egyptian decorative and architectural motifs. However, in the 18th century, the Egyptian style was one of many competing styles, and the rococo, Gothic and neoclassical as well as styles from India and the Far East proved much more popular. The Egyptian style was hardly ever used on its own and remained an extreme, cultivated taste.

'Mania' takes hold

Then, at the end of the century, Ancient Egypt and its architecture, iconography and decorative patterns became all the rage in London. This newfound appeal was the result of the French military campaigns and historic and scientific investigations in Egypt, led and promoted directly by Napoleon Bonaparte (Jeffreys 2003). This was followed by Nelson's dramatic naval victory over the French at the battle of the Nile, an event of national celebration as its secured Britain's supremacy of the sea. The seizure of prized Egyptian antiquities from the French helped to legitimize the culture of Ancient Egypt as worthy of display and study. Prints and caricatures of the French and British in Egypt used the pyramids and temples as a backdrop, popularizing these ancient structures to London audiences. The monuments were seen to be of massive proportions; the statues and wall decorations were distinct and revealed a highly developed culture.

Manufacturers and retailers took up the new style. London-based designers used patterns found in French publications (e.g. Percier and Fontaine 1812) to introduce the Egyptian style. Rundell, Bridge and Rundell, the capital's leading goldsmiths, made use of Egyptian motifs in their neoclassical designs. Sphinxes and winged heads were incorporated into the plate that they supplied to the Prince of Wales. At Wedgwood's showrooms in York Street, a vast array of vases in the Egyptian style was offered for sale (Reilly 1989, 3: 91–96). Curiosity dealers began to sell Egyptian antiquities to a new band of collectors. In 1800, an 'Egyptian Festival' was staged at Drury Lane, keen to exploit the public's appetite for all things Egyptian. Critics panned the production, calling it a "puppet-show on an enlarged scale" though the scenery was praised for its "magnificence" (Dutton 1800). For scene painters, the Egyptian landscape and architecture became an inspiring subject matter.

There were also other presentations held in the metropolis that introduced the public to the landscape of the pyramids and the temples. In 1799, at the Upper Theatre of the Lyceum in the Strand, there were performances of Mark Londsdale's *Aegyptiana*, which began with a 'Hieroglyphic Painting of Isis and Osiris' and an explanation of the 'Art, Manners and Mythology of Ancient Egypt'. This was followed by the examination of the 'accuracy of a Theban Palace' and the 'idea of Cities and Temples of Egypt'. A 'Portrait of an Egyptian Mummy' then featured with a description of the 'art of embalming'. The first section ended with general views of the pyramids and the sphinx. The educative nature of the entertainment continued with a map of Lower Egypt to show locations and the course of the Nile. The rest of the show was devoted to the landscape and everyday life of modern Egypt. Subjects ranged from camels and crocodiles to agriculture and village life. Egyptian city life was represented by a view of the Great Square at Cairo. The landmarks of the ancient world made a reappearance with a view of the 'Pharillon and Harbour of Alexandria' and of 'Pompey's Pillar'. The 'Singular exploits of a Party of English Sailors', perhaps a comic interlude, led into the finale of the 'Grand Illuminated Picture' of 'Lord Nelson's Victory at the Mouth of the Nile', painted by Dodd. *Aegyptiana* must have been a strange theatrical experience. At first, the novelty of its subject matter may have held the public's interest. However, the narrative lacked a story line and drama. Other features such as a 'Gothic Tale' and a reading of Milton's *Allegro* were added in an attempt to widen the appeal of the production, but within a year *Aegyptiana* had closed (Lyceum Theatre folder 1799–1805, Enthoven Collection, Theatre Museum).

Although there were, as already mentioned above, some few Egyptian items in museum collections, the arrival of a major collection of Egyptian antiquities in London in 1802 was an important development in London's perception of Egypt's art and culture. For the first time, many Londoners came face to face with important and unusual artefacts from Egypt. Most of the objects went on display at the British Museum in two temporary sheds in the garden alongside the museum, as there was no suitable space inside old Montagu House. The most noteworthy object, picked out by guidebooks, was the large sarcophagus of variegated marble, covered with hieroglyphics, that was thought to have been the coffin that contained the ashes of Alexander the Great (*Picture of London* 1805: 166–167). Two Roman statues, believed to be of Marcus Aurelius and Severus, were recorded as having been part of the group of antiquities taken from the French in Egypt by the British. On entering the great hall, the guidebook recorded, there were two black marble monuments covered with hieroglyphics understood to have belonged to the mausoleum of Cleopatra that stood near Alexandria. A small Egyptian collection was exhibited in the first room that visitors were shown. It was displayed alongside bronzes from Pompeii and Herculaneum, a cork model of the Temple of the Sibyl at Tivoli and Etruscan vases. The Egyptian case contained some small antiquities as well as "numerous small representations of mummies" thought to serve as "patterns for those who chose and could afford to be embalmed after their decease" (*Picture of London* 1805: 167). It was clear that this material was viewed as 'curiosities', though a better understanding of what they might signify was beginning to emerge.

The sheds housing the larger Egyptian antiquities were an unacceptable location for a collection associated in the public's mind with Nelson's great victory over the French. The Trustees of the Museum appealed to government for extra funds to build new galleries. Despite the continuing war with France, government agreed. But space became a problem again as the museum acquired Charles Townley's collection of Roman antiquities. Thus, in 1808 the Egyptian material occupied only three rooms out of 13 of the new Townley Galleries. Greek and Roman antiquities were clearly considered to be more important than those from Ancient Egypt, the justification for displaying Egyptian antiquities at all lying with the feeling that the Greeks had learnt from the Egyptians (Ucko and Champion 2003). The so-called primitive forms of art could be viewed alongside 'the greatest achievements' of the Classical World (Figure 5:1).

Ancient Egypt remained high on the public agenda. Tales of exciting discoveries of treasure and mummies in Egyptian tombs appealed to the popular imagination of Londoners. Authoritative publications on Egypt and its monuments, with lavish and detailed illustrations, helped to raise the profile of this ancient civilization. For the wealthy, the Grand Tour was extended to take in Egypt as many of the main attractions on the continent were off limits and under French occupation. Travellers acquired unusual Egyptian antiquities on their journeys and on their return wanted to display them in a suitable environment in their homes (see El Daly 2003a). A 'mania', as it was sometimes called, raged in the metropolis (Watkin 1996: 497).

Figure 5:1   View of Egyptian Gallery, British Museum, ca. 1820 (Guildhall Library).

For some people, however, the enthusiasm was short-lived. By 1809, an anonymous writer in *Repository of the Arts* was relating how the fashion for the "barbarous Egyptian style" had been superseded by "classical elegance which characterized the most polished ages of Greece and Rome". So, despite new evidence about Egypt, architects and designers chose to focus on 'the antique', finding in it "more refined notions of beauty". At about the same time, Sir John Soane formulated his measured response to Egyptian architecture, which he presented in his Royal Academy lectures. As one of the leading architects of his generation, his views carried weight and influenced others to reconsider their use of the Egyptian style. In his first lecture, he admitted to being "dazzled and surprised by the magnitude and solidity" of Egyptian architecture. On closer examination, rather than "beauty and variety", he found "uniformity and tiresome monotony". He condemned the "puerile" efforts of some architects to "imitate the character and form" of Egyptian architecture, originally intended for monumental structures, "in small and confined spaces". He was especially critical of its use for shop fronts, such as the newspaper office of the *Courier* in the Strand (Fox 1992: 394). Apart from the Egyptian Hall in Piccadilly (below), few large structures were constructed in the metropolis in the Egyptian style. However, it did find favour when it came to garden ornaments and funerary monuments. Often, the gatehouses and buildings of the new 'out-of-town' cemeteries were Egyptian in character. This suggested that it was a style appropriate for the dead but not for the living. Families commissioning mausolea were attracted by its solidity. As information about Ancient Egypt was disseminated more widely, so the public identified its architecture with death and complex burial rituals, a style that Soane described as "calculated for eternity" (Watkin 1996: 496).

'Mania' in the home

Despite the common association with death, there were still some who saw Egyptian designs as appropriate for the home. Thomas Hope (1769–1831), inspired by the neoclassical, became London's leading exponent of the Egyptian style as applied to the domestic interior (Pantazzi 1994a, b, c; Thornton and Watkin 1987; Watkin 1968). His fortune, stemming from his family's banking operation in Amsterdam, allowed him to indulge in his passion for art and architecture. He helped to popularize the Greek revival style and introduce Egyptian motifs into furniture and metalwork. His eclecticism, including the customs and costumes of different cultures as well as architectural and decorative styles, was based on his lengthy travels and study of different civilizations and cultures. As a young man, he had been an adventurous traveller, his Grand Tour taking over seven years to complete. He was prepared to journey long distances to view some ancient monument or curiosity. In 1797, he travelled to Egypt and became fascinated by the architectural structures and art forms that he found there and he collected a number of Egyptian antiquities. Hope made his mark on London society through a series of spectacular rooms that he created at his house in Duchess Street, off Portland Place. These were used for entertaining and for displaying his collection of art, sculpture and antiquities. The rooms were open to a select public on application or by invitation. There were many styles used in the decoration of the rooms: the 'Egyptian' or 'Black' Room was one of the most spectacular (Figure 5:2). Hope himself had designed all its furniture and fittings in an

Figure 5:2   Hope's Egyptian Room (British Library).

Egyptian style, basing them on what he had seen and recorded during his Grand Tour. Perhaps the greatest influence on the formation of this room came from displays that he had seen in Italy rather than in Egypt. In the mid-18th century, Piranesi (Whitehouse Chapter 3, this volume) had decorated the interior of the English Coffee House in the Piazza di Spagna in Rome with Egyptian motifs and hieroglyphs. He had also published two prints of the design. There were a large number of Egyptian antiquities to be found in Italy, such as those at the Institute at Bologna and at the Vatican's Museum Clementinum, the Villa Borghese, the Villa Albani and the Capitoline in Rome (Hassan 2003a; Paul 2000: 69–75; Rosati Chapter 12, this volume). Hope obtained casts of some of the antiquities exhibited there to help him with the production of the bronze mounts, supports, carvings, inlays and reliefs of the furniture. About four spectacular chairs, Hope (1807: 43–44) revealed that:

> ... the crouching priests supporting the elbows are copied from an Egyptian idol in the Vatican; the winged Isis placed in the rail is borrowed from an Egyptian mummy-case in the Institute at Bologna, the Canopuses are imitated from the one in the Capitol; and the other ornaments are taken from various monuments at Thebes, Tentyris &c.

The publication by Denon (1802), especially the 141 engraved plates, may also have been an inspiration, although Hope had already begun his designs before the appearance of this work. The desire to create an entire environment in the Egyptian taste was certainly novel. Only the most skilled craftsmen were employed. In fact, Hope found it difficult to locate talented furniture-makers and bronze and ormolu workers in London, and he had to use Alexis Decaix, a French 'bronzist', Frederick Bogaert, a carver, born in the Low Countries, and Bogaert's young assistant Francis Chantrey (later Sir Francis). The decorative details used on the ceiling were adapted from those found on mummy cases and the frieze on the walls was adapted from Egyptian papyrus scrolls. Westmacott (1834: 214) wrote that "the prevailing colours of both the furniture and the ornaments are that pale yellow and bluish green which hold so conspicuous a rank among the Egyptian pigments, skilfully relieved by the occasional introduction of masses of black and gold". Colour was also picked out in the statues and vases, in the green basalt of the 'Pastophora, holding the God Horus' and in the black basalt figure of a priest also 'holding the God Horus'. Provenanced antiquities on display included an Egyptian lion in grey basalt from Tiberius' Palace at Capri and an Egyptian urn "in dark oriental granite, mounted in bronze" (Westmacott 1834: 215) found in the ruins of the Canopus at Hadrian's villa. Other vases, urns and sculptures were made of hard stones such as marble, 'onyz alabaster', 'red granite' and veined porphyry, each with their distinctive patinas.

At the centre of the room, balanced on either side by two specially designed low settees with bronze lions on each rectangular corner, stood what was probably the main attraction – a small Egyptian mummy. Westmacott (1834: 215) recounts that it was believed to be "one of the mementos of death which Herodotus mentions to have been carried round at festivals". The mummy was displayed in a glass case placed on a stand with sloping sides and a central opening like a gateway to a tomb or a temple underneath. Two small reliefs of seated priests guarded a "cinerary urn, in Oriental alabaster" (Westmacott 1834: 215), with animal masks on either side of the entrance and a relief of a winged Isis above. Hope (1807: 32) noted that the latter symbol was "emblematic of the immortality of the soul". The black marble fireplace in the

Egyptian Room was unusual in that it copied the façade sepulchre that had been carved from the rock, near Antiphellos, on the coast of southern Turkey. Hope believed that it would convey the massive form and strength of the original. Another fireplace in the 'Lararium', a small room where Hope displayed religious objects from many parts of the world, also had a monumental aspect and was adapted from Egyptian temple architecture. Sydney Smith (1807), reviewing Hope's (1807) book which comprised engraved views of the rooms at Duchess Street and design details of the furniture and fittings shown, felt that the furniture designs were "too bulky, massive, and ponderous, to be commodious for general use". He recognized the beauty of many of the objects but considered them to be "quite unsuitable for articles of household furniture", and he singled out the chairs in the Egyptian Room as being particularly inappropriate. He puzzled why "a fireplace should be made, in one instance, in the form of a façade to a sepulchral chamber, and in another in that of an Egyptian portico". He questioned whether emblems and symbols of "classical mythology" should be applied to furnishings.

> After having banished the heathen gods and their attributes pretty well from our poetry, we are to introduce them habitually into our eating-rooms, nurseries and staircases; and, in the course of our daily business and domestic life, to set constantly before us a chaos of symbols and effigies ... We should expect something like this taste in a vestibule of an academical museum ... but we should be sorry to see it supersede every other in the metropolis of a great and manly and polished people.
>
> (Smith 1807: 484)

Despite such criticisms and the fact that only a few copies of this very costly, 10 guinea, folio book would have been printed, Hope's work had a profound effect on interior design in London. Furniture makers such as George Smith plagiarized and popularized his patterns, introducing Egyptian motifs such as the lotus-flower and leaf, papyrus, palm and sphinx (*Repository of the Arts* 1812: pl. 31; Smith 1808).

Few Londoners attempted such a precise Egyptian interior as that created by Hope, preferring a less radical approach. They were prepared to buy standard household articles such as chairs, settees or mirrors that had Egyptian decorative motifs. But Walsh Porter was an exception. It was reported that he spent £4,000 on 'the embellishment' of Craven Cottage, in Fulham. The front door and hall were copied exactly from illustrations in Denon (1802). The interior was described as being "richly painted in the Egyptian style" with "eight immense columns covered with hieroglyphics" (Faulkner 1813: 432–434). Such unusual Egyptian interiors were essentially private displays, unlike the Egyptian Hall in Piccadilly.

In the public eye

The Egyptian Hall (Figure 5:3; Medina-González 2003: 109–111) was the first London building in the Egyptian style that all could wonder at as they walked along the street or passed by in their wagons and carriages. The building housed the collection of William Bullock, the celebrated showman, entrepreneur and collector. In 1809, Bullock had arrived in London from Liverpool with his collection of natural history material and other historical curiosities. On 4 December, he opened his 'Liverpool

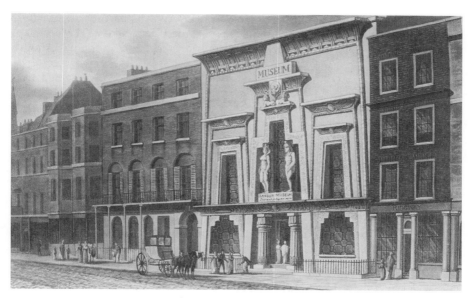

Figure 5:3   Bullock's Egyptian Hall, 1815 (Museum of London).

Museum' to great acclaim at No. 22 Piccadilly. Bell's *Weekly Messenger* of 21 January 1810 reported that the exhibition had "become the most fashionable place of amusement in London" and 22,000 people had visited it since its opening (Altick 1978: 235–252). Bullock was soon searching for larger premises. Nearby, at No. 170–171 Piccadilly, a large plot was under development and Bullock applied to construct "an extensive and substantial Building as a Museum for public exhibition" (*Survey of London* 1960: 266–270). In 1810, the proposal was approved and work on the new building started in early 1811. Bullock's architect was Peter Frederick Robinson, a specialist in historical styles who had worked on the Chinese interiors at the Brighton Pavilion. The façade of the building was loosely based on the late Ptolemaic temple of Hathor at Dendera. The overall elevation was in the shape of a large pylon with an entrance in the same overall form but narrower, flanked by two smaller and lower pylons. Above the entrance stood two imposing sculptures of Isis and Osiris. Other decorative details included sphinxes, lotus-flowers and hieroglyphs. Some critics were quite harsh about the design, arguing that such a style of architecture was inappropriate to the metropolis. However, Bullock had selected the Egyptian style because it was unusual and different. As soon as the outside elevation was completed the building became a London landmark. Bullock had planned to call his attraction 'the London Museum and Pantherion' but it soon became known as the 'Egyptian Temple' and then, a few years later, as the 'Egyptian Hall'.

The interior was quite simply furnished. There was no Egyptian embellishment in the suite of apartments and upstairs gallery. The space was filled mostly with Bullock's extensive natural history collection. Only three Egyptian items were listed in the catalogue when the museum opened in the spring of 1812. These were an "Egyptian Mummy", and two "Mummies of the White Ibis" (Bullock 1816: 94–95), one of which was exhibited in an unwrapped form. Great play was made of the age of the items:

> What are our boasted monuments of antiquity? The dates of our churches and cathedrals (though crumbled and crumbling into dust) are but as yesterday when compared to the age of a few perishable feathers, which had existence on the banks of the Nile perhaps two thousand years before the foundation stone of the first of them was laid.

(Bullock 1816: 95)

Bullock introduced new exhibits to keep the attraction in the public eye. His most successful acquisition was Napoleon's bulletproof battlefield carriage in 1816, bought from the Prince Regent for £2,500. This item along with other Napoleon memorabilia had great appeal to Londoners and attracted 220,000 visitors during an eight month display (Medina-González 2003: Figure 7:2).

In 1819, Bullock sold his collection and converted the Egyptian Hall into a series of exhibition and salerooms. He employed J. B. Papworth, an architect, designer and artist, to redecorate and add a balcony to the main hall known as the 'great room' in the Egyptian style (Figure 5:4). Papworth was known especially for the work that he had carried out at Claremont, Surrey, for Prince Leopold and Princess Charlotte. He designed Rudolph Ackermann's show room and offices at 96 Strand. His decoration for the Egyptian Hall was confident and lively. The gallery railings comprising serpents holding chains appeared quite humorous and the signs of the zodiac seemed to float playfully round the dome of the skylight. The squat columns supporting the gallery had tapered pedestals and strange heads poking out, like gargoyles, directly from beneath the lotus capitals. Most visitors, however, were probably unaware of the inaccurate representation of ancient Egyptian decoration.

Egypt comes to the Egyptian Hall

In 1821, Giovanni Battista Belzoni (Hamill and Mollier Chapter 11: 211–213, this volume; Champion 2003) mounted his display in the Egyptian Hall based on the tomb of Seti I that he had discovered in the Valley of the Kings four years earlier (Pearce 2000; Siliotti 2001: 68–69). At last, the Egyptian Hall's bold architectural style was brought to life by a dramatic Egyptian exhibition which allowed Londoners to experience for the first time the incredible decoration and atmosphere of the interior of a pharaoh's tomb (Figure 5:5). In contrast to the building's decoration, Belzoni's presentation, known as the 'Egyptian tomb', aimed to be extremely accurate. This precision was to be found not only in the 1/6 scale model of the whole tomb but also in the full size re-creation of two of the tomb's rooms – the Hall of Four Pillars and the Hall of Beauties (Siliotti 2001: 322 n. 149). Belzoni and his assistant had made numerous drawings of the actual tomb's decoration, noting especially the range of colours, as well as taking wax impressions of the relief wall paintings. The overall effect of the exhibition was a success. Its main strength was that it focused on just the one site. The public visited it in large numbers – ca. 2,000 on opening day (Siliotti 2001: 322 n. 151) – despite the high admission charge of two shillings and sixpence. Belzoni

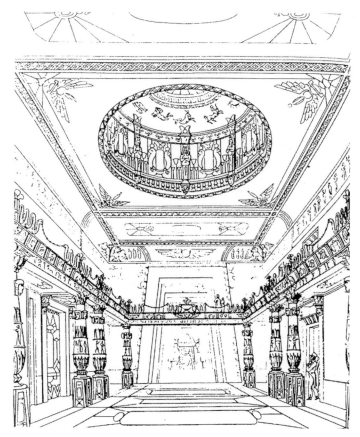

Figure 5:4　Interior of Egyptian Hall, 1819 (Museum of London).

Figure 5:5　Belzoni's display, Egyptian Hall (British Library).

justified this by claiming that the painting and the construction of the model had involved over 16 months of preparatory work.

Belzoni's collection of antiquities was also on show (Siliotti 2001: 322 n. 149). There were at least five large stone figures, including two life-size seated 'giants' with lions' heads, one similar but larger than life and two standing grey granite figures also with lion's heads. Although Belzoni had been employed by Henry Salt, the British Consul General in Egypt, to collect, remove and transport antiquities, he had also been able to amass his own collection of antiquities during his six year stay in Egypt, some pieces of which were very important – such as the sarcophagus lid of Ramesses III, described as a "cover from the king's sarcophagus (Valley of the Kings)" in the exhibition catalogue (Pearce 2000: 122; Siliotti 2001: 192), later donated to the Fitzwilliam Museum in Cambridge in 1823 – the base having been acquired by the Louvre. There were 14 display cases of small idols, vases and scarabs, the largest known papyrus and a "Colossal toe, from the Collosus discovered among the ruins of Carnac, the head of which is now in the British Museum – red granite" (Pearce 2000: 122; Jeffreys 2003). This last item is a reminder of Belzoni's incredible achievement in the transportation of extremely large and heavy items (Hamill and Mollier Chapter 11, this volume). A display case contained "Ancient shoes; and ropes made of the leaves of the palm tree; mummies of various animals, quadrupeds and fish; tresses of hair in a state of wonderfull preservation". In another case, a human mummy was described as having been "opened in England a short time ago". Belzoni claimed that it was "the most perfect" of any that he had unfolded during his time in Egypt and then existing in Europe. All its "limbs" were "entire" and "hair" was "visible on its head". It was displayed in an unusual way at the Egyptian Hall. The catalogue (Pearce 2000: 120) noted that "the box in which it was contained" was "placed above" the mummy. This composite form of display for mummies within the same case became the standard for the British Museum's Egyptian displays. Belzoni may have been the first person to exhibit mummies in this way in London.

Drawing in the public

In the 1830s, Thomas Pettigrew, an anatomist and keen antiquarian, was to popularize the unwrapping of mummies to invited or paying audiences. Belzoni had started him off on this line of investigation in 1820 when he invited him to help him unwrap that 'most perfect' mummy. Of all the aspects of ancient Egyptian culture, it was the way bodies were preserved after death that fascinated Londoners most. In 1844 Pettigrew had 'secured' a mummy that had been obtained by Colonel Needham in Thebes. At a meeting of the British Archaeological Association, the evening began at eight o'clock with Pettigrew reading an essay "on the different kinds of embalmments among the Egyptians". As he unrolled the mummy, he pointed out to the audience various interesting characteristics. He found the linen bandages to be stained with "the usual colour", supposed by him to have been made by acacia gum:

> Bituminous matter having penetrated through the sides, the bandages could not be unrolled from the body; they were therefore cut away, and among them numerous compresses were found, filling all the spaces. Time would not permit of the complete display of the mummy, but the head was fully developed, and the face was found to

have been guilt, large portions of gold-leaf, upon the removal of the bandages, presenting themselves in most vivid brightness.

(*The Archaeological Journal* 1844: 281)

Pettigrew had sought the help of Samuel Birch of the British Museum in deciphering the case's hieroglyphics in an attempt to learn more about the identity of the mummy. Whereas 10 years earlier they would have been a mystery, now, thanks to Champollion's work in solving the mysteries of the Egyptian language, the text could be understood. Unfortunately, it proved impossible to say whether the mummy had been a priest, though Pettigrew thought it likely. The 'unwrapping' had taken up the whole of the evening, resulting in the evening's other papers having to be postponed for a future meeting. Clearly, the audience had been fascinated by the presentation. However, some may have felt that it was wrong to treat an Egyptian in such a public way, especially as he had taken so much trouble to hide and prepare his body for the afterlife.

Since the 1820s, the British Museum's displays of Egyptian statues had been arranged as far as possible chronologically, taking account of recent research and publications (Figure 5:6). A few statues were beginning to be classified as 'art' rather than just as curiosities. Despite the weight of the large sculptures, they had been raised off the ground and placed on large granite blocks. The 'Younger Memnon', a huge bust of Ramesses II that arrived in 1818 as part of the Salt Collection (Hamill and Mollier Chapter 11, this volume: Figures 11:2, 11:3 col. pls.; Siliotti 2001: 73, 75, 102,

Figure 5:6   Interior view of the British Museum, 1841 (Museum of London).

112), was admired and helped to raise the profile of ancient Egyptian art. Percy Bysshe Shelley's poem *Ozymandias* captured the statue's awesome presence:

> ... My name is Ozymandias, king of Kings:
> Look on my works, ye mighty, and despair!
> Nothing beside remains.

Other visitors, such as Nathaniel Hawthorne (1870, I: 313), were less impressed with the display, writing of the gallery as

> all full of monstrosities and horrible uglinesses ... Their gigantic statues are certainly very curious ... Hideous blubber-lipped faces of giants, and human shapes with beasts' heads upon them. The Egyptian controverted Nature in all things, only using it as a groundwork to depict the unnatural upon.

Despite such views, these larger-than-life statues were very popular with the general public. So many people visited the gallery that notices were needed to warn the public against touching the items on open display.[1]

Such statues were rarely seen elsewhere in the capital. In early March 1833, however, Londoners on their day-to-day business around town would have been surprised to see seven Egyptian statues displayed on Waterloo Bridge. There was a representation of Isis "distinguished by the lion's head and the mystical key of the waters of the Nile" as well as other figures surmounted with crescents or hooded serpents. A fine stone sanctuary, carved with the figure of a priestess and priests had hieroglyphics "28 inches high". Perhaps the most remarkable item was a statue of the young Sesostris "in the character of a priest in a kneeling posture, holding a sanctuary with figures of Osiris and Thoth" (*Gentleman's Magazine* 1833: 256). The explanation for this outdoor sculpture event lay with the fact that Sotheby's was holding a sale of John Barker's Egyptian antiquities, Barker having succeeded Henry Salt as Consul-General in Egypt. As the auction room's floors were not strong enough to take the weight of the massive stone statues, it was decided to place them on view on the bridge. The *Gentleman's Magazine* remarked:

> Among the singular circumstances incidental to the changes brought about by the light of Christianity, will be noted the appearance of idols of Egypt, shorn of all their honours and tutelary reputation, for several days on Waterloo Bridge.

> (*Gentleman's Magazine* 1833: 256)

At the sale, the British Museum acquired the sanctuary and the Sesostris statue (Figure 5:7; BM EA 1377, now identified as a nineteenth Dynasty "limestone statue of Panehsy"). In December 1847, the new Egyptian Room on the first floor of the British Museum opened to the public (Figure 5:8). Londoners of all classes were now free to examine one of the world's best collections of artefacts from Ancient Egypt. The gallery was described (*Penny Magazine* 1838: 437) as "chaste and elegant in design", "well lighted from above". The displays took account of the growing understanding of the culture and history of Ancient Egypt. The layout of the Egyptian material had become less like a cabinet of curiosities and more like an ordered and modern museum display. Part of the interest in these new displays was tied to their biblical dimension:

As the relics of a time which has been in some degree rendered familiar to us by the beautiful writings of the Scriptures, and as serving to elucidate many doubtful passages, and to illustrate the many illusions to the manners of the ancient Egyptians so frequently occurring in those writings; the collections made and forwarded to Europe must claim the attention and prove highly interesting to all who are acquainted with the Bible.

(*Penny Magazine* 1838: 436)

The displays may have lacked the excitement and atmosphere of Belzoni's re-creation of the pharaoh's tomb, but the range of material was very impressive, almost overwhelming. "What a number of mummies are here, and ornamented mummy cases! And yet this is London, and not Egypt", noted 'Old Humphrey' (1843). The rows of mummies were undoubtedly the highlight of the new gallery. In the large cases in the centre of the room that ran diagonal to the other cases, mummy boxes were hung on pivots to allow both the decoration of the interior and the exterior to be viewed. Above these, narrow upper cases displayed small items of jewellery and

Figure 5:7   Statue of "young Sesostris" acquired by the British Museum (EA 1377).

papyri. The main run of diagonal cases on either side contained mummies to demonstrate the stages of the burial and preservation process. More boxes were arranged in adjoining cases. Hawthorne (1870, 2: 354) noted how a mummy of "the body of a princess, is unrolled, except the innermost layer of linen. The outline of her face is perfectly visible". Visitors were fascinated and haunted by these displays of ancient Egyptian human bodies.

Contemporary accounts focus on how 'articles of domestic life' had been discovered in the tombs. Whereas Belzoni had included only a small number of items in his display, the museum had amassed a wide range of material, including jewellery, papyri and sarcophagi. Items that proved especially alluring to the museum visitor included a small model of an Egyptian house (from the Salt Collection), a chair and a wig, noted as "1,700 years before Christ" (*Penny Magazine* 1838: 437); Hawthorne (1870, 2: 354) remarked that "the hair is brown, and the wig is perfect as if it had been made for some now living dowager". The preservation of material "30 or 40 centuries old" astonished people then just as it still does today. The *Penny Magazine* (1838: 437) reported overhearing the following remarks about the display of "a fowl

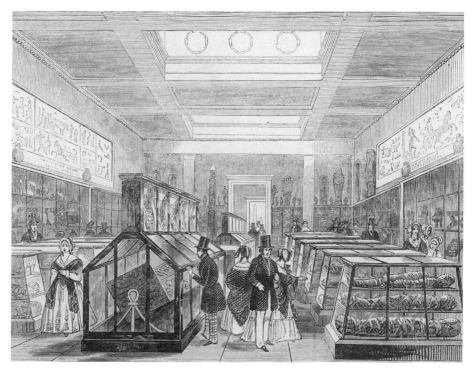

Figure 5:8   Egyptian Room, British Museum, 1847 (Museum of London).

roasted and prepared for eating": "Only think now, May," as we heard a young woman observe, "that them creeturs should eat fowls, and truss them too, just like us!" The British Museum's audiences clearly included not only the connoisseur and the intellectual but also working men and women. Hawthorne (1870, 2: 358) made a similar point, noting that "In all the rooms I saw people of the poorer classes, some of whom seemed to view the objects intelligently, and to take a general interest in them ... I saw many children there, and some ragged boys".

London shows and exhibitions about Ancient Egypt continued in the second quarter of the 19th century. In 1825, Belzoni's widow, Sarah, mounted the Egyptian Tomb exhibition again, but at a different venue, 28 Leicester Square, and with less success than at the Egyptian Hall. Nearby, another Egyptian show at 47 Leicester Square displayed a sculptural copy by M. Casleux of the zodiac of Dendera. The French had removed the zodiac using dynamite and had taken it back to Paris, where it was displayed in the Louvre. A "spirited English speculator" purchased the copy hoping that the Government would acquire it or "some private individual", as it was a "unique gem worthy to grace the first collection in this or any country" (Anon. 1825: 3).

Egypt made easy

Panoramas of famous cities and landscapes were a popular changing attraction in London. Some were moving panoramas that took the audience on a journey from one side of the world to another, often via the landscape of the pyramids and the temples (Hyde 1988: 131–167). This was a Grand Tour of the world enjoyed from a London theatre seat with none of the discomfort of coach, rail and sea travel. Modern Thebes was just one of the many static panorama presentations of cities from around the globe. It showed a city of ruins. Viewers contemplated the great antiquity of the scene and the massive scale of the temples and statues. They resembled passages from the Old Testament that they had read or heard in church or synagogue. Whereas the culture of those that had built the city was obscure and mysterious, it was acknowledged that 'discoveries in hieroglyphics' were beginning to reveal information about Ancient Egypt:

> Every fresh light thrown on the darkness which has so long shrouded Thebes, renders it more interesting; it is like finding something of value while groping in the ruins, that raises our estimation of the mouldering pile.

(Old Humphrey 1843: 106)

Artists were attracted to such scenes. They attempted to reconstruct views of ancient cities with their unusual architectural forms, and they began to interpret some of the dramatic episodes in the life of Ancient Egypt. Their paintings, shown at venues such as the Royal Academy and the British Institution, helped Londoners to visualize places like Thebes at the height of its power. Often these popular works with biblical associations were engraved and so circulated to a very wide audience. For the first time, the dimension of the buildings and statues were set against the human form, making clear their massive scale "so much beyond our pigmy dwellings, and comparatively miniature public buildings" (Old Humphrey 1843: 106; Whitehouse Chapter 3, this volume). The large works of John Martin (1789–1854) interpreted apocalyptic events from the Old Testament (Champion and Ucko 2003: 15–16; Pantazzi 1994d; Whitehouse Chapter 3, this volume). They showed ancient cities and their thousands of inhabitants powerless against the elemental forces of nature and the Almighty. Both Babylonian and Egyptian scenes were painted, though architecture was still subservient to the immensity of the sky and the drama of the distant landscape (Figure 5:9). In the work of David Roberts (1796–1854) a different focus emerged with the detail of the Egyptian buildings more dominant and distinct (Figure 5:10; Whitehouse Chapter 3, this volume). His drawings and watercolours of Egypt were turned into lithographs by Louis Hague and published between 1842 and 1845 to great acclaim.

By the 1860s, artists had moved on to examine everyday life in Ancient Egypt. In April 1865, Ernest Gambart's French Gallery, situated at 121–122 Pall Mall, displayed Alma-Tadema's 'An Evening Party at Nineveh' (Figure 5:11), better known as 'Pastimes in Ancient Egypt (eighteenth Dynasty)' and 'Egyptian Chess Players'. The artist had visited London four years earlier and had been inspired by Egyptian antiquities in the British Museum. In E. J. Poynter's 'Israel in Egypt' (1867; Rice and MacDonald 2003: Figure 1:2) the drama of the scene and involvement of the viewer were heightened by the use of a ground level perspective. This emphasized the scale

Figure 5:9 'The Seventh Plague of Egypt' (1823), John Martin (Francis Welch Fund, © Museum of Fine Arts, Boston).

Figure 5:10 'The Israelites Leaving Egypt' (1829), David Roberts (City Museum and Art Gallery, Birmingham).

Figure 5:11 'An Evening Party at Nineveh' (1863), Sir Lawrence Alma-Tadema (Preston Art Gallery).

and mass of the lion statue, in the centre of the painting, being pulled by the enslaved Israelites with the brightly painted Egyptian buildings in the background. Historical accuracy was considered important although the buildings shown derived from many different sites in Egypt. Poynter had visited Egypt and made studies of statues in the British Museum; the lion was based on the one known as the 'Prudhoe Lion' (Whitehouse Chapter 3, this volume).

Another place that Poynter almost certainly drew inspiration from was the Crystal Palace. When the Great Exhibition in Hyde Park closed in September 1851, a debate ensued about the future use of Paxton's remarkable glass and iron building. Finally, a company was established that acquired the structure, took it down and re-erected it in Sydenham, South London. On 10 June 1854, a new and larger Crystal Palace opened with exhibition galleries, gardens and sculptures. Thousands of Londoners came to visit it, many travelling on the new railways that linked it to the metropolis. Unlike the Great Exhibition, where only modern works of art and industry were displayed, the new Crystal Palace aimed to set out all the different architectural and sculptural styles of western civilization, including ancient Egyptian, Assyrian and Arabic cultures. The displays were devised by two friends, Digby Wyatt and Owen Jones, who had been involved in the establishment and management of the Great Exhibition. To make the displays of the Crystal Palace as accurate as possible, they toured Europe together gathering casts of the finest monuments and sculptures.

The displays at the Crystal Palace were intended, as the company's prospectus specified, "to raise the enjoyment ... of the English people, and especially to afford the inhabitants of London, in wholesome country air, amidst the beauties of nature, the elevating treasures of art" and "to blend for them instruction with pleasure, to educate them by the eye, to quicken and purify their taste by the habit of recognizing the beautiful" (Phillips 1854: 15). The ground floor of the building was divided into courts and the central area was set out as an enormous botanical garden with palm trees, pools and sculptures. Outside on the Upper Terraces were large Egyptian sphinxes copied from originals in the Louvre. By the mid-19th century, sphinxes had become very popular statuary in wealthy Londoners' gardens, but such large examples as set up here were reserved usually for the grounds of country houses or palaces. The Egyptian section, one of the most spectacular elements of the whole display, was the work of Owen Jones and Joseph Bonomi. The structures re-created in the Court were "based on a series of original drawings and measurements" made by Jones during a visit to Egypt with Jules Goury in 1833. He had met Goury, a French architect, in Greece, and together they had visited and recorded ancient buildings in Turkey, Egypt and Spain. Tragically, his friend died from cholera in 1834. His use of primary colours – red, blue and yellow – for the Great Exhibition may have been influenced by what he had seen in Egypt. Jones (1856: 24) wrote how the architecture of the Egyptians was "thoroughly polychromatic – they painted everything", and he believed that there was much "to learn from them" in the way that they used colour and decorative patterns (and see Whitehouse Chapter 3, this volume).

Bonomi (1796–1878) took on "the office both of high priest and chief artist" in the creation of the Egyptian Court (Jones and Bonomi 1854: 7–8). He had spent many years in Egypt studying and recording ancient sites and was familiar with the interpretation of Egypt in popular shows and exhibits, having himself created a successful moving panorama of a river trip up the Nile that was exhibited at the Egyptian Hall (Altick 1978: 460). For the wall paintings in the Egyptian Court, he used a grid system to prepare the outlines of the designs, the same techniques that had been used in Ancient Egypt. Bonomi and his assistant trained "a very small band of mechanics" to decorate and colour the walls and make the sculptures. Through "constant practice", they were able to reproduce the "peculiar character of Egyptian art" (Jones and Bonomi 1854: 7). Such an accurate representation of Egyptian painting in London had not been made since Belzoni's exhibition at the Egyptian Hall. Like Belzoni, a tomb was re-created, in this instance one from Beni Hasan. It was an enclosed and decorated space. Despite the Court's size, it was impossible to reproduce the real dimensions of the different monuments. Nearly everything had to be made on a reduced scale, only some of the columns that divided up the space were of the correct height and proportion (Figure 5:12). This lessened the impact of the original massive structures, especially the model of the Temple of Ramesses the Great, at Abu Simbel (Figure 5:13). However, two of the colossal figures from this temple were built in the main avenue of the exhibition building, Bonomi having modelled the head of the figures from a cast that he had made while in Egypt (Figure 5:14):

> The heads of the figures are moulded from a cast made in Egypt by Mr Bonomi ... the bodies of the figures have been increased by pointing from his model, and built up in their places most skilfully by M. Desady, of Paris, assisted by a very intelligent body of

Figure 5:12   Egyptian Court, artists at work (Hulton Getty).

Figure 5:14   Colossal figures from the Egyptian Avenue of the Crystal Palace at Sydenham (*Illustrated London News*, 22 July 1854) (see also cover of MacDonald and Rice 2003) (Museum of London).

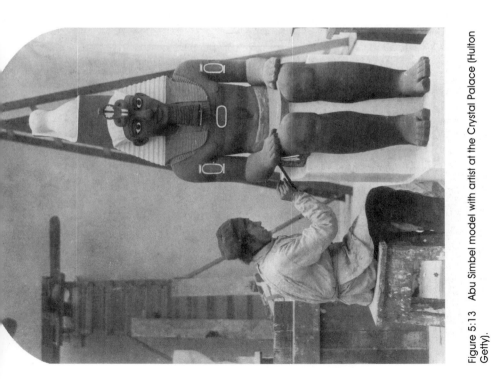

Figure 5:13   Abu Simbel model with artist at the Crystal Palace (Hulton Getty).

French workmen. The (full size) figures between the legs of the statues are modelled by M. Monti.

(Jones and Bonomi 1854: 25–26)

A reviewer questioned the description in the official guide:

> All Egyptian sculpture and architecture were noticeable alike for massiveness and grotesqueness. But the massive and the grotesque are not enough to constitute 'the grand'. There must be some high, if not imperishable, idea and sentiment conveyed by the vast blocks; such as the grief, or the courage, or the self-devotion, or the sense of majesty, or the instinct of love, which are, in their turns, shed over the glyphic productions of Greece and of other lands. Failing these impressions, there must be either exquisite proportion and physical beauty, or exquisite imitation. Neither of these classes of interest is attached to the abnormal and idol-like figures in the garden side of the Nave, sixty five feet in height.

(Illustrated London News 1854: 70)

Despite such criticism, the statues were very impressive, as reflected in contemporary engravings and photographs. A row of sphinxes surrounded by palms led up to the figures, heightening the drama of the setting. Here for the first time, Londoners were able to experience the scale of ancient Egyptian monuments. The large sections of actual statues, displayed at the British Museum, became all the more impressive as a result of this re-creation.

Jones and Bonomi had fun with the hieroglyphics in the Egyptian Court, though few visitors would have been able to decipher the texts (Figures 5:15, 5:16). Only the special guidebook revealed the secrets of the inscriptions. There were cartouches of

Figure 5:15   Construction of the Egyptian Court (Hulton Getty).

Figure 5:16   Egyptian Court, early 20th century (Museum of London).

the names of Queen Victoria and Prince Albert over the three entrances. A text (Jones and Bonomi 1854: 14) heralded Queen Victoria as "the ruler of the waves" and recorded the fact that she "entered this palace and gates" along with "the chiefs, architects, sculptors, [and] painters". The display was identified by thousands: "a thousand columns, a thousand decorations" as well as "a thousand birds and beasts". The aim of those who built 'the palace' was "as a book for the instruction of the men and women of all countries, regions, and districts" (Jones and Bonomi 1854: 15). The text ended with a flourish – "May it be prosperous". Hidden elsewhere in the hieroglyphics were the names of the directors of the Crystal Palace Company. The use of hieroglyphs in this way in the display demonstrated how far knowledge about Ancient Egypt had progressed, largely through the enlightened work of Champollion. A cast of the Rosetta Stone was exhibited in the Egyptian Court. The use of the phrase 'ruler of the waves' also drew attention to the power of Victoria and the extent of the British Empire. In the 1890s, an even clearer correlation between the ancient and the modern empire (Jeffreys 2003) was made when a statue by Onslow Ford of General Gordon on a camel was deposited in the middle of the Egyptian Court. The Crystal Palace was London's premier gallery of contemporary sculpture casts. Clearly, the administrators of the exhibition at this period considered this location to be most apposite for such a work depicting a national hero (Figure 5:17).

The Egyptian Court must be seen as the culmination of all earlier Egyptian displays. Not only was care taken in making the decoration and modelling the statues,

Figure 5:17   Egyptian Court with Gordon sculpture, early 20th century (Museum of London).

but there was also an amalgam of Egyptian sites. Despite the use of casts and copies given over to different historic periods, the Crystal Palace managed to present visitors with a rounded view, displaying what were considered to be the greatest or most representative art works of the age. The architecture, art and especially sculpture of each court were carefully selected. Put together they offered visitors the opportunity to compare and contrast each period of history as they walked through the display. An Egyptian tomb could be viewed alongside a section from the Alhambra or the courtyard of a Pompeiian villa, and colour was faithfully employed in Egyptian and classical contexts.

Such London displays enabled the public before the age of mass tourism and television documentaries (Schadla-Hall and Morris 2003) to 'experience' Ancient Egypt; they served to bring ancient civilizations back to life.

Survivors: Isis and Osiris

Very few 19th century Egyptian-inspired displays and monuments survive in London. Hope's house in Duchess Street was demolished in the 1850s and its fixtures and fittings were dispersed. The Egyptian Hall in Piccadilly was knocked down in 1905 and redeveloped into offices and shops. A massive fire swept through the Crystal Palace on 30 November 1936, destroying the building and its entire interior displays including the Egyptian Court. This makes surviving items or archives from these places, such as the original painted displays from Belzoni's 'Egyptian tomb' in the collection of Bristol Museum and Art Gallery, all the more significant. They provide the only direct physical link to the exhibits and buildings of which no trace remains, widening understanding of how Ancient Egypt was interpreted and displayed in the early 19th century. Recently, the striking statues of Isis and Osiris from the façade of the Egyptian Hall were rediscovered. They reveal one particular style adopted to portray Egyptian deities at this period. Also, they are important as they give a sense of the scale of the elaborate façade of probably England's first major 'Egyptian-style' building.

The statues were believed to have been destroyed, as there had been no record of them since 1905. However, research has since established that they were salvaged when the building was taken down and acquired by a scrap yard in the Kings Cross area. By 1912, they had been bought by a Swedish family living just outside Edinburgh, where they were used as garden ornaments. In 1987, Peter Hone, of Clifton Nurseries, Little Venice, London, rediscovered them. Subsequently, they were auctioned by Sotheby's at a sale in Sussex (31 May 1989) and bought by Christopher Gibbs Ltd. Then, in 1994, they were sold to the Museum of London. Their acquisition was made possible by a grant from the Corporation of London's 'City Changes' improvement programme. They were erected on either side of the Museum's new extended entrance on the Highwalk in the area known as Nettleton Court. The fairly plain entrance with a revolving door was enhanced by these figures.

The statues had been carved in Portland stone in 1811 by the London-Irish sculptor Lawrence Geoghegan, who anglicised his name to Gahagan. He had settled in London in the mid-18th century and by the early 19th century was practising as a sculptor along with his younger brother Sebastian, his son and his daughter. They became respected and skilled carvers. Gahagan exhibited periodically at the Royal Academy from 1798 to 1817. For the Egyptian Hall's sculptures, it is not known whether he worked from prepared designs by P. F. Robinson, the architect, or those by William Bullock, the exhibition's owner, for whom he had been employed some years earlier on the latter's Liverpool Museum. It seems likely that the sculptor was given a general idea of what was required but retained some freedom in the overall representation of the figures. Gahagan did not copy actual ancient Egyptian statuary or employ illustrations from Denon's (1802) work as the design source for his commission. Rather he elected to carve the statues in the classical manner, overlaying them with Egyptian motifs. Isis (Figure 5:18) wears a thin and revealing shift and in her left hand carries a lotus flower and in her right a long palm frond. Osiris (Figure 5:19), clothed in just a loincloth, holds an ankh, a symbol of life, in his right hand and supports a small crocodile on his left arm, probably representing the river Nile. The formalized headdresses of both figures imply an Egyptian style. On the other hand, their relaxed pose and the way their heads are turned to the side does not conform to Egyptian originals. Their faces especially are reminiscent of traditional 18th century representations of blackamoors.

The overall design of the Egyptian Hall façade with its pylon forms was more rigid and formalized than the two sculptures at its centre (Figure 5:3). It would appear that Robinson made use of the latest information about the architecture of Ancient

Figure 5:18   Isis (Museum of London).   Figure 5:19   Osiris (Museum of London).

Egypt whereas Gahagan remained locked into an imagined conception of this civilization. The sculptor created an idealized Egyptian king and queen or god and goddess that remained essentially classical in form and pose. Clearly, he was not interested in working in an 'archaeological' style. The general source for the Osiris figure was probably an Egyptian statue in the Vatican from Hadrian's Villa. In the early 19th century, Coade stone copies were made of it. A pair dated 1800 were formerly at Deepdene, Surrey, Thomas Hope's country house (and now in Buscot Park, Oxfordshire) (Kelly 1990: 94–95). Gahagan adapted and softened the stance. Robinson and Bullock may have intended the statues to be bearers or caryatids that appeared more visibly to be supporting the structure of the building. If their gaze had been rigidly straight ahead then they might have conveyed better the timeless and hypnotic character that one associates with Egyptian figurative sculpture. Nevertheless, at three and a half metres in height, their size managed to convey the monumental and helped to make the building's façade impressive and memorable. It must be remembered that the Egyptian Hall was the venue of some of the most innovative exhibitions held anywhere in London, if not Europe, in the first half of the 19th century. Thousands of visitors each week would have passed under these figures to view displays of large paintings such as Géricault's 'Raft of Medusa' (1820) and of distant cultures such as Bullock's 'Ancient Mexico' (1824; Medina-González 2003). It is more difficult to gauge how the statues were viewed in the first half of the 19th century. Most general descriptions of the Egyptian Hall refer to them as part of the façade but fail to comment on their style. The façade was altered in the mid-19th century; some considered that it had been 'spoiled' as a result (Timbs 1867: 319). One writer described the figures as 'Ethiopians' (Partington 1835: 153). The interpretation of the statues today remains equally problematic, but for very different reasons.

In 2002, the statues were taken down when the Museum of London embarked on further changes to its entrance. The drawn-up plans did not include Isis and Osiris as part of the overall design. After consideration by senior museum officers and by the Museum's architect, Wilkinson Eyre, Gahagan's sculptures were deemed to be inappropriate for the new public entrance. When they were erected initially at the Museum's entrance in 1994, there had been some concern that the public would, on seeing them, expect to find Egyptian antiquities on display inside. The implication was that the public read the sculptures as Egyptian and therefore identified the Museum with the history of Ancient Egypt. Whether such a view was prevalent amongst visitors was never established. However, it was likely that at first glance the statues were taken to be 'historic' items, suggesting antiquity, and therefore in keeping with what one might expect to find at the entrance to a museum. The statues were seen to interest visitors and those passing by along the Barbican Highwalk. Their position at such a key site, at the entrance to the Museum, implied that they were important. Obviously, the interpretative panel explained their 19th century historical context, especially that they came from the first 'London Museum', with the suggestion that the Museum of London was its successor. For the latest entrance, due for completion in 2003, concerns were expressed once more about what the statues would signify to the visitor. Would they suggest to the visitor an 'old style' museum? Were they the most appropriate cultural symbols to convey the Museum's main subject – the history of London? As representations of Egyptian gods, did they appear too authoritarian? Too mysterious? Would the public find them difficult to understand without lengthy exegesis? Such anxieties were understandable as the new entrance needed to convey the right impression to the visitor. On the other hand, it could be argued that the complexity of the statues was what one expected from the best museum objects. There was an interesting story to tell about their history, style and cultural associations. Their London context was central to the history of exhibitions and entertainment in the 19th century metropolis.

The current plan (as of December 2002) envisages that Isis and Osiris will be displayed inside the Museum of London as part of its permanent displays. They will stand on either side of the entrance to the Victorian Walk in the World City gallery that covers the period of London's history from 1789 to 1914. Hopefully, this will be a secure position for these evocative and significant London sculptures. Not only do they record the history of the Egyptian Hall and all its varied displays, "a sort of Ark of Exhibitions" (Timbs 1867: 320), but also the dramatic façade of London's most significant 19th century Egyptian-inspired building.

Note

1   A large warning notice resting against one of the plinths can be glimpsed in an early photograph of the gallery, in the British Museum's Central Archive.

CHAPTER 6

EGYPT IN LONDON – ENTERTAINMENT AND COMMERCE IN THE 20th CENTURY METROPOLIS

Chris Elliott, Katherine Griffis-Greenberg and Richard Lunn

Introduction

Despite its own antiquity, and the length and extent of its associations with Egypt, London has relatively little Egyptianizing architecture. Whereas the Greco-Roman cultural tradition, sustained by the use of Latin and Greek for religious purposes, helped the neoclassical and Palladian styles to flourish, London has no comparable Egyptian tradition. Nonetheless, there has been widespread fascination with things ancient Egyptian, which continues to the present day.

The ancient Egyptian buildings and monuments that were reported, recorded, excavated, and sometimes exported, derived primarily from public religious buildings and elite funerary constructions, not easily adapted to domestic architecture. The early Egyptianizing monuments in London, including funerary monuments, were mainly individual commissions by members of those social groups that could afford to travel to Egypt and collect monuments and artefacts. Popular interest was fed by published material and exhibitions which, with notable exceptions such as those at the Egyptian Rooms in Piccadilly (Werner Chapter 5, this volume), had little or no associated Egyptianizing architecture.

The birth of package tourism in 1868 (El Daly 2003a) made travel to Egypt accessible to more people than ever before, but it was still the relatively affluent who benefited; if they were inspired to build as a result, they built mausolea or monuments rather than maisonettes. Artefacts and monuments from Egypt went into public collections as well as private, but the pious middle classes, for whom Egypt was the land of Moses and the refuge of the Holy Family, were as likely to be inspired by paintings in galleries, or the Egyptian Court at the Crystal Palace (Werner Chapter 5; Whitehouse Chapter 2, both this volume). More than 50 years later, they flocked to the reproduction of Tutankhamun's tomb at the British Empire Exhibition (1924), of which no architectural trace now remains.

The Egyptianizing buildings presented in this chapter were built in the 20th century and are associated with entertainment and commerce. Ancient Egypt provides them with associations of pharaonic luxury and antiquity, and also with practical utility. Each makes a statement, whether intentionally or not, and several have provoked controversy as a result. Despite swings in taste, sustained neglect, the loss of their original commercial justification, and the often overt hostility of professional peers and cultural elites, much of London's significant Egyptianizing architecture has survived, and this in itself is evidence of the enduring power of Ancient Egypt as a cultural influence, and of its hold on the popular imagination.

'Amarnamania'?

Egyptomania received a boost in the 1920s and 1930s. Excavation of the city of Amarna had begun in earnest in 1920, and continued until 1936. Uniquely among Egyptian cities, it had been built and abandoned within a generation, and this stylistic integrity may have exerted more influence on architects than other sites, which had been occupied and built on for centuries. Although the discovery of Tutankhamun's tomb in 1922 was to trigger a popular craze for things ancient Egyptian, the tomb contained little in the way of architecture. As noted by Montserrat (2000: 89), the contemporary British response to Egyptianizing influences in architecture should perhaps be named not 'Tutmania', but 'Amarnamania'.

The clean lines and decorative elements of Amarna architecture had become known to the English public during the early 1900s. The design of the Amarna buildings, with their abundant reliance upon sunlight and their use of varied elevations, would have particularly appealed to a new category of architecture – that of industrial architecture. The ancient city of Akhenaten could be used to conjure up modern, 'factory-like' designs.

In addition to the design of Amarna buildings, the image of an isolated city in the desert, built as a garden utopia for an innovative religion (popularly believed to parallel or prefigure modern Christianity), often held a strong appeal for architects (Montserrat 2000: 74–77). Amarna, and Ancient Egypt in general, represented innovation and a breaking free from traditional forms – in culture, and in architecture (Croad 1996: 5). This view would have had specific appeal to those architects such as Wallis (1933a: 302–303), who rejected classical architecture as a "child's box of bricks" that had been combined in random forms, in favour of an architecture which was bold and innovative, but with good form and proportion.

The Carreras cigarette factory

The 'Arcadia Works' building of Carreras Limited in Mornington Crescent (Figure 6:1 col. pl.; Rice and MacDonald 2003: 8–10) was opened on 3 November 1928. It was designed by architects M. E. and O. H. Collins after the temple of Bubastis (the cat-headed goddess – Naville 1891) (*Illustrated London News*, 10 November 1928).

> To mark the event, Mr Bernhard Baron [Chairman of Carreras] presented every employee with a silver medal specially struck to commemorate the completion of the [building].

> (*The Times*, 23 November 1928)

The building was a cigarette factory. In addition to its size, the owner stressed its hygienic condition, and its "spaciousness and light" (*The Times*, 23 November 1928).

Covering nearly 4 hectares over five floors, it was one of the largest such factories in the world. The owners intended not only that their new factory should express a new and innovative character, but also that it should establish its traditionalism by creating links to an ancient past. Curl (1994: 216) gives a somewhat different perspective:

> The choice of the Egyptian design was deliberately commercial, associated with the excitement generated by the discovery of Tutankhamun's tomb, with the fashion for Egyptian artefacts encouraged by Hollywood spectaculars, and with the Black-Cat trade-mark of Carreras.

The alleged association of Egypt with cigarette smoking luxuries (Montserrat 2000: 85; Rice and MacDonald 2003: 8–10) may also have been an influence.

Whatever the reasons, the architects adopted the newly popular Egyptian style, drawing upon resources such as the Department of Egyptian and Assyrian Antiquities of the British Museum for their ideas (Croad 1996: 10; Andrew Forman, pers. comm.). The opening ceremonies left no doubt about the association of Carreras products with Ancient Egypt. Sand was laid on the ground in front of the building to replicate the deserts of Egypt, while a procession of the cast from *Aida* (Humbert 2003) performed before the temple façade, followed by chariot races, and a parade of "ancient Egyptian types" who cavorted around the structure (William Mitchell, pers. comm.).[1]

The building's design and the association of Ancient Egypt with the luxury of cigarette smoking were easily accepted by the public (Croad 1996: 11). However, the building was criticized by architectural journals as being pretentious (Fry 1928: 736). Carreras moved to other premises in 1959, and by 1962 the new owners of the building had converted it into offices. Many of the remaining Egyptian features were either removed or hidden, to create a more austere 'modernist' façade. With this conversion, the building was renamed 'Greater London House' and lost the individuality which had made it such an impressive structure (Croad 1996: 12–13).

In 1996, again with a new owner, Resolution GLH Ltd, the Carreras Building was restored by Finch Forman Chartered Architects. They consulted the original plans and drawings to re-create as closely as possible 85 to 90 per cent of the original features (Finch and Forman 2001), and the project won a Civic Trust Award.

Externally, the original 'Atlas White' cement construction (tinted to a sand colour) provided a backdrop to the brilliant colours of the columned façade of papyriform bundles. The coloured sections of the pillars were rendered in Venetian glass (Forman, pers. comm.). The columns were reminiscent of the papyriform columns found in some of the tombs at Amarna, noted as specifically influencing other columned London buildings built during the same period (see below, and Montserrat 2000: 89). Other features of the façade did not derive from Amarna: the 'lashed tent-pole' design was used as a framing motif on the doorway, and this design is closely linked with the cavetto moulded lintel, first seen in the Old Kingdom. Both motifs are found together on the entrance façade of a tomb of an official during the reign of Neferkara (third Dynasty; Foucart 1897: 52–53).

The stairs leading to the front entrance originally had a serpentine handrail, held by bronzed human hand sockets (Figure 6:2). The entrance was originally decorated

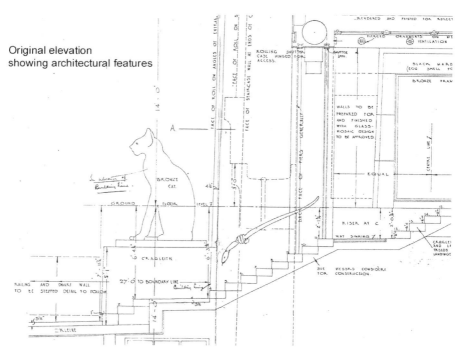

Original elevation
showing architectural features

Figure 6:2   Handrail with human hand sockets leading to front entrance of the Carreras
cigarette factory.

with a portrayal of 'Horus of Behdet'
on the roof lintel and above the doorway (Figure 6:3), which was of the
same sand colour as the columns.
However, this symbol was covered
during World War II as it was thought
to be too much like the war symbols of
the Third Reich (Forman, pers. comm.),
and it was not replaced during the
1990s restoration. Bovine-horned
Hathor lamps (Figure 6:3) stood before
two guardian cat statues, cast in bronze
(Figure 6:4), in front of the building.
Whilst representations of cats in Ancient Egypt are well-known, their inclusion on the Carreras Building was
particularly significant. The Black Cat
had been registered as the first trade
mark of Carreras Ltd in 1886, and it became "a famous and instantly recognis-
able symbol of a cigarette brand"
(Carreras 1976). The two Late Period-

Figure 6:3   Horus decoration on roof lintel
above the doorway of the Carreras cigarette
factory. Note the horned Hathor lamps in front
of cat statues (© Fry 1928).

Figure 6:5   Black cat logo of Carreras cigarettes (© Katherine Griffis-Greenberg).

Figure 6:4   Pair of bronze cast cats in front of the Carreras cigarette factory (© Katherine Griffis-Greenberg).

styled cats (each ca. 3m high) (Figure 6:4; Price and Humbert Chapter 1, this volume: Figures 1:8, 1:9; Rice and MacDonald 2003: Figure 1:5) created the desired impression of the temple of Bast, while the traditional Black Cat logo (Figure 6:5) featured repeatedly across the façade.

The railings around the building incorporate designs that are clearly derived from hieroglyphs. They do not make a totally coherent statement, but are nonetheless appropriate to a modern urban setting – defined lands, inhabited and uninhabited, within boundaries of city and province, which are established, green, and/or dominant. The Carreras Building of the 1930s embodied an Egyptianized Art Déco of a spectacular Hollywood style, designed to promulgate the myth of ancient links with new products, whilst providing ongoing aesthetic enjoyment for the viewer (and see Rice and MacDonald 2003).

The Hoover Factory

The 'Hoover Factory' (now Hoover Building) in Perivale, West London (Figure 6:6 col. pl.), has been called by Curl (1982: 206) "the finest example of the genre in western Europe". It has also been called "offensive" and "atrociously bad" by other critics (Curl 1994: 220). The building, its first stages completed in 1932, was designed by Wallis, Gilbert and Partners. It reflects both Egyptianized motifs and an architectural philosophy in which industrial buildings were built in a streamlined fashion to allow for subsequent refitting for changes in production of goods (Hitchmough 1992: 7).

Wallis (1933a, b), the leading force of the architectural group, was no stranger to controversy regarding his designs, and vigorously defended his architectural philosophy of 'transgressional' design as meeting the modern business client's needs. He had an unerring eye for a striking style that promoted his clients' products by making their offices places of beauty. He rejected the more traditional classical forms of architecture in favour of a style which utilized maximum daylight and was aesthetically pleasing, even to the point of defending his use of coloured faience as being both economical advertising and psychologically beneficial to factory workers (Wallis 1933a: 307).

From a distance, the present-day Hoover Building may look like a nondescript rectangular office building of a type present in any number of cities around the world. Only when the building is approached more closely does one see the use of Egyptian motifs. Wallis had been using such motifs years before the discovery of the tomb of Tutankhamun, and long before the 1925 Paris Exhibition popularized them through the Art Déco style. Hitchmough (1992: 10) explains:

> Perhaps Wallis was drawn to the stark monumentality of Egyptian architecture; the symmetry of the Mastaba tombs with their central recessed entrances and their sides sloping inwards like massive truncated pylons. Certainly he was attracted by the stylized linear decoration in red, blue and yellow, but Wallis adapted ancient Egyptian architecture in much the same way that Hollywood reinvented Egyptian history: as a dramatic spectacle rather than an authentic reproduction.

Wallis had invented an Egyptianizing style through referring to Egyptological archaeological records for ideas (Hitchmough 1992: 10). It had appeared as early as 1919 in the General Electric Company building in Birmingham, but reached its epitome in his industrial style in the construction of the single-storey Caribonum and Firestone Tyre Company buildings of the 1920s. In the creation of these buildings, he utilized northern light as well as eastern and western light, in such a way as to flood the entire facility with natural light (Anon. 1933; Wallis 1933a: 304). Such lighting techniques were new to 20th century architecture, but were not unknown in ancient Amarna architecture with its use of daylight in the Great Temple to the Aten and various sunshade temples, or in the expansive façades of the Deir el-Bahri mortuary temple of Hatshepsut.

The Egyptianizing design of the Hoover Building is evident from the artist's 1931 conception, which is reminiscent, for example, of the front façade of the Temple of Seti I at Abydos. However, Wallis also employed optical illusion to create Egyptianizing designs, simulating such motifs as lotiform designs at both ends of the façade's bevelled columns by using line and minimal use of colour blocks to suggest motifs rather than defining them explicitly. While there is no strict equivalent for this architectural feature in Egyptian art, the use of colour or coloured material to *suggest* floral motifs has precedents in inlay work of jewellery and tile work from the Middle Kingdom onwards (Andrews 1991: 57–58).

The front entrance doorway (Figure 6:7 col. pl.) illustrates the use of angular lines to focus interest towards the centre of the building, whilst retaining symmetry. The harmonizing of form and decoration was a hallmark of Wallis' architectural philosophy, and was appreciated even by his harshest critics. The entrance design was altered before completion in 1932, however, and the plans do not indicate why additional colours and effects (specifically the addition of a gold arrow motif) were used (Hitchmough 1992: 15). A side entrance, referred to in the Wallis plans as the 'Works Entrance', features a battered pylon with a niched pylon effect. Red, blue, sea green, and black are used at the corners of the façade, where coloured tile-work finishes the front in a curved fashion.

The building is best appreciated through subtle changes in its appearance as the light changes. Considering Wallis' preoccupation with the use of daylight, there is little doubt that he would have taken the effects of light and shadow into account in designing the building. All references to choice of location, design styles etc., reflect concern over the lighting *inside* the building, where emphasis was upon enhancing worker productivity (Hitchmough 1992: 16), but Wallis' comments reflect the importance of external visibility, form and façade colour. He considered a building to be the best advertising a company could have, saying it gave "proportionately better results than obtained from the large yearly expenditure so often incurred in usual advertising' (Wallis 1933a: 307).

The building closed in 1980 but was renovated in the early 1990s for the Tesco supermarket chain. As with the Carreras building, the concepts and plans of the original designers were followed closely, but in this case the designs were expanded, with the side buildings and new supermarket in the rear of the building constructed in Egyptianizing style (Anon. 1993).

The Carreras and Hoover buildings may have originally seemed jarring and out of place, and they were criticized for their alleged overuse of decorated design (e.g. Dugdale 1932: 40). Yet time has shown these buildings to have an enduring appeal: the Hoover Building through harmonizing into the surrounding landscape (Wallis 1933a: 303), and the Carreras building by creating through colour and design a strikingly memorable advertisement for its original owners (Wallis 1933a: 307).

Egyptomania goes to the cinema

The Egyptian Hall in London opened in 1812, serving as a museum to house a natural history collection. As related by Lant (1992) and Werner (Chapter 5, this volume), its use changed many times over the years, and in 1896 it opened as a cinema – only the second in England. Egyptomania and the cinema proved to be good bedfellows. Lant (1992: 90) refers to "an association between the blackened enclosure of silent cinema and that of the Egyptian tomb". Tacitly drawing parallels to the adoption of Egyptianizing designs in architecture, she explores why Ancient Egypt, as opposed to other ancient civilizations, should have a particular lure for cinematography; and she compares the appropriation of Ancient Egypt by the cinema to the appropriation of an obelisk by a conquering nation (Hassan 2003a).

Given this context, it is not surprising that some cinemas should have been decorated with Egyptian themes. Indeed, in the short period from 1928 to 1930, four Egyptianizing cinemas were built in London: the Luxor in Twickenham, the Astoria in Streatham, and two Carltons at Upton Park (Figure 6:8) and Islington (Figure 6:9 col. pl.). They were large, the Islington Carlton seating 2,248 and the Astoria Streatham "nearly 3,000" (*Clapham and Lambeth News*, 27 June 1930). They were luxurious, and employed state-of-the-art technology in heating and ventilation, sound and projection equipment, information systems, and safety features. They were also designed to provide facilities in the suburbs to rival those in central London. The Richmond local press (*Richmond & Twickenham Times* 1929, prob. Sept.) spoke glowingly of "Twickenham's Egyptian Palace ... Marvels Of The New Luxor Super-Cinema ...

Figure 6:8   Carlton Cinema, Upton Park, London (© Evans 1993: 139).

Colourful Design And Luxuries Equal To The West End", while the *Clapham and Lambeth News* (27 June 1930) commented on the Astoria, "Everything that modern science can do to cater for the convenience and comfort of theatre audiences has been embodied in this beautiful building".

These four cinemas were not the only ones in London to incorporate elements from Ancient Egypt, and sometimes the Egyptianizing theme was part of a spectacle that could be related to the experience of seeing a film (Montserrat, pers. comm.). The ABC Cinema in Shaftesbury Avenue, for example, displays a series of historic scenes, starting with Egypt in the form of a Tutankhamun mask, and going on chronologically through Greece and Rome. The four cinemas were, nonetheless, a very small proportion of the 300 new cinemas that were being built or planned in 1929 (Elwall n. d.), and they were not the only ones to employ foreign or historical themes: others were built in Chinese, Moorish and Greco-Roman styles. Indeed, the Egyptianizing examples were probably not seen as especially significant. Shand (1930: 19), for example, condemned the "clogging dross of period reproduction and that craving for mere gaudiness which still strangles original design". Nevertheless, they represent the continuing use of Egyptian styles and motifs in London's architecture. Although the four buildings have in common their Egyptian theme, they used it in significantly different ways. The Luxor in Twickenham had an Egyptian façade and interior decoration, the two Carltons had Egyptian façades but more classical or modern interiors, and the Astoria had an Italianate front, but an elaborate Egyptian interior.

The main elevation of the Luxor was described in a leaflet produced to support the planning application (*Richmond Local Collections* n. d.) as "faced with Terra Cotta, the design being a combination of Egyptian and modern architectural details, with the introduction of deep and brilliant colours harmoniously blended". In fact, the only strongly Egyptian elements were six columns with palm capitals across the front over the entrance, which projected from the rest of the building, and two winged pharaoh heads with Nemes headdresses below the parapet of the main front. The rest of the decoration was a mixture of loosely classical elements such as urns and borders with roundels, with tapered glazed lanterns, and an Italianate tiled roof. The foyer was "in a modern style", but the Egyptian theme was repeated in the auditorium, with a cavetto cornice, lotus flower decorative elements, a proscenium framed by combination palm/papyrus columns, a torus moulding, and a winged sundisk and uraeus. The auditorium ceiling was painted to represent a sky and clouds.

The Streatham Astoria was built with a red brick exterior with stone dressings in a hybrid Italianate style. Inside, however, was what the *Clapham and Lambeth News* (27 June 1930) described as

> a vast auditorium adorned with Egyptian paintings and glass mosaics ... The general design is based upon Egyptian traditions in pleasing tones of red, green and gold, ... while the flank walls of the circle are enriched with highly coloured bas reliefs of Egyptian scenes.

The two Carlton cinemas were both designed by George Coles, a prolific designer of hundreds of cinemas in a 50-year career. The one in Upton Park, seating 2,117, incorporated part of an old school building, but its front, set in a parade of single storey shops, was strongly Egyptian in style. It had an inset entrance in which were set twin columns, a composite of palm and papyrus bundles, with a hoarding for cinema posters between them, and the main entrance below. A cavetto cornice ran round the top and sides of the front. Above this was a parapet featuring an extended central section with winged sundisk and uraeus, surmounted by another (unpainted) cavetto cornice, and then a pedestal and flagstaff. Below the lower cornice, and on either side of the wall of the front, were large 'Carlton' signs, and large tapered and glazed lanterns were set either side of the entrance about 3.6 m above pavement level.

The Carlton in Islington (Figure 6:9 col. pl.) was purpose built. Its front was plain at street level, with two entrances, the central one surmounted by a canopy. Above the level of the canopy ran a moulded and painted lotus frieze. From this rose pylon-like tapered window openings at either side, with a cavetto cornice moulding some way above. Between the windows, a higher centre section formed a sort of entablature, slightly set back, with two large papyrus bud columns and abaci supporting a tall lintel surmounted by a cavetto cornice and plain low parapet. Behind the pillars was an upper register of five rectangular panels, and below a torus moulding a lower one of five 'false windows' surmounted by a lotus frieze, with two central papyrus bud pilasters. The interior of the cinema was "on more classical lines than the exterior ... with decorations in a modernised Empire style" (Draper n. d.: 69). Despite its layout being dictated by its function as a cinema, the Islington Carlton uses more Egyptian elements than any other cinema, and largely avoids the eclectic mix of elements found in them. It also happens to be the only one of the four whose Egyptian elements survive today.

Although only a few 'Egyptian' cinemas were built, they were large and important entertainment venues. The use of Egyptian elements was extensive, and went beyond the architectural and decorative; the cover of the Luxor opening souvenir programme featured a winged sundisk and uraeus, and the usherettes wore

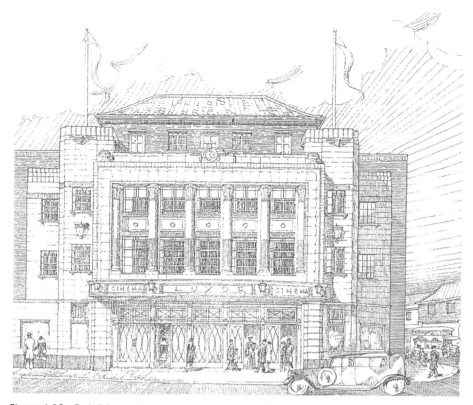

Figure 6:10   Detail from planning prospectus, Luxor Cinema, Twickenham, Middlesex.

Egyptian-style costumes (echoing the opening of the Carreras factory). They employed a mix of styles as part of an overall design that combined modern and ancient elements in a highly functional and luxurious building, accessible to a wide cross-section of the public. The Egyptian style seems to have appealed through its bold use of colour. Antiquity as such was not stressed in contemporary documents, but the planning prospectus for the Luxor (Figure 6:10) noted the "many wonderful examples of ancient craftsmanship" that had emerged from Luxor in recent years, and went on to state:

> The 'Luxor' cinema is giving all that is best in the workmanship and conception of modern cinema construction and organisation, and this, together with pleasing Egyptian design and colour, will bring some of the splendour of Luxor to Twickenham.

The influence of the Egyptophile in the late 20th century

Popular interest in Ancient Egypt remains high to the present day, with unparalleled opportunities through mass tourism to visit its monuments. It has remained a potent inspiration for written and filmed fiction, and there is a wealth of non-fiction books and television programmes on the subject (Lupton 2003; Schadla-Hall and Morris

2003; Serafy 2003). Buildings in Egyptian style continue to be constructed, although the extensive use of modern materials such as glass, heavy modifications and the incorporation of elements from other traditions and styles sometimes make it difficult to decide whether or not a building qualifies as a 'valid' example of the style (Humbert Chapter 2; Price and Humbert Chapter 1, both this volume).

The end of the 20th century saw, in London, the use of Egyptian designs in two retail facilities that could scarcely be more different: Homebase, a modern do-it-yourself superstore, and Harrods, one of the best-known 'elite' department stores in the world. The two stores are united not only in illustrating how a single enthusiast may be responsible for the adoption of Egyptianizing designs; indeed, the designer and team responsible for Homebase were for a time also commissioned to create the Egyptian Hall at Harrods.

Homebase

The Homebase building in Earls Court (Figure 6:11) is a new construction, designed by developer Ian Pollard and completed in 1988. It is fronted by a row of columns and one of the external walls (29 m long x 6.5 m high) is decorated with relief carvings of 10 Egyptian gods. The carvings furthest from the entrance are gilded and coloured, the next figures are partially coloured, and the final representations are not coloured (Figure 6:12 col. pl.). The gods' names are in hieroglyphs (Figure 6:13), and the year of construction is rendered in hieroglyphic numbers. The figure of Seth carries, in addition to his usual sceptre, a power drill (Price and Humbert Chapter 1: Figure 1:4, this volume) (Figure 6:14). The entrance is flanked by more columns, and there are five protective sandstone cobras mounted in the façade, doubling as 'gargoyle' water-spouts. The building was controversial almost from the outset. It is instructive to note,

Figure 6:11   Homebase building, Earls Court, London (© Richard Lunn).

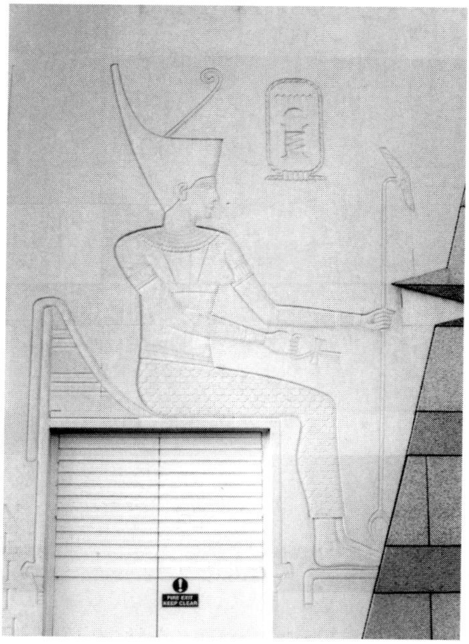

Figure 6:13 Carving of Egyptian deity with hieroglyphic name carved above the figure, Homebase building (© Richard Lunn).

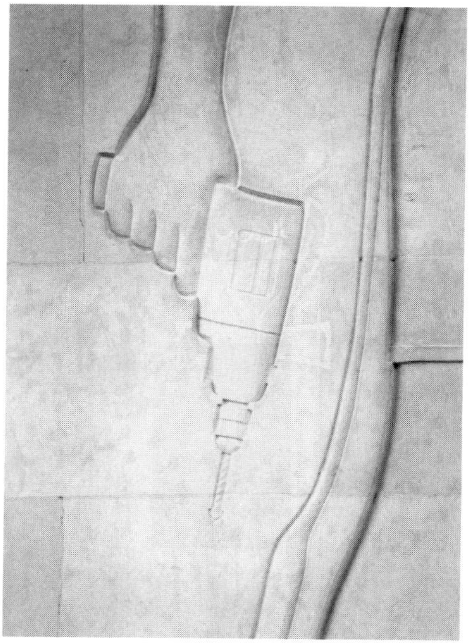

Figure 6:14 Carved power drill in the hand of the god Seth (© Richard Lunn).

however, that the carving of the Egyptianizing elements and motifs (a task that took some eight carvers about seven months) caused no controversy. This Egyptianizing concept had already been developed with Sainsbury's, the owners of the Homebase chain. Indeed, the initial advertising and marketing of the store had been planned as an integrated exercise involving prizes and travel possibilities for customers to visit Egypt. It may have been this publicity which led the editor of *The Architects Journal* (Carolin 1988) to accuse the design of being "advertising, not architecture". But it was Sir John Sainsbury, Chairman of Sainsbury's, who stirred up controversy by announcing that the design "obscured Homebase's trading identity". He ordered the removal of a group of Corinthian columns from the front of the building (allegedly on grounds of cultural incompatibility), and colour was removed from, or painted over, the remaining Egyptianizing columns. A winged sundisk immediately over the entrance was replaced with a Homebase sign (Mallett 1988).

Jencks (1991: 80) categorized the building as "carnivalesque", calling it "the most sincerely hated building in London" although "better than one might think". Pollard himself described it as "populist architecture", and as "something that people would like" (Mallett 1988). It borrows not only from Egypt, but also from classical architecture and from James Stirling's contemporary Staatsgalerie in Stuttgart. The borrowings could be seen to fit into a pattern of eclecticism that has been typified as 'post-modern', and which derives, in part, from the work of architects such as Robert Venturi. Venturi (1977) had examined the design and plan of the Temple of Horus at Edfu, and had placed a series of small, polychrome Egyptianizing pillars on his

Sainsbury Extension of the National Gallery. Venturi admitted that "we didn't think much about the symbolism – we just wanted a lot of detail there at eye-level" (Jencks 1991: 50).

Ian Pollard, the site owner and developer, and Richard Kindersley, the stone-carver, were responsible for the Egyptianizing Homebase designs, and selected the gods to be represented, their order, and the symbols with which they were associated. They did this through reading, visiting museums, and consulting Egyptologists, but the main criteria for their choices were aesthetic ones (Ian Pollard, pers. comm.), together with the overall theme of 'ongoing development' to be indicated by the unpainted section of the frieze becoming a painted section completed by a fully polychrome set of representations. It was Pollard himself who dreamed up the joke of placing a power drill in Seth's hand, replacing a previous ankh sign.

Harrods

Harrods was purchased in 1985 by Mohammed Al Fayed, who approached Pollard's team to develop plans for an Egyptian Hall, and discussions reached the advanced stage of the production of small-scale models – only to be rejected in favour of what was supposed to be a cheaper, less time-consuming and less intrusive set of (moulding) techniques. In 1992, William Mitchell, now Director of Art and Design for Harrods, with advice from James Putnam, then of the British Museum, was commissioned to create an "entertaining retail environment" (Harrods 2000: 1). Within this refurbishment programme, two new sections were introduced: the "Egyptian Hall (room F)" and the "Egyptian Hall and Escalator (room B)".

The Egyptian Hall is decorated with scenes of everyday life and funerary scenes on its upper level, and Opet festival and heb-sed scenes in the lower hall area. The scenes of everyday life and the heb-sed scenes are particularly drawn from Amarna art, such as the water pool floor scene from the royal palace area, which is replicated on the ceiling of the upper hall.

Motifs of Egyptian style are in abundance throughout, drawing both on specific imagery from the tomb of Tutankhamun (as in the ostrich feather fan motif lights) and on stylized Art Déco lotiform designs of Egyptian style (such as the light fixtures within the upper hall area, and display cabinets with similar designs). Cartouches within the Hall speak of its origin; for example, the cartouches at the ends of the escalator contain hieroglyphs which read "Egyptian Hall within Harrods, 1991".

Additional cartouches include those on the lower level, which are phonetic renderings of 'Al Fayed' crowned by royal uraei. The Hall is intended to convey a feeling of luxury and opulence, with a hint of royal trappings. When opened, it was well received by the public, and in 2000 the Department for Culture, Media and Sport upgraded Harrods' listing as a historic building from II to II* (Harrods 2002; W. Mitchell, pers. comm.).

In 1995, Mitchell designed an even more ambitious project – the renovation and redesign of the central area, which had previously housed its lift system. The lifts were to be removed and, in their place, an escalator system was to be installed which was to embody Al Fayed's view of shopping in Harrods as entertainment as well as retail. It was to be of "spectacular architecture and décor inspired by Ancient Egypt, which will certainly bear out his philosophy" (Harrods 2000: 1). The finished escalators measured 29.5 m x 13 m x 18 m, rose some 30 m and ascended through seven floors. The escalators and their accompanying Egyptianesque decoration cost nearly £20 million. Mitchell (in Harrods 2002: 1) reported that "The Chairman of Harrods, Mohammed Al Fayed, also happens to be the owner of Harrods so he has no duty to shareholders, nor is he submerged in a sea of accountants. Fortunately, he is also a bold man who makes decisions which allow exciting projects to be undertaken".

The escalator is themed as a "stairway to heaven" (Harrods 2000: 1), which has Nut (Allen 2003) decorations upon its underside, with the goddess Hathor's disk crown acting as ambient lighting in a moodily lit hall. The goddess' body conjoins with its mirror image along the entire length of the escalator at the winged limbs. The handrail is painted green, to evoke imagery of the flowing of both an earthly and heavenly Nile (W. Mitchell, pers. comm.). The escalator hall decoration is no less dramatic. The lower ground floor contains imagery drawn from Old Kingdom work and floral/faunal scenes. At one end of the hall sit two sphinxes, facing one another. One sphinx bears the image of Al Fayed and holds a model of Harrods within its paws (Figure 6:15), while the other bears the image of Mitchell and holds the carving tool used for creating the hall imagery. Touching scenes of tender moments between an 'Amarnaesque' king and queen, patterned after the Amarna stela called *Promenade in the Garden* (Aldred 1973), evoke memories of the other main feature of this level of the store, the memorial to Diana, Princess of Wales, and Dodi Al Fayed, the owner's son.

Mitchell's carving techniques for the wall decorations required that soft concrete was placed upon the walls of the hall in large blocks. While it was still moist, Mitchell carved his designs by freehand in the soft concrete. The images were then brought to an embossed finish by hand-smoothing, creating a deep-carved effect (Figure 6:16). Traditional Egyptian motifs from the eighteenth Dynasty predominate, with occasional use of Old Kingdom floral/faunal motifs. Scenes of everyday life, mainly fowling and partying, are shown on successive floors. The motifs occasionally matched the goods being sold on each floor (W. Mitchell, pers. comm.); for example, Floor 3, which sold musical instruments, features scenes of musicians.

The overhanging balconies are embellished with pharaonic heads, both male and female. The king's head is roughly modelled upon a nineteenth Dynasty Ramesside style, and is decorated with two royal uraei, which is not a traditional motif for kings of this epoch. The queen's headdress is patterned after the Amarna queen Nefertiti's tall blue crown, although it is expressed in reverse angles from the original, with the sloping inclination of the cap descending from front to back.

Each ceiling is decorated with the repeated *triskelion* motif from the eighteenth Dynasty tomb of Sennedjem, bordered by Art Déco styled lotiform borders. Other

Figure 6:15   Representation of the sphinx in the image of Mohammed Al Fayed, Harrods, South Kensington, London (© Katherine Griffis-Greenberg).

Figure 6:16   Hand smoothed carvings in soft concrete, Harrods, South Kensington, London (courtesy W. Mitchell).

borders include the lashed tentpole design, which is found in Egyptian art since the Old Kingdom. Hieroglyphs, which form a repeating (though incoherent) pattern are to be seen along the stairwell walls in front of the escalators. The luxurious life of ancient nobility is shown best in a huge stained glass rendering (Figure 6:17 col. pl.). The scene is patterned after the fowling scene of Nebamun, a wall relief presently in the British Museum. Its border, however, consists of flattened two-dimensional scenes of a garden surrounding the hunting pool, which is not found in the original rendering.

There are two particularly noteworthy scenes: the first of a seated king holding a *w3s* sceptre before a table of offerings, which is bordered by a quotation from Shelley's *Ozymandias*: "My name is Ozymandias, king of kings/Look upon my works, ye Mighty and despair!" The second is a procession of royal children, located behind a column on Floor 4, which has been enhanced by handprints above the head of each child. Mitchell (pers. comm.) noted that it was customary for a patron of art to place his own mark on an artist's finished product. Here, the mark is left not by Al Fayed, but by his children.

The crowning glory of the Egyptian escalator is on the top level accessible to store customers. Here, the columns, which have run the entire height of the hall, terminate in magnificent bovine Hathor heads, following a roughly Ptolemaic design style, which support a huge lighted ceiling. The ceiling displays a variant of the Dendera zodiac against a dark blue background, in which three large light fixtures are placed centrally, to symbolize the three stars in Orion's belt (W. Mitchell, pers. comm.). The cavetto-corniced border consists of palm branch designs, and at each corner of the ceiling is a crowned Hathor head. The decorations along the wall borders are concerned with the Opet festival, while a side room contains a well-rendered reproduction of the faience mat screen from the Step Pyramid of Djoser. A very large Ramesside kneeling king figure, flanked by military scenes, is positioned along an inaccessible part of the walkway that is seen as the customer leaves the escalator (Figure 6:18).

Figure 6:18   Kneeling Ramesside king figure, Harrods, South Kensington, London (© Katherine Griffis-Greenberg).

The Egyptianizing constructions and decoration of the Egyptian Hall and Escalator comprise both studied motifs with specific meaning, and motifs that are used to create atmosphere. However, it is, in essence, the use of Ancient Egypt as theatrics not education: none of its motifs are labelled with name or date. Its purpose is to entertain and enchant the viewer, to create a backdrop evoking the opulence and luxury which have for centuries been associated with Ancient Egypt, and embodying the personal philosophy of its patron. Indeed, this philosophy was reinforced by the theatrical nature of the opening ceremonies. In an atmosphere that could be described as "carnivalesque", an adjective already applied to Homebase (see above), a procession of 'Ancient Egyptians' assembled outside the store (Figures 6:19–6:21 col. pls.). Strict accuracy and authenticity did not matter: the parade was automatically Egyptianizing because of its association with the Egyptian Hall, which in turn was associated with both modern Egypt (through Mohammed Al Fayed) and Ancient Egypt (through its designs). As with the other buildings described above, Egyptomania was able to inject entertainment and razzmatazz into commerce, utilizing the 'ancient' to sell the 'modern' (Rice and MacDonald 2003: 15–20).

Note

1   It was the memory of this parade that led William Mitchell (pers. comm.), Artistic Director for Harrods Department Store, to replicate a similar ceremony in 1995 for the opening of the Egyptian Escalator at Harrods.

Acknowledgments

We are grateful to William Mitchell (Harrods Department Store) and Andrew Forman (Finch Forman Chartered Architects) for the information that they provided about Harrods and the Carreras building respectively, and to Richard Kindersley and Ian Pollard for information regarding Homebase.

CHAPTER 7

SEARCHING FOR EGYPT: EGYPT IN 19th CENTURY AMERICAN WORLD EXHIBITIONS

Marie-Stéphanie Delamaire

Introduction

On 3 March 1871, the United States' President, Ulysses S. Grant (1822–1885), approved and signed an Act of Congress "to provide for celebrating the one hundredth anniversary of American Independence by holding an international exhibition of arts, manufacturers, and products of the soil and mine, in the city of Philadelphia, and State of Pennsylvania in the year 1876" (H. R. 1478: *Journal of the House of Representatives of the United States* 65: 457). The Centennial Exhibition, as it was to be popularly known, was the first major international exhibition held in the United States. It attracted millions of visitors: one out of every five Americans visited the exhibition. Less than 20 years later, in 1893, the second American world fair took place in Chicago, the World's Columbian Exhibition, commemorating the 400th anniversary of the landing of Christopher Columbus in America.

These two great exhibitions were mounted during a period in which the United States was recovering from the Civil War and was becoming a leading industrial power. It was during this same period that the first major American art museums were founded. Up until then American interest in Egyptology had been characterized by un-coordinated, individual efforts. Two years after the Chicago exhibition in 1895, the first Chair of Egyptology was created for James Henry Breasted (1865–1935) at the University of Chicago, and later George A. Reisner (1867–1942) undertook fieldwork in Egypt with the Harvard-Boston expedition. Thus, professional Egyptology was born in America and gained international recognition.

This chapter is concerned with the preparation and reception of both of the above exhibitions – in the context of Trigger's (1995: 21) claim that there was "an extraordinary fascination with ancient Egypt ... in both the popular culture and the intellectual life of the United States at least a century before there were any professional Egyptologists". It is necessary to appreciate such early American interest in Ancient Egypt in order to place later Egyptianizing architecture into its correct cultural and social context.

The Centennial Exhibition

President Grant officially announced the Exhibition to other nations on 5 July 1873. Official invitations were conveyed to foreign ministers in June 1874. It took one more year for the official participation of Egypt to be announced. Mohammed Tawfik Pacha was to be President of the Egyptian Commission for the Centennial of the United States. The German Egyptologist Heinrich Brugsch (1827–1894) was Commissioner-General, and his brother, Emile Brugsch (1842–1930), was designated Chief of Transportation and Installation. Auguste Mariette Bey (1812–1881), 'Director of the Museum of Antiquities', featured among the several Commissioners (and see Humbert 2003).

The Egyptian exhibits for the Centennial, which were hastily organized, were some of the first to be installed on the exhibition grounds at Fairmount Park in Philadelphia:

> ... the entire exhibit of Egypt has arrived, and to-day three car loads were run into the main building in the sealed cars, and the Custom-house officials broke the seal, and proceeded with their duties in relation to the matter. This is the first arrival of a whole exhibit, and the first that the Government officials have dealt with according to law, and is very satisfactory.
>
> (*New York Times* 1876a: 2)

Commissioner-General Heinrich Brugsch had been in charge of the Egyptian exhibits of the earlier exhibition of 1873 in Vienna (Whitehouse Chapter 3, this volume) and had also worked with Mariette in Paris in 1867. For the American Centennial, he delegated most of the responsibility for directing the installations to his brother, who essentially supervised the exhibition from the reception of the 140 cases that arrived in America in November 1875 to their shipment back to Egypt in December 1876.

Although it had been announced that the Egyptian government would not be erecting any buildings on the exhibition grounds, Heinrich and Emile together directed the construction of an Egyptian court (Figure 7:1) whose entrance was an Egyptianizing façade of a temple, built of wood. This cheap material was probably used for economic reasons since the Egyptian Commission had suffered a sudden financial crisis (Brugsch 1894: 332). Nevertheless, work continued, and Egypt was ready for the opening of the Centennial Exhibition on 10 May 1876. The Egyptian court was located in the main exhibition building to the south of the main aisle and to the east of the Danish section, enclosed by a high wooden structure resembling an ancient Egyptian temple of the Greco-Roman period such as those of Philae and Dendera. This structure consisted of the typical Egyptian battered walls decorated with painted lotus flowers and, above them, the inscription, "Egypt, Soodan, the Oldest People of the world sends its morning greetings to the Youngest Nation". On top of the wall were two plaster busts of pharaohs. Two columns with palm-capitols, a painted winged solar globe, a cavetto cornice and torus mouldings completed the decoration. The hieroglyphic inscription on the lintel was not merely decorative, but read, "The Viceroy has made for the Centennial Celebration, at the city of Philadelphia, a temple" (*New York Times* 1876a). Inside, the walls were ornamented only with the painted cavetto cornice and torus mouldings.

Figure 7:1   The Egyptian Court in the main exhibition hall of the Philadelphia Centennial Exhibition (Free Library of Philadelphia).

Beyond the Egyptian façade, the visitor found himself in the middle of 'Arabian Nights' bric-a-brac, full of products from the land of the Nile including silk clothing, jewellery, gold and silver embroidered saddles, silverware, and magnificent furniture (Figures 7:2, 7:3; Hassan 2003b). The National Museum exhibited a collection of photographs, scenic panoramas and albums, ethnographic collections, publications, earthenwares from Upper Egypt, and a small collection of plaster cast replicas of ancient Egyptian monuments.

Harper's Weekly (1876: 31) announced that a unique collection of casts from the Museum of Bulaq would be displayed at the Centennial:

> The Smithsonian Institution has been officially advised by General C. P. Stone ... of the sailing to America of Dr Brugsch Bey ... to the International Exhibition at Philadelphia. His collection, intended for exhibition by Egypt, fill over 140 boxes ... and among them is a nearly complete collection of casts of the Khedivial collection in the museum at Boulac. These, according to General Stone, will be presented to the United States at the close of the Exhibition, and will consequently form part of the collection of the National Museum in charge of the Smithsonian Institution.

It is difficult today to know precisely the contents of this Bulaq Museum plaster cast collection which was sent to Philadelphia. However, it certainly never consisted of a "nearly complete collection of casts"; it only consisted of a dozen busts, four bas-reliefs, and a model of the pyramid of Cheops (United States Customs Service 1876).

Figure 7:2   Interior of the Egyptian Court at the Philadelphia Centennial Exhibition (Gebbie and Barry 1876, 2: 482).

These plaster casts were not the only exhibits evoking pharaonic Egypt. A reporter for the *Times of Philadelphia* (1876) wrote:

> ... the display in this section that will be sought for by the scholar is that objectively illustrating the progress of handwriting, printing and literature in Egypt since their first institution to the present time. Proof-sheets of Arabic hieroglyphics, specimens of Coptic chirography, books for the blind, manuscripts in hieroglyphics, German, French, and other languages written by Arabic scholars ... are orderly arranged in elegant cases, and cannot fail to command attention. Mr Brugsch has also a portfolio filled with drawings of sheets of papyrus, covered with hieroglyphics, and perfectly representing the decayed and falling-apart originals. These works were executed after years of labor by Mr Brugsch himself.

Figure 7:3   Bric-a-brac in the Egyptian Court (© Marie-Stéphanie Delamaire).

All in all the Egyptian section had been expected to be a great draw for the exhibition. The special correspondent of the *New York Times* (1876a), for example, enthusiastically announced the probable participation of Egypt, reporting that the celebrated tomb at Beni Hasan, which was reproduced in 1873 in Vienna in all its brilliant colours (*Centennial* 1875: 2), would be set up again in Philadelphia. In the event, however, the Egyptian display at the Centennial was not able to meet American expectations. The *New York Times*, for example, which had originally been so enthusiastic, commented (1876b):

> Neighboring Denmark is Egypt, whose archway is a feeble attempt to imitate Karnak, which can scarcely be considered a happy thought. The colours of the lotus-leafed capitals are dingy purple and dirty green, and the small plaster casts of the colossal Memnon heads are also great failures. The internal decorations are of the same character though far less pretentious.

Not all the critics were so bitter (e.g. McCabe 1876: 436–437). What stands out about both the prior "anticipation", and the ensuing American reactions to the display is how accurately the writers were informed about the previous Egyptian exhibitions in Paris and Vienna, leading them to expect that the most attractive part of the Vienna exhibition – replicas of monuments from Egyptian antiquity – would be sent directly to Philadelphia.

The Paris Exposition Universelle of 1867 was one of the earliest to have featured an important Egyptianizing pavilion (and see Werner Chapter 5, this volume). Mariette, "Directeur des travaux d'antiquités en Égypte" and Director of the Bulaq Museum, had supervised its contents, which consisted of four buildings: an Egyptian temple, an Arabic palace, an 'okel' with its outbuilding and café, shops, workshops, accommodation for the Egyptian staff, and a room dedicated to the study of Egyptian mummies and skulls. The temple (Figure 7:4) was designed by Mariette to be "in some

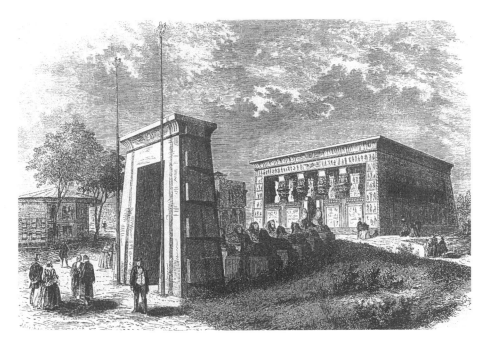

Figure 7:4   The Egyptian Temple at the 1867 Parisian Exposition Universelle (© Jean-Marcel Humbert).

ways an example of the essence of archaeology" (David 1994: 172) and a "museum and example of pharaonic art" (Mariette 1867: 9). Mariette intended the temple to present different phases of Egyptian architecture and also to house a chronologically representative collection of antiquities from the Bulaq Museum (and see Edmond 1867). He (Mariette 1867) also published a 'Description of the Egyptian Park', for the public, to describe and explain the didactic purpose of what he called the 'temple-museum'. This temple was built of blocks of plaster covered with sand to imitate sandstone and was divided into three sections: the centre part was Old Kingdom, the corridor New Kingdom, and the colonnade of the peristyle, Ptolemaic. A monumental gate and a dromos lined with 10 sphinxes (copying sphinxes in the Louvre – Edmond 1867: 90) led to the entrance of the temple.[1]

As with his opera designs (Humbert 2003), Mariette was extremely concerned about the accuracy of details. For instance, the colouring of the reliefs used a range of samples deriving directly from the original monuments in Upper Egypt. Inside the temple (Figure 7:5), original reliefs, statues, and objects from the collections of the Bulaq Museum were exhibited, including some pieces of exceptional interest such as the diorite statue of Khephren, the Cheikh el-Beled, and the famous jewels of Queen Aah-Hotep.[2]

When Egypt decided to participate in the 1873 Vienna Weltausstellung, organized to celebrate the 25th year jubilee of the Emperor Franz-Joseph, Heinrich Brugsch was designated General Commissioner. He had been Director of the new school of Egyptology in Cairo since 1869, but had had to close the school because the

Figure 7:5   Egyptian antiquities from the Bulaq Museum inside the Egyptian Temple of the 1867 Parisian Exposition Universelle (Musée du Louvre, Département des Antiquités Égyptiennes).

organization of the Egyptian exhibits for Vienna was taking all his time (Brugsch 1894: 315). Mariette was in charge of the creation of the replicas of the reliefs of the tombs of Saqqarah and Beni Hasan that would be exhibited in Vienna (David 1994: 217). The Khedive had credited the Egyptian Commission with one million francs for this exhibition. A group of buildings which included two mosques, an Egyptian house and a fellah village were erected on the exhibition grounds to house the Egyptian exhibits (Brugsch 1894: 318). Mariette was granted permission from the Viceroy to forbid any genuine antiquity from the Bulaq Museum from being sent to Vienna: "I am always fearful that these antiquities will not be returned. How could the Viceroy refuse a request to keep them if the idea came from the Austrian Emperor?" (Auguste Mariette to Edouard Mariette, 27 March 1873; quoted in David 1994: 228).

Chicago's World Columbian Exhibition

Seventeen years later, at the 1893 Chicago Exhibition, a huge 'Street in Cairo' was allocated to Egypt in the Midway Plaisance. The Midway was formerly a wooden drive connecting Jackson Park with Washington Park, catering mainly for recreation and entertainment. Visitors could enjoy a kind of world tour, passing from a 'Dahomey Village' to the Irish, or Turkish, visiting 'Old Vienna' or the 'Japanese Bazar' and admiring the 'Eiffel Tower'. But they could also enjoy a ride on the 'Ferris Wheel', or the 'Ice Railway', as well as being entertained in the 'Brazilian Music Hall' and the 'Electric Scenic Theatre'.

It was between Algeria, Tunis and a German village that the attractive 'Cairo Street' (Figure 7:6) was located, one of the biggest complexes of the Midway Plaisance, and one of the most popular: "The street in Cairo, with its Egyptian temple annex and its Soudanese additions, is the centre of attraction" (*Vanished City* 1893). Modelled on the rue des Nations at the 1889 Paris exhibition and designed by Chicago architect Henry Ives Cobbs, it comprised a temple, a mosque, a theatre and 62 shops. The combination of old and modern Egypt clearly excited the visitor's imagination. Visitors were invited to wander in the bazaars in the midst of Egyptian snake charmers, dancers and performing monkeys. They could also ride on a donkey or a camel, and – once a day – could admire a wedding procession.

At the west end of the street was the Luxor temple (Figure 7:7), with its outdoor wall inscribed "Egyptian Temple, Luksor, 3400 Years ago, Pharaonic Royal Mummies, Sacred Tombs of Apis and Thi", and described as a "close copy of the one near Thebes, built around 1400 BC" (Bancroft 1893: 868). In front of the temple were two obelisks inscribed with the names of Ramesses II and United States President Grover Cleveland (R. Fazzini and E. Bleiberg, pers. comm.). Inside, "in cases about the room were replicas of the recently-discovered mummies of Thothmes III, Sesostris, Seti I, and a dozen others of the most important people who have yet lived on earth" (*Dream City* 1893). Once a day, there was a procession carrying a statue of the bull Apis, led by a priest wearing a typical Egyptian priest's leopardskin outfit.

Cairo Street and its temple were not the only exhibits of the fair showcasing Ancient Egypt. The University Museum[3] exhibited a collection of antiquities in the anthropology building, mainly deriving from W. M. Flinders Petrie's (1853–1942) recent excavations at Naucratis, Tell Defenneh, Meidum, Tell el Amarna, and in the Fayum, and acquired by the museum through its association with the Egypt Exploration Fund (Jeffreys 2003). Additionally, the Austrian antiquities dealer Theodore Graf (1840–1903) exhibited a collection of 75 portrait panels found in the Fayum and Armand de Potter exhibited a collection consisting mostly of bronze statuettes of Egyptian gods and goddesses.[4]

Figure 7:6   The 'Cairo Street' at the 1893 Chicago World Columbian Exhibition (*Vanished City* 1893).

Figure 7:7   The Luxor Temple at the 1893 Chicago World Columbian Exhibition (*Dream City* 1893).

Comparisons

The success of the Chicago Exhibition was in stark contrast to the 1876 Philadelphia Exhibition. Philadelphia, with its modest collection of casts (dispersed in the middle of all the other products exhibited by Egypt), appears quite humble in comparison not only to the Columbian Exhibition but also to the earlier European fairs' temples, palaces and mosques, and their extensive collections of antiquities and ethnography. Unlike Mariette's educational intent and attention to the smallest archaeological detail, or Brugsch's concern with education in Vienna in 1873, the Centennial Exhibition presented an untidy display of a few plaster casts with various other assorted artefacts from different categories. Nor can Egypt's financial plight be seen as a sufficient explanation for the mediocre Egyptian display of the Philadelphia Exhibition, for Egypt still participated at the last minute in the Paris Exhibition of 1878 at the Trocadéro. Then the Egyptian Commission, along with the Compagnie Universelle du Canal Maritime de Suez, constructed an Egyptian pavilion containing an Egyptian house which, under the direction of Mariette, tried to re-create for the public an archaeologically accurate Egyptian house (Figure 7:8) based on then recent excavations at Abydos (Mariette, quoted in Humbert 1998a: 133). Mariette was concerned about the details of the house and tried to solve all the architectural problems by sticking as close as possible to the archaeological data:

> Separate limestone fragments of sills and lintels are the only evidence for windows, which were reconstructed following those of Ramesses III's pavilion which were the only existing parallel. The small columns which divided up the windows in the Trocadéro were reconstructed after a small lotus-shaped capital which was found in the ruins of Abydos and which could only have been part of a carving of this sort.

Inside the house, replicas of the reliefs of the tomb of Beni Hasan and Saqqarah were again presented and, as before, a short pamphlet was available for purchase by the visitor.

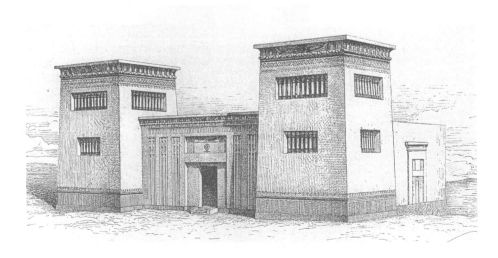

Figure 7:8   The 'Egyptian House' at the 1878 Parisian Exposition Universelle.

Nothing of the kind occurred at Philadelphia. In his autobiography, Brugsch (1894: 329) explained his own lack of enthusiasm for the Philadelphia Exhibition with reference to the Khedive's financial situation. Whatever the real cause, his disinterest in the undertaking was palpable. No catalogue or pamphlet was published separately, and he spent very little time in Philadelphia. Additionally, he did not give any details about his intentions for the construction of the façade, nor any guidelines for the collections to be exhibited. Overall, the poor quality of the Philadelphia Centennial must have been mainly a consequence of the organizers' ignorance and indifference to the American taste for Egypt.

On the other hand, the Columbian Exhibition's 'Street in Cairo', with its huge 'Luxor Temple', clearly reflected a different attitude. Inside the temple were exhibited copies of the royal Egyptian mummies found by Emile Brugsch in 1881. The huge display clearly demonstrated that its builder, Professor Mosconas (a Greek orientalist of Alexandria and a student of Heinrich Brugsch) did not underestimate the lure of Egypt for the American public. At the same time, the collection exhibited by Theodore Graf responded to the taste of the American collector. The strong fascination with Ancient Egypt in both popular and intellectual culture was no longer being ignored by European Egyptologists and art dealers.[5]

Museum collections

Most of the plaster casts exhibited at the Centennial Exhibition were bought either by Clement Miller Biddle (1838–1902) on behalf of the 'Permanent Exhibition' that was to become the origin of the Pennsylvania Museum and School of Industrial Art[6] or by the Museum of Fine Arts of Boston for its newly opened Egyptian Gallery (United States Customs Service 1876).

It was in Boston that the first permanent collection of Egyptian art was opened in any American museum, the outcome of a popular and scholarly interest in Ancient Egypt whose roots can be traced back to the early 19th century, with Boston's increasing commercial and missionary interests with the Near East. It was also in Boston that an Egyptian mummy was presented to Massachusetts General Hospital where trustees arranged for it to be examined and the results published "for the satisfaction of the public" (Warren 1823: 164). Again it was in Boston that George Gliddon (1809–1857), first American Consul in Egypt (from 1836 to 1844) and first American Egyptologist, inaugurated his series of lectures on Ancient Egypt (Gliddon 1843). And finally the Museum of Fine Arts, Boston (1876: 10) opened to the public at the time of the Centennial, with the first permanent collection of Egyptian art in America.[7]

From the 1840s, Philadelphia also expressed a recurring interest in Ancient Egypt and Egyptology through various learned societies. The American Philosophical Society regularly published papers on subjects related to Egyptian history (e.g. Morton 1844). A little later, the Philomathean Society of Pennsylvania University published the first American work on Egyptological philology after a plaster cast of the Rosetta Stone was presented to the Society in 1855 (Hale *et al.* 1859). The casts bought by Biddle for the Pennsylvania Museum and School of Industrial Art did not belong to any of the disciplines on which the museum intended to focus in order to create an industrial art collection, and they show the strength of the perceived need for an institutionalized Egyptological collection. The museum received only a few further Egyptological objects, and its entire collection of Egyptian antiquities was subsequently transferred to the University Museum (founded 10 years after the Centennial).

Conclusion

The centennial year of the United States can be seen as a turning point in America's involvement with Ancient Egypt and Egyptology, an outcome of both a scholarly and popular interest in Ancient Egypt which had begun early in the 19th century, first in Boston, and then in Philadelphia. 1876 can perhaps be regarded as the birth of institutional Egyptology in America, when Heinrich and Emile Brugsch brought to light the Egyptological potential of the New World for Europeans – well before Henry Breasted and George Reisner. The importance and success of the Luxor temple of the Columbian Exhibition was one of the consequences of this realization.

Notes

1   Some of these sphinxes can still be seen today in the property that Victorien Sardou bought in 1863 in Marly-le-Roy (Yvelines) – Humbert 1998a: 129.

2   Mariette refused to present these jewels to the Empress Eugénie who had asked the Khedive Ismail to give them to her. After this unfortunate incident, Mariette decided to forbid any further loan of antiquities from the museum to future international exhibitions.

3   The 'University Museum of Archaeology and Anthropology' (Philadelphia) was founded in 1887, and officially named from 1892 to 1913 the 'Free Museum of Science and Art' but was commonly referred to as the 'University Museum'. It will be called University Museum throughout this chapter.

4   The Armand de Potter collection was lent to the University Museum after the Columbian Exhibition and purchased from his widow by the Brooklyn Museum of Art in 1908.

5   For instance, Anthony Joseph Drexel (1826–1893), founder of the Drexel Institute of Philadelphia, assembled a collection of Egyptian antiquities which he bought from Emile Brugsch. He presented his collection to the Drexel Institute in 1895. Part of this collection belongs today to the Harer Family Trust Collection (Scott 1992: ix–x). His brother Joseph William Drexel (1833–1888) gave a collection of Egyptian plaster casts to the then recently founded Metropolitan Museum in New York, in 1881.

6   Historically, the Philadelphia Museum of Art was a legacy of the Centennial Exhibition: Memorial Hall, the art gallery during the exhibition, remained open as the Pennsylvania Museum and School of Industrial Art (founded in 1876, and today the Philadelphia Museum of Art). Clement Biddle was elected president of the committee in charge of spending $25,000 for the acquisition of a collection of industrial arts for the museum.

7   This collection consisted of part of the Robert Hay (1799–1863) collection (sold to the Reverend C. Granville Way and presented by his son to the museum in 1872) and the collections of Egyptian antiquities gathered together by the American traveller John Lowell Jr (1799–1836) and donated by his heirs to the museum in 1875 (Museum of Fine Arts 1876: 10).

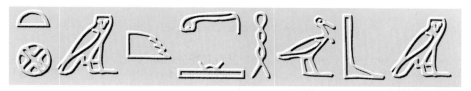

CHAPTER 8

'EGYPTOMANIA' AND AMERICAN ARCHITECTURE[1]

Richard A. Fazzini and Mary E. McKercher

In the one monograph that has been written on American Egyptianizing architecture, Carrott (1978) argued that the true Egyptian Revival in architecture was limited to the first six decades of the 19th century.[2] His reasons for this are simple, if somewhat Amerocentric (cf. Humbert 1989: 95): it was then that in the United States a significant number of Egyptianizing buildings were designed and/or built by important architects in various major urban centres. Moreover, if these buildings displayed a stylistic evolution, they also encompassed a significant number of types of structures, and many of the uses of the style reflected and resulted from associations brought to mind by Ancient Egypt. Such associations had, of course, existed before the growth of interest in Ancient Egypt and in Egyptian archaeology that began during the late 18th century and continued into the 19th century. However, increasing awareness of Ancient Egypt and factors conducive to eclecticism (including symbolic eclecticism in architecture) made such associations of broader interest.

Associational symbolism

The associational symbolism of Egyptianizing architecture of the period is the main concern of Carrott's book, beginning with a project he describes as an early comprehensive use of Egyptian revival style: Benjamin Latrobe's 1808 design, never executed, for the interior of an otherwise Classicizing United States Library of Congress (Carrott 1978: 3, 64–66, pl. 97). For Carrott and some others, one reason for the use of this pharaonic style here was the old, but still current, idea of Egypt as a land of wisdom in general and, in particular, the home of the famed Library of Alexandria (Carrott 1978: 110–111; Butler Chapter 15, this volume), despite the fact that the latter was not pharaonic in form.

As Carrott noted, Egypt had a long reputation, based in part on Herodotus and Manetho, as a land not only of learning and wisdom, but also of significant medical knowledge (see various chapters in Ucko and Champion 2003). This could explain the selection for the style, interior as well as exterior, for Thomas S. Stewart's 1884 Medical College in Richmond, Virginia (Carrott 1978: 111–112, pls. 102–103).

Egyptianizing forms came to be used in designs for suspension piers and suspension bridges as early as the 1820s in Europe. Examples include the Brighton Chain Pier of 1823 (Carrott 1978: 123 n. 11, pl. 81) and a bridge of 1825–1826 in St

Petersburg (Humbert 1989: 80, 312 n. 187; Whitehouse Chapter 4, this volume). The latter was replaced with another Egyptianizing bridge in the early 20th century (Humbert 1989: 224). In the ca. 1826 design for another suspension bridge in St Petersburg, the gateway suspension supports were inspired by a large gateway at Karnak, with Russian double eagles replacing the disk in the winged sundisks, and reliefs depicting Czar Alexander I's victories over Napoleon (Humbert *et al.* 1994: 322–325). In north America, Egyptianizing forms for piers and bridges were introduced in the 1830s (Carrott 1978: 104–105, pls. 79, 80, 82, 83). One motivation for the use of Egyptian battered gateway forms and obelisks (thicker at the bottom than the top) for suspension bridges was that they were functionally well-suited as suspension supports. However, the choice of Egyptianizing forms for bridges could also reflect an interest in Egyptian style for aesthetic reasons and/or its novelty. There is also written evidence that the qualities associated with Egypt (a 'land of wisdom') and its architecture (ingenious, strong, solid, stable, time-defying) were used to help allay public suspicion of the new type of bridge (Carrott 1978: 102–105). Some of these bridges were railroad bridges and economy of construction costs, a desire for the fashionable, and associations with the wise and enduring were also reasons the 1830s and 1840s saw the design, and sometimes the construction, of Egyptianizing stations in England and the United States for the still-new railroad (Carrott 1978: 102–104, pls. 38–41).

Other technological structures that sometimes used an Egyptianizing style were reservoirs and pumping stations, massive battered Egyptian walls being very well suited for reservoirs. The most impressive was the Croton Distributing Reservoir in New York City, built between 1837 and 1842 (Carrott 1978: pls. 86–87). There is no general agreement on whether specific symbolism was associated with this reservoir. Carrott (1978: 107) seems to suggest that the Croton Reservoir and other Egyptianizing reservoirs or waterworks may have been associated with ideas relating to the annual flood of the Nile and Egypt's irrigation-based economy, an idea rejected by Humbert (1989: 80), who sees the forms as reflecting aesthetic concerns. Covering two city blocks, with walls over 15 m tall, the Croton Distributing Reservoir was one of the most impressive Egyptianizing monuments ever constructed. It was also, to quote Carrott (1978: 107, pl. 85), "much more archaeological" than its likely prototype, the somewhat more ornate wall of the first partially-Egyptianizing reservoir built in Albany, New York in 1811, which also included Islamicizing structures. Nevertheless, even that wall indicates that its designer had done some research on ancient Egyptian architecture. Indeed, the architects and engineers responsible for all these structures were aware of current archaeological knowledge, including that stemming from Bonaparte's Expedition (1798–1801) as published by Vivant Denon (1802).

The symbolism of public monuments

Perhaps not unsurprisingly, the first Egyptianizing monument in the United States that seems to be clearly influenced by Denon was by the French émigré architect, Maximilian Godefroy (ca. 1765–ca. 1845), whose Baltimore Battle Monument, begun in 1815, commemorating the city's defenders against the British in 1814, appears to have used Denon (1802: pl. 80; Alexander 1958). Most of the monument is, however,

Classicizing, and Godefroy transformed a pharaonic-style gateway into a pedestal for a Roman column surmounted by a personification of Baltimore.

Godefroy's combination of the Egyptian and classical was hardly unique in American architecture of the first half of the 19th century, as evidenced, for example, by the winning plan for the monument commemorating George Washington (d. 1799) in the capital named after him. Robert Mills' proposal of 1833 (Figure 8:1) featured an obelisk 150 m tall that was to rest atop a 30 m tall base in the form of a circular Doric colonnaded building 75 m in diameter and with a tetrastyle portico (Zukowsky 1976: 575, fig. 2), a design not without at least partial parallels in earlier European works (Humbert 1974).

As it happens, there were also proposals for George Washington to be buried in Washington, DC in a pyramidal mausoleum (Gutheim 1951: 139–140), as

Figure 8:1   Robert Mills' design (1883) for the Washington Monument, Library of Congress, Washington.

well as for a pyramid-shaped monument there (Sky and Stone 1983: 283, fig. 445), the latter neither the first nor the last proposal for a pyramid as a public monument in the United States (Fazzini with McKercher 1996: 254 n. 22). The obelisk was by far the most favoured Egyptianizing form for public monuments in the United States, however, Carrott (1978: 139–141) listing 24 large obelisks built as "specific monuments" in the United States between 1792 and 1860.

In its erection of public monuments in the form of obelisks, the United States was following the lead of Europe and England. Nevertheless, monumental commemorative obelisks, especially hollow ones with internal observation platforms, were particularly popular in 19th century America. Most of them celebrated military victories or presidents as military commanders, the presidential monuments differing from battle monuments in having temple-like bases to house documents or art related to the president (Zukowsky 1976: 574, 578, 581).

Had it ever progressed beyond its cornerstone ceremony, one of the most impressive presidential monuments would have been a New York City monument to George Washington designed in 1847 by Minard Lafever. He advocated the use of the Egyptian style for national and private memorials because of its massiveness, strength and permanence, and saw the obelisk as an appropriate monumental form because it was visible from afar (Landy 1970: 136). This monument, based in part on a slightly earlier Lafever-designed private grave monument, consisted of a hollow obelisk rising from two levels of multiple pylons, both base and obelisk being adorned with Egyptianizing motifs derived from publications such as Denon's *Voyage* (1802; Carrott

1978: pl. 35; Landy 1970: 132–146; Zukowsky 1976: 577). Its total height would have been 150 m.

Figure 8:2   The Washington Monument (© Sam Serafy).

Other proposals for American obelisks utilize the idea that the vistas visible from some of them were associated with American expansionism, and that the Pharos of Alexandria, even though it was not an obelisk, may have been an iconographic source for the United States' monumental obelisks, which would symbolize liberty enlightening the world (Zukowsky 1976: 579–581). It has also been argued that the George Washington Monument of Washington, DC can be seen as the use of Egyptianizing forms to evoke Burkean sublime emotions associating the country's founding father with scale and power and ideas related to obelisks: phallus-father, unifying god, military victor, masonic warrior for freedom (Pierce 1980: 77–105).

The Washington Monument as completed (Figure 8:2) – an unadorned obelisk without ornate base (Carrott 1978: pl. 136) – may better suit Burkean artistic theories than Robert Mills' original design, but that is not why it lost its original colonnaded base with portico. Work on the project began in 1848, but stopped in 1856. It was not until the 1870s that serious efforts to restart the work led to a reassessment of Mills' plan and a consideration of new proposals, one, submitted by H. R. Searle, showing an Egyptianizing base supporting an obelisk (Pierce 1980: 97–98, fig. 41). However, in 1880 the Washington Monument Commission, part of the federal government, decided to complete the monument as a simple obelisk. In this they were influenced by George P. Marsh, a US diplomat in Rome who had also served in Egypt, who was responsible for the proportions of Mills' obelisk being changed to agree with those of ancient obelisks (Pierce 1980: 101–102). This change reflected the growing value being placed on archaeological accuracy.

A grandiose architectural project where archaeological accuracy was a major concern was a scheme of 1891–1900 developed by Franklin Webster Smith (Fazzini with McKercher 1996: figs. 36–37). Strange as it may seem now, it eventually became a serious proposal in the United States Senate, being published by the US Government in 1900 (Smith 1900). The central aspect of this scheme (Smith 1900: fig. 44) called for the creation of an American Acropolis on which would stand, among other structures, a 50 per cent larger-than-life Parthenon as a memorial to American presidents and, behind it, a large Gallery of American History. A processional way was to lead from the Acropolis to the Capitol Building, and was to have been flanked by eight galleries, each one representing by its form and contents one of eight great civilizations of the past, among them Egypt. The processional way was to have included an Egyptian gateway and an avenue of sphinxes, while scaled-down reproductions of the Great Sphinx and the pyramids of Giza, hollow, to serve as auditoria or storerooms, were to grace other parts of the capital.

Although his proposal was not without serious supporters, all that Smith built was a Hall of the Ancients (Smith 1900: fig. 45) as a small example of what the proposed national galleries would be (Figure 8:3). As Smith indicated in the Senate proposal, the largest columns in the Hall of the Ancients imitated those of the Hypostyle Hall of Karnak's Amun Temple, but there were also other columns, such

THE EGYPTIAN HALL OF GODS AND KINGS IN THE HALLS OF THE ANCIENTS

Figure 8:3   Drawing of Franklin Webster Smith's 'Hall of the Ancients', from his 1891–1900 proposal for enlarging and beautifying Washington, DC.

as those based on the Temple of Hathor at Dendera. He also credited various elements of the Hall's decoration to the *Description* (1809–1828) and to publications by Egyptologists such as Champollion, Belzoni, Wilkinson and Lepsius. Indeed, some elements of the structure's decoration are specifically credited as being inspired by the Egyptianizing decoration arranged by Lepsius for the Neues Museum in Berlin (Lepsius 1870), as well as by some of the Egyptian objects in that museum (Humbert *et al.* 1994: 342–343). If it is borne in mind that the great obelisk of the Washington Monument was to be incorporated into this aggrandizement, the scope of its Egyptianizing is truly impressive.

Notwithstanding these examples, archaeological accuracy hardly became the prime goal of Egyptianizing in American architecture. Indeed, most of the time it remained of little real interest, as evidenced, for example, by the Franco-American Constant Desiré Despradelle's 1900 design for a 450 m tall obelisk with fantastically elaborate base. Called the 'Beacon of Progress' because of the powerful light it would have at its summit (to which one could travel by elevator), it was to be located in Chicago, where it was to commemorate both the 1893 World Columbian Exposition, which included several Egyptianizing buildings (Fazzini with McKercher 1996: 255, no. 34; Delamaire Chapter 7, this volume) and "the apotheosis of American civilization" (Sky and Stone 1983: 86–87, figs. 118–119).

Equally interesting and archaeologically inaccurate are the two 'obelisk' designs submitted in the 1922 competition for a new administrative building for the *Chicago Tribune* newspaper. One design, by Alfred Fellheimer and Steward Wagner of New York City, which won an honourable mention, can be described as an ornately adorned obelisk (*Chicago Tribune* 1980: pl. 158). The other, featuring a 22-storey obelisk-shaped office tower atop an eight-storey Egyptian temple-shaped structure, was submitted by Chicago architect Paul Gerhardt, who, in 1920, built two Egyptianizing buildings in Chicago faced with multi-coloured glazed terracotta tiles (*Chicago Tribune* 1980: pl. 159). Glazed tiles were a very popular architectural art form in Chicago, and the most spectacular of Chicago's Egyptianizing buildings adorned in this manner was the Reebie Storage and Moving Company (Humbert 1989: 88, and illustrations on 84–85, 120–121). This building, whose colourful decoration and inscriptions were designed specifically to represent and symbolize the company, may have been inspired in part by the discovery of the tomb of Tutankhamun in late November 1922.

Gerhardt also submitted a second Egyptianizing plan to the *Chicago Tribune* competition, this one having the same base but a large tower in the form of a papyrus column (*Chicago Tribune* 1980: pl. 160). It had visual prototypes of a sort in the 1838 and 1849 Egyptianizing entrances, each surmounted by a large Egyptianizing column or pier, to cemeteries in Rochester, New York and Philadelphia (Carrott 1978: 89, 95, pls. 74–75). The design received very little interest, however.

Funerary monuments

Cemeteries are – and include – funerary monuments, and funerary monuments are one of the two most prominent categories of Egyptianizing monuments in the United

States during the first half of the 19th century. They have also flourished in at least some of the years since that time. This no doubt derives from the long history of real and/or symbolic associations of many Egyptian forms with the funerary or with ideas relevant to the funerary, despite the objections of some to the use of pagan imagery in non-pagan religious settings (Carrott 1978: 82–86).

The earliest group of significant Egyptianizing tombs in the United States dates to ca. 1813–1815 and is in the Westminster churchyard cemetery in Baltimore (Allen 1978: 18; Fazzini with McKercher 1996: fig. 2). Designed by Godefroy, they were not very archaeologically correct. The tall proportions of one tomb's pyramidal top, for example, were based ultimately on the famed 12 BC pyramid of Caius Cestius in Rome (Humbert 1989: 11), the inspiration of so many earlier and quite a few later pyramids in America and elsewhere. However, the tomb in the form of a rectangular 'temple' with Egyptianizing columns and cavetto cornice represents a step beyond the obelisk/pyramid tomb marker then more normal for America. It would have numerous and varied descendants until the 1930s, when financial factors helped put elaborate mausolea out of style, although elaborate burials 'à l'égyptienne' have still not entirely vanished.

Godefroy also designed the Westminster churchyard's small carriage gateway, which consists of a pair of pillars surmounted by cavetto cornices and adorned with engaged obelisks with winged hourglasses (Carrott 1978: 97, n. 10, pl. 56). It was between 1813 and 1850 that Egyptianizing cemetery gates first became fashionable in the United States and, in fact, enjoyed their true heyday. Sometimes these structures appear to depend, at least in part, on specific images of ancient Egyptian monuments made available as a result of Bonaparte's Expedition to Egypt. For example, Alexander Jackson Davis may have based the central doorway element of his 1828 project for a cemetery gate on a drawing of a Theban gateway in Denon 1802 (Carrott 1978: 53, pls. 66, 68). And the 1844–1848 gateway to the Grove Street Cemetery in New Haven, Connecticut – a *distyle in antis* portico with papyrus bud columns, battered walls, torus mouldings, cavetto cornice and winged solar disk – possibly stems from plates in Denon 1802 or the *Description* (1809–1828) of *pronaoi* of Egyptian temples (Carrott 1978: 92, pls. 69–71). Such Egyptianizing monuments could also themselves be influences. It is possible, for example, that the 1848 cemetery gate in Roxbury, Massachusetts and a ca. 1850 cemetery gate in Farmington, Connecticut were based on the New Haven gateway (Carrott 1978: 92–94, pls. 72–73).

The most famous of America's Egyptianizing gateways was that of Mount Auburn Cemetery in Cambridge, Massachusetts, which represented an important step in the rural cemetery movement, and acted as an influence (including in its use of Egyptianizing elements) on other American cemeteries. Mount Auburn's gateway with lodges was originally built of wood painted to imitate granite, then rebuilt in granite in 1842 (Figure 8:4). Its designer, Joseph Bigelow, was one of the cemetery's founders, a physician and a Harvard University Professor of the Application of Science to the Useful Arts. As noted by Carrott (1978: 87–88, pls. 59–60), Bigelow's statement that his main sources were Karnak and Dendera makes it likely that he was influenced by the Napoleonic *Description*'s reconstructions of large gateways in the temenos walls of those sites. However, it has also been argued that Bigelow, who studied publications of the Napoleonic Expedition with Alexander Jackson Davis,

Figure 8:4   Entrance to Mount Auburn Cemetery, Cambridge, Massachusetts (Joseph Bigelow, 1831, rebuilt in granite 1842).

may also have been influenced by Davis' designs inspired by Karnak or Dendera, or even by an engraving of the tomb of G. Monge in Père Lachaise (Curl 1994: 160, fig. 115; Linden-Ward 1989: 262–263, figs. 10.9–11). Bigelow included a simplified drawing of a fanciful Louis-François Cassas (pre-1798) reconstruction of a pyramid with temple, obelisks and processional way in his 1840 book, which reminds us that archaeological accuracy was not the only factor at work in the design of Mount Auburn's gateway (Linden-Ward 1989: 260, fig. 10.5).

The symbolism of Mount Auburn is complex. Stated most simply, the gateway's style could be seen in terms of Ancient Egypt's association with permanence and the long-term protection of the dead, as is also evidenced by Bigelow's statement that the "size of the stones and the solidity of the structure entitle it to a stability of a thousand years" (Carrott 1978: 88).

In a different vein, and related to far more than Mount Auburn, Champollion's 1822 decipherment of the Egyptian hieroglyphic script was a significant factor for Egyptianizing in the United States, as elsewhere, especially as it fostered debate on the origins and nature of many things. It has been proposed that this, together with reinterpretation of The Fall as humanity's discontinuity with the natural world, helped make it possible for the Egyptian style to represent the restoration of naturalism and thus be an appropriate style for a garden-like cemetery (Linden-Ward 1989: 262). Be this as it may, some of the developers of Mount Auburn Cemetery, familiar with a first century BC commentary by Diodorus of Agyrion, traced to Ancient Egypt the practice of "placing the tomb in the midst of the beauty and luxuriance of nature" and equated all of Mount Auburn Cemetery with "the great Egyptian cemetery ... on the farther shore of the Lake Acherusia, near Memphis, ornamented with trees and water-courses" (Linden-Ward 1989: 129, 265). This was not reliable Egyptology, and was partially propaganda for a rural cemetery. It also goes well beyond the usual associations for Egyptianizing funerary monuments and shows how erudite and complex such associations could become.

Prisons and courts

A certain degree of complexity of symbolic associations is also to be found in the second most prominent field for the use of Egyptianizing designs in the United States up to the Civil War (1861–1865): prisons and courts. Some of the most significant were designed by John Haviland, one of the most important architects of the early American Egyptian revival. His first Egyptianizing design for a place of incarceration was the New Jersey State Penitentiary in Trenton, built between 1832 and 1836 (Carrott 1978: pls. 106–107, 110). This penitentiary and its yards were housed in a large rectangular space delimited by "a long high battered wall with cavetto cornices and torus moldings ... relieved otherwise only by battered niches recalling flag-pole holders in temple pylons such as Edfou" (Carrott 1978: 66). The penitentiary's entrance is in the form of two pylon towers turned at right angles to the wall with a colonnaded portico between them. As has long been realized, this portico's design, with its inscriptions of King Amenophis III, was derived from images in the Napoleonic *Description* (1809–1828) of a bark station on Elephantine Island (Carrott 1978: pl. 109; Roos 1940: 219, fig. 2, 222), which is not to say that Haviland slavishly followed his archaeological sources. For example, one might see an inspiration, if not a true prototype, for such a porch in a side view of an Egyptian temple (Carrott 1978: 114, pl. 108). Moreover, as Carrott has noted, Haviland's portico and the wall above it have corbelled arches which appear to have entered western Egyptianizing art through the designs of Piranesi published in 1769. Carrott (1978: 114) is wrong, however, in his belief that such arches were unknown in Ancient Egypt; corbelled constructions in Ancient Egypt are described, for example, by Arnold (1991: 185–191).

With its massive enclosure wall and exotic portico, the New Jersey State Penitentiary must have been an impressive edifice, perhaps even 'sublimely' impressive. But Haviland began work on an even more monumental building before the Trenton prison was completed: the New York City Halls of Justice and House of Detention (Figure 8:5), built between 1835 and 1838 (Carrott 1978: App III, 146–192, pls. 111–112, 114, 116–118, 121–123, 127–128, 134). This building, in turn, seems to have influenced the design of New Orleans' Sixth Precinct Station (1897), a relatively rare late building of this type (Allen 1978: 20; Carrott 1978: 128–129 n. 67).

In arguing that the American interest in things Egyptian has been somewhat more morose or lugubrious than that of the French, Egyptologist H. G. Fischer (1986: 21) quoted the words of a character from a Herman Melville work, a prisoner in the New York City Halls of Justice and House of Detention: "The Egyptian character of the masonry weighed upon me with its gloom."

This, together with the fact that the building came to be better known as 'The Tombs', suggests that the building may not have lived up to its goals. Like the penitentiary in Trenton, The Tombs was a structure connected with prison reform. And if Haviland and the committee that selected him felt that an Egyptian style could and should be appropriately massive, solid and secure, the goal was not for it to be terrifying and gloomy (Carrott 1978: 160–161). On the contrary, and as argued by Carrott, they may have hoped that the forms of Egyptian architecture and Egypt's association with wisdom and the eternal would invoke the sublime nature of the law as timeless and righteous, transcending the moment and the individual. Moreover,

Figure 8:5   New York City Halls of Justice and House of Detention, New York (John Haviland, 1835–1838).

and whether or not it was always actually true, they might also have felt that an Egyptianizing prison was economical to build (Carrott 1978: 131–135, 164).

Haviland's design for The Tombs may have been influenced by earlier (and not all Egyptianizing) buildings in France, Britain and Russia (Carrott 1978: 116–118, 189–190 n. 53, pls. 104, 126). However, he also made use, for example, of the Temple of Ramesses III at Medinet Habu in the choice of column types, and he may have been influenced by the form of the main Dendera temple in his tripartite plan of the entrance hall and courthouse. Indeed, in the announcement of the winners of the architectural competition, it was stated that "the design is from one of the most approved examples contained in Napoleon's Egypt", i.e., the *Description* (1809–1828; Carrott 1978: 164).[3]

Unlike most American Egyptianizing buildings, significant parts of the interior of The Tombs were also in the Egyptian style. Its main entrance hall would have been more ornately Egyptianizing if Haviland had had his way. In a discussion of The Tombs in a guidebook to New York City of 1839, it is noted that the columns in the main entrance hall "bear the character of an order taken from the colonnade of the temple at Medynet Abou" and that "attached to the antes opposite these columns, the architect originally designed to place the Egyptian cariatides [*sic*], so highly spoken of by the French artists in Napoleon's great work on Egypt, published by Paukonche [*sic*]; and he feels assured that the board will yet be of his opinion, and finally adopt these splendid and imposing figures in this entrance hall" (quoted in Carrott 1978: 166–167).

It remains uncertain precisely which sculptures were intended for inclusion in The Tombs. However, whichever they were, they would have been a remarkable addition to the near total lack of American Egyptianizing sculptures before the Civil War, the major exception being William Wetmore Story's 1858 sculpture 'Cleopatra' (Hamer 2001: 308, fig. 11.5), which was actually made in Rome. Even Hathor-headed column capitals seem not yet to have graced the New World, and the United States continued to lag well behind Europe in the production of sphinxes and seldom, if ever, witnessed the creation of an Antinous-figure.[4]

Associative symbolism in decline: residential architecture

If, during the first half of the 19th century, Egyptian hieroglyphs assumed significant symbolism for such important writers as Poe, Emerson, Hawthorne, Thoreau and Melville (Irwin 1980: 12), hieroglyphs and other Egyptian elements had as little influence on American painting during the first half of the 19th century as they did on American sculpture. And it has been argued that Egyptianizing in American decorative arts was almost non-existent in the first half of the 19th century, partly because Ancient Egypt (unlike Greece and the Roman Republic) did not have associations deemed appropriate for the democracy of the United States. This situation did not change until aesthetics became more important than associational symbolism in the decorative arts (Stayton 1990: 6–7). By this time, the 'official' Egyptian Revival had come to an end for several reasons. Among those often cited are the decline of the acceptance of symbolic eclecticism, religious reaction to the heathen associations of Egypt (and even Greece and Rome) and, to quote Carrott (1978: 136), the Egyptian style's lack of "deep cultural values germane to the American sociological psyche". In fact, Carrott (1978: 55–56, 136, pls. 37, 92) notes that there was very little in the way of residential Egyptianizing, exterior or interior, in the United States, and that "it seemed that anyone associating Egyptian architecture with tombs, cemeteries and prisons would hardly wish to live in it or be surrounded by it". All of this may be true, but there were more later Egyptianizing residential interiors and buildings in the United States than is generally realized.

Perhaps the grandest of these buildings is in Wesley Hills, New York (Fazzini with McKercher 1996: figs. 5–6, 8). Built in 1915 by architect Walter Robb Wilder, it was a summer residence on 600 acres for one Joseph M. Goldberg, who had spent much time in Egypt for health reasons and had become interested in Egyptian archaeology. Known locally as the 'Egyptian House', the main structure's form and the placement of kiosks/gazebos on two corners of the terrace on which the house sits are at least as much European or classically influenced as Egyptianizing. Nevertheless, the house is Egyptianizing to a considerable extent throughout. That it is also known locally as the 'Luxor Temple' stems from the Luxor Temple-like colonnade between house and guest house (Figure 8:6), as well as the use of similar columns for the main house's portico and the kiosks.

Figure 8:6   The 'Egyptian House', Wesley Hills, NY (Walter Robb Wilder, 1915): the colonnade.

After Goldberg's death, the house slowly deteriorated and lost most of its acreage. Since 1984, however, its new owners, Debra and Steven Preston, have restored the house except for the polychrome decoration known to have adorned the column capitals and bases, which they plan to restore as well. A brief publication (Anon. 1992: 6) concerning the Egyptian House notes that "the few surviving domestic examples of the [Egyptian] style tend to have superimposed Egyptian columns on otherwise Greek Revival – or Italianate – style forms", and that "the existence of a free-standing temple-form Egyptian revival building such as the Egyptian House is perhaps unique and certainly rare in this country". The first statement is contradicted by some of the houses to be mentioned below, but the second statement is certainly true and quite possibly reflects the personal experiences, preferences, and/or symbolic associations of Egypt for its first owner.

Egyptianizing architecture is not totally absent from Northern California. There are, for example, the Fine Arts Building constructed for an 1894 fair in San Francisco and the Rosicrucian World Headquarters in San José with, for example, its temple, university and Rosicrucian Egyptian Museum (Fazzini with McKercher 1996: fig. 9). Allen (1978: 24–25) has said of these latter structures, built at various times between the 1920s and 1960s, that they "illustrate changing concepts of what Egyptian architecture looks like", the buildings ranging "from 'Moorish' through frankly American buildings decorated with Egyptian motifs to unusually correct and sensitive 'Egyptian' structures". Humbert (1989: 94) says much the same about the Rosicrucian buildings, noting also that they reach greater Egyptianizing heights than is generally true of Masonic lodges. However, residential architecture in Egyptian style appears to be far more a phenomenon of the southern part of the state.

In the catalogue for an exhibition on Egyptomania in Los Angeles, it was observed that the discovery of Tutankhamun's tomb in November 1922 was certainly a major influence for Egyptianizing, but that other factors were also at play, among them the growth of the film industry, which contributed to the Hollywood sense of 'larger than life' permeating local architectural styles (and see Serafy 2003). One result of this was that "apartment buildings, with semi-pylon façades and hieroglyphs were built with astounding rapidity in Los Angeles" (Glenn *et al.* 1977: 8).

One of these buildings was a bungalow court at 1428 S. Bonnie Brae (Polyzoides *et al.* 1992: 193), built in 1916 and thus demonstrating that some Egyptianizing in Los Angeles predates the discovery of the tomb of Tutankhamun. It is described by Gebhard and Winter (1977: 202, no. 31) and in an unpublished list of Egyptianizing buildings in Los Angeles by R. Marks.

Plans for an Egyptianizing movie theatre were published as early as 1917 by architect and theatre specialist Edward B. Kinsilia, although it was never built (Kinsilia 1917). The tomb's discovery did have an immediate effect on at least one motion picture theatre. Grauman's Egyptian Theatre in Hollywood, which opened to the public shortly after the discovery, was originally intended to be in the Moorish style, but was rapidly changed to a pharaonic theme to capitalize on the new wave of Egyptomania. And it was essentially in the mid- to late 1920s that Los Angeles became home to a significant number of Egyptianizing apartment complexes, many of which are mentioned in Marks (1978). Some had names like the King Tut Court, the King Tut Apartments, the Egyptian Court, the Osiris Apartments, the Amasis Apartments, and the Amun-Ra Apartments; others were unnamed; and there was even one with an Arab name: the Ahmed Apartments. On the other hand, two essentially 'Arabicizing' apartments bore pharaonic names: the Ramesses Terrace and the Luxor Egyptian Court. The appearance of many of these buildings also related to the fantasy and sometimes stage-set-like 'façadism' in much of southern Californian architecture influenced by Hollywood (Glenn *et al.* 1977: 8).

While Los Angeles may have been the main centre for southern California's Egyptianizing residential architecture, San Diego was also important in this regard. It is thanks mainly to Hobbs-Halmay (1992) that there is now information concerning the Egyptianizing structures of San Diego and environs which were influenced by the discovery of Tutankhamun's tomb; by the motion picture industry, in terms of historically eclectic and fantasizing domestic architecture; by the 1920s' atmosphere of 'anything goes'; and possibly by the fact that southern California's sunny and dry climate was suitable for Egyptianizing flat roofs and open courtyards.

As indicated by the 1905 Egyptianizing gateway to a centre of the Theosophical Society (Hobbs-Halmay 1992: 96), Egyptianizing architecture in and around San Diego did not begin with residential architecture. In San Diego itself the earliest Egyptianizing buildings of the 1920s were electrical power substations, some of them also passenger terminals, built in 1923–1924 for an expanding electrical transportation system. In a newspaper's publication of architect E. M. Hoffmann's sketch for one substation/terminal (Fazzini with McKercher 1996: fig. 10), it is said of the building that it is "a solid, substantial building of unique architectural design and is an important asset in the beautification of the site on which it is built at Ocean Beach" (*Evening Tribune*, 1924). The first part of this sentence is an interesting, if probably fortuitous, echo of ideas associated with Egyptianizing railroad stations in the previous century, while the second part indicates that aesthetic considerations were not without significance.

Technological advances in electrical wiring and the growing importance of motor buses and the automobile as means of transportation made most of the trolley substations unnecessary soon after they were built, but not all have vanished. The substation at the intersection of Euclid and University Avenues was remodelled into a garage in 1925 (Fazzini with McKercher 1996: fig. 11), and in 1927 was enlarged by an addition that included a semi-obelisk and a relief of the god Thoth. The addition has a row of pilasters topped with cement pharaohs' heads matching those on the earlier part of the building and those of the substation at Ocean Beach.

Similar pharaoh-headed pilasters appear elsewhere in cement architecture in San Diego, for instance on the Park Egyptian Apartments (formerly the Pharaoh's Court Apartments) of 1928 on Park Boulevard. Indeed, on a two-block stretch of this street several Egyptianizing buildings survive: the above-mentioned Park Egyptian Apartments; the Egyptian Court Apartments (1926, Fazzini with McKercher 1996: figs. 12–13), recently restored; parts of an Egyptianizing gasoline station and automobile garage (1926); a movie theatre (1926), part of whose original Egyptianizing form remains; and an Egyptian-style door, with corbelled-arch-shaped windows, added in 1932 to a 1928 Italian Renaissance Revival building when the building was renamed the Nile Apartments. A testament to the influence of one building upon another and/or to the spirit, commercial or otherwise, in a neighbourhood, the same block once also contained an Egyptianizing combination shop and office building (1926), a restaurant called the Garden of Allah, built in 1946 in Egyptianizing style to be in keeping with the neighbourhood, and the Egyptian Miniature Golf Course (prior to 1927). Some of these buildings are described in Hobbs-Halmay (1992: 99–103).

Hobbs-Halmay (1992: 101; and cf. Allen 1978: 23) has described the 1926 Egyptian Court Apartments (Fazzini with McKercher 1996: figs. 14–15) as "classic Egyptian Revival Art Déco" in style, saying of the frieze of flowers across the entry (Figure 8:7) that "these flowers were a design of marguerite daisies copied from the Malkata Palace of Amenophis III ..., the palace in which King Tut is believed to have been born". Be this as it may, few of the decorative details of this complex of apartments, which has a central garden and a pond and is flanked by two small shops, can be linked to monuments associated with Tutankhamun.

The same is true of the 1928 Pharaoh's Court Apartments, which has apartments above shops. Here the façade of the main building, the bungalows in the garden behind it and the staircase leading to the garden all have pharaoh-headed pilasters related to those on San Diego's electrical substations. Harold Allen, photographer *par excellence* of American Egyptomania, once observed that the Pharaoh's Court Apartments had details copied from Grauman's Egyptian Theatre in Hollywood (Fazzini with McKercher 1996: fig. 16). By this he probably meant both the pharaoh-headed pilasters and the corbelled motifs, of which an elaborate version forms the Egyptian Theatre's proscenium (Allen 1978: 23).

Figure 8:7   Egyptian Court Apartments, San Diego, 1926.

It must be remembered that Egyptianizing influences had already entered the realm of American theatres in the previous decade, whereas Egyptian buildings for exhibitions had long since included the fantastic and playful. Hence, although the discovery of Tutankhamun's tomb did help to make Egyptianizing architecture much more popular than it had been, Fischer (1992: 226) is not truly correct in saying that "it was not until the discovery of Tutankhamun's tomb enchanted the easily dazzled decade of the 20s that a more playful adaptation of Egyptian architecture began to be applied to theatres and other structures in the USA". If the discovery of Tutankhamun's tomb did make Egypt and Egyptianizing more popular and, sometimes, more sensational in the United States, Ancient Egypt did not lose its allure for serious artists. Indeed, that interest has grown again dramatically during the past few decades: Red Grooms and Lysiane Luong, for instance, created a serious work of art that is also humorous and functional: the 1986–1988 Tut's Fever Movie Palace in New York City's American Museum of the Moving Image (Figure 8:8; Carliss 1988).

As for the Egyptianizing structures of San Diego, if the discovery of Tutankhamun's tomb helped to spur their construction, it appears to have had very little influence on their appearance. This is certainly true of the pharaoh-head pilasters and the one other significant piece of architectural statuary that the group boasts: the female Egyptian figure that is part of the fountain of the 1928 Pharaoh's Court Apartments (Hobbs-Halmay 1992: 92; Fazzini with McKercher 1996: fig. 17). The ultimate prototype for this figure is surely a New Kingdom 'cosmetic spoon' and, given the rarity of the combination of long sidelock and the crossbands on the body of the fountain's figure, perhaps specifically the 'spoon' illustrated 50 years earlier (or the illustration itself) by Prisse d'Avennes (1878: pl. 94, 2nd row). However, the figure bears an even stronger resemblance to a relatively common Egyptianizing incense burner (Fazzini with McKercher 1996: fig. 18). It is thus possible that this incense burner, perhaps itself dependent on Prisse d'Avennes, was the fountain figure's prototype. A new version of this incense burner has been marketed for sale in the United States since 1993, while somewhat different figures of this type graced European purses and an English automobile radiator cap in the 1920s and 1930s (illustrated in Humbert *et al.* 1994: 542–543).

Figure 8:8   Egyptianizing seat cover in Tut's Fever Movie Palace (© Jean-Marcel Humbert).

It must also be mentioned that San Diego's Egyptianizing architecture includes at least two single-family houses (Fazzini with McKercher 1996: figs. 19–20). One, built ca. 1925, was remodelled, but still maintains some Egyptianizing details, including a very unusual – and hardly archaeologically correct – door in the form of an upside-down cartouche or, possibly, of an *aper*-amulet. The other, built in 1926, has a cavetto cornice identical to that on the 1926 Egyptian Court Apartments, which raises once again the question of whether this reflects the stylistic influence of one building upon the other and/or the availability of certain stock forms in concrete. This house also had battered walls and corbelled porch openings (Hobbs-Halmay 1992: 109).

Two other Egyptianizing houses in Encinitas, north of San Diego, were built by a land developer and builder called O. L. Steel in an attempt to develop an Egyptian-style housing colony for moderate-income families (Hobbs-Halmay 1992: 107–109). Unfortunately the idea proved too exotic for potential buyers, but at least one of these houses was built in 1923, which means that not all the region's Egyptianizing housing post-dates or was necessarily influenced at all by the Egyptianizing electrical substations.

In general, the few private homes that are entirely Egyptianizing in style, such as the 1915 home in Wesley Hills, have been built by fairly wealthy amateurs of things Egyptian. This is certainly true of a large residence built by a non-Egyptologist amateur named Jim Onan in Wadsworth, Illinois. Begun in 1977, it includes a house in the form of a 16 m tall pyramid plated in 24 carat gold, with three smaller subsidiary pyramids and a long driveway lined with sphinxes (Figures 8:9–8:11 col. pls.). This complex was inspired by the builder's interest in 'pyramid power', and for several years the entire residence was an admission-charging tourist attraction. In 1988, however, the house reverted to being a residence, while plans were made for a full-scale reproduction of King Tut's tomb to become the main tourist attraction. That archaeological accuracy does not reign supreme in Wadsworth is reflected in Onan's reference to plans for "stone statuary poured from the same molds that were used to conjure up reality in Hollywood movies like 'The Ten Commandments'" (Humbert 1989: 90–91, 124; Weber 1988). It is perhaps not surprising that Ramesses II and Tutankhamun are prominent in the imagery of Onan's estate.

To be sure, a pyramid-shaped house is not an invention of Onan or of the last quarter of the 20th century. However, noting that "la pureté de lignes et la sobriété des formes de l'obélisque et de la pyramide en font des symboles de l'art contemporain", Humbert (1989: 94–95) refers to a number of 1970s and later pyramidal structures made for various purposes, including resort living and offices.

Post-modernist Egyptianizing

Following the near-banishment of historical references in modernist architecture, post-modernism's reaction against what has sometimes been called 'avant-garde amnesia' has made it possible for architecture again to include forms that either seem to be – or actually are – Egyptianizing. Among the most common are the pyramids forming or adorning a growing number of roofs. However, other Egyptianizing forms also exist, as is evident in the columns and decorative metalwork on The Alexandria, an apartment building with shops built at Broadway and 72nd Street in New York in about 1990 (Fazzini with McKercher 1996: fig. 21).

Near The Alexandria is one of New York City's most spectacular Egyptianizing buildings, now an apartment building. Designed by Thomas W. Lamb when he was one of the United States' leading designers of theatres, this 1927 structure (Fazzini with McKercher 1996: fig. 22) was built as a temple for the Knights of Pythias. Its front elevations have been described as:

> ... a bizarre combination of Sumerian, Assyrian, and Egyptian motifs, stepping up in three stages to a blind screen of polychromed Doric columns, Babylonian crenelations, and twin towers capped by reconstructions of the gilded basin set up by Solomon in the temple at Jerusalem – complete with their supporting cast of attendants gazing into the Street below.

(Stern *et al.* 1987: 197–198)

The Egyptian motifs include four colossal, glazed-tile statues of seated pharaohs in New Kingdom style (Figure 8:12 col. pl.).

While the adornment of the Pythian temple is very clearly Egyptianizing in part, it is also difficult not to see evocations of Ancient Egypt in the 1990 Mellon Bank Centre in Philadelphia (Fazzini with McKercher 1996: fig. 24), whose shapes resemble cavetto cornices and obelisk/pyramid. And it is tempting to speculate that the use of such forms was not totally devoid of the association of ancient Egyptian architecture with conservative, long-term stability that is evident in several periods in buildings built for similar purposes. One such structure is the Bankers Trust Building (ca. 1912) in New York City, a tall tower that may recall the mausoleum of Halicarnassus, but is nevertheless surmounted by what was then a "distinctive stepped pyramidal roof"

(Stern *et al.* 1987: 75, 586, 602). It is perhaps also associational symbolism that accounts for an old Bankers Trust coin bank being much more pyramid than supporting tower.

The Egyptianizing battered walls and cavetto cornices on the lower storeys of the Sun Trust Bank building on Church Street in Nashville, Tennessee, built about 1986, may also be due in part to associational symbolism. However, the presence on the opposite side of the street of the historic and well-known Downtown Presbyterian Church, which is Egyptianizing inside and out, must have influenced the architects in their choice of style.

The Pennsylvania Fire Insurance Company building in Philadelphia (Fazzini with McKercher 1996: fig. 25), whose façade has been preserved as a historic monument, was designed by John Haviland. It was built in 1838 and doubled in width (following the same design pattern) in 1901. Carrott (1978: 103, pl. 42) has expressed the altogether plausible belief that the associations of Egypt with ideas of solidity, endurance and agelessness would have made an Egyptianizing style appropriate and beneficial to a building for an insurance company. He saw the Prudential Insurance Company's use of the Rock of Gibraltar as their trademark as a different example of this type of association. One cannot help but see similar ideas and motivations in the Metropolitan Life Insurance Company (Met Life) advertising campaign of the late 1980s that featured Egyptianizing images with Charles Schulz's cartoon characters. In fact, such messages are made clear by the words accompanying an image of the dog Snoopy as the sphinx at Giza:

> The stability of Met Life is monumental ... we've proven we can stand the test of time. For over 100 years ... we plan to be around for centuries to come.

'Memphite Egyptomania'

Some of the whimsy of Snoopy as Giza sphinx is also found in the avenue of animals (rather than sphinxes) leading to the entrance to the Memphis (Tennessee) Zoo and Aquarium (Fazzini with McKercher 1996: fig. 26). On the other hand, the forms and decoration of the park's 1990–1991 pylon gateway are very clearly Egyptianizing. Just as early 19th century publications of the Temple of Ramesses III at Medinet Habu influenced some early American Egyptianizing buildings, the figural decoration of the Memphis Zoo gateway owes a debt to the much more recent publication of scenes in the same temple showing the presentation of defeated enemies to the deities Amun and Mut (Epigraphic Survey 1930: pl. 45; Hölscher 1934: pl. 24). Moreover, thanks to some help from local Egyptologists, the gateway's inscriptions do read, possibly with the first phonetic renderings in hieroglyphs of words like 'kangaroo' and 'shark'.

In some ways the entrance to the Memphis Zoo and Aquarium is a late descendant of the famous Egyptianizing elephant pavilion of 1855–1856 in the Antwerp Zoo, and the well-known ostrich pavilion of 1901 in the zoo in Berlin (Humbert 1989: 70–71, 78). However, it also has pre-World War II American ancestors of sorts in the Detroit Zoo of the Detroit Zoological Institute. Here there are interesting Egyptianizing paintings on the hippopotamus building and the giraffe building (Fazzini with McKercher 1996: fig. 2, 27–28), which also includes Egyptianizing sculptures. Unlike their European predecessors and the Memphis Zoo and Aquarium gateway, however, the Egyptianizing inscriptions of the Detroit Zoo demonstrate that bogus hieroglyphs never went entirely out of fashion simply because of Champollion's great achievement. They also demonstrate that archaeological accuracy need not be a major consideration in Egyptianizing, even for public and educational buildings.

The animal pavilions in Antwerp, Berlin and Detroit, as well as the entrance to a California ostrich farm that featured a banded pyramid with *distyle in antis* portico and a pair of sphinxes (Hobbs-Halmay 1992: 100), testify to the long-lived belief that Egyptianizing forms and decoration are appropriate for structures housing African animals. However, the Memphis Zoo and Aquarium's Egyptianizing encompasses the fauna of a range of geographical regions, which may be a reflection of Memphis, Tennessee as a city with a long history of Egyptomania, public and private. As noted by some, including Linden-Ward (1989: 262–263), in the last century

> the Egyptian style ... captured the imagination of arbiters of American culture intent on finding new symbols representative of their nation. Many Americans in the 1830s equated their country with Egypt, another 'first civilization' capable of providing an alternative cultural idiom to that inherited from England. They nicknamed the Mississippi the 'American Nile' and gave the names of Memphis, Cairo, Karnak and Thebes to new towns along its banks.

General James Winchester, one of the city's developers, gave Memphis its name sometime between 1818 and 1820, before the era described by Linden-Ward. Nevertheless, some of these ideas may already have been at play, and it is a moot point whether Winchester's selection of a name for the city expressed a hope that it would become a seat of political power (as was Memphis, Egypt) or whether it was a promotional ploy (Harkins 1982: 18). Whatever the reason, the choice of a name had a long-term effect on Memphis, Tennessee, although not all Egyptianizing architecture there relates to the city's name. According to the company, the Egyptianizing decoration of the 1917 Ballard's Obelisk Flour building (Fazzini with McKercher 1996: fig. 29), which included a prominent use of applied obelisks, relates to the company's name, not to its location in Memphis.

Nevertheless, Memphis, Tennessee did become involved in Egyptomania, even if there was often more than one reason for the creation of a building. A case in point is the City of Memphis' pavilion at the 1897 Tennessee Centennial and International Exposition in Nashville, Tennessee. Expressing the belief that Memphis could not rival the various classical, Gothic, Renaissance, oriental and American designs that the fair would include, the pavilion's Memphite architect, J. B. Cook, proposed an Egyptian design evoking the city's ancient namesake. His design was a pyramid with temple-like porticoes on all four sides (Harkins 1982: 6, 107) which, like pyramids with only one or two porticoes, finds parallels in earlier and later architecture in America and elsewhere (Carrott 1978: 30, 43–44 n. 45, pls. 25, 28, 29; Curl 1991b: 212). It also represented the pyramid of Kheops, scaled down to a height of 100 feet (30 m), representing Tennessee's 100 years. Built of wood stuccoed to resemble stone, the pavilion was originally intended to be dismantled and rebuilt in Memphis, but this proved too expensive. As a result, Memphis, Tennessee had to wait close to a century before it acquired a monumental pyramid.

Figure 8:13   The Great American Pyramid, Memphis, Tennessee (1991; © M. E. McKercher).

Thanks in part to 'Memphite Egyptomania', heightened by several recent special exhibitions of Egyptian objects in Memphis, and in part to the aspirations of promoter/developer Isaac Tigrett (creator of the Hard Rock Cafe), Memphis now has a 96 m tall 'Great American Pyramid' (Figure 8:13; Humbert Chapter 2: Figure 2:9, this volume). Opened in 1991, it contains a radio station and a 22,000-seat arena. It was intended to be part of a 'festival park' whose main theme was to be American music, but was also to contain a reproduction of a king's burial chamber in which a hologram of a pharaoh would discourse on the Mysteries of the Great Pyramid (Seal 1990). The theme park has succumbed, at least temporarily, to financial problems.

Egypt as entertainment

Finances are unlikely to be a problem for the United States' even more recent large-scale pyramid: the main structure of the Luxor Hotel/Casino in Las Vegas, Nevada that opened in the autumn of 1993 (Figure 8:14). According to Early (2000: 180–181), Circus Circus, owners of the Luxor, originally intended to build a vaguely Mayan-looking, U-shaped building but realized that the pyramid shape would allow a larger casino. It would also allow them to claim (inaccurately) to have built the first pyramid in a desert in 6,000 years. The pyramid is 30 storeys tall and is fronted by a sphinx-shaped entrance that is 50 per cent larger than the sphinx at Giza, the builders having decided that a Giza-sized sphinx would seem too small when placed directly before their pyramid (Circus Circus Enterprises 1994). The Luxor has proved so popular that a major renovation and expansion took place in 1998. The new wing includes what is in effect half a step pyramid whose reflections in the adjoining glass tower provide the full step pyramid effect.

The major context of this edifice is the essentially recent and growing trend for Las Vegas gambling casinos to become family resorts as well, built around special themes. On one level, the Luxor Hotel/Casino can be viewed as 'Egyptland'. Indeed, in the original version, one could take a guided 'archaeological cruise' along a very narrow 'Nile' inside the pyramid, circling the large casino on the hotel's lower level and passing evocations of some famous Egyptian monuments. This proved impractical (and not very popular), and so was eliminated in the hotel's remodelling. Instead, a monumental gateway with colossal statues and sphinxes forms the main entrance to the casino level, whose decoration is profusely and exuberantly Egyptianizing, if not always archaeologically accurate (Fazzini with McKercher 1996: figs. 32–35). While some areas blend carefully rendered scenes from monuments such as the tomb of Nakht at Thebes or a painting from the Theban tomb of Nebamun now in the British Museum, other areas reveal the influence of 19th century paintings, or are pure fantasy (Figure 8:15). The entrance to 'Pharaoh's Pheast', the new cafeteria on the lower level, incorporates three-dimensional versions of elements from paintings by David Roberts and Elihu Vedder. The cafeteria itself imitates an archaeological site, with half-excavated coffins, tomb entrances, and even a 'dig house'.

There is also another level of 'Egyptianizing' in the hotel/casino. For example, the spotlight on top of the pyramid, claimed to be the most powerful in the world, evokes 'pyramid power'. Like the laser light show that is generated from the sphinx's eyes and plays on the fountains between the sphinx and the obelisk, the spotlight-pyramidion is just one of the many elements of the Luxor Hotel/Casino that involve

Figure 8:14 Luxor Hotel and Casino, Las Vegas, Nevada (1993): general view in 1993 (© M. E. McKercher).

Figure 8:15   Luxor Hotel and Casino, Las Vegas, Nevada (1998 renovation): sphinxes flanking a painting inspired by 19th century orientalist paintings (© M. E. McKercher).

science fiction, contemporary fantasy, 'new age' mysticism, and Hollywood showmanship and special effects. In the casino's original incarnation, a major part of its entertainment programme was a three-part, three-theatre play that included virtual reality, film, and live theatre, and covered the past, the present, and the future, dealing with the search for a magical obelisk of great power. This, too, has disappeared in the revisioning of the complex, although the obelisk and vaguely pre-Columbian temple (originally one of the three theatres) on the Attractions Level (above the casino) remain (Fazzini with McKercher 1996: fig. 35). They represented some of the remains of the 'Luxor Archaeological Site', which were those of the advanced, pre-ancient Egyptian civilization of the virtual reality play. The official style of these remains is 'Crypto-Egypto', defined as Egyptian forms modernized and made of sophisticated materials so they will not appear handmade (Circus Circus Enterprises 1994). In a way this style reminds one of Southern California buildings in a style sometimes termed 'Egypto-Mayan'.

The new Luxor Casino now features the Ra Nightclub, whose influence is more of the motion picture *Stargate* and heavy metal than new age, and whose entrance is guarded by two over-life-size statues of buxom warrior-maidens. Inside the club, much use is made of Art Déco-inspired silver metal wall panels and the place is dominated by a colossal seated, winged figure with a hippopotamus head and an enormous kneeling, winged male figure wearing a Nemes headdress and a decidedly unfriendly expression. It is Egypt the dark and mysterious that is being recalled here, not Egypt, land of enlightenment.

The Luxor Hotel/Casino is not totally without precedent. For example, Caesar's Palace in Las Vegas (a Greco-Roman fantasy) has for some years had an Egyptianizing

'Cleopatra's Barge' restaurant, and in 1991 Trump's Taj Mahal Casino in Atlantic City, New Jersey ran advertisements with an invitation to "Behold the Magic of the Pyramids. Discover their secrets with our new 'pyramid power' slot machines". Needless to say, the Luxor Hotel/Casino goes much further in its Egyptianizing, although perhaps not as far as suggested by its local architect's statement that "we have an obligation to build the ultimate buildings" (Gormon 1993: 47). Be this as it may, in many ways the buildings and decoration of the Luxor Hotel/Casino (both original and renovated) reflect much of the old/updated/new symbolism associated with Ancient Egypt: Land of Magic and Mystery, Land of Wisdom, and heir to Atlantean or alien knowledge. As is often the case with Egyptianizing architecture in the United States, the archaeological accuracy of the forms used in the Luxor Hotel/Casino or the relationship between the modern symbolism of those forms and their actual ancient Egyptian symbolism is not of paramount importance, although numerous attempts are made in the Luxor at visual archaeological accuracy.

Egypt-as-entertainment is a theme that has continued into 21st century architecture. The Muvico Company, which builds and operates multiplex movie theatres primarily in the south-east, has created two thoroughly Egyptianizing theatre complexes: the Paradise 24 in Davie, Florida, and the Egyptian 24 in the Arundel Mills Mall in Hanover, Maryland, which opened in late 2001 (Figure 8:16). The exterior of the Arundel Mills Mall theatre features a long, battered wall (the exterior of the temple?) and a columned kiosk and portico, complete with an over-life-size statue that appears to be the god Seth. Its 'stone walls' show the stress of time: cracks run through parts of the wall, and the paint on the columns most exposed to the sun is more 'faded' than columns that are in the shade. Once inside, moviegoers purchase their tickets at a small temple or from a machine set into the base of an obelisk before entering the concession area, guarded by two colourful sphinxes. The concession area is dominated by two Abu Simbel-inspired colossi with glowing red eyes and, like the ticket area, is heavily decorated with paintings adapted from well-known tombs and ancient monuments.

Those who prefer outdoor activities may visit 'Pharaoh's Lost Kingdom Adventure Park' in Redlands, California. Designed by James Cioffi of Palm Springs, California, it was completed in the summer of 1996. Pyramids rise above the walled park, which is entered between the paws of a large sphinx (Figure 8:17) that is deliberately related in style to the sphinx of the Luxor Casino (Figure 8:14 above). Within the walls are the attractions of several types of amusement parks and Egyptianizing elements of art and architecture such as an Egyptianizing colonnade, a fanciful array of colossal statues and fantastic sculpted creatures, and a pyramid grill if one gets hungry.

Both the Muvico theatres (Figure 8:16) and 'Pharaoh's Lost Kingdom' make a nod at archaeological accuracy, but as in the past, accuracy is not the goal. In the 21st century, as in the 20th century, it is exotic (yet increasingly familiar) Egypt that is being used to draw people, whether to gamble, watch a movie, or otherwise enjoy themselves.

Figure 8:16   Muvico Egyptian 24 Theater, Hanover, Maryland (2001; © M. E. McKercher).

Figure 8:17   Pharaoh's Lost Kingdom, Redlands, California (1996): entrance (© W. Benson Harer).

Notes

1   This chapter is an updated version of a paper published in French (Fazzini with McKercher 1996). Many of the monuments described in this chapter are illustrated there, and priority has been given here to illustrations that have not been published before. Fazzini with McKercher (1996) also contains a large number of footnotes that have been omitted here. The editors have inserted some cross-references to other chapters in books within the series.

2   There was nonetheless some Egyptianizing in North America before the 19th century, of which the most famous example is the Great Seal of the United States, with its topless pyramid and eye, approved by Congress in 1782 and printed on each dollar bill (Gombrich 1989). And in 1792, the Chevalier d'Anmour, French Consul in Baltimore, erected on his estate in that city a large brick and cement obelisk for Christopher Columbus, possibly the first commemorative obelisk in the United States not associated with a grave (Eckels 1950).

3   For comparisons between The Tombs and various ancient Egyptian monuments, see Carrott (1978: 117, 170–171, pls. 113, 119, 120). Carrott's "unidentified temple, Fayoum" (xvi, pl. 120) is the temple at Qasir Qarun/Dionysias, and is *Description* (1802–1828) A. Vol. IV: pl. 69, rather than Vol. III: pl. 69.

4   Sponenburgh (1956) speaks of a lack of competent sculptors as a reason for the lack of Egyptianizing sculptures in the United States until the later 19th century. No such lack existed on the opposite side of the Atlantic, where by the mid-century a bias toward the later (and more western) Egyptian or Roman-Egyptianizing style was gradually giving way to a preference for earlier Egyptian forms. Owen Jones (Jones and Bonomi 1854: 5) could speak of the "artistic character" of Egyptian sculpture as "constantly in a state of decline from the earliest known examples", and could say of the Egyptian sculpture made by Joseph Bonomi (Werner Chapter 5; Whitehouse Chapter 3, both this volume) for the Crystal Palace that "it possesses a character of the intermediate stage between the Pharaonic and the Ptolemaic period. He has not been able to attain to the perfection of the Pharaonic period, but he is yet far above the Ptolemaic".

Acknowledgments

We are grateful to the many people who have contributed to this chapter, including Jeff Baxter, Promotions Manager for Pharaoh's Lost Kingdom Adventure Park; Edward Bleiberg, formerly of Memphis State University's Institute of Egyptian Art and Archaeology and now a curator at the Brooklyn Museum of Art; Jasmine Day; Louis D. Fontana; Mary Gow, Assistant Librarian at Wilbour Library of Egyptology, Brooklyn Museum of Art; William Hammond, former Executive Director of the Detroit Zoological Institute; W. Benson Harer, Jr MD, for photos of Pharaoh's Lost Kingdom; William H. Peck, Curator of Ancient Art at Detroit Institute of Arts; Debra and Steven Preston; Nancy Thomas, of the Los Angeles County Museum of Art; Glynis Waldman of the Museum of the Masonic Temple, Philadelphia; and Sally West of the San Diego Historical Society.

We are indebted to Jean Galard, Chief of the Service Culturel of the Louvre Museum, for permission to include the updated version of Fazzini with McKercher 1996 here.

CHAPTER 9

ANCIENT EGYPT IN MELBOURNE AND THE STATE OF VICTORIA, AUSTRALIA

Colin A. Hope

From 17 August 1988 until 11 June 1989, the exhibition 'Gold of the Pharaohs' (Hope 1988) toured Australia to mark the bicentenary of white settlement. Attendance surpassed that at any previous international exhibition in Australia, and catalogue sales were substantial. This showed clearly the interest in things Egyptian and, of course, the allure of gold.

This was not, however, a recent phenomenon. Since the earliest decades of the 19th century, ancient Egyptian images and some of its characteristic architectural forms have been appropriated for use in Australia. Throughout the country and abroad obelisks have been erected by Federal and State governments and local councils as memorials to those who died in combat, while private individuals have erected memorials to family members in this form. Events of national and local significance have also been commemorated by the erection of obelisks, while the current and potential achievements of the various States have been similarly characterized at international and national exhibitions. Other memorials have taken their inspiration from temples, being either close copies or utilizing particular architectural elements in their design. The architecture and decoration of Egyptian temples has inspired the form of synagogues, Masonic temples (Hamill and Mollier Chapter 11, this volume) and Theosophical Society buildings, the entrance to public water catchment areas, banks and a variety of other secular buildings. Coincident with such use has been the creation of national collections of Egyptian antiquities of varying sizes in most of the States, and also of library holdings.

The Australian use of Egyptianizing forms does not equal in quantity that encountered in various parts of Europe or the United States of America, which may account for the absence of any detailed study of all such monuments in the country (but see Apperly *et al.* 1994: 50–51). Nevertheless, it forms an interesting component of the Australian tendency to copy the trends of those regions and, in some cases, serves as a marker for cultural affiliation and aspiration (Merrillees 1990, 1995, 1998). It is the contention of this chapter that the formation of the collections of Egyptian antiquities currently housed by the National Gallery of Victoria (Hope 1983a, b, 1997) and by the Museum Victoria (Hope 1984; Hope and Miller 1984), and the holdings related to Egyptology in the State Library of Victoria, is inextricably intertwined with Australia's use of Egyptianizing monuments. Aspects of their formation and availability illuminate certain elements in Melbourne's, and the State of Victoria's, use of Egyptian themes. Thus the latter, as it relates to architecture, cannot be studied without reference to other areas of interest in things ancient Egyptian, which provide a broader context in which to understand the phenomenon. They can be seen as providing a means of access to Egyptian architecture and design in a country far removed from their land of origin.

This chapter focuses upon Melbourne as an Australian case study and also presents information on buildings elsewhere in Victoria. The timeframe covered is from the first documented appropriation of an Egyptian architectural form in 1851 until 1939.

The State Library and antiquities collections

White settlement of Port Phillip Bay commenced in 1834; in 1835, Batman made a treaty with the local Aborigines and acquired Melbourne. Independence from New South Wales came in 1850; this was followed in 1851 by the announcement that gold had been discovered. Within two months the mines of Victoria were producing more gold than elsewhere and life within the new State was changed irrevocably. Gold was to be the basis for the rapid development of the State and Melbourne, and for a new social hierarchy that challenged the ideologies of the earlier settlers and at times created much turbulence, even anarchy. It was against the backdrop of these momentous changes that a public library and university were founded in 1853, each intended to be a 'civilizing' agency within the State and to reinforce the old order (Fox 1988). The driving force behind both was Redmond Barry, who became the first Chancellor of the University of Melbourne and Senior Trustee of the Melbourne Public Library; it was he who determined the course each was to take in the formative years and to determine their character.

Barry was of Anglo-Irish descent, born in 1813 into a family that, in the 18th century, had played a significant role in Freemasonry (Galbally 1995). Throughout his life he maintained an interest in classics and developed the belief that, as European culture was based upon those of Greece and Rome, knowledge of classical culture was of advantage to all and an essential component of tertiary education. He emigrated to Australia in 1839 and quickly became part of the social elite of Melbourne. As early as April 1840 he delivered a lecture at the Melbourne Mechanics Institute on the 'History of the Art of Agriculture' and presented his idea that it was agriculture that distinguished civilized people from hunter-gatherers. In a further lecture in 1847, he stated his belief in the supremacy of the classical tradition, but illustrated his familiarity with some aspects of Ancient Egypt and Denon's (1802) publication (Barry 1847: 6–7). He (Barry 1847: 7) does not appear to have been overly impressed by Egyptian achievement:

> ... we find no mention of walls or fortifications encircling the cities; ... no allusion (at least until the time of the Emperor Probus about AD 270) is made to quays, baths, bridges, or theatres, hospitals for the sick, or houses of refuge for the aged and infirm; nor do we discover anything to remove the impression that while her kings squandered so much human life and treasure, on buildings the ruins of which are still to be seen, they were inattentive to many of those matters which the polished nations

of the present day consider of perhaps paramount importance, and indifferent about the comfort and convenience of their subjects.

The accuracy or source of these beliefs is irrelevant here; it is significant to note that he had obviously read both ancient and contemporary authors on Egypt. Admiration for the achievements of the Ptolemies, however, is clear, and it is of importance to read that Barry focuses upon the establishment of the Alexandrian Library and Museum (and see Butler Chapter 15, this volume):

> It was not until Egypt was governed by Ptolemy Lagos ... that the polite sciences *revisited their cradle*, and found at the Court of the Egyptian Monarch protection and encouragement. He commenced the formation of a library, which ultimately contained 700,000 volumes, and which, to the infinite grief of the learned, was destroyed by fire when Julius Caesar was besieged in Alexandria (BC 47). He gave up a portion of his palace to the use of a society of learned men, and established a museum, the first of its kind, the members of which, maintained at the public expense, were employed in philosophical researches.

(Barry 1847: 7–8; emphasis added)

In 1853, when plans were announced for the creation of a public library and a university, Barry came to the fore, having energetically argued for both. He was elected the Chancellor of the University of Melbourne and Senior Trustee of the Public Library. The latter was to be secular and amongst its first four foundation professors was to be one of classics; the library was to collect in all areas, except contemporary literature which he abhorred, and would be open to all. Barry regarded the role of the Library as central to the cultural life of the Colony, which was to mirror that of contemporary Europe (Fox 1988: 14).

He set about acquiring books through purchase and donation. Naturally, for one whose education was based upon classics, he purchased liberally in that area but also desired the collection to have major holdings relating to all ancient cultures of the Mediterranean. The Library opened in 1856 containing 3,846 volumes. On Egypt, by 1864 it had acquired the *Denkmäler* (Lepsius 1849–1859), a donation from the King of Prussia, Lepsius (1853), *Description* (1809–1828), a volume of Firth's photographs, French and English editions of Denon (1802), and many more works. This policy was to be followed until the early 1900s.[1]

Plans for a museum attached to the Library date back to 1854; in this Barry was ardently supported by McCoy, first Professor of Natural History at the University. McCoy argued for a Museum of Fine Arts and Antiquities, and suggested that the casts of "classic statuary, antiquities and architectural decorations" that had been displayed in 1851 at the Crystal Palace Exhibition should be acquired for display in Melbourne (Fox 1988: 16; Galbally 1995: 110; Werner Chapter 5, this volume). In 1859 Barry announced plans for an extension to the Library building including a Museum and Statuary Gallery. Resulting from the failure of earlier exhibitions of paintings elsewhere in Melbourne in 1853 and 1856, and Barry's suspicion of the impact contemporary art would have upon the colonists, it was decided that the first acquisitions should include photographs, casts of classical sculpture, medals, coins and gems (Cox 1970: 9–10; Fox 1988, 24); no Egyptian material was included. The

Museum of Art (Sculpture Gallery) opened in 1861, and the National Museum of Victoria soon followed.

In 1856, Weidenbach, one of the artists on Lepsius' expedition to Egypt in 1842–1844, and who was resident from 1848 in Australia (Merrillees 1990: 8–10), offered a selection of antiquities to the Library for purchase. Whilst it seems that this was declined, his description of a mummified head with small pieces of gold foil attached to the face fits that of one now in the Museum Victoria (X83763). However, the first certain date recorded for an Egyptian piece entering the collection is 1862, when some scarabs and beads were donated, and Egyptian material continued to enter the Museum of Art collection in a small and sporadic fashion in the 1870s and 1880s. It is clear that no emphasis to establish a reputable collection of antiquities matched that which drove the Library acquisition policy. Even the munificent donation by Sir Charles Nicholson of his antiquities collection to the University of Sydney, which Barry saw and admired in 1862 (Galbally 1995: 114), did not act as a catalyst, despite the competitive nature of relations between Victoria and New South Wales. Another offer of antiquities, this time from the collection of the French Consul Le Compte de Castelnau, was made in 1880 and again was declined. His collection of antiquities had featured in a highly successful exhibition of fine arts in a new extension to the Museum in 1869 that attracted 14,634 visitors in 94 days.

As documented elsewhere (Hope 1983a; Merrillees 1990), the collecting policy for Egyptian antiquities had an uneven history. Material from excavations in Egypt was acquired largely through subscription from 1899–1932, the first important collections coming in 1899 from Petrie's excavations at Dendera and Diospolis Parva. The antiquities were usually shown in the Museum on their arrival. Of a more imposing nature was the very popular, so-called Egyptian Room in the Melbourne Exhibition Building. There, two mummies and their coffins donated by J. S. Gotch were displayed in a room that had a pylon-shaped entrance; on its walls were hung paintings copying Egyptian tomb scenes (Dunstan and Graham 1996: 249). One of these bodies was unwrapped in a theatrical manner in 1893 before a public lecture (Dunstan and Graham 1996).

1850 to World War I

At the London International Exhibition held in 1862, one of the most popular sections was that celebrating the achievements of the Colony of Victoria. Over the display of various produce, paintings and other manufactured items towered a tall, slender pyramid 45 feet high and 10 feet square at the base (Sweet 1996: 104, 106; 2001), made from gilded plaster (Figure 9:1). Allocated a prominent place within the Exhibition, its volume matched the quantity of gold that had already been discovered in Victoria. It was designed by Knight, one of the architects of the Victorian Parliament building, and was first seen in Melbourne in 1861 when the entire Victorian display was previewed there (Galbally 1995: 118, illustration opposite 148). Knight supervised the installation of the Victorian exhibits in London (Knight 1865). This was the first use of a pyramid within Melbourne. It has been suggested that its significance in the context of an international exhibition was that "It affirmed Australia as a rewarding place of

Figure 9:1
J. G. Knight's
pyramid
displayed at
the London
International
Exhibition in
1862 (La
Trobe
Collection,
State Library
of Victoria).

settlement, and it symbolized the economic wealth of the British Empire" (Sweet 2001: 91).

Sweet (2001: 91) has seen the use of a pyramid form as "a metaphor for intellectual and artistic sophistication" in the colony. The achievements and potential of Victoria may have been likened to those of Ancient Egypt and thus one of the greatest symbols of its achievements could appropriately represent the State. It is, however, uncertain what was actually the immediate source of Knight's inspiration. The shape of his monument (Figure 9:1) resembled more that of the pyramids erected over private tombs of the New Kingdom and the royal burials of Napatan and Meroitic times in the Sudan, rather than a classic Egyptian royal pyramid. Drawings of such pyramids had already been published,[2] while throughout the history of Egyptian revivalism it is the steep-sided pyramid that occurs most regularly either in actual built form, such as that of Caius Cestius (Curl 1994: 25, pl. 15), or in drawings and paintings (Curl 1994; Humbert 1989; Humbert et al. 1994). Knight had emigrated to Australia in 1852 (Serle

1949: 503), and he may have had the opportunity to view such representations, or he may have been inspired by the Egyptian Court at the Crystal Palace Exhibition in 1851 (Curl 1994: 193–194; Werner Chapter 5, this volume), which is said to have included an obelisk form (McKay 1998: 318 n. 318) It is also possible that he had seen the so-called obelisk erected in 1818 in Macquarie Place, Sydney, or the 1855 memorial to Major-General Sir Robert Nickle (Figure 9:2, and see below), the shape of both of which his 1861 pyramid resembles. Despite the popularity of Knight's pyramid and the appeal of representing the quantity of gold discovered in Australia in this imposing manner, after the Paris Exhibition of 1867 it became impractical to do so, and Australians had to select another form to symbolize both mineral wealth and cultural achievement. Another quintessential Egyptian form was chosen: the obelisk.

As McKay (1998, 2001) has documented, from 1862 and for most of the following 50 years Australian exhibits regularly featured obelisks in all the international exhibitions, whether overseas or in Australia, as symbols of the country's gold or other mineral output. By 1880 they were being termed 'goldometers'; their numbers

Figure 9:2 Tombstone of Major-General Sir Robert Nickle, 1855, Melbourne General Cemetery (© Colin A. Hope).

began to proliferate at each exhibition and their use became so common that boredom with the image began to set in. The largest, however, was displayed in Melbourne in 1888: standing 60 feet tall, it represented the 2,524 tons of gold mined in Australia to date. When their use was beginning to wane, Queensland persisted in employing them, and when a Coat of Arms was designed for that State and granted in 1893, the gilded obelisk was inserted in one of the quadrants (McKay 2001: 160). The spectacular nature of such symbols of Australian achievement was intended to impress and attract capital to the country. Whilst the obelisk was dominant in such displays, the pyramid occasionally made its reappearance, as in London in 1886, but on a reduced scale; at that event a triumphal arch into Victoria's display was surmounted by a gilded female figure holding a cornucopia that, like its Ptolemaic precursor, symbolized prosperity and peace (McKay 2001: 153–154).

The obelisk was used not only within exhibitions; it is found in a wide variety of other commemorative contexts throughout Victoria and the rest of Australia. In a recent study of Australian sacred places, both inside and out of the country, Inglis (1998: 160) estimated that Australia has 10 obelisks for every cross raised. As memorials for Australians killed in battle overseas or, rarely, at home, they have been erected since 1884, the first in Camperdown, Victoria.

Major events in national and regional history have been remembered by the erection of obelisks. Examples in Victoria include the deaths during the Eureka Stockade rebellion by goldminers in 1854 and at Ballarat in Victoria in 1856, the fateful 1860–1861 Burke and Wills expedition in Castlemaine in 1863, and the discovery of gold at Ballarat, in 1897; while in New South Wales at Kurnell, in 1870, such a monument was raised to mark Captain Cook's landing place (Apperly *et al.* 1994: 50). Australian cemeteries display a large number of tombstones in the form of obelisks, some on horned altars; in Melbourne they have been employed since 1851, by Christians and also Jews, until relatively recently. One of the oldest has an unusually wide base and thus resembles a combination of pyramid and obelisk. It stands in the Melbourne General Cemetery in commemoration of Major-General Sir Robert Nickle, Commander of Her Majesty's forces within the Australian command, who died in 1855 (Figure 9:2). The oldest use of such a marker appears to have been erected sometime just after 1838, in Rokeby, Tasmania (Apperly *et al.* 1994: 51). At the former Melbourne Observatory yet another obelisk was erected in 1886–1887 to serve as a collimating marker.

It should be noted, however, that the oldest 'obelisk' in Australia is to be found, not unexpectedly, in Sydney and dates to 1818 (Herman 1970: fig. 14; Merrillees 1990: ill. 37). It was used to mark distances from the city and stands in Macquarie Place; designed by Greenway (Freeland 1970: 35–41), it was erected at the command of Governor Lachlan Macquarie. This obelisk also bears some resemblance to a narrow-based pyramid; its base recalls a horned altar. Another Sydney obelisk is actually a vent for the city's sewers (Apperly *et al.* 1994: 51, no. 79; Merrillees 1998: 275). Obelisks were also a feature of the architecture of the now dismantled York Street Synagogue in Sydney consecrated in 1844, which incorporated other elements of Egyptian temple architecture and housed an Ark of the Covenant in the form of an Egyptian naos (Merrillees 1990: 56). Three other synagogues – in Adelaide, Launceston and Hobart, all consecrated between 1844 and 1850 – also contained various degrees of

Egyptianizing architecture (Merrillees 1998). No similar structure was erected in Melbourne.

Some authors (Inglis 1998: 12; McKay 1998: 318 n. 318) have attempted to explain the popularity of the obelisk by alluding to the occasional Egyptian practice of erecting obelisks to commemorate victories over enemies. Obelisks as symbols of victory either over or in Egypt can certainly be seen throughout Europe, and others are found as indicators of political or economic influence over Egypt, e.g. those in London, New York, Paris. Whether those responsible for the Australian usage knew of the ancient Egyptian practice is doubtful, and it is more likely that they were influenced by Roman and more recent uses (Carrott 1978: 21–57, 82; Curl 1994: 25 ff; Humbert *et al.* 1994). It may be, as Davison (1996: 13) has suggested, that the shape was selected because it "suggested both bulk and height, achievement and aspiration", while, as Inglis (1998: 25–26) notes, in a secular society it did not possess Christian significance. Part of the reason may also lie in the beliefs of Freemasonry. Both Macquarie and Greenway were Freemasons (Merrillees 1995: 79; 1998: 275), as was Thornton who erected the Hyde Park obelisk (Merrillees 1998: 275), and there was a strong link between Freemasonry in Australia and the Jewish community (Merrillees 1998). It is worth noting, however, that Macquarie had served in Egypt with Abercromby in 1801 (Pike 1967). The use of the obelisk within cemeteries may have been inspired simply by European practice (Curl 1991b: 190–218; 1994: 161).

Within Victoria the ideological link between Freemasonry and Ancient Egypt (Curl 1991b: 28–38, 135–68; 1994) is given its clearest, earliest and most spectacular realization in the decoration of the Zetland Lodge's Hall in Kyneton.[3] This structure, and other Masonic Temples in Melbourne, necessitate a revision of Merrillees' (1998: 275) statement: "Strangely enough the Freemasons in Australia did not to any significant extent make use of ancient Egyptian imagery for their architecture or motifs." Originally constructed in 1866 as an Oddfellows Hall, the original structure appears not to have had any Egyptianizing aspect but rather a slightly classical reference in its use of pilasters and a pediment; classical form was employed for the early Masonic temples elsewhere in Victoria, e.g. in Bendigo (1873) and Warnambool (Saunders 1966: 201, 240). The Lodge purchased the building in 1904, and two rooms were added on either side of the entrance to the hall, giving a more monumental, pylon-like, appearance. The decoration of the hall commenced in 1905 and continued until 1911, with some additions as late as 1919, all the work of Levick, a member of the Lodge. The decorative scheme comprises wall panels, framed by pilasters painted to imitate marble and with Egyptian capitals, some of which contain murals and others blocked windows or the doors into the hall. The doors, windows and other features have timber surrounds in the form of the front of a naos or doorway within a temple surmounted by a cavetto cornice. The doors carry images of the open blue lotus flower and the open papyrus *umbel*. The ceiling has a beam structure, between which the panels are painted to simulate the sky with stars; one beam supports a representation of the winged scarab rolling before it the solar disk. The wall pilasters are so arranged to imply that they support the ceiling beams.

Four of the wall panels carry murals, and it is these that are by far the most imposing elements in the decoration (Figure 9:3). The dominant one, set within an arched frame, represents the famous kiosk built by Trajan on the Island of Philae. The

Figure 9:3   Part of main wall panels in Zetland Temple, Kyneton, painted by T. F. Levick, 1905–1911 (© Rob Hickman, reproduced courtesy of the Zetland Lodge).

selection of this image is significant because of Freemasonry's belief in its connections with the cult of Isis (Curl 1991b: 28–38; Hamill and Mollier Chapter 11, this volume). The scenes in the three other panels are painted as though viewed from within the kiosk and thus considerable space is devoted to showing varying numbers of columns with a *trompe l'oeil* effect. Immediately to the left of the panel with the kiosk is one showing a minaret and domed building behind a market scene; this panel accords considerable space to a roll of honour commemorating locals who died during World War I, which was added in 1919. The other two panels contain depictions of the Giza pyramids viewed at the time of inundation and with the sphinx partly cleared. The paintings are extremely well executed and their images are intended to emphasize the antiquity of Freemasonry, through medieval into Roman and then back to the pharaonic Egypt of the Old Kingdom.

The sources of inspiration for the panel paintings come from published illustrations in volumes that, when Levick was working, were housed in the Melbourne Public Library. The major source is Roberts and Brockedon (1846–1849), acquired for the Library between 1865 and 1880. The view of the Philae kiosk is an almost exact copy of one entitled 'The Hypaethral Temple at Philae, Called the Bed of Pharaoh', though Levick increased the height of the rock upon which the building was shown and changed the arrangement of the boats and palms. The scene of the pyramids appears to be derived from several such images drawn by Roberts, while the Islamic panel may have been inspired by those showing the tombs behind the Cairo citadel. The idea of showing three of the scenes as though from within a building may also derive from Roberts' penchant for such, and the details of the pilaster columns clearly replicate those of Ptolemaic temples shown by him, for example at Edfu and Philae, the colouring used by Roberts also being copied. A different source inspired the image of the sphinx, namely the illustration entitled 'View of the Sphinx during the Excavations' (Vyse 1842) acquired by the Library in 1870. The distinctive view with the front part of the sphinx revealed during excavations in 1818 to show the chapel between its legs makes this identification certain. Levick did not slavishly copy the originals, but added his own touches, composition and colour schemes.

Contemporary with his decorative scheme for Kyneton, and again inspired by the Philae kiosk, is the David Syme Memorial in Melbourne's Boroondara General Cemetery at Kew (Clerehan 1982: 24–25; Merrillees 1990: 61, frontispiece; Searle 1992). Work on this monument commenced after Syme's death in 1908 and was finished in 1910. It consists (Figure 9:4) of the kiosk upon a platform approached by two steps,

Figure 9:4   The David Syme Memorial in Boroondara General Cemetery, Kew, 1908–1910, designed by Walter Butler (© Colin A. Hope).

with small courts at front and rear framed by squat, tapering pillars between which are balustrades; the monument is open to the air. True to the original, it has the cavetto cornice atop short piers (*abaci*) on the column capitals, which are elaborate and vary in detail, but the lintels over the doors are continuous and the screen walls are reduced in height, thus differing from it. The sides of the entrances are decorated as though open doors made of panels. The entire cornice is decorated with friezes of uraei, both inside and outside, crowned with solar disks; the lintels have winged solar disks. The tops of the sides of the pillars are decorated with winged scarabs, excepting where the balustrades are set into them, and here the fitting has four plaques ornamented with scarabs. The scarabs on the sides of the pillars are topped by solar disks and below them are segments of others; this composition resembles the writing of Khakheperra, the *praenomen* of Sesostris II. The gates in the mausoleum are openwork, and within an arched top there are three uraei with solar disks and a small central, male head wearing the Nemes headcover. On the metal cover into the burial crypt, above the name of David Syme, is another winged disk. In each corner of the interior space is an arrangement of four tiles, the decoration on which combines to depict four scarabs rolling a single, central solar orb. Their wings are marked, recalling the drawing of open papyrus *umbels,* and are coloured blue; they are quite narrow and resemble those on the winged disk on the inner face of the lintel of the sanctuary of the Deir el-Medina temple. The wings of the scarabs on the exterior pillars are represented in a similar manner; the overall effect of the internal corner tiles has a strong Art Nouveau feel. The monument is built in granite with copper decorative fittings. In his will (State Library of Victoria, MS 9751.1277), Syme had requested that his trustees have constructed a "family vault in or over his grave in the form of a Doric Temple or any other structure thought appropriate", and the design of the structure was entrusted to architect Walter Butler, with whom Syme had many dealings before his death.

As the will indicates, the first choice might have been a pseudo-Doric monument, but Butler chose otherwise.[4] Searle (1992: 30) has intimated that Syme was "fascinated by Egyptian architecture and symbolism", but cites no authority for this; the biographies of Syme do not allude to it (MacDonald 1982; Sayers 1965). In a letter to Mrs Syme (Searle 1992: appendix E), Butler implies that he selected the Egyptian design because of Syme's interest in the soul, the significance of Osiris in Egyptian conceptions of the afterlife and the worship of Osiris and Isis at Philae. In the same letter he outlines the significance of the scarab as a symbol of resurrection, the function of the winged disk and the uraeus as "the emblem of leadership and power". The latter symbol, Butler says, was chosen "as significant of Mr Syme's character"; this is of interest in the context of Syme's domination of the Melbourne newspaper, *The Age,* from 1859.

The stonemasons who built the Syme Memorial, A. and G. Ballantine, also provided several obelisks between 1893 and 1909 that now stand in the Melbourne General Cemetery and also the tomb of Sarah Jane and Henry Perrin Wallace. Sarah was interred in 1901 and Henry in 1905. Its form is clearly Egyptianizing (Figure 9:5) with corner and side pilasters, horizontal torus moulding and cavetto cornices. The lower parts of the side walls are not painted and resemble screen walls; the white-painted front, rear and upper side walls present the appearance of copying open areas with light shining through, and thus the monument may simulate the form of a peripteral chapel, but certainly resembles Roman period mud-brick mausolea. In the

Figure 9:5   The tomb of Sarah Jane and Henry Perrin Wallace in the Melbourne General Cemetery, 1901 (© Colin A. Hope).

Boroondara Public Cemetery another interesting memorial was erected in 1910 for Richard Lohn (Figure 9:6). This comprises a central memorial tablet flanked by columns supporting a lintel and pediment that resembles a door, flanked by low side walls and with a walled area in front. The tops of the columns only are fluted, in a manner that later, in the 1920s to 1930s in Melbourne, would be used in the representation of palmiform capitals within an Egyptianizing context.

From World War I to World War II

Many of the elements of Victoria's use of Egyptianizing architecture prior to World War I also occur subsequently. Obelisks as memorials within cemeteries occur until at least 1958; one, in honour of Herbert Manning Knight, erected in

Figure 9:6   Richard Lohn Memorial in Boroondara General Cemetery, Kew, 1910 (© Colin A. Hope).

Melbourne's Box Hill Cemetery by his Masonic friends, is triangular in section, recalling the shape of a sundial and, as such, the earliest Masonic monuments erected in Scotland in 1714 (Curl 1991b: 48–50).[5] Obelisks to commemorate those who died during the wars are encountered from 1924; there are such memorials for Australians in France, Belgium, Turkey and Papua New Guinea, the latest being erected at el-Alamein in 1989. The form was used to commemorate those who died during World War I as the official state memorials in Tasmania, at Hobart in 1925, and Western Australia, at Perth in 1929 (Inglis 1998: 283–290); and Jewish soldiers who died in World Wars I and II erected in the Melbourne General Cemetery. The official memorial in Melbourne, however, took quite a different form, as did that in Canberra.

In 1923 Sir John Monash chose the design for the Melbourne memorial, clearly influenced by the Lincoln Memorial in Washington and the tomb of Ulysses S. Grant in New York (Inglis 1998: 315–329). The former reproduces aspects of the Parthenon and the latter of the Mausoleum of Halicarnassus. It was opened on Armistice Day, 11 November 1934 at 11 am, at which precise time a ray of sunlight passed over the word 'love' in the text "Greater love hath no man", incised upon the black granite slab at the centre of the Crypt (Inglis 1998: 315; Richards 1998: fig. 9.8). This event occurs naturally only at that precise time annually and, according to one source, it had been suggested for the Shrine by the State's premier, Sir Stanley Argyle (Inglis 1998: 315), who had served in Egypt as an officer and had noted such an event in one of its temples. Thus, the most solemn moment in the commemorative service held in the Melbourne Shrine of Remembrance might be based upon the illumination of the statues in the sanctuary at Abu Simbel (but see Goad 1999: 124).

The Australian War Memorial in Canberra, inaugurated in 1929 and opened in 1941, comprises an imposing domed chamber preceded by a long entrance colonnade flanked by two tall towers. Merrillees (1990: 33–34) has proposed that the final plan may have elements inspired by the standard Egyptian temple architecture. A crucial role in deciding the final form of the Memorial was played by C. E. W. Bean, official historian of the Australian Imperial Force, who had been in Egypt during World War I and was a member of the Theosophical Society.

In 1929 a second Egyptianizing Syme family memorial was erected, this time in the Box Hill Cemetery, Melbourne. Commemorating David Syme's son John Herbert, it simply comprises a memorial tablet in the form of a closed door or screen wall, topped by a cavetto cornice, flanked by two columns with papyriform capitals that support a short abacus and an architrave with a cavetto cornice, with two low side walls (Figure 9:7). The design resembles a segment taken from that of the first Syme memorial and, likewise, was probably designed by Butler (*contra* Clerehan 1982: 24)

During the same decade in which John Syme's tomb was built, Egyptianizing architecture in Melbourne took quite a different form from previously. Two Masonic temples were constructed with façades and interiors distinctly in Egyptian style; the new headquarters of the Theosophical Society and the Melbourne chambers of the Bank of New South Wales were constructed in the Modern Style with various Egyptian elements; while the Richmond Town Hall underwent renovations that introduced similar features.

Figure 9:7   John Herbert Syme Memorial in Box Hill Cemetery, 1929 (© Colin A. Hope).

The Masonic temples are the best examples of their type in Victoria. 'Emulation Hall', built between 1928 and 1930 for Emulation Lodge No. 141 at 3, Rochester Road in Canterbury (Figure 9:8), was designed by Reynolds, a member of the Lodge (Butler and McConville 1991: 248–249). Its façade is that of a temple pylon approached by a flight of steps, with a large central entrance flanked by two attached columns leading to a porch. In the front of each tower of the pylon there is a lower tall, partly-closed window, given the form of side doors, and an upper smaller window above which is a large winged disk below a cavetto cornice. In the sides of each tower there are also lower windows similar in form to those at the front, and upper winged disks. The area between the towers is closed at the rear and the wall supports the image of a black scarab with gilded wings, with upper and lower, gilded solar disks. Cornices atop the main entrance, all windows and the top of the towers are coloured blue, as are the winged disks over the main entrance and the upper windows, and the capitals of the entrance columns. The uraei that flank the disks are coloured black. Cavetto cornices top the side and rear walls; in the side walls are two rows of windows of similar form to the upper ones in the towers but without the colouring on the cornices. The interior of the hall has a ceiling decorated with 10 sets of signs of the zodiac; on the walls on the side of each set are pillars decorated to resemble bundles of papyrus tied at top and bottom, with open lotiform capitals. The lotus is employed regularly in wall and ceiling decoration; the Eye of Horus is represented in each corner of the room, and a winged disk flanked by uraei is represented above the stage in the refectory.

Figure 9:8   Emulation Lodge, Canterbury, designed by Dunstan Reynolds, 1928–1930 (© Gayle Jenes).

In a lecture delivered in 1986 to the Lodge, one of its members, Holborn, identified the building as a replica of the Philae Temple of Isis, although clearly it is not an exact copy. He emphasized Freemasonry's links with Egypt and the 'Mysteries of Isis and Osiris'. The entire layout of the interior is explained by use of numerology to relate to the Egyptian calendar, and even the number of nomes, while in relation to the use of the winged disk he noted:

> Many hand made tapestries bearing this motif and the Scarab were brought back from Egypt by Australian soldiers returning from the first world war, and probably accounts for much of the inspiration behind the erection of Emulation Temple.

The façade of Emulation Temple also recalls those of the London Egyptian Hall (1811–1812), Devonport Library (1823), the Penzance Egyptian House (ca. 1835), Brown's Egyptian Pavilion (1842) (Curl 1994: 157, 160, 165, 188), and the 1845 Hobart Synagogue (Merrillees 1998: 264–266). The columns flanking the entrance, rather than relating to any symbol of Osiris, may, as in many Masonic temples, represent those in front of Solomon's Temple (Curl 1991b: 28–38; 1994: 134–135), although they could simply be inspired by 19th century structures.

The second temple is at 23, Abbott Street in Sandringham (Figure 9:9), again with distinctive tripartite façade, but here the central section is dominant, projecting forward of the side sections. It is thus far less a copy of an Egyptian temple style than Emulation Temple, and more an interpretation in a modernist style. The entrance comprises a porch with two slender columns with palmiform capitals at the front and open side windows with grills in the form of stylized columns with papyrus-bundle

Figure 9:9   The Sandringham Masonic Centre, 1931, designed by G. J. Sutherland (© Colin A. Hope).

capitals. The same form of column and capital occurs as the support for the balcony atop the entrance porch. Both the entrance porch and balcony have cavetto cornices, and the central and side sections of the façade are crowned with the same, as is the front part of the side walls. There is a very stylized winged disk on the lintel supported by the porch columns, and a more naturalistic rendering on the parapet wall of the balcony. The upper and lower rows of windows at the front and sides are framed and have an upper cavetto cornice at the front only. The final element of note in the external architecture is the use of two small obelisks in front of the porch, the tapering tops of which are triangular in shape, and thus resembling sundials.

The internal decoration is similar to that of Emulation Temple, and many of the decorative moulds used for the latter were employed for the decoration of the Sandringham Temple, as in the lower and upper halls and the stairway and halls (Figures 9:10, 9:11); woodwork throughout is of fine quality and also adopts Egyptianizing design elements. The walls and ceilings of both halls are divided into panels flanked by pilasters, which are painted to resemble bundles of papyrus with palm-frond capitals on the walls, and either columns with papyrus capitals or floral bouquets on the ceilings. The windows and doors are all framed and capped with cavetto cornices, and the lead-light windows have winged solar disks flanked by uraei, a motif that also occurs on the ceilings. Several of the doorframes are ornamented with double columns supporting papyrus-*umbel* capitals, between the shafts of which are interlocking, S-shaped spirals and sprays of jasmine. The focal point of each hall is at the west end; in the lower hall this comprises a dais flanked by pilasters with the double-column motif found on the doorframes, above which is the winged disk. In the upper hall there is an elaborately carved wooden frame with

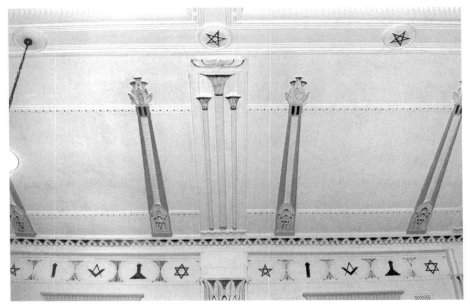

Figures 9:10, 9:11   Decoration of the interior of the Sandringham Masonic Temple, 1931 (author's photos, reproduced courtesy of the directors of the Sandringham Masonic Centre).

columns, cavetto cornice and winged disk that marks the location of the seats, with tapering backs, of the Lodge's master and senior members. Masonic symbols, signs of the zodiac, the Star of David and the pentangle complete the decorative scheme.

The motifs employed throughout the building are of a general Egyptianizing form, although the ceiling pilasters in the upper hall with the central taller papyrus stem flanked by shorter ones closely resemble one of the decorated pillars erected by Tuthmosis III at Karnak before the sanctuary of the main temple. The prominence given to the frontal columns and the structure of the portico bear a striking resemblance to the Freemason's Hall of 1860–1863 in Mainridge, Boston, Lincolnshire (Curl 1994: 196–198). Quite distinct from the decoration of the interior of both Emulation Lodge and the Sandringham Masonic Centre is that now in the headquarters of the United Supreme Grand Chapter of Mark and Royal Arch Masons at 23–25, New Canterbury Road in Petersham, New South Wales (Foster and Sykes 1998). This presents a copy of the vignettes from the Papyrus of Ani. It was executed in 1927, originally housed within the Royal Arch Temple in College Street Sydney, and installed in its present location in 1977.

The façade of the Theosophical Society building at 181, Collins Street in Melbourne is a further example of the Egyptian temple design, but here it is part of a five-storey building and stands three storeys high. The building,[6] the most elaborate of all those of the Theosophical Society in Australia, was constructed 1936–1937. Two slender columns with palmiform capitals are set within a frame topped with an angular cornice, meant to represent the entrance to an Egyptian temple. The choice of this feature must be based upon Theosophists' ideas concerning the antiquity of their movement and its beliefs, and thus, as in the case of the Masonic temples, the Egyptian elements relate to the commissioning body and not to the individual architect's/ architects' wishes. There is a tripartite aspect to the design, which is also encountered in another central Melbourne building of slightly earlier date, the Melbourne chambers of the Bank of New South Wales, constructed between 1929 and 1931. Here a rendering of the same idea as found on the Theosophical Society building – the entrance to an Egyptian temple – occupies the entire upper five storeys of the façade of the building. The columns are flattened into piers and crowned with capitals that contain only volutes; the same elements occur at the top of the side walls, which are reduced in width to resemble piers. Below a cavetto cornice there is a winged solar disk the width of the central part of the façade. Other elements in the design have classical reference.

In 1934–1936 the Richmond Town Hall in Melbourne was remodelled according to a design which comprised the addition of a portico with four frontal and two side columns all with palmiform capitals, and pilasters framing the doors into the building proper with the same type of capital. The alterations commemorated Victoria's centenary and in the National Trust file for the building it has been suggested that the columns were "no doubt symbolic of the power which lies within". On the chimneys of a 1923 apartment building at 36, Eildon Street in St Kilda are what resemble *nb*-baskets, and there is a stylized rendering of the solar disk with three dependent rays on the upper front of the building. The rays end in a small square that may be intended to represent the hands on the rays of the standard representation of the Aten. The Egyptianizing decoration on two hotels in Johnston Street in Fitzroy is of uncertain date (probably 1930s), both having a first-floor balcony with columns supporting very stylized palmiform capitals, and tall narrow windows, and the Tankerville Arms having winged solar disks flanked by uraei adorning the exterior of the upper ground floor.

The policy of acquiring volumes on Ancient Egypt for what is now the State Library of Victoria continued throughout this period but on a much-reduced scale. The collection of Egyptian antiquities in the National Gallery of Victoria received its last major additions in 1939–1940.[7] In 1939, the Trustees of the Felton Bequest purchased 46 antiquities in Cairo, some quite major pieces, for the gallery; while in 1940, again through the Felton Bequest, seven portrait paintings were acquired (Connor 1978; Hope 1983b, 1997). On the arrival of these pieces a new display was inaugurated in a room hung with textiles ornamented with Egyptian themes. Here the mummified human remains then in the State's collection were also displayed, comprising principally the early twelfth Dynasty mummy and coffin of Tjeby (Hope 1984) and the two Late Period bodies and their coffins donated by Gotch, referred to earlier.

Conclusions

In attempting to understand the interest in, and the appropriation and use of ancient Egyptian architectural and decorative forms within Melbourne and Victoria, a variety of factors and influences must be considered simultaneously. Individuals such as Barry were educated according to 19th century British norms and held firm beliefs in the supremacy of their cultural traditions and the importance of an understanding of the classical tradition for cultivated society. These were to be grafted onto a fledgling society especially through his dominance of cultural institutions, primarily the Public Library. In instituting a collecting policy that was catholic, he ensured that Melbourne artists and architects, as well as the public at large, had access to volumes that would inform them of the arts of the ancient world. At the same time, architects trained in Britain who emigrated or were forcibly removed to Australia brought with them knowledge of the prevailing traditions within Europe, amongst which was a firmly established use of Egyptianizing themes. The appropriateness in the 19th century of the use of the pyramid and obelisk, in addition to classical architecture, in the context of cultural achievement and aspiration, by a country newly inhabited by Europeans, is easy to understand. Elements of personal preference must also be considered, as in the suitability of Butler's choice for David Syme's memorial or in the selection of the obelisk for a grave marker. Whilst the latter was one of the standard forms used, it is possible that exposure to the use of obelisks in Egypt, and also in Britain and Ireland by those undertaking the trip back to their family's place of origin, could have prompted its regular use in Australia. Visits to Egypt as part of such a trip became more common after the opening of the Suez Canal, and Australian soldiers regularly served in Egypt or passed through it on their way to service elsewhere. The obelisk lacked specific religious association within the contemporary world and could, therefore, appeal to a society that was becoming less sectarian. Souvenirs brought home appear also to have been of influence, as observed in the decorative scheme of Emulation Temple in Canterbury.

Freemasonry played a significant role within the Australian use of Egyptianizing architecture. The beliefs of the group at large or of an individual member clearly prompted the use of obelisks as tombstones, the decoration and architecture of temples, as well as the use of obelisks within a public sphere. It also impacted strongly upon the architecture of various synagogues.

The discovery of the tomb of Tutankhamun in 1922 prompted a major revival of interest in Ancient Egypt, and another phase of 'Egyptomania' followed. The discoveries were broadcast in Australia by the media, and caused a renewal of interest. Reflecting this, in New South Wales, might be the entrances to the Cordeaux and Avon Dams (van Daele and Lumby 1997: 160–161; *National Trust Magazine* 33 [1986]: 11), the pylon-like towers of the Sydney Harbour Bridge, and Burley Griffith's obelisk-like tower on the Leichardt incinerator, as might the Australian National War Memorial in Canberra, and the façade of the Melbourne chambers of the Bank of New South Wales. So too the Canterbury and Sandringham Masonic temples, and the façade of the Theosophical Society building in Melbourne, although here the beliefs of the organizations for which they were constructed may well also have been significant. The desire by the National Gallery of Victoria to increase its holdings of Egyptian antiquities in 1939–1940 may have resulted from interest in the material culture of Egypt that surged in the wake of the Tutankhamun find. The acquisitions that were made and displayed along with other antiquities in the Egyptian Room with its wall hangings representing mortuary themes would continue to remind Victorians of the achievements of ancient Egyptian culture for several decades.

Notes

1   For the earliest acquisitions see Overell 1991, 1997.
2   Amongst the holdings of the National Gallery of Victoria is a collection of 98 anonymous, original pencil drawings mostly of ancient monuments in the region south of Aswan and in the north of the Sudan that include representations of such pyramids. They appear to have been acquired in the last decades of the 19th century. There is no evidence that they have ever been on display and thus it is uncertain whether they may have had any impact upon Egyptianizing architecture or design in Victoria.
3   Information is derived from a Shire of Kyneton Conservation (Heritage) Study and the text of an address to the Lodge by Alan Willis, provided to me by Heritage Victoria.
4   A Kew conservation study lists the architect as Arthur Peck, following Clerehan (1982: 24); in a telephone conversation with the present writer on 30/04/2002, Mr Clerehan acknowledged that he was mistaken.
5   These monuments appear to contradict the claim that "Egyptian rites and embellishments do not seem to have entered Freemasonry seriously before the 1780s" (Pevsner and Lang 1968: 32).
6   Information on this building derives from a conservation study (1988) commissioned from Meredith Gould by the Architects Branch, Melbourne City Council and G. Butler's (1985) Central Administrative District Conservation Study; no discussion of its architecture appears to have been published until now.
7   Subsequently the only major pieces to enter the collection have been a limestone bust of a female from Behnesa (1973 – Cullican 1973/4), and a painted and gilded, cartonnage head-covering (1994 – Hope 1997; Potts *et al.* 1997).

Acknowledgments

It is my great pleasure to thank all of the following for their assistance during the course of the preparation of this study: Gayle Jenes, Research Assistant in the School of Historical Studies, Monash University, who diligently sought out much primary source material; Joanne Boyd and Andrew Jamieson of Heritage Victoria for providing information and access to files and images; Professor Graeme Davison, School of Historical Studies, Monash University, for drawing Inglis (1998) to my attention; Alan Willis of the Zetland Lodge, Kyneton, for information and photographs; Ivan Foster of the Sandringham Masonic Centre for kindly providing access to the Sandringham Temple and a copy of the text of the lecture by R. W. Holborn on the decoration of Emulation Temple; Grace Giannini of the Matheson Library, Monash University, and Shona Drewer and Brian Hubbard of the State Library of Victoria for assisting me in locating the text and for providing me with a copy of Barry's first 1847 lecture; Des Cowley, Rare Books Librarian at the State Library of Victoria, for acquisition details on various holdings and for bringing Overell (1991) to my attention; Olaf Kaper, for comparing elements of David Syme's memorial with the Deir el-Medina temple; Judith McKay of the Queensland Museum, who kindly supplied me with a copy of her 2001 article before its publication; John Shannon of Boroondara General Cemetery at Kew, for access to a copy of Peter Searle's study of the Syme Memorial; Lionel Sharpe, Australian Centre for Jewish Civilization, Monash University for providing me with a copy of Merrillees 1998; Jonathon Sweet, Deakin University, Melbourne, for providing me with access to his 2001 discussion of the pyramid prior to its publication, and also copies of several other of his articles; Tom Taylor of Royal Arch Lodge in Sydney, for a copy of the published discussion of the decoration of their Egyptian Room at Petersham; and finally, to my colleague Dr Gillian Bowen, of the Centre for Archaeology and Ancient History at Monash University, for assisting in documenting Egyptianizing monuments in Melbourne and proof-reading the manuscript of this chapter.

CHAPTER 10

EGYPT IN PARIS: 19th CENTURY MONUMENTS AND MOTIFS

Cathie Bryan

Introduction

Although Bonaparte's Egyptian Campaign was a failure in military terms, France nonetheless accorded a new prestige to Egypt in the early 19th century. Egyptian civilization was acknowledged as the precursor of Greece, which was in turn superseded by imperial Rome. Thanks to Napoleon, the French Empire had become the latest cultural and political *ne plus ultra*, at least in the eyes of the French, if not the world. Western culture, including its underlying Christianity, was held to be of the highest order. Along with other European nations, France had a duty (*mission civilisatrice*) to bring the less developed and 'heathen' world into the light. Parallels between the Roman Empire and the French Empire became dominant themes of the arts under Napoleon, with both Empires having a common Egyptian connection.

Art, architecture and iconography during the reign of Napoleon: 1804–1815

Civilian scholars had accompanied the Egyptian Campaign to undertake a scientific documentation of Egypt. The written and graphical documentation resulted in the publication of *Description de l'Égypte* (1809–1828), which converted the achievements of Ancient Egypt into an icon of French power and leadership. Although the Campaign secured Egypt for France for a mere three years, the symbolism of Egypt became fused with Napoleon. Contained within the frontispiece of the *Description* is a cleverly-coded association between Napoleon and Egyptian divine royalty, which can be seen in the cartouches containing the bee which flank Napoleon's monogram. Even before the decipherment of hieroglyphics, Napoleon and Denon, first Director of the Louvre, would have been aware, largely through the writings of Ammianus Marcellinus (ca. 325–391) (Iversen 1993: 49–50, 132–133), that the bee was understood by the Romans to be associated with the title of the Egyptian king. Such symbolism became incorporated into Napoleon's subsequent mythology (Boime 1990: 6; Humbert 1989: 12), and continues to affect the French view of him to the present day.

The 'Old Boys from Egypt', both military and civilian, held key positions in Napoleon's government (Bergeron 1990: 52–53), thus ensuring a team of supportive capability and talent. Napoleon openly exercised censorship and controlled the flow of information across the media and arts. Artists were not only the instruments of propaganda, but were themselves subjected to the same propaganda. Whether in open support or in covert opposition to Napoleon, much art of the period was intentionally political (Boime 1990; Durant and Durant 1975).

In painting, Napoleon had his person and rule linked with previous military emperors of antiquity and France. The portraits of the heroes of his reign were shown in classical mode and sometimes even employed an obelisk or an allegorical personification of Egypt. A reference to Ancient Egypt could also point to Imperial Rome, thus reinforcing the comparison between the Roman and the French Empires.

In architecture, Percier and Fontaine – the foremost designers of the Empire period – were responsible with Denon for much of the monumental propaganda. They insisted, for example, that the rapid improvements to the Louvre[1] were undertaken not to create a monument to their patron but to provide him with a bigger and better palace than other European sovereigns. In June 1803, when Bonaparte was still First Consul, Denon tried to change the name of the Louvre to 'Musée Napoléon' (Romi 1969: 53), thereby signalling a change in the function of the palace.

Egyptianizing monuments and buildings of the Empire display the traditional symbolism relating to Egypt that had been in use since the Renaissance. Further inspiration was drawn from *Description* (1809–1828), from Denon (1802), and from objects in the Egyptian collection at the Louvre. Ptolemaic temples and their elements were favoured models for public Egyptianizing architecture. For example, the temple of Hathor at Dendera, complete with Hathor-headed capitals, was the inspiration for a memorial to two heroes of the Egyptian Campaign, Desaix and Kléber.[2] Other popular elements in the French Egyptianizing repertoire included the pyramid, the obelisk and the pylon-form with steeply sloped walls surmounted by an Egyptian gorge cornice, also called cavetto, with torus moulding beneath. Buildings or monuments in the Egyptian style often incorporated the winged sundisk, hieroglyphics and Egyptianate reliefs or sculpture including the sphinx, the lion, and historical and mythological figures. A Nemes-coiffed bust or a vulture-headdressed queen were used frequently to allegorize Egypt.

Alongside traditional images and symbolism of Ancient Egypt, re-worked symbols and new themes were introduced as part of Napoleon's iconography of self-promotion and legitimization. These were often inseparably intertwined with the 'politically correct' social theory of the day. For example, the ornamental fountain with its combined functions of spectacle, water source and sanitation, was a visible and potent vehicle for governmental publicity. In 1806 Napoleon decreed the construction of 15 public fountains, of which six (at the Palais des Beaux Arts, de l'Apport-Paris, popularly called the Fontaine du palmier or Fontaine de la Victoire, du Fellah, du Boulevard Montmartre, du Château d'Eau, and de la Paix et des Arts) were designed to honour himself and the Egyptian campaign (Humbert *et al.* 1994: 268–269). The Fontaine du Fellah[3] (Figure 10:1) in the rue de Sèvres features a copy of Antinous, a Roman Egyptianizing statue in the hellenistic style from Hadrian's Villa. The naos or gateway with cavetto cornice within which he stands bears the Napoleonic eagle instead of the more customary Egyptian winged sundisk. In the Roman sculpture, Antinous as the god Osiris wears the Nemes – one of the pharaohs'

Figure 10:1   The 'Fontaine du Fellah' (© Tony Bryan).

head coverings. The sculptor of the fountain, Beauvallet, was apparently not aware of the incongruity of depicting a peasant (*Fellah* in Arabic) as the deified Antinous wearing the Nemes (Humbert 1989: 50). Beauvallet was not alone in his misunderstanding, as the fine and decorative arts of the 19th century contain numerous examples of non-royal Egyptians with the Nemes.

In 1803 the government decided to commemorate the death of General Desaix (Jeffreys 2003) at the Place des Victoires, the same site that had been considered for the memorial temple to honour Desaix and Kléber. The monument incorporated a colossal (5.3 m) bronze statue of Desaix as an heroic nude, with a Nemes-coiffed Egyptian head at his feet (both by Claude Dejoux), set against an original Egyptian rose granite obelisk (Figure 10:2).[4] The 6 m marble Egyptianizing pedestal was by Lepère. Scandalized public reaction to the nudity of Desaix ensued after the inauguration of the monument in 1810. The monument was demolished in 1814, and was replaced by a statue of Louis XIV. The statue of Desaix was recycled, and in 1815 the obelisk was returned to the Albani estate, from which it was sold on to Munich (Humbert 1998a: 80–82; Humbert *et al.* 1994: 213–215).

With the encouragement of Denon, numerous designs for obelisks to embellish the Pont Neuf were received during the Empire period. Louis XVIII cancelled the obelisk project, and in 1818 an equestrian statue of Henri IV was re-erected at the foot of the bridge (Wagner 1997: 296).

Specific individuals from mythology and history, notably the goddess Isis, were important to the Egyptian imagery associated with Napoleon and France.[5] The significance of a cult of Isis in Paris during Romano-Celtic times was not lost on Napoleon, as Imperial Rome and the French Empire both 'owned' Egypt. 'Evidence'

Figure 10:2
Monument to
General Desaix in the
Place des Victoires.
Anonymous print,
1810.

for an early association of Paris with Isis through the Roman Empire in France made Napoleon's achievements in Egypt seem all the more noble and legitimate. Indeed, in recognition of the 'Isiaic origins' of Paris the city seal of 1811 depicts her seated on the prow of the *Nautes* guild boat, the symbol of Paris (Humbert 1998a: 106; Humbert *et al*. 1994: 255). Moreover, Isis is a witness to the inscription of the name of Napoleon on the tablet of history (Humbert 1998a: 96–98), as represented on the façade of the Cour Carrée. Isis in Egyptian regalia, with sistrum and cat, has pride of place next to Moses the lawgiver, thus relating Egypt to biblical history as well as to classical civilizations.

In the private sector, residential architecture of the wealthy was occasionally inspired by Egypt, without ever becoming a widespread theme. The general attitude amongst architects and designers about use of the Egyptian style was almost the same in France as in Great Britain: "Never ... adopt, except for motives more weighty than a mere aim at novelty, the Egyptian style of ornament" (Loudon, quoted in Lewis and Darley 1986: 119). The mansion acquired by Josephine's son Eugène de Beauharnais in 1803, now housing the German Ambassador's Residence, provides a spectacular example of the Egyptian style. The new owner commissioned an Egyptianizing addition to the 18th century façade.[6] A pylon-form portico, supported by two tapered outer piers and two inner palmiform-capital columns, terminates in a gorge cornice decorated in traditional Egyptian fashion with the winged sundisk. The piers are decorated with a relief of the goddess Mut, an unusual motif within the Egyptianizing repertoire. The niche cut into each pier, which admits light to the stairway, is said to have originally held statues of Antinous, which are now on display at the Marmottan Museum (Humbert 1989: 51). Simultaneous remodelling of the interior of the hotel included the Salon des Saisons and a Turkish boudoir (Wischermann 1997: 97). Interior decoration of the Salon des Saisons realized a Greco-Roman theme (Martin 1945: pls. VII, IX, 44) that incorporated the Napoleonic eagle as a dominant feature of the ceiling and the frieze.

Ornamental Egyptianate elements and motifs were more common in residential architecture of the Empire period than were major structures in the Egyptian style. In 1807, Josephine's residence at Malmaison was adorned with two French-designed obelisks of the 17th century, salvaged from the recently demolished château of Cardinal Richelieu at Poitou. The obelisks were installed on a bridge over the moat, overlooking the gardens (Chevallier 2001: 13). Apart from the reused obelisks, Egyptian influence at Malmaison was minor, and limited to furniture mounts and 'fire dogs'.

Long before Napoleon, the sphinx (normally female, deriving from the ancient Greek sphinx) had symbolized protection, and could be found as 'guardians' at the entrances to buildings (Humbert 1989: 258; 1996b: figs. 3, 4, 7). After the Egyptian Campaign, the sphinx as architectural ornament acquired masculine gender and became more Egyptian in appearance and pose (Humbert 1996a: figs. 15, 20 for those at the entrance to Hôtel Mailly at 1 rue de Beaune and at the entrance to a garden pavilion in the Marmottan Museum Park). Both these sets of sphinxes date to approximately 1800 (Humbert 1998a: 46).

Funerary architecture provides a further area in which the influence of Egypt is clearly apparent. Egypt had been associated with death and eternal life since the Roman period (Humbert 1989: 302). The pyramid, Osiris, Osiris-Canopus, the anthropoid coffin and the mummy could all be used to represent death and eternal life. Use of these Egyptianizing motifs expanded as a consequence of major reforms introduced by Napoleon which were to radically change Parisian funerary practices.[7] Nonetheless, Egyptian influence did not feature alongside more traditional memorials until after the deaths of those involved in the Egyptian Campaign (see below). By contrast, the obelisks carved into the walls of the catacombs are of a somewhat earlier date. Quarries which had served as the main source of construction stone since before the Middle Ages were converted into catacombs for burial in 1786. They immediately received the disinterred remains from the 'Cemetery of the Innocents' (Culbertson and Randall 2000: 165). Between 1810 and 1811, the catacombs received further skeletal remains from other intramural cemeteries. Nicholas Frochot, who had worked for Napoleon on many of the burial reforms, decided that the remains should be presented decoratively (Willms 1997: 116). This task was delegated to the quarry masons, many of whom were also Freemasons. It is possible that the numerous pairs of obelisks carved and painted on many of the support piers were part of the new decorative scheme. Obelisks greatly outnumbered carved and painted crosses.

The spectre of Napoleon from the Bourbon Restoration through the Second Empire (1815 to 1870)

The Restoration period during the reign of Louis-Philippe saw the unveiling of several monuments which honoured Napoleon (Tudesq 1965: 16), with reference to Egypt. The Arc de Triomphe de l'Etoile, which was started in 1806, was completed by Louis-Philippe (unveiled 1836) with an altered sculptural programme that was intended to assure harmony and reconciliation of the different streams of French politics (Rosenblum and Janson 1984: 207–208). Most surprising was the juxtaposition of a sculpture popularly known as 'La Marseillaise' (F. Rude) and 'The Apotheosis of Napoleon' (J-P. Cortot). Ancient Egypt figured in the frieze of the arch in the decoration that dealt with the triumphal procession of the armies. A sphinx resting upon an obelisk in an ox-drawn cart are trophies from the Italian Campaign – perhaps a reference to the Albani obelisk which featured in the monument to Desaix (Humbert 1998a: 172).

The installation and dedication in 1836 of the Luxor obelisk officially launched the cult of Napoleon (Humbert 1989: 304; Humbert 1998a: 117). It was installed at the Place de la Concorde, a hallowed revolutionary location. This rose-granite obelisk, originally erected in the third year of the reign of Ramesses II (ca. 1276–1275 BC), surmounts a modern pedestal which bears gilt reliefs detailing the engineering of the dismantling of the obelisk in Luxor and its re-erection in Paris. In a Latin inscription on the west face of the pedestal, Louis-Philippe acknowledges the obelisk as a gift from Egypt while under Ottoman rule (see Hassan 2003a), and dedicates the monument to the memory of the Nile Campaign (Humbert 1998a: 158–161).

As imposing as it is independent of any adornment, the obelisk and its immediate landscape became a magnet for ephemeral Egyptianizing decoration which intensified the association between Egypt and Napoleon. In 1848, on the occasion of ceremonies to mark the adoption of the Constitution, four Egyptianate columns designed by Charpentier were erected on the Concorde bridge. For the celebration of the second anniversary of the Republic in 1850, the Concorde bridge was decorated with pyramids and the obelisk was enriched with a pedestal façade bearing four sphinxes *couchant* and four seated, Nemes-coiffed caryatids. The obelisk was adorned in Egyptianizing fashion for the same anniversary holidays in 1852 and 1866. For the latter celebration, an Egyptian palace mock-up with Hathor-headed columns surmounted by several imperial eagles and the monogram of Napoleon surrounded the obelisk (Humbert 1998a: 116–123).

The Luxor obelisk provided a complex set of messages. It simultaneously enriched and empowered France by the physical possession of Egypt's past, and it signified the rescue of that past from oblivion by Napoleon and indirectly by Champollion. A contemporary Parisian notice advertising the spectacle of the erection of the monument erroneously ascribed the obelisk to Tuthmosis III – "the Napoleon of Ancient Egypt" – in a clever association between Napoleon and a pharaoh famed for his military conquests and empire building (Vercoutter 1992: 144). The role of France in safeguarding antiquities for 'world heritage' was another message. Champollion, Curator of the Louvre's Egyptian collection, had negotiated the acquisition of the obelisk. In his view, "A single column from Karnak is more of a monument in itself than the four façades of the Cour Carée" (Solé 1997: 87).

If France had not lost the Rosetta Stone to England (see Jeffreys 2003), that too would have underscored France's role in rescuing Ancient Egypt from oblivion. Notwithstanding the absence of the stone, every hieroglyphic interpretation undertaken after 1822 – whether accurate or fantasy – was a reminder that Champollion of France had 'won the race' to understand the language of Ancient Egypt. Bartholdi's 1875 statue of Champollion with his foot on a fragmentary pharaonic head (Figure 10:3) publicly declared French primacy in the discovery and interpretation of Egypt's past (Humbert 1998a: 174, 176–177). A pensive Champollion regards the shattered Egyptian head, but his posture has overtones of a *conquistador*.

Figure 10:3 Statue of Champollion, by Frédéric-Auguste Bartholdi, 1875, in the entrance court of the Collège de France (© Tony Bryan).

The sculpture is located in the courtyard of the Collège de France, thus commemorating the scholarly achievement of Champollion in an educational setting.

An original Egyptian obelisk and the significance of hieroglyphics decoded by Champollion were hard acts to follow. However, the sphinx (as an element in public monuments and architectural ornament) continues as an exotic, yet familiar, symbol of Ancient Egypt. Those brought to Paris as military trophies from the Siege of Sebastopol by General Pélissier (1855) maintained the traditional role of guardians outside the Tuileries Palace (Humbert 1998a: 46). At the same time, they also reminded the public of French victory in the Crimea and they associated the reigns of the two Napoleons.

The Fontaine de la Victoire was originally constructed in 1807 by J. M. N. Bralle and located in the Place du Châtelet. It featured a subtly Egyptian palmette column inscribed with Napoleonic battles (Humbert *et al.* 1994: 271–272). In 1858 it was rendered more dramatically Egyptianizing when it was enhanced by Alfred Jacquemart with four sphinxes as fountain spouts (Figure 10:4) (Curl 1994: 144; Humbert 1998a: 50). The more obviously Egyptian fountain reinforced the association of Napoleon III with Napoleon I. In addition, the new sphinxes as bearers of water allude to a heritage in European *grotesque* ornament inspired by Roman art.[8]

There is another example of the sphinx as *grotesque* at the entrance to 64 boulevard de Strasbourg. Whereas all other decoration embellishing this building is in the classical style, the siren-tailed, female winged sphinxes reveal an eclectic mix of

Figure 10:4   Two views of one of the sphinxes added to the Fontaine de la Victoire (1807) by Alfred Jacquemart in 1858, Place du Châtelet (© Tony Bryan).

ancient Egyptian and Classical art. They wear the Nemes headdress usually seen on the male sphinxes of the period. Despite their transformed appearances, the sphinxes still act as guardians of the building, as indicated by their position over the door.

Like his uncle Napoleon, Napoleon III enhanced and enlarged the Louvre. The Louvre of the Second Empire was inaugurated in 1857 after five years of work, but the completion of sculptures that were commissioned to decorate the Cour Carrée and the rue de Rivoli took considerably longer to achieve (Pingeot 1989: 112). The French Hall of Fame decorating the façade of the Louvre on the rue du Rivoli includes Desaix by Honoré Aristide Husson (1856). In military uniform, Desaix appears with an Egyptian bust with Nemes headdress that acknowledges his involvement in the Egyptian Campaign. (Ironically, the figure of Kléber in the adjacent niche has no allusion to Egypt.)

Two sculptures in the new decorative programme of the Cour Carrée featured Egyptian personalities. Cleopatra (commissioned by F. Fannière in 1865, and completed by F. Faivre in 1902 – Humbert 1989: 275) appears as one of the seductresses of Antiquity and the Bible, keeping company with Bathsheba and Helen of Troy (Pingeot 1989: 114). As Antinous was the model Egyptian male, so was Cleopatra the model female. During the 19th century it was Cleopatra's vampish aspect as 'prostitute queen' which was most often depicted in the arts, and the Cour Carrée sculpture is a rare appearance of Cleopatra in architecture.

H. Daillion's sculpture 'Archaeology' (1891) introduces Akhenaten, often acknowledged as the world's first monotheist (Figure 10:5). Akhenaten was modelled upon a statue from the Amarna period, which was purchased for the Louvre in 1826.[9] Given what was known and published at the time about Amarna art and the religion of its monarch (Montserrat 2000: 55–71), this work is seen to revere Akhenaten as 'the best' of Ancient Egypt. To be held in the arms of Archaeology suggested that it was the new science which had revealed Akhenaten to the world. Archaeology personified as a classical Greek suggested the passing on of the legacy from Egypt to Greece and, simultaneously, the superior civilization of Greece.

The winning subject of the 'Grand Prix de l'Empereur' for architecture in 1869[10] is subtly Egyptianate (Figure 10:6). The principal symbolism of Joseph-Louis Duc's 1868 façade of the Palais de Justice relates to law and justice. While the architectural influence is predominantly classical, seen in the columns (or pillars of justice), capitals and decorative sculpture (of fairness and force),[11] the geometry, volume and effect are reminiscent of the *pronaos* of an Egyptian temple (Humbert 1998a: 168). The screen of the façade that bears the sculpture, between the columns, is like the screen wall that closes off the lower front of the Ptolemaic *pronaos*. Because of their transparency, the tall glass windows of the Palais de Justice give the impression of open space between the columns, as in an Egyptian temple. The three entrance doors are gently pylon-shaped, and the windows feature Egyptianizing columnettes. The most overt references to Egypt are the pair of lions flanking the central grand stairway, symbolizing force (Van Zanten 1987: 214). Duc's lions are modelled after the lions of Nectanebo I, which were discovered by Mariette at the Serapeum in 1851 and are now on display in the Louvre (Humbert *et al.* 1994: 345–346). Napoleon and the French Empire are symbolized by the two imperial eagles on the roof. The building thus

Figure 10:5 'Archaeology',
by Horace Daillion, 1891,
with detail of Akhenaten.
Cour Carrée of the Louvre
(© Tony Bryan).

associates Ancient Egypt with law and justice, and points to Napoleon as the rationalizer and consolidator of the French *code civil*.

The Egyptian building at the Place du Caire (1828) is the best example of Egyptianizing domestic architecture of the period after Napoleon (Humbert 1998a: 147–150). Adherence to the ancient Egyptian forms are seen in the Hathor heads (Price and Humbert Chapter 1: Figure 1:4, this volume) and in the columns. The relief frieze is evocative of Ancient Egypt, but the hieroglyphs on the cornice are pure fantasy. This re-created exoticism of Egypt was an apparent marketing device for the ground level boutiques and café. The immediate neighbourhood of the Egyptian building recognizes the Egyptian Campaign in many of the street names, e.g. Damietta, Aboukir. The street names Place du Caire and Passage du Caire were established in 1798, and an 'Egyptian café' opened in the Passage du Caire in 1805 (Humbert 1998a: 147). This has caused some scholars of the Egyptian Revival to conjecture whether an earlier Egyptianizing structure may have predated the building of 1828.

Less permanent examples of Egyptian motifs in architecture were represented at the Universal Exhibitions of 1867, 1899 and 1900. The Egyptian pavilions of 1867

Figure 10:6   Façade of the Palais de Justice, by Joseph-Louis Duc, 1868, rue de Harley (© Tony Bryan).

provided a mini parade of the Suez Canal, the Viceroy's Palace, and Auguste Mariette's Egyptian Temple (also see Medina-González 2003; Werner Chapter 5, this volume). The latter was modelled upon the Temple of Dendera, and featured an avenue of sphinxes fronted by a pylon entrance (Delamaire Chapter 7: Figure 7:4, this volume). Exoticism, the allure of armchair travel as a choice for enjoyment of leisure time, education and the close ties between France and Egypt are the possible intended messages. The Universal Exhibitions attracted people from all socioeconomic levels and, in 1900, one of the star attractions was the opportunity to see the new moving pictures (Abel 1994: 1). The association of Egypt with exoticism and entertainment was further reflected in the interior decoration of some theatres.

From the 1820s onwards, the greatest surge of Egyptianizing was to be found in the funerary architecture of Paris. Père Lachaise cemetery showcases the tombs of several scholars from the Egyptian Campaign. The memorials to the mathematicians Gaspard Monge (1820) and Joseph Fourier (1830) adjoin Champollion's monument of an unadorned obelisk (1832) in a prime location off the *rond-point*. Both show a pylon-shaped naos with a gorge cornice decorated by the winged sundisk. Fourier's tomb features an Egyptianizing relief of lotus and papyrus on the sides of the pedestal, but the front face of the pedestal bears a 19th century symbol of death, the downturned torch. The intention to be identified with the accomplishments of the Egyptian Campaign is obvious in the tombs of the two scholars; however the classical portrait busts within their monuments acknowledge the importance of Imperial Rome in the arts and architecture of the Empire period. Close by, but in not as prestigious a location, is a simple obelisk (1830) bearing a relief cross and a list of the battles in which Jean-Simeon Domon, one of Napoleon's generals, had participated.

The obelisk memorial was a natural choice for Champollion: Egyptologist, translator of hieroglyphs, and negotiator of the Luxor obelisk acquisition for Paris. The selection of an obelisk for others without such a strong connection to Ancient Egypt, however, may also be related to the number of obelisks to be found in Rome, the seat of Catholicism. Adoption of the obelisk as a suitable Christian memorial thus had a venerable history in Europe. The obelisk as a funerary memorial for the tombs of the wealthy had precedents in 17th century France, such as the heart monument for Duke Henry I de Longeville (designed by F. Anguier, 1604–1669), now at the Louvre. Two sides of the obelisk show attributes of the arts, whereas the other two bear military trophies. The pedestal has two brass reliefs of battles in which the deceased participated. The obelisk memorial to General Turenne (Le Brun, Tuby and Marsy, 1684) now at the Hôtel des Invalides, a necropolis for French military heroes (Gray-Durant and Robertson 1998: 124), undoubtedly contributed to the popularity of this form. Both monuments established a military association for the obelisk that was earlier than Napoleon and the Egyptian Campaign.

The memorial to Le Bas (1873), the engineer who erected the Luxor obelisk, depicts the obelisk's installation. It too is an obelisk, prominently located at the principal entrance. The adjacent Egyptianizing tomb of Louis Poinsot (1859), member of the Academy of Sciences of the Institut de France, is pylon-form, surmounted by a gorge cornice. A cameo-like portrait of the deceased appears in the centre of the winged sundisk. Close to these tombs is the showpiece monument of Père Lachaise, also Egyptianizing: the 'Monument aux Morts'.

The 'Monument aux Morts' by Paul Albert Bartholomé (1892–1895, installed 1899) dominates the summit of the avenue of the principal entrance. The monument is acknowledged to be a masterpiece of Symbolist sculpture comparable to Rodin's 'Gates of Hell' (Turner 1996: 231). Functionally, it provides the façade to an ossuary (Burollet 1998: 141). The architecture features a receding pylon with twin towers and a larger central pylon-form (Figure 10:7) that provides the backdrop for the sculpture. The sculpted figures represent the march of humanity to death, whilst the sculpture of the lower register represents resurrection (Turner 1996: 231), accompanied by a quotation from Isaiah. The two flanking pylons fit the ancient Egyptian pattern of a classical New Kingdom temple, but the dominant central mastaba tomb, although erroneously depicted as a pylon, alters the significance of its interpretation.

The writings of the sculptor acknowledge inspiration from the tomb of the Archduchess Maria Christina (Antonio Canova, 1798–1805), which employed a pyramid relief as the set design for the sculpture of a funerary procession (Burollet 1998: 138; Rosenblum and Janson 1984: 105–107). Bartholomé appreciated the strong association between Egyptian architecture and the concept of an afterlife, which he wanted to incorporate in the monument. However, he wanted an Egyptian structure that conveyed the same message as the pyramid, but which was more democratic and 'universal' than a pharaoh's tomb (Burollet 1998: 138). Hence the choice of the mastaba tomb. In 19th century Europe, the pyramid and the mastaba (employed by Egyptian nobles as well as early royalty) were understood to be 'rebirth' machines as well as tombs. Bartholomé's knowledge about ancient Egyptian architecture, however, was insufficient to let him differentiate between an element of the temple (pylon) and a mastaba tomb. The frequent use of the pylon-form associated with Egypt throughout

Figure 10:7 'Monument aux Morts' by Paul Albert Bartholomé (1892–1895, installed 1899), Père Lachaise Cemetery (© Tony Bryan).

the 19th century had prepared the public and artists to recognize it as unmistakably Egyptian and to establish it as having endurance, like the pyramid. Bartholomé succeeded in representing what could be recognized as an Egyptian tomb, but without the royal monopoly on resurrection conveyed by the pyramid. The monument may be argued to honour ancient Egyptian religion whilst linking through hope of resurrection to Christianity.

Egyptianizing memorials were also selected by people who had nothing to do with Egypt or the Egyptian Campaign. Presumably this was because of the long-standing symbolism that associated Egypt with eternal life, linked with the appeal of Egyptian architectural forms made more accessible by publications after the Egyptian Campaign, and reinforced by the Egyptian style in French public monuments and the arts. By far the most rare were the tombs that were purely Egyptian in inspiration. The Wallerstein Tomb (1851) is in the form of a classical Egyptian shrine or kiosk, complete with gorge cornice and winged sundisk. Located in the cluster of Egyptianizing tombs radiating from the *rond-point*, the tomb of the brothers Bis (1855) is another – a large pylon or mastaba surmounted by a gorge cornice. The tombs inspired by Egyptian architecture as the only source thus relied upon Egypt to represent the hope of resurrection. However, the Egyptian chapel and mastaba or pylon-form and their elements of decoration had become compatible with Christian imagery in the same manner as the obelisk.

Other tombs in the Egyptian style employed a mixed vocabulary of classical forms and Christian symbols. The Feuquières-Lecomte family tomb (1844) is pyramidal with classical and Christian elements. Set inside a portico with a winged sundisk appended to the pyramid, the door contains a cut-out papyrus design. The tomb's windows are cruciform, and it thus combines Egyptian design with Christian iconography. The pyramid chapel of the Collin-Gellé family likewise features a cross. Possibly the associated Christian and Egyptian symbols of resurrection were considered to be doubly 'potent' and complementary, which could explain the proliferation of tombs which were simultaneously Egyptian and Christian.

In 1806, the Montmartre cemetery in the north of Paris was made available for Parisian burials. The tomb of the Minodet family (1829) is a simple classical chapel, but it has a pair of Antinous carved into each side of the doorway. As has been established earlier, Antinous was popular across the arts and recognizable as Egyptian. The Minodet chapel thus presents Antinous, a personification of Egypt, as an unusual symbol for belief in the afterlife. The pyramidon vault of the Waldeck-Rousseau family (ca. 1900) is pierced by cruciform windows and thus provides a further example of Christian iconography in association with Egyptian forms.

Egyptianizing funerary architecture also features at Montparnasse cemetery (1824) in the south of Paris. De Charmoy's cenotaph of Baudelaire (d. 1867) exhibits a unique use of Egyptian imagery (Figure 10:8). The poet emerges from a column terminating in a fantastic capital – a bat with partially unfurled wings. Head on hands, the author of *Les Fleurs de Mal* contemplates the mummiform supine figure beneath the column. The symbolism related to Egypt conveys transcendence of Baudelaire's spirit from his physical remains. The Egyptian mummy instead of a more traditional skeleton as a *momento mori* is novel, but understandable in light of a trend in international fiction which presented the mummy as a supernatural being able to survive death. The bat is an image from Western symbolism that represents the night, perhaps in this case the long night of death, and it also conveys the connotation of evil. The cenotaph may thus be said to acknowledge Baudelaire's most famous poetry as well as his definitive French translation of the fiction of Edgar Allan Poe (Chauprade 1996: 214–232, 341), including *Some Words with a Mummy* (1857).

The other Egyptianizing tombs of Montparnasse cemetery are interesting in their simplicity and similarity, and indeed, they may have been mass-produced. The De Champagny de Cadore tomb provides a good example of the style: a vaguely pylon-form chapel with gorge cornice, complete with a stylized winged sundisk, terminating in a simplified classical pediment with *acroteria*. The reason for so many standardized Egyptianizing tombs may point to the residence in the neighbourhood of an artisan who specialized in the Egyptian style (Humbert 1998a: 167).

Egypt in Paris of the *Belle Epoque* through the early 20th century

With the end of the Second Empire, a Republican government and new trends in *fin de siècle* Paris, the Egyptian Revival took new directions. Increasingly, Egypt represented exoticism associated with tourism in the pursuit of leisure, often with a mass appeal and linked with the latest popular culture. An important change in the social structure of France – a *bourgeoisie* with higher purchasing power and increased leisure time – was a strong factor in the choice of Egyptianizing architecture and decoration. The appeal of Egypt also served as an effective marketing device to encourage consumerism (Rice and MacDonald 2003).

The site of a large theatre from the 1900 International Exhibition on the outskirts of Paris was acquired by Gaston Akoun for an American company in 1908 (Langlois 1998: 60). Akoun had much experience with public amusements. He assisted with aspects of the fabulous 'Trip to the Moon' attraction in the original Luna Park in Coney Island, New York, where he was manager of the 'Streets of Cairo' attraction (Stanton 1998). Luna Park, an American-style amusement park, opened in Paris in 1909, and was enormously popular (Langlois 1998: 60). It was a modern, urbane and

Figure 10:8
Cenotaph of
Baudelaire by
De Charmoy in
Montparnasse
cemetery (©
Tony Bryan).

sophisticated alternative to traditional French country fairs and cabaret
entertainment. Luna Park attracted all ages and social classes and encouraged
attendance by families.

The amusement park was the heir of the World Fairs in that it harnessed the
newest electrical technology to offer public entertainments (Nasaw 1993: 85). Vintage
photographs show rides full of action, thrills and chills as well as a number of more
static attractions invoking exotic locations. The latter were reminiscent of the national
pavilions at the International Exhibitions that had included Ancient Egypt, but with a
dramatic difference. The intention was not educational, nor was the rendering of
Egyptian architecture and iconography accurate. The architectural theory behind
amusement park design is best expressed in the words of Frederic Thompson, the
creator of Luna Park in New York. Thompson purportedly relegated his architectural
"books and plans onto the ash-heap and decided to start after something new ... I
stuck to no style ... One result is Luna Park which is utterly unlike anything else of its
kind ... An exposition is a form of festivity, and serious architecture should not enter
into it if it will interfere with the carnival spirit" (Nasaw 1993: 83).

The 'Crypte des Pharaons' at Luna Park, Paris (Figure 10:9) was a fantastic
mixture of Egyptianate motifs and elements, combined with Islamic architectural
features (Humbert 1998a: 142–143). A staircase emerged from the top of a pylon,
fronted by two obelisks inscribed with fantasy hieroglyphics. Six mini-sphinxes
couchant bordered the edges of the stairway and a colossal sphinx *couchant* presided at
the summit. We do not know the nature of the attraction nor what lay behind the
choice of images. However, extrapolating from Middle Eastern attractions in
American amusement parks and with the knowledge that Akoun managed the Cairo
attraction on Coney Island, we may conjecture with confidence. The 'Streets of Cairo'

Figure 10:9   The 'Crypte des Pharaons' at Luna Park, Paris, 1907 (private collection of
François-Xavier Bouchart).

genre of entertainment usually featured 'belly-dancers' (Nasaw 1993: 85). The crypt theme specified in the lurid name and the blatant proliferation of fantasy pharaonic images gives another hint to what the attraction offered, namely disorientation or fright, possibly associated with the pharaoh's mummy. The fiction of Poe, Gautier, Rider-Haggard and Stoker, involving mummies, reincarnation, a type of life after death, etc., provided a respectable pedigree for an Egyptian themed mock-scary fairground attraction. Furthermore, the scary amusements permitted girls to scream and the courageous males to protect and comfort, as was undoubtedly the case for early horror films.

Cinema was another entertainment made possible by new technology, and it surpassed amusement parks in popularity. By 1909, there were 100 cinemas in Paris, many of which were located in areas already dedicated to shopping or entertainment. The first luxury cinemas, called 'palaces', opened in 1911 and were owned by the Gaumont chain. The scale and architecture of the cinema palace has been compared with the 'Palace of Electricity' of the 1900 Universal Exhibition (Abel 1994: 7, 30–31, 54–55). The 'Louxor Palais du Cinéma' (Figure 10:10) by Ripey and Tibéri (1920–1921) exploited the presumed exotic aspect of Egypt, and in itself amplified the fantasy and change of scenery of the film industry. The sloping walls of the theatre were suggestive of a pylon-form and brightly coloured mosaics were used for all the two-dimensional decoration. The entrance was topped by a portico in which papyrus bud columns were interspersed with piers decorated with the lotus in bloom. The portico terminated in a gorge cornice bearing three winged sundisks. Lotus blossom columns demarcated the entrance to the cinema, complemented by alternating lotus-papyrus decoration. The Egyptian theme continued in the interior decoration of the cinema (Figure 10:11), so the exoticism of Egypt was not merely a device to entice people in.

The fluted frame surrounding the screen contained the vulture Nekhbet in flight, and a large winged sundisk was central in the frieze above. Each side of the frieze contained a procession of Egyptian figures, meeting at the sundisk. The walls surrounding the screen continued decoration in the Egyptian style, with a shrine decoration uncannily similar to the engravings of Prisse d'Avennes. Winged sundisks decorated the balcony lodge (Anon. 1922).

Exoticism and escapism are not the only reasons why Egypt in particular may have been associated with the architecture of entertainment, particularly cinemas. It certainly had nothing to do with the subject of the films, although some were set in Ancient Egypt (e.g. Lupton 2003; Serafy 2003). To understand, we must look to 19th century orientalist paintings of *odalisques*, literature, and popular entertainment which included the stripping of glamorous female mummies. In art, Ancient Egypt represented the 'Dolce Vita' and the beauty of love (Humbert 1989: 302). Use of the exotic Egyptian scene as the respectable filter of antiquity gave the pretext for showing nude women within the intimacy of the harem (Thornton 1994: 122). Ingres' *odalisques* are the ultimate representations of 'woman' as 'object' on view for the delectation of men, and paintings such as 'Ramsès dans son harem' (Jules Jean A. Lecomte du Noüy 1885) as well as numerous Cleopatra canvases[12] of the period are part of the genre. The depictions of scantily clad females in paintings set in Egyptian antiquity were clearly intended for a predominantly male audience, who were absolved of voyeurism by the reference to events taking place in the distant past.

Figure 10:10   Louxor
Cinema Palace by Ripey
& Tibéri, 1920–1921, at rue
Magenta, as it appeared
soon after its opening.

The Egyptian ambience that was more exotic and romantic than the real world
was also luxurious. An excerpt from an American analysis of the popularity of the
cinema palace, in general (Lloyd 1929), could have been written about the Louxor:

> All of this splendour has been planned for her [the customer's] delight, and with a
> luxuriance that she had imagined was enjoyed only in Cleopatra's court, oriental
> harems ... She strolls voluptuously through lobbies and foyers ... her feet sink in soft
> rugs, she is surrounded by heavy Renaissance tables, oil paintings, and statues of
> nudes ... When she takes her seat, she is further flattered by the same colourful
> magnificence on the stage as in the lobby ... The royal favour of democracy it is: for in
> the 'deluxe house' every man is a king and every woman a queen.
>
> (Lloyd, quoted in Nasaw 1993: 239)

Although the 'Louxor Palais du Cinéma' was completed before the discovery of
Tutankhamun's tomb in 1922, it was well placed to profit from the discovery and from
the subsequent enhanced fascination with Ancient Egypt. Both Paris and the world as
a whole were to experience a new wave of Egyptian Revival, accompanied by the Art
Déco movement in art and architecture.

Figure 10:11   Interior of Louxor Cinema Palace, ca. 1921.

Conclusions

The Empire style of architecture, as created by Percier and Fontaine, contained many references to antiquity within a framework that may be described as neoclassical. Egyptian forms and motifs joined the repertoire of antiquity, but there was a desultory use of the Egyptian style, and the classical influence continued to predominate. Starting in early 19th century Paris, the traditional images and symbols of Ancient Egypt were enhanced and enlarged as a consequence of the publications deriving from the Egyptian Campaign and the establishment of an Egyptian collection in the Louvre. For the first time, the source of Egyptian iconography was acknowledged, instead of being confused with Imperial Roman Egyptianizing as seen in the monuments of Rome.

This resurgence of the 'Egyptian Revival' – one that included new associations with Napoleon and his mythology – was a particularly French phenomenon. The Egyptianizing motifs that were to be seen in publicly commissioned works were inseparably linked with Imperial Rome, as part of Napoleon's long chain of legitimization. Augmenting Napoleon's deliberate identification with Ancient Egypt, his successors consolidated the trend. As has been seen, the re-erection of the Luxor obelisk by Louis-Philippe officially launched the cult or myth of Napoleon. By the dedication of the obelisk to Napoleon and the Egyptian Campaign, some of that glory was reflected upon the king, in addition to an association with the Revolution. A myth of Napoleon that incorporated Egypt was particularly beneficial to Napoleon III, the eventual inheritor of Napoleon's 'dynasty'.

MacKenzie (1995: 51) doubts whether, in Britain, there was any direct link between imperialist colonization and the popularity of oriental themes in the visual arts. He is still less convinced that collectors sought objects that symbolized imperial domination and the moral ascendancy of the West. However, in France the chief patron of the arts was the government itself. Even the Academy of Arts and the Louvre were effectively arms of the government. Throughout Napoleon's reign, the Bourbon restoration and the Second Empire, Egyptianizing monuments, architecture and art that were commissioned by the government carried direct and subtle state publicity. From the evidence presented, it becomes clear why reference to Egypt was such a natural and potent vehicle for Napoleonic propaganda, despite the military failure of the Egyptian Campaign.

As a military man, Bonaparte's main objective in invading Egypt was conquest and colonization. At that time, the intellectual aspect was secondary. After the military failure, the spirit of the age allowed the objectives to be reversed. The commissioning of public monuments that highlighted Egypt promoted the success of the intellectual achievements of the Egyptian Campaign, and thus introduced a 'spin' which down-played the military loss. Perhaps Bonaparte and his advisors on publicity felt that there was no option but to "accentuate the positive, eliminate the negative" (Bing Crosby) if his military reputation and political career were going to be salvaged. Once the idea of an intellectual victory was established in the public's mind, this would be easy to continue and even build on. Recognition of the intellectual victory was to make people more aware of the meaning of some of the Egyptian symbols and motifs, as a result of which they began to be used as grave markings (often in association with Christian symbolism) in the new cemeteries that were being established around Paris. These were particularly in evidence on the graves of military men and the *savants* who had taken part in the Egyptian Campaign, who otherwise might have preferred not to be associated with its doubtful military outcome.

Several facts and observations serve to support the theory. Bonaparte had included *savants* in his first Italian Campaign, but felt no need either to publish an imperial report or to invent new Roman symbolism. As may be seen in popular engravings in the Parisian press from the time when Bonaparte made his clandestine departure from Egypt, the ground was already being prepared for his 'apotheosis'. Instead of an ignominious return, after what could be viewed as his first military failure, Bonaparte was received as a hero. The first Egyptianizing monuments were commissioned by the Directory Government immediately after the Nile Campaign. Denon's report on Lower and Upper Egypt in 1802 was in the vanguard of publications resulting from the Campaign, thus establishing him and his engravings as associated with the success of the Egyptian interlude. Politically, it also associated the accomplishments in Egypt with Bonaparte in a flattering fashion. Pleased with the 'publicity', Bonaparte rewarded Denon with the appointment as Director of the Arts (Humbert *et al.* 1994: 204). From about this time, the military aspects of the campaign could be forgotten altogether and the intellectual achievements became the principal outcome. This was very much in the spirit of the times, which accounted for the *savants* being sent to Egypt in the first place.

Analysis of the forms and motifs employed to build up the Egyptianizing repertoire shows a selective, limited set which allowed for quick absorption into the public subconscious, in the fashion of modern advertising's 'brand recognition'. The pyramid, the sphinx and the obelisk were all forms already known and used in France, with the obelisk as a particularly suitable emblem for French military glory, since the 17th century. The newest forms and images to emerge which evoked Egypt have been shown to emphasize temple architecture, the mastaba, the historically accurate sphinx, figures inspired by Antinous, a bust wearing a Nemes headdress and the vulture-headdressed Egyptian queen, often Cleopatra.

A commentary upon the rapid and successful establishment of the Egyptian icons that were then related to Napoleon may be seen in a political cartoon of the Empire period, 'The Apotheosis of Napoleon' (Figure 10:12). In a celestial setting in the presence of military heroes from across the ages, Napoleon is invited to enter the Temple of Glory[13] by an ancient Egyptian. The temple bears many of the Egyptianizing elements – it is pylon-form with winged sundisk, enhanced by Hathor columns and sphinxes *couchant*. In case of any doubt, the pyramids of Giza appear in the background.

Figure 10:12   Engraving by J-B. Thiebault after a drawing by D. Georgin of 'The Apotheosis of Napoleon' (Image d'Épinal).

There is no evidence that Napoleon himself was an Egyptophile before or after the Nile Campaign. His personal use of Egyptian motifs at Malmaison and references to Egypt in the new decorative programme of the Louvre were all minimal, as compared with constant references to Imperial Rome. The choice of an Egyptian portico by Prince Eugène de Beauharnais to enhance his new Paris residence was a dramatic gesture which may be said to show solidarity with his step-father and the public Egyptianizing of the Empire period. But Beauharnais did not choose an Egyptian themed interior decoration. Denon, 'the eye of Napoleon', also had much to gain personally from presenting Egyptian motifs in favourable association with Napoleon. Denon's project, the competition to design the best obelisk for placement on the Pont Neuf, is revealing as an example of just how far the Egyptianizing linked to the glorious Nile Campaign could have proceeded.

It is equally interesting to look at what was included in the publications of the Egyptian Campaign, but omitted in the 'Egyptian Revival' of the Empire period. For the most part, the Egyptian images both subtle and dramatic, such as the variety of pharaonic crowns and the profusion of animal-headed gods, were not widely used in the arts and architecture of the Empire or even the Second Empire period. One senses a deliberate restraint, introduced so as not to dilute the potency of the Egyptian association of the preferred set of elements.

The other consideration in the use of Egyptian themes and motifs in 19th century France concerns popular taste. Propaganda aside, the French public admired the strong geometry of Egyptian architectural forms combined with an exotic appeal. The traditional French use of the sphinx as a guardian of the home continued, and could be seen in the residential architecture of the middle class as well as the wealthy. Funerary architecture in Parisian cemeteries provides the strongest evidence of a public acceptance of ancient Egyptian forms and motifs to symbolize the hope for eternal life. With the turn of the century, French use of Egyptian themes and motifs was influenced by international trends in literature and the architecture of public entertainment, especially from America. Moreover, 70 years had passed since the decipherment of hieroglyphics, resulting in the translation of Egyptian texts and inscriptions, which then led to a fuller understanding of ancient Egyptian culture. Where the commission warranted it, architects and designers who chose to use the Egyptian style could be more confident about their choices and the original meanings behind them. But where a more frivolous product was required, designers also had the flexibility to fall back upon stock Egyptian architecture and iconography to effect a blurry mixture of fantasy, orientalism and ancient Egyptian 'mythologizing'.

Notes

1   Enhancements to the Louvre during the Empire included the revival of the master plan of the Bourbon kings – linking the Louvre with the Tuileries Palace. Artists and others who were living within the environs of the Louvre were evicted, and their dwellings were demolished. A Roman-style triumphal arch honouring Napoleon and the army, designed by Percier and Fontaine and carved by the best sculptors of the day, was erected within the Carrousel. The arch served as the entrance to the Tuileries (D'Archimbaud 1997: 22–23, 49). The decorative programme of the Cour Carrée was updated, relocating some of the original sculpture of Jean Goujon to less central locations of the Louvre (Bresc-Bautier 1989: 103–104). Percier and Fontaine designed and commenced construction of the Pavilion de Rohan, which was completed during the Restoration period (D'Archimbaud

1997: 22–23, 49). Under the directorship of Denon, the Louvre's collections grew to become a major centre of the arts, often enriched by spoils from the Napoleonic campaigns.

2   This had been planned for the Place des Victoires but was not realized then; Chalgrin, designer of the Senate, erected a model of the temple at the Place des Victoires in 1800 (Humbert 1998a: 76–77).

3   The Fontaine du Fellah was made by François-Jean Bralle and Pierre Nicolas Beauvallet (sculptor) in 1809. The present statue of Antinous at the fountain is a copy by Gechter (1844). Several statues of Antinous wearing the royal Egyptian kilt and Nemes headdress were installed at Hadrian's Villa (Humbert et al. 1994: 46–48, 268–271). One of the original statues was in the Louvre as a war trophy of the Italian Campaign (Humbert 1989: 50).

4   The obelisk had been taken to Rome in antiquity, and was re-discovered in the 17th century. In 1770 it was acquired by Cardinal Alessandro Albani. It was inscribed with accurate hieroglyphic writing, including a dedication to an Emperor – possibly Claudius – and also to an individual named Titus Sextius Africanus (Humbert 1998a: 80).

5   During the Revolutionary period, the Fontaine de la Régénération, which mixed ideology of the French cult of Nature with that of Isis, was erected at the site of the former Bastille. This was an ephemeral decoration to celebrate the first anniversary of the Republic (Humbert et al. 1994: 158–160). A century later, the Art Nouveau sculpture by Lacombe (1895), on view at the Musée d'Orsay, repeated the image of Isis as the incarnation of Nature and the source of life.

6   Built by Boffrand in 1714 at 78 rue de Lille. Nicolas Bataille added to the façade, ca. 1807 (Humbert 1998a: 98–99). By the time of the remodelling of the hotel, Prince Eugène de Beauharnais was Viceroy of Italy (1805) and had been officially adopted by Napoleon (1806) (Hubert 1969: 118).

7   The Revolution and the Reign of Terror had disrupted previous burial rites in churchyards. The corpses resulting from mass execution and disease had been disposed of in shallow mass graves, without Christian burial rites. This contributed to problems of public sanitation and disease, as well as a lack of security or hope for a Christian afterlife (Willms 1997: 113). Napoleonic funerary reforms included the introduction of burial regulations, the closure of intramural cemeteries, the creation of new cemeteries outside the city limits, and the introduction of 'perpetual' concessions for burial plots (Willms 1997: 115–116).

8   The discovery of Nero's Golden House had revealed Roman painting to Europe. The location of the palace in 1488, far beneath street level, had given rise to a belief that the Emperor enjoyed subterranean residence in a grotto. The motifs and creatures featured in the palace's decorative scheme were named *grotesque*, implying 'from the watery world of the grotto'. Raphael was the first to design an entirely *grotesque* interior decoration for the Vatican Logge (1516) which featured sphinxes (Fleming and Honour 1989: 370–371). Whether conscious or not, Jacquemart's use of the sphinx as fountain spout was the legacy of Renaissance revitalization of the Egyptian motif via ancient Rome.

9   N. 831, a seated royal statue without cartouche, was purchased from Henry Salt (and see Werner Chapter 5, this volume) by Champollion as part of a lot of 4,000 objects. At the time of its acquisition, it was thought to represent Smenkhare, but during the reign of Napoleon III it was identified as Akhenaten (Humbert et al. 1994: 376–378).

10 Other competitors for the 1869 prize were Garnier for the Opéra and Labrouste for the Bibliothèque Nationale (Van Zanten 1987: 219).

11 Van Zanten (1987: 214, 304 n. 82) incorporates primary sources describing the decoration and symbolism of earlier parts of the Palais de Justice which are in harmony with Duc's façade.

12 Paintings that exemplify Cleopatra as vamp within a harem-like setting include 'La Mort de Cléopâtre', by Jean-André Rixens, 1874 and 'Cléopâtre essayant des poisons sur les condamnés à mort', by Alexandre Cabanel, 1887 (probably inspired by Gautier's 1834 story, *Une Nuit de Cléopâtre*).

13 The name of the temple is undoubtedly meant to refer to the real-world Parisian 'Temple of Glory' completed during the Empire period, the Madeleine (Vignon).

Acknowledgments

Many thanks to Kate Mueller-Wille for her valuable comments on earlier versions of this chapter. My greatest thanks go to my husband, Tony, for his encouragement and interest, and for his original photography in many far-flung *arrondissements* of Paris.

CHAPTER 11

REBUILDING THE SANCTUARIES OF MEMPHIS: EGYPT IN MASONIC ICONOGRAPHY AND ARCHITECTURE

John Hamill and Pierre Mollier

Freemasonry is the world's oldest secular fraternal society. It teaches moral lessons and self-knowledge through participation in a series of ceremonies which are learnt by heart and performed within each lodge. There are many theories as to the origins of Freemasonry, the general consensus amongst Masonic historians today being that it developed either directly or indirectly from the organizations of the stonemasons who built the great cathedrals and castles of the Middle Ages. The earliest evidence for Freemasonry comes in the late 16th and early 17th centuries, a period of great religious and political turmoil in Great Britain, when differences of opinion split families and eventually led to civil war. It is believed that those who formed and developed Freemasonry were seeking a means of bridging or removing those differences to enable men of differing views to come together in harmony to see what they had in common and how they could build on that commonality for the good of society as a whole. It is for that reason that the discussion of politics and religion has always been barred at Masonic meetings. Allied to the idea of building a better society is the ideal of the individuals building within themselves a spiritual temple. With building as a central theme the originators looked to the world of the stonemason, which in addition to providing the basic unit – the lodge – provided a wealth of tools to be used as symbols on which to hang moral precepts. For example, the mason's square teaches morality, the level equality and the plumb rule, justness and uprightness of life and actions.

The oldest Masonic documents – collectively known as the 'Manuscript Old Charges' – provide the first link between Freemasonry and Egypt. Some 130 versions of this manuscript have survived. The earliest, the 'Regius Poem', dates from ca. 1390 and the later versions are 18th century antiquarian copies of versions which appear not to have survived. The versions have a common form: a 'history' of the masons' trade followed by a series of 'charges' or rules to be followed by the mason. The history traced the development of building in stone from Adam through biblical and later periods up to its reintroduction into England by St Alban and the holding of a great assembly at York during the reign of Athelstan. According to this history, when Abraham went into Egypt he taught the Egyptians the seven liberal arts and sciences and had with him Euclid, who taught the Egyptians "... the science of Geometry in practic, for to work in stones all manner of worthy works that belonged to building of temples and churches, castles, manors, towers, and all other manner of buildings". In addition, Euclid gave the Egyptian masons a series of 'charges' or rules of conduct to cover their personal, professional and public lives. Thus, according to the anonymous author of the 'Manuscript Old Charges', was Masonry re-established on a firm basis and then exported throughout the known world.

In this way the precursors of Freemasonry unwittingly gave rise to the later theory that Freemasonry had its origins in Ancient Egypt (Haycock 2003: 148). That idea was echoed in England in the early 19th century. In 1813 the two Grand Lodges in England came together to form the present 'United Grand Lodge of England', the governing body of Freemasonry in England and Wales. That event was an opportunity to bring about a certain amount of standardization in English Freemasonry, including ritual matters. Ritual had been passed on by word of mouth and was not permitted to be written down or printed. As a result, regional variations had grown up in addition to differences between practices under the two former Grand Lodges. In 1814 a 'Lodge of Reconciliation' was set up to reconcile the two former systems and to establish a standard ritual. In each of the three ceremonies there is a 'Tracing Board': a pictorial symbolic representation of the lesson of the particular ceremony. The 'Lodge of Reconciliation' produced a 'Lecture' to explain each of the three Tracing Boards. That for the Tracing Board in the first ceremony ('Entered Apprentice') begins: "The usages and customs among Freemasons have ever borne a near affinity to those of the ancient Egyptians. Their philosophers, unwilling to expose their mysteries to vulgar eyes, couched their system of learning and polity under signs and hieroglyphical figures, which were communicated to their chief priests or Magi alone ..." Thus was perpetuated the myth begun in the 'Manuscript Old Charges' that the origins of Freemasonry, if not in Ancient Egypt, were at least influenced by the Ancient Egyptians.

The introduction to the first degree Tracing Board, however, was not an invention of the 'Lodge of Reconciliation' but comes from the 'Lecture' system of the foremost English Masonic educator of the late 18th century, William Preston. Preston (1742–1818) was born in Edinburgh and came to London to work as a printer. He entered English Freemasonry in 1763 and was to have a considerable effect on the development of the philosophy and ritual of Freemasonry. Until Preston began his work, the three ceremonies had been very simple, passing on to the candidate by catechetical 'Lectures' the principles, tenets, history and symbolism of Freemasonry. It was a very simple system of morality with a symbolism based on the building of Solomon's temple and the working tools of an operative stonemason. As a printer, Preston had read widely and as a deputy to the Grand Secretary had contact not only with Freemasonry in England but also in Europe. From the early 1770s Preston began to expand the simple catechetical lectures, importing a great deal of new material, strengthening the philosophical and spiritual basis of the institution and introducing a more complex allegorical and symbolic framework. It is from the fourth section of Preston's 'Entered Apprentice Lecture' that the prefatory paragraph of the 1814 'Entered Apprentice Tracing Board Lecture' was taken. To understand why Preston should have reintroduced Egypt – to which there is no reference in the pre-Preston catechetical 'Lectures' – it is necessary to turn to what had been happening in Europe.

Freemasonry was introduced into continental Europe from the British Isles and by the 1730s was becoming established in France, Holland, the German and Italian states and Scandinavia. Unlike the British Isles, where the membership of Freemasonry was a microcosm of contemporary society, membership of Freemasonry in Europe was limited to professional and aristocratic circles. It would appear that the Continental Freemasons soon became dissatisfied with the simple Masonic system, based on an artisan craft. From the 1740s they began to invent a myriad of Masonic Orders and systems with increasingly complex rituals, flamboyant regalia and ostentatious titles. This development coincided with a growth of intellectual interest in two other areas: medieval orders of chivalry and Ancient Egypt, both of which were to impact on the development of these additional Masonic systems.

Central to the revival of interest in Egypt was the publication of Jean Terrasson's *Séthos, histoire ou vie tirée des monuments, anecdotes de l'ancienne Égypte* (1731). In this lengthy tome, Terrasson describes the life of Sethos, an Egyptian prince who undergoes various trials to prepare him for initiation into the mysteries of Isis. After a life full of travels and adventures, Sethos eventually retires to a temple of initiates of Isis. Terrasson's book was an immediate best-seller and English and German translations appeared in 1732, with an Italian version in 1734. From the evidence of the library catalogues and inventories of 18th century Continental Masonic Lodges it is clear that Terrasson's book was well known in European Masonic circles. It was to give birth to other literary and musical works. In 1773 in Salzburg the first performance was given of *Tobias Philipp*, a play by Freiherr von Gebler, which became the opera *Thamos, König in Ägypten*, the music for which was provided by the young Mozart. Von Gebler was a Freemason and his play may have been Mozart's introduction to the concepts of mystical initiation, hermetic ideas and Freemasonry. Mozart was to become a Freemason in 1784, when he was initiated in the 'Lodge zür Wohltatigkeit' in Vienna. In his opera *The Magic Flute* he took the combination of Ancient Egypt and Freemasonry to its greatest artistic height.

The influence of Egypt on Freemasonry was brought to its lowest depth by the activities of Giuseppe Balsamo (1743–1795), the self-styled Count Alessandro Cagliostro. Whilst in London in 1777 Cagliostro became a Freemason in the 'Esperance Lodge', a lodge whose members were predominantly French. Moving to France he claimed to have been initiated into an Egyptian Rite of Freemasonry whilst in London. The Rite was of six degrees or ceremonies of great complexity, combining elements of Freemasonry, alchemy, Swedenborgianism, pseudo-Isiac mysteries and Rosicrucianism. He set up his first Egyptian Lodge in Strasbourg in 1779 under the patronage of Prince Cardinal de Rohan. Unfortunately, with de Rohan he became involved in the affair of Queen Marie Antoinette's diamond necklace and was imprisoned in the Bastille. On his release he returned to London, and at the Freemasons' Tavern gave demonstrations of his Egyptian Rite, as well as dispensing quack medicines. His visit to the venerable 'Lodge of Antiquity' in London on 1 November 1786 was lampooned in an engraving by Gillray. Cagliostro removed himself to Rome where he set up a new Egyptian Lodge. By this time he was describing himself as the Grand Kophta of Egyptian Freemasonry and claimed to be in possession of "the Great Secret". His activities in Rome brought him to the attention of the Inquisition, by whom he was imprisoned in 1789. He died in captivity six years later and his Rite died with him.

The next link in the chain, and the first to have a real effect on Masonic iconography, is Napoleon Bonaparte's expedition to Egypt. There is no evidence that Bonaparte himself was a Freemason, despite claims that he was initiated in Malta on his way to Egypt. Within his army and the large group of civilians who formed his expedition, however, there were many Freemasons. There is no doubt that there were those amongst them who were looking for evidence of early Freemasonry (Hassan 2003a; Jeffreys 2003) and it seems more than a coincidence that from this period we see a proliferation of pyramids, obelisks, sphinxes and other Egyptian motifs in European Masonic engravings, documents and regalia. Nor can it be safely argued that this was simply a Masonic adaptation of what was happening in the decorative arts in general at this period.

In 1807, Alexandre Lenoir explained the seven degrees of the 'French Rite' – the Rite practised by the great majority of Lodges in continental Europe at the time – in light of ancient Egyptian religion. Lodges subsequently developed 'museums' – little more than cabinets of curios – in which Egyptian antiquities were centre-stage. Egyptianizing designs were mostly to be found in the furniture and interior decoration of the Lodges. The furniture of 'La Parfaite Harmonie' lodge, at Mulhouse, which was manufactured in 1806, represents one of the best examples of this *retour d'Égypte* style. Masonic workshops continued to produce similar furniture throughout the 19th century, and examples can be found in the Paris Museum of Freemasonry and in the Nantes Lodge 'Paix et Union, Mars et les Arts Réunies'. An outstanding example of interior decoration is provided by the Masonic Temple in Douai, which in 1824 was decorated with vast Egyptian frescoes[1] designed by Brother Felix Robaut (1799–1879), a lithographer and bookseller (Figure 11:1).

The revival of interest in Egypt caused by Bonaparte's expedition coincided with the birth of Masonic historiography. Organized Freemasonry was almost a century old and thinking Freemasons were beginning to collect records and begin the long search for the origins of Freemasonry, a search which continues to this day. To the 18th century the 'East' was the eastern end of the Mediterranean, and it was there that, both biblically and historically, 'civilization', learning and knowledge had begun. Not surprisingly it was to that area that those who were beginning to seek the origins of Freemasonry turned their attention. Even amongst the educated, the historical portions of the 'Manuscript Old Charges' were accepted as historical fact. If they stated that Euclid revived geometry and Freemasonry in Egypt at the time of Abraham, then that must have been the case.

This was very much so with one of the 19th century founders of Egyptology, Giovanni Battista Belzoni (1778–1823). Born in Padua, he came to England in 1803 after various adventures in Italy, Prussia and Holland. He had very little formal education or training, but possessed great strength and stood at 6' 6" in height (1.98 m). He became an entertainer – often being billed as the Patagonian Samson – travelling around the British Isles with occasional forays into Europe. Shortly after his arrival in England, he married a Sarah Banne, who was to share his many enthusiasms. The Belzonis were in Malta in 1815, en route to Turkey, when they met the agent of the Pasha Mohammed Ali, the Turkish ruler of Egypt. He persuaded them to change their plans and sail to Egypt to assist in restoring that country to prosperity.

Figure 11:1 Masonic Temple in Douai, France, 1824 (Douai Public Library).

In Cairo they met J. L. Burckhardt, the Swiss explorer who developed their interest in Ancient Egypt and introduced them to Henry Salt. Salt had been sent to Cairo in 1816 as the British Consul General, but his real task was to seek out 'antiquities' for shipment to England. Belzoni had already visited Thebes and persuaded Salt to undertake the removal of the nineteenth Dynasty head and 'colossal bust' (ht. 2.67 m) of Ramesses II for shipment to London (Figure 11:2 col. pl.). Belzoni achieved this and the bust (Figure 11:3 col. pl.) is now in the British Museum (EA 19), although Salt and Burckhardt were given the credit for securing it.

Between 1816 and 1820 Belzoni carried out excavations at Abu Simbel, Thebes, Philae, the Valley of the Kings and Fayum. He made many discoveries which he carefully noted, making extensive drawings of the temples, tombs and wall decorations that he discovered. His major discovery was the tomb of Seti I with its magnificent, but empty, alabaster sarcophagus and unique wall paintings. Returning to England in January 1820, he set about writing up his experiences and discoveries. His *Narrative* (Belzoni 1821) was an instant best-seller, reaching a third impression within 12 months followed by French, German and Italian translations. In 1821 he hired the Egyptian Hall in Piccadilly (Werner Chapter 5: Figure 5:3, this volume) to exhibit his Seti I treasures, models and drawings. The antiquities were eventually auctioned and are now in the British Museum. A modern writer (Coon 1985: 4) commented that Belzoni's "methods would, of course, be described today as unscientific and destructive, but they were acceptable at the time and his many and important discoveries went far towards excusing them".

Belzoni was a Freemason. It is not known where he entered Freemasonry but in 1820 he became a member of the 'Royal Arch' in the 'School of Plato Chapter', Cambridge, and in 1821 was received into the 'Masonic Knights Templar' in Norwich. His sponsor into the 'Royal Arch' had been the Reverend George Adam Browne, a senior Freemason of the day and a member of the inner circle of HRH Augustus Frederick, Duke of Sussex, 'Grand Master' of the 'United Grand Lodge of England' from 1813 to 1843. Browne introduced Belzoni to the Duke, who was presented by Belzoni with a silver replica of the gold medal which had been conferred on him by the City of Padua and a set of his coloured drawings of the wall paintings in the tomb of Seti I.

After Belzoni's death from dysentery in Benin City in Ghana, West Africa, his widow Sarah tried to keep his name and achievements alive. Throughout his *Narrative* he makes no mention of Freemasonry, but in 1844 Sarah presented a copy to the 'Grand East of the Netherlands' (the governing body of Freemasonry in that country), accompanied by an essay written by herself on Antediluvian and Egyptian Masonry, illustrated by sketches of what Belzoni had found in the tomb of Pharaoh Osirei in the valley of Baben-el-Maloch, near Thebes. She claimed that the decorations on the tomb showed the pharaoh in a triangular Masonic apron being taken through the various degrees of Freemasonry. The Dutch were much impressed with her paper and ordered it to be printed and circulated to all their Lodges. In 1849 she was living in Brussels and an American Freemason, Dr John A. Weisse, and his wife lodged with her. She gave Weisse some of Belzoni's papers and drawings out of which, much later, Weisse (1880) produced a book that is the most outlandish of the publications that claim that Freemasonry originated in Egypt and that Freemasons were responsible for the building of the pyramids and obelisks.

Mrs Belzoni's theories were given publicity in two influential English-Masonic periodicals. Her 1861 paper on Antediluvian and Egyptian Masonry was summarized (Anon. 1861), giving in detail her explanation of the supposed depictions of the pharaoh progressing through the Masonic degrees. The article inferred that the tomb itself was an ancient Lodge Room. The same information was repeated in Belzoni 1880. Articles quoting extensively from her work appeared in the *New York Herald* on 16 and 18 February 1880, possibly in connection with the publication of Weisse's book.

The Belzonis were to have a tangential connection with an event that evoked great public interest in Egyptology in the late 1870s. In 1819, the Viceroy of Egypt presented an obelisk to Great Britain, now known as Cleopatra's Needle (Hassan 2003a: Figure 2:5). It was a tremendous gift, but it raised enormous problems: how to get it to Alexandria and then on board a ship for transport to England, to say nothing of who was going to pay for the expensive operation. Belzoni organized transport to the coast, but there the obelisk was to lie for almost 60 years as successive British governments refused to consider paying for its shipment to England (Bierbrier 2003). It was another Freemason who came to the rescue. Sir Erasmus Wilson became aware of the existence of the obelisk and provided most of the money and technical expertise to bring the obelisk to London. There were major arguments as to where it should be sited, but the building of a new river roadway – the Victoria Embankment – linking the Houses of Parliament with the City of London was the popular choice. Wilson and his circle of Masonic friends raised further finances to have a proper base constructed, the foundation stone of which was laid with Masonic ceremonies. The attendant publicity in both the public and the Masonic press revived Masonic interest in Ancient Egypt as a possible source for the origins of Freemasonry. The kindest word one can use to describe the resulting papers and books is 'speculative'. Those who saw echoes of Masonic symbolism and rituals in Egyptian wall paintings gave full reign to their imaginations, including 'proofs' that the Great Pyramid at Giza had been constructed not as a burial chamber but as the original Masonic Lodge Room.

This mid-19th century interest in Ancient Egypt coincided with the development of Masonic architecture (Curl 1991a, b). Despite the central allegory of Masonic ceremonies being building and the traditional links with architecture and stonemasons, architecture was the last of the arts to be influenced by Masonic symbolism and ideals. This was because, wherever in the world it was practised, in the 18th century Lodges met in private rooms in taverns and coffee houses. The ceremonies were fairly simple, much of the meeting being spent around a table at which the new members were instructed in the principles, tenets, symbolism and 'history' of Freemasonry by means of catechetical lectures. There was thus no need to have an elaborate setting for the meetings. However, in 1775 the senior Grand Lodge in England bought a property in Great Queen Street, London, and built the first Freemasons' Hall, to designs by Thomas Sandby. It was built in the classical style of the day. With one or two exceptions, individual lodges were slow to copy the Grand Lodge's example. When the two English Grand Lodges united in 1813 it was an opportunity to bring standardization into what had been a very informal organization. The standardization of ritual and ceremony necessitated a formal setting – Lodge Room – and from the 1820s began the development of local Masonic Halls. Allied to standardization was a growing respectability, leading to a desire to leave taverns and inns and move at least to formal rooms in hotels if a lodge or group of lodges did not have the finances to acquire property.

In continental Europe, among the first known instances of an Egyptianizing Masonic building is one to be found in Valenciennes, close to the border between France and Belgium, where the lodge erected a temple in 1840.[2] The town itself has Masonic roots, with 'La Parfaite Union Lodge' establishing itself in 1733 and being very active during the 18th century. In 1811, the city's two lodges amalgamated to become 'La Parfaite Union et Saint-Jean du Désert Réunis'. At the end of the 1830s, the Lodge entrusted one of its members – the neoclassical architect Bernard – with the task of rebuilding its temple. The new building appears to have been erected on the same spot as the old lodge, re-using its foundations. The inauguration was featured in the local press, shedding light on the inspiration behind the temple's design. In its edition of 4 April 1840, *L'Echo de la Frontière* wrote:

> The inauguration of the new temple of Valenciennes' Masonic Lodge was celebrated last Sunday with a banquet for 180 people, which included dignitaries from both of Lille's Lodges, and from those of Douai, Mons, Cambrai, etc. The new building incorporates an Egyptian temple that represents a copy of what remains of the ancient towns of Thebes and Memphis. Fortunately, Mr Bernard – the architect who directed the work – used for inspiration the figures from the scientific commission of Egypt's excellent book [*Description* 1809–1828]. The façade consists of a peristyle supported by low, Theban-style columns protruding from the building. At the top, there is a large wall without any openings, which gives the monument the serious and severe appearance that is required of it. Two large obelisks covered in Egyptian hieroglyphs break this uniformity and decorate the front, giving it an imposing aspect.

When one looks at "the façade of the temple, as viewed from the garden" (Figure 11:4), one can tell without difficulty – even through the style of the lithography – that it did indeed clearly resemble one of the illustrations in the *Description* (1809–1828).

Curiously, there was no mention of the unusual architecture in the 78 pages of speeches that were delivered during the inauguration of the new building (Figure 11:5). It seems that the resemblance of a Masonic temple to a Memphis sanctuary was, for Masons at least, so obvious that it did not need to be highlighted. Following Valenciennes' lead, the Flanders region – between France and Belgium – was to be transformed by a whole series of 'Egyptian' Masonic temples into a 'new Memphis'.

By contrast, no real Masonic style developed in England. The major building took place from about the 1860s and tended, particularly in the growing cities, to emulate the current style of municipal and other public buildings – from heavy Victorian classical to high Gothic revival. As there was no central direction of Masonic buildings or clear Masonic architectural style, individual lodges were able to decide what they wanted.

It must have been something of a surprise to the inhabitants of Boston, Lincolnshire, between 1860 and 1865 when the local lodge built a Hall, which is still in use today. To quote Curl (1986: 582):

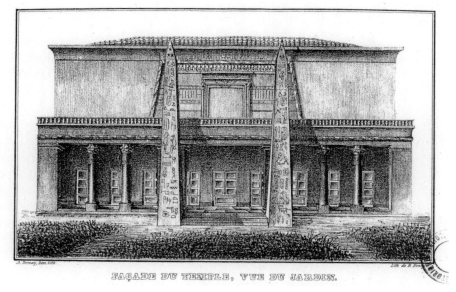

FAÇADE DU TEMPLE, VUE DU JARDIN.

Figure 11:4   View of the Valenciennes Temple "from the garden" (Grand Orient de France Library).

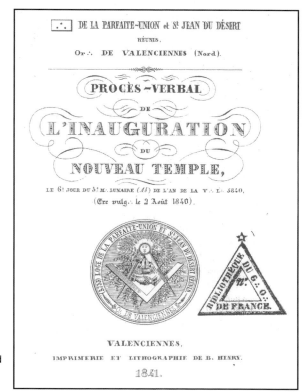

Figure 11:5 Lithograph of 1841 by B. Henry (Grand Orient de France Library).

At Boston, the Freemasons' Hall, again with the distyle in antis arrangement of columns, is based on Ancient Egyptian prototypes from Dendera, Edfu and Philae, as illustrated in the seminal works of Denon and of the Commission des Monuments set up under Napoleon at the beginning of the century. The interior was coloured chocolate, with ornament of gilt bronze, and the ceiling was dark blue with gilt stars. Eschewing all modesty, the splendid pylon-like front, made of brick with stone dressings, proclaims in hieroglyphs that its foundation dates from 1860.

Curl's comment on the sources for the style and decoration at Boston is important. With one possible exception, there was a conscious effort on the part of the architects and designers of the various Egyptian-influenced Masonic Halls and Lodge Rooms *not* to produce a pastiche of ancient Egyptian style, but to go to the sources and reproduce accurately Egyptian architectural features and decorative schemes. This reached its apogee in the early 20th century in Sydney, Australia, when the local 'Royal Arch' Masons were building a new Hall. The Lodge Room walls and ceiling cove were decorated with meticulous copies of scenes from the Papyrus of Ani, also known as 'The Judgement of the Soul of Ani the Scribe', now in the British Museum. The wall decorations were an art work in themselves, being coloured, low relief in fibrous plaster. As a result, when the building was vacated in the 1970s for smaller premises the Egyptian Lodge Room was dismantled in sections and re-assembled in the new building (Hope Chapter 9, this volume).

Whilst the Boston Masonic Hall was being built, the 'Grand Lodge of Ireland' was considering building a headquarters in Dublin. It decided that each of the rooms would be devoted to a particular Masonic Order and be decorated accordingly. For the Royal Arch Room they decided on an Egyptian theme, although it is difficult to understand why. The Royal Arch follows on from Craft Freemasonry, and has as its central allegory either the repair of Solomon's Temple under King Josiah or the preparation of the ground for the building of the second Temple by Zerubabel. No mention of Egypt! The design of the Royal Arch Room in Dublin is somewhat reticent when compared to later designs, but the placing of 'Egyptian heads' at head height on the walls is somewhat startling to visitors. In the great burst of Masonic building in the late 19th and early 20th centuries in both Europe and North America, there was a tendency to have a Royal Arch Room in Egyptian style if the building was to serve more than one Masonic Order. The finest example in North America is possibly that in the Grand Lodge of Pennsylvania's Masonic Hall in Philadelphia (1923). Externally reminiscent of a Gothic cathedral, each of its Lodge Rooms is of a different architectural style, following the history of Masonry given in the 'Manuscript Old Charges' – Egyptian, Romanesque, Gothic, Classical (an amalgam of Greek and Roman revivals) and Colonial. In the Egyptian Room the detail is carried through the whole scheme, including furnishings and light fittings, all copied from discoveries in Egypt or facsimiles of 'Books of the Dead'. A few other American temples were entirely Egyptianizing, such as those at Colorado Springs, Denver and Meridian (*Theatre of the Fraternity* n. d.), whilst the Masonic monument to George Washington, Alexandria, sets out to be a replica of Alexandria's famous lighthouse (El Daly 2003b: Figure 3:1). However, the majority of Masonic buildings built between 1880 and 1930 in the United States were strongly neoclassical in style (Rich and Merchant 2001), albeit with sphinxes flanking a staircase or Egyptianizing designs on part of a façade, as at the 'House of the Temple' in Washington (Fox 1996).

This late 19th century revival was probably inspired by the publication of E. W. Budge's (1897) monumental 'Egyptian Book of the Dead'. In England at that period the new Masonic Hall in St Saviour's Gate, York, and two new Lodge Rooms in two London Hotels – the 'Great Eastern' at Liverpool Street Station and the 'Horseshoe' on Tottenham Court Road (sadly now demolished) – certainly used Budge's work as their source book. Unlike the 1860 Boston Masonic Hall, however, the Egyptian columns in these later designs had no practical purpose and were simply half-rounds used to articulate the wall spaces and frame the painted scenes. The finest example of this late flowering in the British Isles was the Chapter Room built 1901–1902 in Queen Street, Edinburgh by the 'Supreme Grand Royal Arch Chapter of Scotland' (Figure 11:6 col. pl.). Built to designs by Peter Henderson (1849–1912), its columns at least have the appearance of serving as supports. The design was carried through the whole room, including the carpet and furniture, in the most vivid colours.

In continental Europe, Belgium was the most fertile centre of Masonic 'Egyptomania' during the late 19th and early 20th centuries. In Brussels, the rue des Sablons temple – which no longer exists – was decorated in several stages, probably between 1835 and 1857, with Thoth, Apis and Anubis heads, and with the Osiris-Isis-Horus 'trinity'. In 1876, the 'Amis Philanthropes Lodge' launched a competition to transform the recently acquired building on rue du Persil, which was won by the architect and mason Adolphe Samyn (1842–1903). His astonishing design aroused the interest of the architectural journals *La Chronique des travaux public* and *L'Emulation* (Anon. 1884), both of which published photographs of the Egyptian temples. The largest had a capacity of 1,000 people and was decorated with papyriform columns between which 12 paintings illustrated Masonic doctrine (Figure 11:7). Ancient Egypt played a central part in the design, which included cobras, winged sundisks and scarabs, as well as the vulture goddess Nekhbet.[3] At the time of the building's inauguration, on 26 January 1879, the Venerable Master of the Lodge proclaimed:

> Going back into the distant past, we have borrowed from ancient Egyptian wisdom what, according to its supreme divinity, was regarded as the essence of life: *I am what is. I am what has been. I am what will be. I am the Being par excellence whose form is forever hidden.* This inscription was engraved in hieroglyphs a long time ago on the pediment of the Temple of Saïs, dedicated to the goddess Isis, as noted by Herodotus and Plutarch …

(Anon. 1880: 23)

The most impressive example of Masonic 'Egyptomania' in continental Europe is probably the 'Lodge of the Grand Orient de Belgique', which was built on rue de Laeken in Brussels in 1910 (Celis 1984: 25; Neve 1984: 69–80). The project was assigned to Paul Bonduelle, a 30-year-old architect and Freemason with only two prior buildings to his credit. The choice was not a bad one. Bonduelle would – between the two World Wars – become one of the great names of Belgian architecture and the figurehead of Brussels' neoclassical movement. The Masonic Egyptian Temple was completely atypical of his later work. The contract was considerable, since it consisted of three temples, the largest of which was almost 400 m². The architect also supervised the furnishing and interior decoration, using iconography that represented the mysteries of Egyptian initiation. The project was run very efficiently: authorization to build was given on 20 April 1909, the first stone was laid on 3 June of the same year,

Figure 11:7   Grand
temple of the Amis
Philanthropes Lodge
(1879), rue du Persil,
Brussels, Belgium
(EDOM).

and the solemn inauguration took place on 17 December 1910. Immense in volume
(25.15 m x 14.93 m x 13.3 m), the largest temple is bordered by 26 colossal polychrome
columns with papyriform capitals along the north and south walls, and 10 on the two
other walls. The 10 columns support an architrave decorated with gilded statues of
rams in sphinx position and crowned with sundisks framed by cobras. The ceiling
rests on the rams and is decorated with a zodiac carried by Horus and Isis. The
temple's nave is bordered on each side by a high gallery. Bonduelle's attention to
detail and the quality of his work can probably be explained by his numerous visits to
the Louvre during his studies in Paris, and by his interest in archaeology.

Just as Lenoir had helped to justify the use of Egyptianizing architecture by
Masonic Lodges in the first half of 19th century, Eugène Goblet d'Alviella (1846–1925)
played an important part in legitimizing Masonic Egyptomania during the 1900s. He
created one of the first Chairs in the History of Religions in Europe at Brussels' Free

University (1884), and was devoted to his work on masonry. He was a defender of the 'migration of the symbols' theory, which was the title of one of his books (D'Alviella 1894).

The rue de Laeken temple (Figure 11:8 col. pl.) was built during the period in which Goblet d'Alviella's ideas were becoming very popular. This was particularly true among Freemasons, for whom he represented an intellectual beacon. If Egyptianizing architecture was often conspicuous and spectacular for the public, this was not the case here. The passers-by in rue de Laeken could not have imagined that, behind the façade of this 18th century middle-class house, there was a secret sanctuary dedicated to the mysteries of Memphis! It is also worth noting that the project took place in strict confidentiality. Unlike the rue du Persil temple, architectural journals made no reference to this unusual work. The architect himself never spoke about it and did not refer to it in any of his publications. Similar neo-Egyptian buildings were built in Antwerp ('The United Friends of Trade and Perseverance') and Mons and, only a few kilometres away in France, the 'Grand Orient' Freemasons built a splendid Egyptian temple in Lille, immediately before World War I. The architect, Brother Baer, was undoubtedly influenced by the Belgian temples.

Douai, Valenciennes, Lille, Mons, Brussels, Antwerp ... Beyond Flanders, one can certainly find other examples of Egyptianizing Masonic architecture, and these are sometimes spectacular, but in no other part of the world can one find such a high density of Masonic temples reproducing the 'Sanctuaries of Memphis'.

The 1920s came, and with them the Tutankhamun discoveries by Howard Carter. Surprisingly, perhaps, they had no impact whatsoever on Masonic design or architecture. By that time the study of Masonic history had moved on. In 1886 a research lodge had been founded by the 'United Grand Lodge of England', the 'Quatuor Coronati Lodge No. 2076', which brought together a formidable group of Masonic historians who began to apply to Masonic studies the disciplines of scientific research. Through their work, and that of their colleagues in Europe and North America, the old legendary histories of Freemasonry were systematically examined and rejected, and the present theory of Freemasonry having developed in England or Scotland in the late 16th century out of operative stonemasonry began to emerge. No Masonic student would now seriously believe that Freemasonry existed in Ancient Egypt, but their predecessors' fascination with, and acceptance of, the old legend of Euclid reviving Freemasonry in Egypt has produced an important heritage of Masonic buildings with decoration in the Egyptian style.

Notes

1   The temple no longer survives, but five photos of the interior and one of the exterior, dating from around 1900, are held in the Douai public library (MS 1723).

2   The temple was in use for only 10 years or so. Following Napoleon Bonaparte's *coup d'État*, Freemasonry met with strong opposition. The Valenciennes Lodge became dormant and was sold in 1856. The neighbourhood became very run-down, but some of the Lodge's walls survived. In the mid-1990s, the Valenciennes Freemasons bought back the remains and restored them to their original initiatory function. Only a few Egyptianizing elements have been salvaged: a few columns, a portico and part of a funerary monument.

3   The original elements of the architecture were ruined by the renovations of 1936 and 1954.

Acknowledgments

We are grateful to Frank LaNgenaken, librarian of the 'Grand Orient de Belgique', and to Jacques Lamblin, curator of the Douai public library, who found the photographs of the Douai Temple and gave permission for their reproduction. Roland Allender drew them to our attention and Jacques Trehout made the copies.

CHAPTER 12

NEO-EGYPTIAN GARDEN ORNAMENTS IN FLORENCE DURING THE 19th CENTURY

Gloria Rosati

Interest in Egyptian art was widespread throughout Italy during the second half of the 18th century. Even garden ornaments reflected an Egyptian style, and theorists emphasized the geometric simplicity, formal purity and architectonic immediacy of many Egyptian monuments. Egyptian designs were chosen for their aesthetic value and adapted to different contexts and purposes. In 1796, for example, the architect Giuseppe Manetti (see below) chose a pyramidal shape for the ice-house in the Cascine park in Florence (Figure 12:1), which he had been restoring since 1787. Nearby there is a fountain dedicated to Narcissus, which was built around the same time in the form of a thick obelisk.[1]

Figure 12:1   Pyramidal ice-house in Cascine park (© Gloria Rosati).

In general, Egyptian or neo-Egyptian patterns found as garden ornaments can be explained as peculiar to an eclectic taste, and their presence reflects how receptive Italian – and in this specific instance Tuscan – architects were to such new trends originating from abroad, and from Enlightenment thought (e.g. Cresti 1989: 139; Zangheri 1984: 17–18). Since the first decades of the 18th century the well-known fashion of landscape gardening had spread out all over Europe from its native source, England. The so-called 'English' or 'Anglo-Chinese' gardens showed an idealized view of the world, where 'spontaneous' nature and vegetation was exalted and supported by means of scenic settings. Such settings, called *fabriques* in France, were constructed combining different styles, distant in time and place, to create a 'scene', or an 'episode'. Architectural elements and remote styles were reinterpreted on the basis of their psychological effects or symbolic value (Patetta 1991: 9; Phillips 1986; Tagliolini 1994: 320). One of the most sensational Italian examples is no longer extant but is documented in an 1812 plan (Tagliolini 1994: 321): it is the 'English' garden planned soon after 1787 by G. Pregliasco for the park of Racconigi (Cuneo). The architect was able to gather together several 'episodes', ranging from Swan Island to the Merlin Temple, a grotto, a Gothic church, a hermitage, a Chinese bridge, Roman ruins, Turkish ornaments, Egyptian sphinxes and inscribed Egyptian stelae, a mosque, and a medieval castle.

Interest in Egyptian antiquities increased at the start of the 19th century as a result of Bonaparte's campaign. In 1803, during the Kingdom of Etruria established by Bonaparte, the funerary display of Ludovic I in the church of St Lawrence was built in Egyptian style (Cresti 1989: 139 n. 19; Del Rosso, see below): a columned porch with papyrus capitals, and a pyramid on the catafalque. In 1808, a richly illustrated translation of Denon (1802) was produced by Fontani. Then in 1824, immediately after his accession, Grand Duke Leopold II (1824–1859) bought the collection of Giuseppe Nizzoli, Chancellor of the Austrian Consulate in Egypt.[2] In 1827, Leopold gave support for the Franco-Tuscan Literary Expedition to Egypt, and a double exhibition was subsequently arranged in Florence and Pisa, consisting of the antiquities, paintings and drawings that were brought back. In this atmosphere of patronage, Seguin's St Leopold and St Ferdinand suspension bridges,[3] near the Cascine park and at the eastern end of the town, were built in an Egyptianizing style between 1835 and 1837: they had obelisk-like piers with recumbent lions in front of each one. This design was highly fashionable, and the choice of Egyptian style has been interpreted (Curl 1991a: 94; 1994: 167) as suggesting durability and stability. Moreover, the Egyptian style was considered by contemporaries as highly suitable for metal engineering, being solid, simple, easy to reproduce and inexpensive (Patetta 1991: 106–107).

During this same period, renewed interest in the primeval, pure forms of architecture was related to the cultural debate about the origins of classical architecture, which was lively at the end of the 18th century, following the 1785 initiative of the Académie Française to hold a competition regarding the Egyptian legacy to Greek art, and the general opinion to emerge was an unfavourable criticism of Egyptian art. The winner, Quatremère de Quincy (1755–1849), denied any European legacy and he classified Egyptian art, though admirable, as monotonous and lacking in proportions (Curl 1994: 107). Jacopo Belgrado (whose dissertation was published in Parma in 1786) called its architecture "rough and coarse" (Patetta 1991: 103). The architect Giuseppe Del Rosso (1760–1831, born in Rome but working in

Florence) entered the competition, arguing that Etruscan art originated from the Egyptian (a view that he shared with Piranesi). His essay (Del Rosso 1787) agreed with the Academy's view that the vitality and sense of proportion of Greek art was superior to the grandeur and solidity of the Egyptian. Nevertheless, he acknowledged the enterprise of Egyptian art, and strongly supported the study of ancient iconology.

Del Rosso's rival, Giuseppe Manetti (1762–1817), was receptive to the concept of landscape gardening, whilst at the same time wishing to revive the use of symbolism in architecture. After his work in the Cascine park, he announced that the garden should be a philosophic-initiatory place: he dedicated and entitled his plan for the Corsi garden in Via Romana (1801–1810) "To Friendship", and on a seat there can be found the maxim: "Wise men must submit to fate" (Dezzi Bardeschi 1986: 34). Unfortunately a magnificent project he designed for the Poggio Imperiale garden was never realized because it was regarded as too expensive (and was finally abandoned when Ferdinand III re-ascended the throne in 1814), but it can arguably be regarded as the prototype for other English-style gardens of the period.[4] Manetti's main source of inspiration was ancient mythology, revivified in a Romantic sense. Among symbolic and very evocative settings, one of the most significant monuments, and one of the first in the neo-Gothic style in Italy, was a three-sided Pantheon dedicated to Renowned Men (Greeks, Romans and Contemporaries), to be compared, most probably, with the first neo-Gothic building at Stowe, the Temple dedicated to Freedom, designed with a triangular base by James Gibb around 1740 (Reinhardt 1989: 89). Manetti's *fabrique* has been interpreted (Dezzi Bardeschi 1984: 114; 1986: 35, 38) as an allusion to new ideals and the need for social renovation, that is to the aims and ideals of initiated minds. Moreover, other episodes were envisaged to exalt the theme of human value and qualities. A pyramid was dedicated to Ancient Virtue, and Manetti describes it rather precisely: square base, height one-and-a-half times the size of its sides, faced with marble, with different decoration on each face. One face was to be decorated with 'Egyptian symbols' (hieroglyphs, as he writes expressly in a page of notes), one with bas-reliefs in Etruscan style and two in Greek and Roman style. To honour Modern Virtue he chose a column with a sequence of rings decorated with bas-reliefs in Italian, French and German style. Not far from them, Egyptian symbolism returned, with an obelisk, which "should have the same proportions as the Egyptian ones and any feature resembling them" (Manetti, Archivio di Stato di Firenze, fondo Possessioni, Piante nn. 537, 588). In this instance, the order of the *fabriques* may be explained as elements of an initiatory walk, the garden being designed as a ritual setting, whether or not the 'initiated' were followers of a Masonic lodge.

The influence of Freemasonry and its subject matter in garden architecture has already been recognized, especially with regard to Egyptian patterns (Curl 1991b: 125; 1994: 134–136; Staehelin 1990 for pyramids). There is still an open and lively debate concerning the possible role of Masonic symbols in the first half of the 19th century. Supporters of the role of Freemasonry include Reinhardt (1989), Dezzi Bardeschi (1989), Maresca (1989) and Humbert (2001: 181), while the sceptics include Cresti (1989) and Mosser (1990). Nonetheless, as shown below, there are some unequivocal instances of Freemasonry among Tuscan architects in Florence.

The Torrigiani Garden dates from the same period, and is closely reminiscent of Manetti's projects. It is situated close to the southern end of Boboli Gardens, near the Porta Romana. It was planned by the architect Luigi de Cambray Digny (1778–1843), who worked there for only one year (1813–1814). Marquis Pietro Torrigiani took over the project in collaboration with the architect Gaetano Baccani from 1819 onwards. The *Guida al Giardino Torrigiani* (Anon. 1824) makes it possible to recognize the garden's surviving monuments, and to trace an itinerary that has been interpreted (Cini 1997: 185–196; Grifoni and Negri 1998: 99–100; Maresca 1986, 1989: 171–172; 1993) as a complex iconographic system, where the garden is conceived, as at the Poggio Imperiale, as a place of initiation. The client and the architect Digny were both liberals, and both were Freemasons (Cresti 1989: 138; Maresca 1986: 56 n. 2). The Egyptian inspiration was restricted to the entrance to the garden. Near the main gate, on top of the southern wall, is the first of two sphinxes that were designed by Torrigiani for the gate itself, but which proved to be oversize. Only one can be seen from the road (Figure 12:2), where it appears to maintain its protective and evocative power, while the other is placed about 30 m behind. The torso of a white marble Osiris/Antinous-type statue was placed in front of the gate, emerging from a deep niche-shaped bush (Figure 12:3). He holds a double slab resembling the Tablets of the Law, and the whole appears to represent a theme of self-regeneration and spiritual rebirth. Among features that were typical of the Romantic garden, paths led the visitor into a world which was once enlarged by means of *trompe-l'oeil* paintings on the boundary walls, and where marble hands once indicated the way. Admiration for the beauty of nature was intended to cause introspective meditation. The *Sepolcreto*, a tomb described by Maresca (1993) as being in the neo-Egyptian style, was originally designed as a hill, and it is still half covered by the slopes of a small one; on top of it a pointed skylight allows a little light to enter the inner room, just like many other initiation grottos. Further on, other 'stations' lead toward self-consciousness and hope. The highpoint of the itinerary was the tower, the first neo-Gothic monument to be built in Florence. It is 22 m high, with a wealth of Masonic symbolism. The few Egyptianizing patterns in this garden appear however to be deeply meaningful (cf.

Figure 12:2   Sphinx near the main gate of the Torrigiani Garden (© Gloria Rosati).

Figure 12:3   'Osiris' statue at the entrance to the Torrigiani Garden (© Gloria Rosati).

the association of Osiris with rebirth), and they probably marked the turning point of the initiatory walk.

The Stibbert Garden and Villa provide one of the most remarkable instances of eclectic taste in Florence. They were the property of Frederick Stibbert (1838–1906), who collected an outstanding number of works of art from around the world (ranging from paintings and statues to costumes, suits of armour, furniture, and antiquities). The garden reflects his passion for antiquity. In 1859 he engaged one of the most famous architects in Florence, Giuseppe Poggi,[5] to design some new buildings for the garden. Stibbert himself probably planned its ornaments (Del Francia 2000; Pagni 2002). From the Villa, paths wound their way downhill until they reached an artificial lake with an Egyptian temple (Figure 12:4). A short avenue (*dromos*), flanked by terracotta sphinxes, led to the entrance of the building (Figure 12:5). Although small, it was built in true pharaonic style, with a torus and a cavetto cornice on top, and biaxial opening.[6] Each door was flanked by standing statues representing pharaoh as Osiris, with double crown, Nemes headdress and crossed arms holding sceptres. On the vertical strap is a hieroglyphic inscription of part of the titulary of Ptolemy Caesarion, the son of Cleopatra VII and Caesar (Del Francia 2000: 40 nn. 51–52). It was probably copied from Champollion's (1835–1845) *Monuments de l'Égypte et de la Nubie*, bought by Stibbert in 1864. The same work was presumably used as the source of the wall decoration consisting of scenes from the temples of Abu Simbel and Beit el-Wali, and from the tomb of Ramesses III.

An obelisk was built on the northern side. The view from the lake side is spectacularly impressive: the building stands out on a small peninsula, two lions[7] flank the door and a stairway, with a sphinx at both ends, leads to the water (Figure 12:6). Del Francia (2000: 36) points out the resemblance to Karl Friedrich Schinkel's

Figure 12:4   Stibbert Garden: the Egyptian temple, southern side (© Gloria Rosati).

Figure 12:5 Stibbert Garden: pharaohs and painted decoration of the Egyptian temple (© Gloria Rosati).

Figure 12:6 Stibbert Garden: the Egyptian temple viewed from the lake (© Gloria Rosati).

stage-sets for Mozart's *The Magic Flute*, to be staged in the Berliner Schauspiele Opernhaus production in 1815 (Baltrusaitis 1985: 47; Curl 1994: 151–152; Humbert *et al*. 1994: 404–408; Martellacci 1989), and believes that the lake was intended as the Nile. The lake contains little islands and a grotto. Although Stibbert was a Freemason (Del Francia 2000: 36), the composition as a whole does not immediately suggest any deep hidden meaning, but rather an aura of sophisticated satisfaction combined with sheer enjoyment. Nonetheless, there are also two free-standing columns which, together with the Egyptian themes and the grotto, could be seen as more in character with an initiatory walk than mere gardening fashion (Maresca 1989: 173; Pagni 2002: 72–73).

Poggi also designed several new English-style gardens in Florence. In 1855 he was entrusted with the renovation of Villa Strozzi 'al Boschetto' on the hill of Monteoliveto, by which time he had already gained much experience (for example, in the Poniatowski garden, in the Villa Guicciardini, Villa Guadagni at San Domenico, and Villa Archinto 'alle Forbici') (Pozzana 1996). The celebrated park after which the Villa had been named since the 17th century probably retained much of its original appearance at the beginning of the 19th century (Trotta 1990). It extended on steep slopes, and had been designed during the 16th century without regard for Italian fashion. This 16th century wild look and manneristic style was now maintained and even stressed, in order to impress the visitor, with the creation of cliffs, stone bridges, grottos and waterworks. It was renowned for combining 'the wild and the domesticated', and as such it anticipated the so-called English fashion. Poggi

redesigned the south-western part, to which he moved the main entrance (originally on the north side). A farm was transformed into a park, where the road to the main building twisted and turned up and the landscapes changed at every turning. The northern part of the park, the so-called 'old wood', was reserved for walking, and is probably not very different now from its ancient appearance. Poggi designed paths, restored some architectural ornaments (Poggi 1909: 61–63) and added a few new ones. The staircase with helical ramps, here crowned by a masonry bridge, is characteristic of his style. And here is Egypt again: a couple of terracotta Antinous-type statues, about 50 cm high, were placed on the balustrade in front of the ramps, but they subsequently had to be moved to protect them from damage. A statue of a severe-looking pharaoh, slightly larger than life, seated on his throne with Nemes headdress, was placed in front of the balustrade (Figure 12:7). This

Figure 12:7   Villa Strozzi al Boschetto: the pharaoh (© Gloria Rosati).

familiar representation was accompanied, however, by a figure of a naked girl, kneeling, prostrate with grief, and sprawled on the pharaoh's legs. It is not clear whether these figures were chosen by Poggi. The composition is unusual and its significance has still to be researched and understood.

Finally, there is one instance of an Egyptianizing garden ornament that was chosen as 'the latest fashion': it is the wall-fountain (the only one extant of two) in the Villa Rospigliosi Pallavicini, then Ginori, in Carmine Square (Cini 1997: 177–180). It combines Egyptian style (temple façade, with cavetto cornice) with Doric, and includes a sundial. It is considered to date from the end of the 18th century or the beginning of the 19th, when Egypt and Egyptian patterns were most fashionable.

Florence and its surroundings contain other examples of parks which do not conceal their philosophic-esoteric meaning, but no Egyptianizing patterns are generally to be found, whereas neoclassical or neo-Gothic overtones are dominant. Only in the park of Villa Puccini at Scornio, Pistoia (the most complete work by Luigi de Cambray Digny, 1821–1828: *Monumenti del Giardino Puccini* 1845; Dominici and Negri 1992) is Egypt referred to, and there only twice: a bust of G. B. Belzoni, honoured for his enterprise and discoveries, and a figure of Cleopatra, seen as a very negative figure.

Near Pistoia, in the park of the Villa di Celle at Santomato, is a very peculiar monument (Figure 12:8) (Cei 1994: 54–55; Chiostri 1989: 164; Gurrieri 1974: 43–46). It was planned and designed by Giovanni Gambini between 1840 and 1850. Among very scenographic and pleasant settings and a range of small, charming buildings, Gambini constructed a sepulchral monument to honour the Fabroni family (owner of the Villa), which he called 'Egyptian', but which actually combines a sort of truncated pyramid or thick obelisk, over a temple-like structure, decorated with a winged disk on the front. It also resembles a sarcophagus with four columns at the edges, with Assyrian details, and with hieroglyphs and symbolic elements incised; the basement is reminiscent of a subterranean cavity or crypt. It looks like a summation of several symbolic elements, and it is difficult to distinguish one single source of inspiration. The pyramid-like monument, however, retained its funerary function as a mausoleum.

Figure 12:8   Villa di Celle at Santomato, Pistoia: funerary temple of the Fabroni family (© Gloria Rosati).

Architect Agostino Fantastici (1782–1845) worked in Siena and in southern Tuscany, earning fame with his designs for neoclassical furniture (Calderai and

Mazzoni 1992). His decorative repertoire was very rich (although he appreciated the Greek style in particular), as was his imagination: his stage-designs also reflected the exotic and esoteric. For example, his striking stage-design probably for 'Maria Stuarda' by Vittorio Alfieri imagined Egyptian capitals for a columned hall with Romanesque and Venetian elements, but in a Gothic ensemble, and with imaginative architecture in the background (Martellacci 1992: 173, cat. 48A). In 1834 he designed the Romantic garden for the Villa di Arceno, Castelnuovo Berardenga (Siena), and in the years 1825–1835 the Villa il Pavone near the Roman Gate in Siena, where Egyptian inspiration is evident in the interior decoration, in the furniture, and at the main entrance of the garden. The gate is crowned, as very often, with two sphinxes surveying the main path, originally flanked by palms. In front of the visitor is a dark pyramid (Figure 12:9), a memorial to the owner's family (Bianchi Bandinelli). The tomb is underground, and the entrance to the pyramid, resembling a pylon with a winged disk, leads into a chapel: over the entrance of which, on the pyramid itself, is written – with golden letters: DEO VERO / OPTIMO MAXIMO (To the true, the perfect and greatest [or supreme] God). Inside, the few original ornaments have been described as typically Masonic (triangle, columns, etc.). The monument was clearly intended to impress, but its message appears deeper than just a search for purity of form combined with a taste for the exotic. It represents a further example of Masonic influence exerted by both client and architect (Borgogni 1992: 61; but see Cresti 1989: 139); Cresti (1992: 14) agrees that it does not fit the poetics of ruins nor does it draw romantic parallels, but it gives substance to different meanings and creates a proper setting for secret and elite rituals.

The same authors stress the architectonic rationality of the pyramid, being both an expression of Enlightenment research and a symbol of the supremacy of rationality

Figure 12:9   Villa il Pavone, Siena: the pyramid (© Gloria Rosati).

over nature, and the attention for Masonic themes could confirm that Fantastici was a follower of Enlightenment thought (Cresti 1992: 14; Borgogni 1992: 59). Others, however, examine the villa with its furniture and decorations and the 'scenographic' garden as a whole, and regard such a complex as an intimate place of memories, related to the new Romantic sensitivity (Calderai and Mazzoni 1992: 76–77).

This survey, although restricted to evidence from a small part of Tuscany, confirms the quick spread there of landscape gardening fashion and also local appreciation for Egyptian patterns. Pyramids, obelisks, lions and sphinxes are obviously preferred monuments, inspired by the Roman evidence, and they were used, as elsewhere in Europe, to create evocative settings, stimulating meditation. Once at least (Stibbert Garden) it was a printed scientific publication that was used as a source to reproduce pictures and inscriptions. On the other hand, the typical Egyptian monuments seem to be regarded as endowed, in themselves, with symbolic or 'moral' values (Humbert 2001: 182–183; Reinhardt 1989: 89) and connections with Masonic thought and themes are often manifest. In Naples and in Florence, Egyptian motifs were taken on by Masonic affiliates much earlier than elsewhere (1728 and 1733 resp.; Jaeger 1995: 35–36, fig. 1.1, pl. II, 2).

Egyptian inspiration for garden ornaments had its highpoint within the first half of the 19th century and then declined, but without waning completely. Pyramids, however, are occasionally found later, even if not in gardens, as inexhaustible symbols of eternal memory: for example, in 1921 a pyramid was built as a memorial at Montaperti (near Siena), on the hill overlooking the plain where on 4 September 1260 a famous battle between Guelfs and Ghibellines took place.

Notes

1   Nowadays it is nearly ruined and has lost the evocative force that was perhaps felt by the poet Shelley: he chose it as his favourite place to sit and meditate while composing his 'Ode to the West Wind'.

2   Leopold's predecessor, Ferdinand III (1769–1824), had declined the collection, along with the Egyptian collection of Bernardino Drovetti, considering that the expense would not be justified.

3   The bridges were demolished, in 1932 and 1939 respectively, but six of the eight lions are extant, two in the Cascine park and four at both ends of Viale del Poggio Imperiale. They are copies of the famous ones in Rome, on the ramp to the Campidoglio, and they reproduce the one (which is now number 16 in the Musei Capitolini) with its tail on its right side, even to the minutest details: on its mouth a small orifice reproduces the hole for the water-pipe.

4   Thus, for example, Grand Duchess Elisa Baciocchi Bonaparte entrusted Manetti with renovating the gardens of both the Poggio a Caiano and the Poggio Imperiale Villas in 1809 to 1811. She herself was well versed in modern gardening fashion, being the owner of the splendid Royal Villa at Marlia (Lucca), transformed in the neoclassical and 'English' style. Two successive plans, with notes, for the Poggio Imperiale are kept in the Archivio di Stato di Firenze, fondo Possessioni, Piante n. 537 and n. 588: Dezzi Bardeschi 1986: 35 ss; Parigi 1998: 106–109.

5   A few years later, Poggi was to be entrusted with the task of renovating Florence and preparing it for its new role as the capital of the Kingdom of Italy from 1865 to 1871.

6   However, an old photograph reveals the astonishing fact that the three large openings on each long side, as windows, were closed with shutters.

7   These lions also are copies of the ones on the ramp to the Campidoglio in Rome.

CHAPTER 13

EGYPTIANIZING MOTIFS IN ARCHITECTURE AND ART IN BRAZIL

Margaret Marchiori Bakos

Introductory context

Brazil is the largest and the only Portuguese-speaking country in South America. The history of its settlement and colonization is fascinating. Spanish, Dutch, French and English, among others, disputed ownership of its territory with the Portuguese explorers and with the Native Indians. Africans also arrived here from the 16th century onwards. During the 19th and 20th centuries, countless waves of European and Asian immigrants arrived, to complete this continent-sized melting pot.

The history of the country and the mixture of the cultures led to a unique cultural context, characterized by a balance between renewal and permanence. With reference to Egyptianizing motifs, permanence has been achieved through instruction and teaching of ancient history, and renewal through the dynamic variation of the appropriation of Egyptian elements for different purposes.

This complex Brazilian cultural process combines knowledge of details with imaginative power and an exotic artistic sensibility. The Portuguese influence is still evident through the encouragement of the study of Egyptology and ancient history in schools and universities. Admiration and respect for all the symbols, monuments and culture of the Egyptian civilization is maintained, often manifest by the frequent utilization of images of obelisks for commemorative purposes. Such references to obelisks are not exclusive to Brazil, as Buenos Aires, capital of Argentina, has the tallest obelisk in South America. However, in addition to the conservative and respectful usage of Egyptian symbology, Brazil also developed its own lighter way of dealing with these symbols, at times satirical and even bordering on irreverence. A new example is the usage of Egyptian motifs from the exhibit 'Pharaonic Egypt', in Rio de Janeiro, adapted this year for the typical Brazilian festival, the 'Carnival'. This excellent exhibit was brought from the Louvre to the 'France-Brazil House', and its motifs inspired a 'Carnival Group'. The Group was named 'Isis'. All its members were dressed accordingly, although dancing and singing the Brazilian *samba*. Carnival in Brazil is a unique and world-famous event characterized by irreverence, freedom and rule-breaking (DaMatta 1990: 66). The use of a historical event as the inspiration for a satirical and typical festival like the Carnival is a very Brazilian phenomenon, unlikely to be observed in any other Latin American country.

The permanence of Egyptian elements in art, architecture and other forms of cultural manifestations in Brazil not only has deep roots in the history of the country, but also relies on the traditional, although distinctive, Brazilian practice of qualitative appropriation of cultural elements of other peoples and eras.

This chapter deals with the presence of Egyptianizing motifs in Brazil since the early 18th century. These elements can still be encountered in commemorative monuments, public and commercial buildings, and private houses; mainly in the form of obelisks and pyramids. The presence of Egyptian symbols in paintings, decorative arts and commercial logos is evident in Brazil.

No systematic work on Egyptianizing motifs in art and architecture in Brazil has been undertaken to date, but at least one can say, in the same way that Carlos Saguar Quer (1996: 307) does in respect of Spain, that "the interest in ancient Egyptian culture started a very long time ago in this country".

The acquisition of the first Brazilian collections of Egyptian antiquities must count as one of the most significant early steps in Brazil's relationship with Ancient Egypt. Its most important public collection of Egyptian artefacts is housed at the National Museum in Rio de Janeiro. Kitchen and Beltrão (1990: 5) consider it to be "... probably the oldest and the most important in South America". The earliest part of the collection was assembled before the beginning of the Republic, during the Brazilian Empire. After the decipherment of hieroglyphs and the birth of Egyptology, a strong movement developed in Europe to rescue and value Egyptian culture. This fashionable trend extended to the Americas, receiving the sponsorship of Dom Pedro I and his son Dom Pedro II in Brazil, both members of the Portuguese Crown.

At the beginning of the 19th century, the Portuguese royal family was the influence behind Brazil's acquisition of knowledge about ancient Egyptian civilization. The most important European period in Egyptology was a result of Bonaparte's expedition to Egypt (1798–1801). The expedition triggered the first acquisitions of Egyptian antiquities by the Brazilian Royal Family. The largest part of the Egyptian collection at the National Museum was purchased at a public auction in 1824 by His Imperial Majesty, Dom Pedro I, from the Italian Nicolao Fiengo, who originally had planned to sell the collection to Argentina but had been unsuccessful in so doing.

Before the decipherment of hieroglyphic writing by Champollion in 1822, only a small number of early 19th century travellers had dared to visit Egypt. Those that did had the opportunity to visit temples and tombs which no longer exist. With time, travel to this 'mysterious' country became more accessible to a wider public. Dom Pedro II was able to visit Egypt for the first time in 1871. Still on display in Rio de Janeiro is a beautiful painted coffin from the Saite Period that was presented by Khedive Ismail to Dom Pedro II during his second visit to Egypt in 1876.

Other private collections in Brazil were created at the end of the 19th century. In 1963, Mrs Vera Bezzi inherited 36 pieces of Egyptian antiquities from her grandfather, and this collection was then used to form the Museum of Art and Archaeology at the University of São Paulo (Brancaglion 2001: 23). Other objects were later given to this museum by private contributors, and others were purchased through the Fundação de Apoio à Pesquisa do Estado de São Paulo (FAPESP), a grant-giving research foundation.

There is another collection of 22 Egyptian antiquities in the Museu de Arte de São Paulo Assis Chateubriand (MASP). This collection was donated to the museum in 1976 by the former Director and Curator Pietro Maria Bardi and his wife Lina Bo Bardi. The Foundation Eva Klabin Rapaport in Rio de Janeiro also possesses a small collection of Egyptians objects (Brancaglion 2001: 25).

Despite the presence of ancient Egyptian art and artefacts in the above collections, many people living in Brazil still have little or no opportunity to learn about the civilization of Ancient Egypt. In spite of this, since the end of the 19th century, especially after 1869 with the opening of the Suez Canal, new interests in Ancient Egypt arose throughout the world. In Brazil a wave of using Egyptianizing elements in architecture and arts began. These can be easily observed in the early monuments and civilian buildings of that period, which were used to legitimize and add an air of solidity to State practices.

Egyptianizing architecture

The interest in Egypt continued to evolve with diverse and divergent readings of ancient Egyptian forms. Egypt was regarded not only as a land of wisdom and justice, but also as a land that possessed the happiness of eternal life and a land acquainted with spectacular structures and ornamentation (Humbert *et al.* 1994: 312). The heightened interest in Ancient Egypt was brought to Brazil in a variety of different ways.

One influence can be traced to the work of 'Mestre [master] Valentim' (Valentim da Fonseca e Silva, 1745–1813), who is recognized by scholars in Brazil as having produced the most significant artistic output in Rio de Janeiro during the 18th century. At this time the city was elevated to become the new capital of the Vice-Royalty, situated at the centre of the power of the colony, where aesthetic standards would be created and diffused to the whole country (Monteiro de Carvalho 1999: 7).

Very little is known about Valentim's history, beyond the fact that he was the son of a noble of Portuguese origin and a black Brazilian (Franco 1996). His creations, from sculpture and architecture to urban elements, can be seen as part of the process of enlightenment for the 'Carioca'[1] society in the 18th century. The primary objective was to respond to the needs of very important governmental and secular institutions. For instance, Valentim designed and constructed several monumental civilian buildings in Rio de Janeiro such as the 'Public Promenade', as well as several impressive fountains. He also carried out important work for churches as well as for non-religious institutions.

The programme of 'enlightenment' in Rio de Janeiro is very evident in the plans and construction of the 'Public Promenade' – the most popular place for public relaxation (Monteiro de Carvalho 1999: 15). The model chosen for its plan consisted of a monumental public garden, representing nature, and human control of it, together with an important fountain for people's use.

From 1779 to 1883, in order to sanitize the swampy and unhealthy lagoon of Boqueirão da Ajuda, Valentim created two pyramids that were intended to be placed facing the sunrise. These pyramids are considered by some authors such as Maria Eugenia Franco (1996) to be "important by themselves: dislocated in their time, but created to have more significance and importance in the future". Starting from a pure geometrical form, the triangular pyramid was put on a rectangular base, over a cornice, the latter being an architectonic element often used in the baroque period. Small, triangular and quadrangular pyramids, either alone or considered with other elements, were often used over doorways and façades in Brazilian baroque architecture. As Franco (1996) says, "to emphasize the character and mark of the obelisk, Mestre Valentim encrusted an oval medallion in each of the pyramids". These medallions are made from a light marble of local granite, contrasting with the dark carioca granite: "the skill of the sculptor managed to retain the taste of the period for the romantic and the picturesque; on each medallion is engraved 'À saudade do Rio' (To the nostalgia from Rio) and 'Ao amor do público' (To the love of the public)" (Franco 1996).

These pyramids, which by their shape and non-figurative characteristics differ from all other of Valentim's sculptures, are sometimes considered as the precursors in Brazilian sculpture of the emancipation of the artist from the constraints of figurative representation.

The 'Public Promenade' could be defined as a 'court-like garden', similar to some 16th, 17th and 18th century European gardens. Such gardens were meant to create for the observer an architectural illusion of geometrical character. Their decoration consisted of geometric and figurative sculptures in the form of symbols from ancient history such as pyramids, arches, columns, temples, and of fountains and waterfalls (Monteiro de Carvalho 1999: 15). From a plan of 1808, it can be seen that Valentim envisaged the 'Public Promenade' as hexagonal in shape. The doorway still remains and preserves some of the old decoration, such as exotic Chinese details on the iron gate. Valentim represents the 'enlightenment', uniting art with utilitarian purposes (Monteiro de Carvalho 1999: 29). The triangular pyramids gave a new look to the carioca metropolis, public statuary with a non-religious character (Monteiro de Carvalho 1999: 38).

Valentim was also the artist responsible for the adoption of certain Egyptian structures to embellish utilitarian areas. One of the oldest and best examples in Brazil is the 'Fountain of the Pyramid', located in the Praça XV square in the centre of Rio de Janeiro (Figure 13:1 col. pl.). In 1780, the Swedish engineer Jacques Funck had been contracted by Viceroy Vasconcelos to improve the existing fountain, which was in ruins and no longer providing the necessary water supply. He urged the construction of a new fountain near to the quay (Monteiro de Carvalho 1999: 9). The resulting pyramid was actually the work of Valentim, who remodelled the old structure of the fountain with two intentions in mind: to supply the ships and the population with water deriving from the Carioca Reservoir, and to create a masterpiece which would embellish the city.

It was Funck's idea to fuse the reservoir and the fountain into one block and to fashion the composition to resemble a church tower. But it was Valentim's version of the fountain, still maintaining the idea of a vertical bell tower and made from dark local granite, that was built. It possesses both baroque and rococo marble ornamental elements, such as cushions, balustrades and garlands. It can be described as a great prism with a rectangular base, almost a cube, which supports a smaller pyramid (Monteiro de Carvalho 1999: 45).

The oil painting by Leandro Joaquim (Figure 13:1 col. pl.) shows that the fountain dramatically dominated the maritime scenery of the wharf, having on its left side the 'Paço' and on the right a building belonging to Teles de Menezes, one of the richest men in the city. In the background stand the monastery and the churches of the First and the Third Religious Orders of the Carmo. The central part of the construction is rectangular, with uneven sides. The alternate concave and convex lines create surprising lighting effects on the surface, contributing to the overall impression of ascension and steepness of the monument. The sides are composed of superposed stones of granite, forming columns. At the top is a classical urn made of granite with a marble pyre, a symbolic representation of the sacred fire of Greek temples. Above this used to be the Portuguese coat of arms (removed in 1842 and replaced by a metallic sphere, sustaining a Brazilian crown). A door in the front façade, facing the sea, leads to a terrace, with a wonderful view of Guanabara Bay. On the opposite façade (towards the Carmelite cloister and church) is an oval marble tablet, engraved with the name of the Viceroy, comparing his deeds to those of the god of light.

Another very important example of this kind of ancient fountain, the 'Fountain of the Saracuras', was also the work of Valentim (Monteiro de Carvalho 1999: 49), built at the end of 18th century. It was originally to supply water to the Convent of the Ajuda, in Rio de Janeiro, and was Valentim's last work for public consumption.

The 'Fountain of the Saracuras' was sponsored by the Sisters of the Order of the Clarissas, and was intended to commemorate the Count of Rezende (1790–1801), the Viceroy of Brazil. The Clarissas Convent was built in 1748 by Brigadier General Engineer Alpoim, occupying a large area in central Rio de Janeiro. In 1795, its fountain was intended for the inner court of the cloister, where it became a place for relaxation. In 1911, it was presented to the municipality by Archbishop Joaquim Arcoverde Cavalcanti, and it now stands in General Osório square, in Rio de Janeiro.

The 'Fountain of the Saracuras' is made from dark local granite and contained both functional and ornamental details in bronze, such as faucets in the shape of a bird ('saracura'),[2] a turtle and the heraldic symbols of the Viceroy in marble. The plan has at its centre a cup-shaped fountain surmounted by an obelisk in 'needle style', which is mounted on a circular base. On the top of the monument stands a bronze Christian cross.

This monument simultaneously contains elements and styles of the Renaissance, the baroque and the rococo. The composition displays a harmonious articulation in a single block that integrates different architectural principles. As described by Anna Maria Monteiro de Carvalho (1999), the fountain itself recaptures the idea of centrality (mother/earth), the origin of life (water) and the ideal of eternity (sky/youth), present in old ancient oriental tradition. According to Monteiro de Carvalho (1999: 52), Valentim had recaptured in the 'Fountain of the Saracuras' the idea of centrality/ eternity present in Bernini's fountain in Rome and, by adding the Latin cross, he had given a sense of transcendency to the monument.

In 1808, Dom João VI, at this time Prince Regent of Portugal, landed in Rio de Janeiro, bringing with him around 15,000 members of the Portuguese court. Rio became the capital of the Empire, blossoming as a city with the construction of public buildings and establishing its own architectural identity.

The obelisk, a single tapering rectangular block of stone, is particularly associated with Ancient Egypt. It is the most frequent Egyptianizing motif adopted in Brazilian urban architecture. The obelisk is also commonly used in commemorative monuments. Due to its impressive features, it is a constant source of inspiration for those who aspire to enduring memorials. The Brazilian urban landscape contains several obelisks, erected by both public and private groups. These symbols are associated with all the major moments of Brazilian history, and memorialize events ranging from major battles to city foundations.

The exact number of obelisk-like monuments in Brazil is not known, pending the completion of an inventory being undertaken through a national research project. Thus far, several dozen obelisk-like monuments in several states of the country have been documented (www.egyptomania.hpg.ig.com.br). Nor is there any register of original Egyptian obelisks in Brazil. All the obelisks so far observed are copies or adaptations of originals. They are generally placed in urban settings, erected singly, not in pairs as in Ancient Egypt, their function being purely decorative or commemorative. Several good examples can be found throughout Brazil. One of the best in Rio de Janeiro is a granite obelisk called the 'Obelisk of the Rio Branco Avenue',[3] erected in 1906 in homage to the opening of the former Central Avenue (Figure 13:2). Another fine example of a commemorative obelisk is encountered opposite the main entrance to the docks of Porto Alegre, built in memory of the city's bicentennial.

São Paulo was founded between the rivers Tamanduateí and Anhangabaú, in the plains of Piratininga, far from the coast. Some historians see this location as having been chosen as an act of disobedience towards the Portuguese metropolis, settlements on the coast being encouraged in order to hamper attacks from other European countries. A small school for teaching catechism to the natives was founded in 1554 on the plains of Piratininga, by the priests of the Society of Jesus. On St Paul's day, an inaugural mass was celebrated in that school, which became a very important location for the development of the settlement. In 1711, the 'village' was placed in the category of a city. In the

Figure 13:2   Granite 'Obelisco da Avenida Rio Branco', Rio de Janeiro (1906).

beginning, the city was very quiet and tranquil but later changed when the diocese was established in 1745. The urban nucleus was enlarged with more buildings with additions on their façades. Wealth changed the way of daily life and required the opening of roads. In 1814, in commemoration of the opening of the road to Sorocaba, Marshall Daniel Pedro Müller, who derived from European ancestry and had completed military and mathematic studies in Lisbon, ordered an obelisk to be erected in the 'Ladeira dos Piques' (Slope of the Piques). He contracted Vicente Gomes Pereira (Master Vicentinho, a well known stoneworker) to build a stone obelisk, measuring 8.78 m high and 1.78 x 1.8 m at its base. It is now known as the 'Obelisk of Memory' (Castanho 1987: 85) and its appearance in 1847 was captured by Miguel Dutra, in a watercolour called 'Pyramids and Fountain of the Piques' (Figure 13:3 col. pl.). Vicentinho was born in Itu, a small town in the state of São Paulo, and is well known for his numerous skills (Petri 1981); he is considered one of the precursors of plastic arts in Brazil. He was self-taught, and his paintings capture a 'naive' realism, scenes and customs of the time. The obelisk was built where the muleteers and cattle drivers passed on their way to Sorocaba, now in the middle of the city, in the neighbourhood of Pinheiros. Some record that it was built to mark the provision of canalized water to the city. It stands over a circular masonry basin with iron grids, a sort of fountain reservoir at its lower level. Water used to be channelled from this tank, through hills and boroughs until reaching the central lake of the Botanical Garden.

The 'Fountain of Memory' was finished in 1872. In 1919, to commemorate the forthcoming centenary of the Independence of Brazil from Portugal, the Mayor of São Paulo decided to restore the sculptures, masterpieces of the past. The pyramid was maintained in its original place and a new fountain was built in front of a large wall. The glazed tile lining, including the ones decorating the benches and walls, were all painted with ancient landscapes by the artist, J. Wasth Rodrigues. The stairs were conceived in an Art Nouveau style. By the end of the 19th century the fountain was surrounded by high iron grilles. In this enclosure trees grew wild, giving the impression of a small forest. It is surprising to find in such a small area, lost in the middle of a jungle of concrete, so many masterpieces of sculpture, including the 'Fountain of Memory' and the 'Pyramid of Memory'.

The influence of Egyptian style can also be seen in the art of one of the best 19th century Brazilian painters: Minas Gerais' Honório Esteves do Sacramento (1860–1933). Honório Esteves was one of the early Brazilian academic painters whose works were ever-present in the everyday life of Minas Gerais State. He made oil paintings, pastels, portraits, and charcoal drawings. Honório, the son of a carpenter, had a very humble upbringing, and remained very religious and deeply appreciative of local traditions. At the age of 11 he had started to study art at a design school in Ouro Preto, and it was in 1880 that he visited Rio de Janeiro for the first time. Four years later, by special appointment of the Emperor Dom Pedro II, he moved there, and studied with famous Brazilian painters such as Pedro Americo and Victor Meirelles. Esteves' talent was very well recognized during his studies at the Imperial Academy of Fine Arts, where he received several prizes.

While living in Rio de Janeiro, he produced his 'Egyptian Shepherd' (Figure 13:4). The main subject of the painting is a human figure with Egyptianizing elements, but also with some connection to the artist's own surroundings. Thus, the Nemes and the

Figure 13:4   Oil painting by Honório Esteves of an Egyptian shepherd (date unknown) (Museu Mineiro, Belo Horizonte).

loincloth are Esteves' interpretations of Egyptianizing motifs, while other elements of the composition – including the face of the shepherd, the box on which he is seated, his staff, and the curtain in the background – represent the painter's environment.

Between 1870 and 1920, many painters were impressed by the art of Sir Lawrence Alma-Tadema (Werner Chapter 5: Figure 5:11; Whitehouse Chapter 3: Figure 3:6, both this volume) and attempted to follow in his artistic footsteps. It is possible that there was a group of orientalist painters at this time in Brazil (certainly there must have been some influence from such painters whether in Brazil or Europe) to have inspired Esteves. Indeed, one can detect similarities between some of the colours and design effects, clothes and hairdressing worn by Esteves' Egyptian shepherd in the portrait made in 1887, and the seated man on the right in Alma-Tadema's oil painting of 'Egyptian Chess Players' dating to 1865 (and see Coli 2001: 387).

Public and private buildings in most major cities in Brazil show some Egyptianizing motifs in their architecture and decoration. For example, in Porto Alegre, in Rio Grande do Sul, at the Public Library, there is a fine example of the use of Egyptianizing elements for decorative purposes: the 'Egyptian Room' (Figure 13:5 col. pl.). The building was started in 1911 by Afonso Herbert, a German architect, and was opened to the public in 1914 (Bakos 2001). The building still reflects some signs of the strong influence of positivism in Rio Grande do Sul at that time, as its façade is decorated with images of Auguste Comte's calendar. The rising bourgeoisie in Rio Grande do Sul embraced positivism and Comte's philosophical system and religion provided the underpinning to support an elaborate structure for social planning (Nachman 1977: 7).

Due to its cultural importance the building needed to be expanded, and its Director wished to redecorate the interior. The result was a series of thematic rooms decorated by a local artist, Fernando Schlatter, with the assistance of some of the most gifted local painters found in the artistic community, mainly immigrants. The redecoration began in 1919 and was completed three years later. The themes which Schlatter used to decorate all the rooms were copied from a German book by Dolmetsch (1889), which was adapted in a much simplified form for the Public Library in Porto Alegre. The decoration as a whole was mainly in Roman or Greek style, based on classical inspiration. However, some walls and ceilings show details based on Egyptian themes, such as animals from the Nile Valley, serpents, ibises, and winged disks (Bakos 1998: 90). The atmosphere created in the Egyptian Room is probably the only example of this kind in a public building in Brazil. The motifs for the painting of the ceiling and a series of wall panels reveal an emotive imagination, "fused with an exceptional command of dramatic effect, on occasion pushed to delirium ..." (Humbert *et al.* 1994: 69). In the 'Grand Salon' of the Public Library, flanking the Egyptian Room, stands a statue of a breasted Nemes-wearing sphinx (Figure 13:6). The sphinx is widely known, and occupies a special position in the history of the survival of ancient Egyptian imagery: it is the element that has been used almost uninterruptedly in the western world. It evokes a dual symbolism in the western mind, being both enigmatic and cruel. In this case, wearing the royal Nemes, the Egyptian sphinx is a manifestation of the pharaoh (Humbert *et al.* 1994: 86, 138).

Another fine example of Egyptianizing motifs in architecture is an elegant, still-standing, four-storey building in downtown Rio de Janeiro. It is located in the heart of

Figure 13:6   Marble Nemes-wearing sphinx (author and date unknown) (Public Library, Porto Alegre).

the old city, at the corner of two of the best known streets, the 'Ouvidor' and the 'Rio Branco Avenue'. Its exact construction date is not known, but it was already built by 1930. With the exception of the ground floor, all the others have balconies. On the fourth floor, these are made of cement, with columns of two sizes, while on the other two they are of iron, decorated with figures of winged scarabs. Inserted into the balconies on the second floor are two exquisite iron statues of winged human figures, similar to caryatids. A man and a woman hold a large cup-shaped bowl covered by a smaller dome-shaped lid above their heads. Both wear elegant Egyptian Nemes, pectorals, and loincloths, and stand in the place of honour on the balcony, easily seen by all passers-by (Figure 13:7). The walls are painted in light pink, with ivory stucco friezes on the third floor, and green garlands composed of spirals and small lotiform flowers on the second.

Humbert *et al*. (1994: 21) state that in all western countries, without exception, people have tried to adapt Egyptian art and make it their own. Brazil also follows the rule. Obelisks and pyramids are the most popular forms of Egyptianizing motifs adopted in this country. Other Egyptian symbols can be observed in art, construction and decoration. Through the 19th century, the use of Egyptianizing motifs grew more popular in architecture and in the arts. They can be found in isolation or associated with other styles of decoration.

Freemasons and Rosicrucians also incorporated Egyptianizing motifs within the architecture of some of their lodges and temples (Figures 13:8, 13:9 col. pls.; Humbert *et al*. 1994: 451). Equally remarkable is the presence of Egyptian styles on some burial and family memorials in several cemeteries in Rio de Janeiro, São Paulo and Rio

Figure 13:7 Bronze statue of a winged Nemes-wearing woman on an Egyptian style balcony, Rua do Ouvidor, Rio de Janeiro (© M. M. Bakos).

Grande do Sul, where monuments in the forms of sphinxes, pyramids and temples imitate Egyptian originals.

The increasing use of ancient Egyptian names by local construction companies is evident today. Such names are applied to both construction firms and buildings and are apparently successful in delivering a message of solidity and long-lasting quality. In Bento Gonçalves city, the firm 'Pyramids Real Estate Enterprise' has named some of its buildings: 'Khephren', 'Ibis', 'Ramesses I', 'Apis', 'Isis', 'Amun Ra', 'Horus', 'Tuthmosis' and 'Kheops'. Similar examples are found in other southern Brazilian cities, but also in the northern city of João Pessoa, where 'Pyramid Constructors' call their apartment buildings '1st Pyramid', '2nd Pyramid' and so on. Brazilian companies believe in the 'positive energy' transmitted by such names.

As observed in other countries (e.g. Brier 1993: 40) the use of ancient Egyptianizing motifs always had a single purpose: to attract customers. Egyptianizing references are used to highlight the solidity, permanence and quality of products, by associating them with models that have survived throughout the centuries.

For aesthetic purposes, private houses and residential buildings today are decorated on a smaller scale with Egyptianizing components such as small pyramids and obelisks, for example, a house in Pelotas, where a pyramid forms the roof of the main entrance hall (Figure 13:10). In the commercial sector, images of Egyptian architectural elements are often used in an imaginative manner. For example, a physical fitness academy in Natal is the 'Pyramid Fitness Academy', and is a building with pyramid-like roof and four concrete extensions to form the sides of the pyramid (Figure 13:11). It was built and named specifically to create a reference to the ancient Egyptian traits of strength and endurance. The massiveness of certain Egyptian forms, like the pyramid, whose weight and solidity are universally appreciated, are perfect for calling attention to simple buildings, and they have been used exactly for this purpose.

The widespread and growing tourist industry in Brazil occasionally uses Egyptianizing symbols to call attention to its buildings. In Natal, on the seashore, the modern 'Pyramid Hotel' displays a white pyramid on its roof, facing a luxurious lake-shaped complex of swimming pools, surrounded by coconut trees and thatched-roof bars for refreshments. The exoticism of this architecture and its evocative power (Humbert *et al*. 1994: 314) are frequently used for commercial purposes.

'Faraó's Motel', in São Bernardo do Campo, in the state of São Paulo, has a façade with scenes showing stylized and somewhat satirical human figures of nobles and

Figure 13:10   Pyramid-shaped roof of a private house, Pelotas (© Viviane Adriana Saballa).

Figure 13:11   Piramide Fitness Academia, Natal (© Rodrigo Otávio da Silva).

servants in leisure activities. Painted columns seem to sustain a fretwork surmounted by several stylish pyramids intermingled with vases. At the main entrance, a seated figure of a pharaoh is flanked by two vertical cartouches painted with symbols imitating hieroglyphs, and two columns of concrete supporting a marquee (Figure 13:12). Several other cartouches with fantasy hieroglyphs and human figures and vases are located around the building. An inner court, with painted walls, shows human figures, lion goddesses, birds and feathers. The rooms are equipped with brass wall-mounted lanterns with figures of a cobra serpent holding over her head a flame-like glass lamp (Figure 13:13). Some suites are called 'Mycerinus', 'Khephren', 'Kheops' and 'Thebes'.

Over the last 300 years Brazil, the largest South American country – and very distant from the land of the pharaohs – has been influenced by the worldwide and age-old fascination with Ancient Egypt. Evidence of Egyptianizing motifs can be seen throughout the country, mostly in architecture and art. From the 18th century obelisk-like fountains and commemorative monuments to today's modern hotels and buildings, such Egyptianizing motifs have been used in different ways, but their links have always been to the stability, solidity, royalty and mystery of that ancient civilization.

Figure 13:12   The main entrance of 'Faraó's Motel', São Bernardo do Campo (© André Chevitarese).

Figure 13:13
Uraeus-like wall-
mounted lantern
in 'Faraó's Motel',
São Bernardo do
Campo, brass (©
André
Chevitarese).

Notes

1   *Carioca* is a term used to refer to people or things living in or coming from Rio de Janeiro. It derives from the word *karioka*, from the 'tupi' language, and its original meaning was 'white people's house'.

2   *Saracura* is a very wary and suspicious local bird. It stays hidden in the vegetation of marshes and swamps during daylight, and comes out from its hiding place at sunset to eat insects, crustaceans and small fish.

3   This obelisk is particularly famous because in 1930, at the end of a revolution, a group of horsemen from the winning side and deriving from the South, more specifically from Rio Grande do Sul, tied their horses to the obelisk, a landmark of Rio de Janeiro, to symbolize their victory over the government and the end of the civil war.

Acknowledgments

I gratefully acknowledge the important contributions to this chapter of André Chevitarese (Rio de Janeiro), Antonio Otávio de Paiva Moura (Minas Gerais), Bianca Hennies Brigidi (Porto Alegre), Carolina Machado Guedes (Rio de Janeiro), Ciro Flamarion Cardoso (Niteroi), Fábio Vergara Cerqueira (Pelotas), Fernanda Coimbra C. Pereira (Espírito Santo), Gilvan Ventura da Silva (Espírito Santo), José Antonio Dabdab Trabulsi (Belo Horizonte), Luis Augusto de Lima (Museu Mineiro-Minas Gerais), Nathalia Monseff Junqueira (São Paulo), Pedro Paulo Funari (São Paulo), Raquel Glezer (Museu Paulista – São Paulo), Rodrigo Otávio da Silva (Rio Grande do Norte), Welcsoner Silva da Cunha (Pelotas), and Faraó's Motel (São Bernardo do Campo).

Financial support was provided by a grant from Conselho Nacional de Pesquisa (CNPq). Mrs Sherril Hookem revised the manuscript.

CHAPTER 14

EGYPTIANIZING MOTIFS IN SOUTH AFRICAN ARCHITECTURE

Izak Cornelius

The crest of Cecil John Rhodes in South Africa House, London, and in Rhodes House, Oxford, was designed by the architect Sir Herbert Baker. It shows the mountains of the moon and the source of the Nile, the Zimbabwe birds and the southern cross (Merrington 1995, 2001), and thus represents a fitting link between Egypt and South Africa.

This chapter surveys some South African examples of the 'Egyptian Revival'. It indicates, for the first time, the way in which Ancient Egypt has served as a source of inspiration for South African architecture (cf. remarks in Claassen 1987: 112, 118; Greig 1971: 174; Oberholster 1972: 16).

Egyptianizing motifs occur in several buildings. The 'Gymnasium Primary' in Paarl, 50 km north of Cape Town (Figures 14:1, 14:2), is notable for its elaborate Egyptianizing decorations (Fransen and Cook 1980: 201–202; Greig 1971: 174; Oberholster 1972: 90–91; Picton-Seymour 1977: 141). It was opened in 1858 and proclaimed a national monument in 1968. It is still in use as a primary school for boys and girls. The school was originally established as a church school to train boys before they went to the Theological Seminary or to study in Europe. One of the teachers was responsible for teaching "Classical Languages, Ancient History and Mythology" (Oberholster 1972: 90). One of its buildings, which dates from 1868–1869, clearly reflects ancient Egyptian influences. The main entrance is in the form of a giant Egyptian temple pylon, with typical tapering sides and a crowning cavetto cornice. The cavetto pattern is also to be seen on the side walls. The windows are crowned with this pattern, decorated with a winged sun. A comparison from the Egyptian Revival period (cf. Curl 1994: 236) might be Bullock's Egyptian Hall from 1812 (Curl 1994: 156–157, fig. 110; MacKenzie 1995: 78, 81, fig. 71; Medina-González 2003; Werner Chapter 5, this volume) with its pylons and cavettos with winged sundisks. In the case of the Paarl school, the idea does not seem to have been copied from any specific model of a known Egyptian temple but rather is generic in origin.

The building is decorated with Egyptian motifs in stucco. On the central clock tower there are many Egyptian decorations: floral patterns and a winged sundisk with uraei. Around the spot where the clock would have been, there is a row of circling scarab beetles flanked by floral patterns. Below this is a frieze with Egyptian

Figure 14:1   Paarl Gymnasium (© Izak Cornelius).

Figure 14:2   Paarl Gymnasium: main entrance (© Izak Cornelius).

uraei with sundisks on their heads, and more winged sundisks and stars. Directly above the main wooden door with its gabled window is a large sundisk with wings and four crawling scarab beetles.

On the gables of the two wings are various decorations. Notable are the head of the goddess Hathor and the sphinx. The Hathor head is shown with *naos* and a sundisk with horns inside it. Other decorations include the vulture goddess Nekhbet, and another winged sun with rays and other patterns.

One can trace the origins of these Egyptian motifs to the founder of the school, Reverend Van der Lingen, who had a direct influence on the decorations and even spent some of his own personal funds on them. He has been described as being extremely conservative, very anti-English and opposed to the public schools of the time. He had studied many oriental languages (De Villiers 1874: 240) and was apparently well read, with a personal library of 10,000 volumes (Kitshoff 1972: 263). A list of 1870, the *Catalogus van een Belangrijke Verzameling Goed Gekonditioneerde Boeken*, drawn up by a teacher at the school, includes many volumes on Egypt and the Orient such as the *Description* (1809–1828; cf. Kitshoff 1972: 267). Van der Lingen also owned copies of Denon (1802) (in the Dutch 1803 translation of this work), Vyse (1841), Birch (1857) and Salt (1825). It is known that he studied Piazzi Smyth's (1867) speculations on the Great Pyramid, but was not convinced by them (De Villiers 1874: 242). One biographer noted that he studied 40 books to create his Egyptian style of building (De Kock 1983: 136). He was an admirer of ancient Egyptian culture and is said to have studied Egyptian hieroglyphs (Fransen and Cook 1980: 210), but it has not yet been possible to determine the scope of his studies.

Merrington (1995: 649 ff; 2001: 332) deals with the 'Cape to Cairo' motif and also refers to the school in Paarl. He draws a possible relation between some Egyptianizing motifs and the Dutch tradition of Freemasonry at the Cape. However, it should be noted that Van der Lingen himself spoke very negatively about the Cape Freemasons (Cooper 1986: 150).

The motto of the school, *Sol uistitiae illustra nos* ("The sun of justice shines on us", taken from the Hebrew Bible, Maleachi 3:20), which was adopted from the University of Utrecht in the Netherlands where Van der Lingen had studied, also strengthens the solar symbolism and the connection with Egypt. It was also the motto of the Stellenbosch Theological Seminary (1863). The motto is no longer visible on the school walls, but is said to have appeared beneath the window in the tower (Kitshoff 1972: 137). It also appears on the front gable of the Dutch Reformed Church in the same town, the so-called *Paarl Strooidak* (thatched roof) church (1805), where Van der Lingen preached.

Nothing comparable to the architecture and decoration of this school occurs on buildings from the period after the discovery of Tutankhamun's tomb, nor in contemporary buildings in South Africa. It stands as a unique example and as the jewel of Egyptianizing motifs in South African architecture.

The oldest buildings in the Cape which reflect the style of the Egyptian Revival are in the Cape Town Gardens (Figures 14:3, 14:4) next to Parliament. Here, just below Bertram House on the right hand side of the *Laan* (Avenue), is the 'Egyptian building' (Fransen and Cook 1980: 47; Greig 1971: 94; Oberholster 1972: 16), the oldest building

Figure 14:3   Egyptian building of the University of Cape Town (© Izak Cornelius).

Figure 14:4   Side of Egyptian building of the University of Cape Town (© Izak Cornelius).

still remaining of the first 'European' University, dating from 1841. Thus it could perhaps have provided an example for Van der Lingen, although the Paarl building is much more elaborate in its decorations.

In 1829 the South African College was established and in 1838 the Governor, Sir Benjamin D'Urban, gave property to the College. James Adamson, Professor in English and Nature Studies, designed it and Colonel G. G. Lewis of the Royal Engineers revised the design. The College was opened in 1841 and proclaimed a national monument in 1969.

There are open papyrus-like Egyptianizing pillars, but these are not decorated. Egyptianizing pylon-like decorations occur in plaster relief on the side wings. The roof also has a cavetto cornice pattern and on the side of the 'Avenue' there are more pylon decorations with sundisks as well as adapted winged sundisks above the windows.

The reasons for using an Egyptian style have yet to be established. They might have included the continuing effect of Bonaparte's expedition (1798) and ongoing publications about it (final volume of the *Description* published in 1828), although Merrington (1995: 650) prefers to see the style's origins in the Egyptianizing Freemasonry of the Cape. The tradition of regarding Egypt as a place of learning and wisdom may also have been influential.

The oldest Jewish community in South Africa dates back to 1841 and the first synagogue was built in 1849. It was called *Tikvath Israel* ("Hope of Israel"), a reference to "[the Cape of] Good Hope". The present synagogue was consecrated on 13 September 1863 (*contra* Claassen 1987: 112, who gives 1882; Fransen and Cook 1980: 49; Greig 1971: 96) (Figure 14:5). Above the entrance is a façade in the form of a pylon with a large cavetto cornice with a vertical linear pattern. The pillars in front are also Egyptian, but are not exactly comparable to any Egyptian examples. One might expect that the capitals would be lotus- or papyrus-shaped, but close examination reveals what look like papyrus-shaped capitals with perhaps vine leaves. On the lower base there are palm-like decorations. Greig (1971: 96) describes these as "a mixture of decorative acanthus and palm leaves and lotus flowers".

Synagogues in similar style are also known from elsewhere, especially in the USA (Curl 1994: 189; Fazzini Chapter 8, this volume; Wischnitzer 1975: 347) and no specific reasons have so far been ascertained for the adoption of the Egyptianizing style in South Africa.

Figure 14:5   Old synagogue in the Cape Town Gardens (© Izak Cornelius).

Figure 14:6   L'Agulhas Lighthouse (© Izak Cornelius).

The Lighthouse of L'Agulhas (Figure 14:6), which was also called the 'Pharos of the South', was used from 1849 and is the second oldest lighthouse in South Africa. The original plans in the Transnet Archives date from 1848. The old limestone tower was replaced in 1962 and after restoration it was reinstated in 1988. It has a pylon-shaped entrance with windows in the centre. Above the central entrance is a decoration of a winged sundisk with uraei (part of which has fallen off and is now in the museum). The roof and the windows also reflect the cavetto pattern. The British Governor at the time of its construction, Sir Harry Smith, asked that the Lighthouse should reflect culture and civilization at this rugged outpost (Van Bart 1993). Using Egyptianizing motifs and constructing a lighthouse in the tradition of one of the (lost) wonders of the ancient world (the Pharos lighthouse in Alexandria) therefore seemed most appropriate.

The best-known building in South Africa with known Egyptian influence dates from August 1820 and was declared a national monument in 1938. It is a steep-angled pyramid on Donkin Hill in old Portuguese Algoa Bay, where the first British settlers set foot on South African soil. It was built by the Acting Governor, Sir Rufane, in memory of his wife Elizabeth, who died in India in 1818 and after whom the city was named. The inscription reads:

> To the memory of one of the most perfect of human beings, who has given her name to the town below.

(Oberholster 1972: 133–134)

Pyramids are synonymous with Egypt in many people's minds (and see Humbert Chapter 2, this volume), and there are many later examples (Lehner 1997: 240–243). However, according to Harradine (1991), this particular pyramidal shape had its origins in Britain, where pyramid shapes (such as the example at Castle Howard, Yorkshire, cf. Curl 1994: 84) were very popular from the 1700s. The model for them was the very steep-angled pyramid tomb of the tribune Caius Cestius at the Porta San Páolo in Rome (12 BC) (Curl 1994: 25–26, fig. 15; Humbert 1994: 114). In later times in Ancient Egypt pyramids were also constructed to indicate tombs, such as the one at Deir el-Medina. One example (cf. Lehner 1997: 193) also has a steeper angle, which suggest that Curl's (1994: 25) argument that the Caius pyramid derived from the steeper pyramids of Nubia may not be entirely justifiable.

After the completion of this chapter, Dr Hans Fransen informed me of another pyramid tomb outside Caledon (112 km east of Cape Town) above the hot baths. This tomb was built by a Dr Johann Friedrich Hässner (1764–1821) for his wife, who died in 1817 while giving birth to twins. It is almost 3 m high and plastered and was restored in 1988 (cf. Brand 1998: 75–77). This pyramid is comparable to the Donkin pyramid which was also built for a deceased wife, but of interest is that the Caledon one is older and the fact that the wife was buried there.

In the small town of Kakamas near the border of Namibia is the so-called 'Transformer' building. It resembles the pylon shape of an Egyptian temple with its cornice, but not the typical concave cavetto or *gorge*. It was built by the Swiss architect A. B. Hangartner in 1914, and has been a museum since 1998 (Hopkins 1978: 130–131). The name of the town itself is written in Phoenician letters, which is another link to the ancient world.

It is said that Hangartner opted for an Egyptianizing style because Kakamas was situated on the same longitude as Egypt (28° 44') and because of the intense heat in both countries. To this might be added the fact that the river is so prominent. Kakamas is indeed a 'gift' of the Orange River – as the Mississippi is sometimes described as the "Nile of America" (Wischnitzer 1975: 349). The river creates a paradise in a very dry region, much as is the case with the Nile in Egypt.

The Women's War Memorial in Bloemfontein (Figure 14:7; Van Schoor 1993) is a sandstone obelisk 36.5 m high, with a bronze tip designed by the Afrikaans sculptor Anton van Wouw; the monument was unveiled on 16 December 1913 to commemorate the more than 20,000 women and children who died in the English War (also called the Anglo-Boer War) of 1899–1902.

Another commemorative obelisk is the small one erected in Kakamas in 1998 to commemorate the forced removals under the apartheid regime and the desecration of the tombs of coloured and black people. The inscription in Afrikaans reads:

> In memory of 150 Brown and Black loved ones who passed away and were laid to rest here. Their tombs were destroyed in 1986 by the forced removals of the apartheid years. We honour their memory.

These two obelisks date respectively before and after the discovery of the tomb of Tutankhamun. In each case the obelisk was chosen to commemorate the memory of the dead, although representing quite different ideologies.

Following the discovery of the tomb of Tutankhamun in 1922, the Art Déco style with its Egyptianisms took hold in Europe and America (Curl 1994: 211–220, 230; Humbert 1994: 508 ff). Not only were many mummy and Cleopatra movies made at this time (Lupton 2003; Serafy 2003), but the trend is also reflected in the architectural styles of cinemas and theatres which were built during this period. A South African example of this is the Colosseum theatre in Johannesburg, which was built in the 1930s but unfortunately demolished in the 1970s. Martin (1987: 23–24) described it as having had a façade with six Egyptianizing pillars with bronze papyrus capitals and freestanding female figurines in niches. The original designers thought they were building in "Old Roman Style" – hence the Latin name.

Figure 14:7   Obelisk in Bloemfontein (© Izak Cornelius).

This is the only clear Egyptianizing example from the post-1922 period. In contrast to the other examples from the 19th century (which were places of learning or worship, commemorative monuments and an electricity transformer), Egyptianizing motifs were used in this instance in a building intended for entertainment. A contemporary example of Egyptian motifs used as 'kitsch' is the restaurant called 'Cleopatra's Table' at the casino in Gauteng near Johannesburg (website www.caesars.co.za/entertainment/default.htm). It is decorated with large statues reminiscent of the statues of Antinous (Curl 1994: fig. 19) which were very popular in Rome. The guests are seated in an Egyptianizing boat which imitates the one in which Cleopatra met Marc Antony and which is described by Plutarch.

Conclusions

Egypt can act as a source of inspiration over a variety of spheres. Although the examples from South Africa are limited in number and hardly comparable to those in Europe and the USA, it is noteworthy that the revival style still found expression in a place as far removed from Europe as the Cape of Good Hope at the most southern tip of the African continent. It is ironic that this inspiration came via Europe and not from the continent that it shared with Egypt.

Acknowledgments

I am grateful to Pierre-Jacques Venter, Jo-Marie Claassen, Mimmie Seyffert, René Fourie, and Anlen Boshoff. I also want to thank Mr M. V. Carstens and Mrs Ria Basson of the Paarl Gymnasium as well as Mr I. Arendse and Mrs E. Powess. Marlene Goosen informed me about the building in Kakamas. I sincerely thank Debbie Aggenbag for her and her husband's kindness during our stay in Kakamas. Margaret Harradine provided information on the Port Elizabeth pyramid and Dr Hans Fransen on the Caledon pyramid.

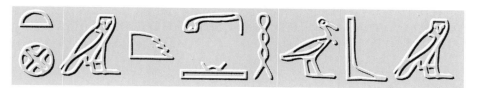

CHAPTER 15

'EGYPTIANIZING' THE ALEXANDRINA: THE CONTEMPORARY REVIVAL OF THE ANCIENT MOUSEION/LIBRARY

Beverley Butler

Despite its loss, or rather because of it, the ancient library has never lost its hold on the European imagination ... What had been not the only, but perhaps the most famous library, museum and even garden of the Hellenistic period was banished to the attics of legend and myth ... Today, this interest in the past is being encouraged by a vision of the future – the Bibliotecha Alexandrina, an ultra modern library and conference centre, developed under the auspices of UNESCO and the Egyptian government, and rising on the shoreline of Alexandria, near the place where the ancient buildings are thought to have been. The international enterprise is dedicated to the advancement of knowledge, and will attract scholars from many countries. It will celebrate the cosmopolitanism that is the city and culture of Alexandria, and the traditions of internationalism, critical questioning, and freedom of enquiry that were at varying times the hallmarks of the ancient library.

(MacLeod 2001: xi)

Discrepant cosmopolitanisms guarantee nothing politically. They offer no release from mixed feelings, from utopic/distopic tensions. They do, however, name and make more visible a complex range of intercultural experiences, sites of appropriation and exchange. [In] these cosmopolitical contact zones ... nothing is guaranteed, except contamination, messy politics and more translation.

(Clifford 1998: 369)

The Bibliotecha Alexandrina project[1] – which aims to revive the ancient Alexandria Mouseion/Library (built in the third century BC by Ptolemy Soter) – represents a very specific intervention and engagement with the use of ancient Egyptian architectural motifs and constructions. The revival of the ancient Alexandrina marks an inversion or reversal of the usual flow of translations and transmissions from Egypt across the world. What I investigate is the 'Egyptianization' – the often problematic, return 'home' of this potent 'lost' monument of Alexandria's Greco-Roman past to the contemporary city. (Intriguingly, the contents, appearance and location of the ancient library are largely unknown, but it is best understood as a composite of a temple of the Muses, a 'universal' library, philosophical academy and a planetarium.) Moreover, as MacLeod (2001) suggests, cosmopolitanism is the key motif mediating return, and as such it has afforded contemporary revivalism an opportunity both to re-work Alexandria's ancient cosmopolitan role as the 'meeting point between East and West' and to serve as a medium for a series of re-engagements between the city's ancient pasts and its contemporary concerns and agendas.

The aim of this chapter is to map the process of this Egyptianizing movement which takes the Alexandrina from the attics of legend and myth (the exclusive hold of the European imagination) in order to recast it in terms of future visions for Egypt. Combining insights from ethnographic work undertaken in Alexandria with recent theoretical framings of 'cosmopolitanism', the defined levels and layers of the Bibliotecha Alexandrina's contemporary potencies as a "cosmopolitan contact zone" (cf. Clifford 1998: 369) are interpreted through the project's movement from an 'idea' revived by academics from Alexandria University; its re-inscription as a 'partnership' between Unesco and the Egyptian government; its emergence as an architectural object; and its continuous re-workings as the project is shaped, translated (and often contested) via a series of institutions (governmental and non-governmental organizations), groups and individuals at local, national, and international levels.

What emerges alongside the Bibliotecha Alexandrina's own emergence as architectural object is both an 'official' celebratory revivalist thesis and a complex 'messy politics' born of the intimacies, tensions and discrepancies between this dominant thesis and co-existent struggles to particularize, pluralize and popularize the Alexandrina's cosmopolitics. This is an experience which is not without its points of trauma and crisis, and with no absolute 'guarantees'; the scene of revivalism has also been subject to what is the most potent fault-line to haunt the Alexandrina's (and also cosmopolitanism's) genealogy – the 'Clash of Civilizations' thesis.

From the academy to international project

Two 'anecdotes' provide some deeper context to both Alexandrina's old and new, and to revivalism's Egyptianizing dynamic. They were told to me by Mostafa El-Abaddi, Professor of Greco-Roman Studies at Alexandria University. Abaddi, who first raised the idea of revivalism in the 1970s (subsequently securing the support of his colleagues within the academic domain), described these 'anecdotes' as acting as 'catalysts' to the contemporary revivalist scheme. The first concerns the former US President Richard Nixon's state visit to Egypt, made in 1974 at the invitation of the then Egyptian President Anwar Sadat. Part of Nixon's itinerary included a visit to Alexandria where Abaddi and his colleagues from the university were drafted in as specialist academic 'tour guides'. Of the occasion Abaddi commented:

> Nixon displayed the interest that many foreigners do. He had an idealized image of Alexandria already formed in his imagination and obviously felt a certain affinity and a nostalgia for Alexandria's golden-age: its Greco-Roman, Hellenistic, and cosmopolitan pasts. This became particularly obvious when Nixon asked us if we could show him the site where the ancient 'Universal' Library and associated Mouseion once stood.

Abaddi then added with some irony:

> Of course we couldn't show him anything ... The exact location of the Great Library is not known to us – there are no archaeological traces. Not so much as a single stone survives.

Not long afterwards a form of role-reversal took place as Abaddi was invited to the US to attend a meeting at the Library of Congress. He told me how he was greeted with a special warmth by the Chief Librarian, who said how pleased he was to meet a delegate from Alexandria, proclaiming that "The Alexandria library was the prototype of our own institution: its ancient ancestor". The compliments continued as Abaddi was then asked if he could give information concerning the appearance and architecture of the ancient institution so that, as a tribute, a model could be made and placed at the entrance of the Library of Congress. In what Abaddi called "a near repetition of the Nixon encounter", he told me, "of course, I couldn't show the Chief Librarian anything – not so much as a single record or image survives of the Alexandrian Library". Abaddi concluded that the two encounters left him "much amused".

What emerged in this interview was the centring of two main trajectories: first, it critically rehearsed the processes by which the ancient Alexandrina and cosmopolitanism have been claimed possession of as 'Western objects', and second, as Abaddi reiterated throughout our meeting, the contemporary revivalist's project objective to re-appropriate these 'objects' for Egypt both intellectually and operationally.

Myth of Return

The Alexandrina's 'Westernization' has been well-rehearsed (although typically uncritically) and relates to what the cultural theorist Foucault articulates as Alexandria's "Myth of Return" (see Errera 1997: 138). Here Foucault describes the empathetic identification made by the West with an idealized, imaginary Alexandria, one which is bound up in modernity's Grand Narrative searches for 'authentic' cultural homelands; for ancient origins; for a 'Greek' heritage; a birthplace and thus for "its very beginnings" (Errera 1997: 138). A privileged Western genealogy thus imposed itself on the city, affording modernity's so-called 'universal' histories to claim possession of Alexandria's myth and memory as exclusively Western concerns. By these means the West's mappings of the ancient site have been powerful in characterizing the ancient hellenistic monumental, marble city as an extension of the 'Greek' landscape, as the 'New Athens' and as synonymous with the West's roots/ routes of culture (cf. Clifford 1997).

This 'Westernization' has also afforded the canonization, as 'Western objects', of Alexandria's associated legendary personalities – such as Alexander the Great, who founded the city in 332 BC, and Cleopatra (69–30 BC), famed for her glamour and seductions – and of equally legendary monuments, including Pharos, the lighthouse which was one of the Wonders of the Ancient World, and taking the central position within this potent landscape, the Alexandria Mouseion/Library (Errera 1997: 138). True, Alexandria is not 'in' the West, or even 'of' the West *per se*; nevertheless, in this genealogy a deep resonance is given to Alexandria's ancient characterization as *Alexandria ad Aegyptum* – Alexandria *by*, not *in*, Egypt – a city 'separate' or 'detached' from wider Egyptian landscape (Brown and Taieb 1996: 7). Alexandria thus assumes an integrity with the 'Greek/Western' landscape and, by these means, makes strategic re-attachments too with a wider cosmopolitan framing as the "liminal city *par excellence"* (Gregory 1997: 52), which ultimately affords the city its identity as the "meeting point of East and West".

City and archive

The ancient Alexandrina occupies a central position within this mythologization as a potent locus of modernity's memory-work. Both the lack of historical details of the institution and the relative poverty of archaeological evidence (what Abaddi described as its 'enigmatic' qualities) have allowed the institution to re-emerge as an object of the imagination (Abaddi 1990: 15). This process also affords the West the acquisition of a golden-age fantasy of originary unity in which the Alexandrina is idealized further, as a metaphorical vision of essential wholeness. The archive's destruction is subsequently read by the West as the traumatic loss of an ancient ancestor and embeds the institution, like the city itself, in an entropic, romantic poetics of nostalgia and loss (the kind that Nixon's own romantic impulse alludes to) – not least because of the lack of material traces. Crucially, the Alexandrina also presents a myth of redemption bound up in the potent notion that one could recover and redeem the archive as 'lost' object. This enactment of a 'return' – either in metaphysical or more literal terms – positions both city and archive as a 'resource' or a well-spring of ancient inspiration – aspiring to effect a liberation or cure: the rebirth, re-enchantment or redemption of Western culture (Errera 1997: 138).

This redemptive quality underpins the revival, retrieval and re-workings of the Alexandria paradigm during the key 'nodal' moments of Western genealogies (e.g. the 'European' Renaissance and Enlightenment). As the Librarian of Congress' comments attest, modernity's staging of the Alexandrina as a 'template' articulates a further dynamic in which substance is given to myth. As the ancient institution is objectified in architectural, material form, it becomes the West's 'archetype' for archival and museum spaces (see Butler 2001).

Ancestor cosmopolitanism

An equivalent search for an 'ancestor cosmopolitanism' has given added potency to this 'Westernizing' genealogical trope. 'Traditional' accounts of the origins of cosmopolitanism map out both its Greek etymological roots and the ancient 'abstract' sources of cosmopolitanism. These typically rehearse attempts to define a 'world citizenship' (*kosmo-polites* is a composite of the Greek for 'world' and 'citizen') by focusing in on the 'initial elaborations' of philosophical schools such as those of the Cynics and Stoics (Anderson 1998: 268; see also Yerasimos 1999: 34–39). However, it is argued that "... through Alexander the Great's programme of cultural fusion and his far-reaching world conquests" philosophical cosmopolitanism was "translated" into operational culture (Anderson 1998: 267–268). This shift is couched in terms of epic acts of 'separation' and 'de-attachment' as the 'West as History' moved out from the confines of the *polis* to push forward and map out the parameters of the rapidly expanding 'known world' and, in so doing, confronted new 'universal', cosmopolitan spheres of dwelling, knowledge and cultural contact (Ferguson 1973: 25–26).

Most crucially, these authors position the city of Alexandria and its archive as the summit of Alexander's dreams and as the symbolic 'home' or 'birthplace' of cosmopolitanism proper. Moreover, the 'intrinsically cosmopolitan' character of the dynamic of hellenism, it is argued, saw its greatest expression in Alexandrian culture (Ferguson 1973: 25–26; Zubaida 1999: 20).[2] Traditional accounts thus characterize the ancient Alexandrina archive as an almost utopian space which functioned both as a refuge (in a world increasingly subject to rupture and displacement) and as a site of intellectual and empirical experimentation. The latter brief is best expressed in projects, located at the Alexandrina, to map, measure, define and extend knowledge of the 'known world': this included not just the earth but, with the planetarium, the heavens too.

Separation and re-attachment

The city and archive as both a 'world in microcosm' and a 'dynamic fusion of cultures' is celebrated further as the 'meeting point' which brought together intellectuals of "all cultures and all creeds" and which nurtured a "communal solidarity ..." (Zubaida 1999: 20) based upon the "ideal of [cosmopolitan] detachment" (Robbins 1998: 3). This latter 'ideal', the central core of cosmopolitanism, is hailed as the key to defining 'world citizenship' (Robbins 1998: 2–3). The logic here asserts that only once 'outside' or 'separated' from one's usual 'boundaries' can 'multiple (re-) attachments' be made with diverse cultural contexts and viewpoints (Robbins 1998: 3). The creative channelling of the newly mediated cosmopolitan perspective into "cultures and fields of intellectual endeavour" not only aspired to relocate diverse communities upon "neutral common ground" (Zubaida 1999: 20) but developed an oppositional politics (one that Abaddi and many others argue is still resonant) which pitches the cosmopolitan viewpoint as a challenge to all "exclusive orthodoxy" and "restricted perspectives" (Anderson 1998: 267; Zubaida 1999: 20). In the ancient world, this was argued to combat a number of exclusive phenomena including the restrictiveness of the *'polis'*, of 'ritual', of 'law' and increasingly of the "monotheistic religions" (Anderson 1998: 267; Zubaida 1999: 20). It is further argued that the Alexandrina's central role as a site of translation and transmission was not only bound up in its legendary attempts to accumulate 'universal', encyclopaedic knowledge (best expressed in attempts to create a library of 'all known texts') but on a more metaphysical level too, in attempts to make sensible dramas of separation and creative re-attachment.

It is, however, in that final drama of separation, the destruction of the ancient institution, that life is given not only to seductive desires to revive the institution but also to projects to retrieve and re-work the dynamic of cosmopolitanism. Thus within dominant Western genealogies, cosmopolitanism too re-emerges, "by way of the *esprit cosmopolite* of Renaissance humanism" to become bound up in "later cosmopolitanisms" which further essentialize its qualities in terms of the 'liberal' enlightenment values (Cheah 1998a: 22–23). The latter subsequently came to dominate the paradigm and rendered it synonymous with the Kantian project to attain "a universal cosmopolitan existence" based upon "a perfect civil union of mankind" (Cheah 1998a: 22–23). This intervention effectively redeemed the "ideal of detachment" as a moral-ethical resource, which its apologists understand as affording positive, intimate links to the development of a 'cosmopolitan' rights culture. (Interestingly, revivalism's key culture broker Unesco is bound up in this culture, as detailed later.) Its critics, however, would argue that this cosmopolitan dynamic is also complicit in an exploitative culture of commodification and of colonialisms old and new (see Spivak 1998).

Reclaiming the cosmopolitical

Contemporary 'Egyptianization', therefore, exacts a challenge to the academic purchase on the old Alexandrina paradigm. First, Egypt's return or re-attachment to the Alexandrina is coming at a time when the 'Western' academy is strategically detaching itself from the Alexandria paradigm by making explicit its rejection of the discourse of ancient origins and of its elitist, colonial, universalizing cosmopolitics (Cheah and Robbins 1998). Ironically, even as postmodernity's never-ending return has squeezed the city and archive of all metaphor, elsewhere in the academy, new critical returns and new intimacies are being articulated in terms of postcolonial theory's relationship with the cosmopolitical dynamic. As Cheah states, "... postcolonial cultural studies grew out of a critique of cosmopolitan culture but is currently reclaiming the term cosmopolitical" (Cheah 1998b: 291).

There are sympathies, resonances and correspondences between postcolonial theory's reinvestment in cosmopolitanism and the contemporary process of 'Egyptianization's' own reinvestment of the Alexandrina/cosmopolitan paradigms. Postcolonial theorists and the authors of contemporary 'Egyptianization' argue that any new return to the discourse of the cosmopolitanism/Alexandrina paradigm should be made only at a critical pitch (Cheah and Robbins 1998; Meijer 1999). Also, by using theoretical insights in order to recast the contemporary scene of revivalism as a 'cosmopolitical contact zone' (cf. Clifford 1998: 369), this not only offers critical depth in terms of understanding both historical and contemporary subtleties of exchange and encounter, but has the critical capacity too to address what is at stake in the more oppressive, distopic underside of the discourse of cosmopolitanism and that of the Alexandrina's genealogy, the 'Clash of Civilizations' thesis. This latter motif, as mentioned earlier, has emerged alongside contemporary revivalism's own celebratory rhetorics, and demands to be addressed.

'Clash of civilizations'

The 'fault-line' which appears in traditional 'Western' accounts of the destruction of the institution and which pitches this as an event synonymous with the burning of the site, is the result, so the narrative goes, of incomers imposing a more fundamental view on the city and archive (see Flower 1999). Here the West's insistence on an emotive – violent, traumatic – narrative of loss more specifically casts this act as the outcome of an encounter with an intolerant, obstinate 'other'.[3] More provocative still (particularly for contemporary revivalism) is how a dominant genre of Western history writing has particularized this 'clash' further as the first in a series of 'major encounters between Islam and the West' by repeating one (now discredited) account of the destruction, first related by Gibbon in *The Decline and Fall of the Roman Empire* (Ahmed 1992: 94–95).[4] This trajectory has given the Alexandrina's myth its full force and intimacy within the 'Clash of Civilizations' discourse.

This discourse – the antithesis of the cosmopolitan 'world of mixture' – characterizes East and West (and more specifically Islam and the West) as essentially oppositional and antagonistic entities by locating them within separate worlds, radically distinct genealogies, reductive identities and in an 'Us versus Them' pseudo-history (see Said 2001). In this sense one could argue that the Alexandrina can be read too as the 'birthplace' of, and 'template' for, the 'Clash of Civilizations' thesis. Moreover, this latter characterization has also been effective in assisting Western desires to split the world into the categories of 'civilized' and 'barbarian', and in putting into motion a related desire, that of seizing the dominant or superior position in projects to reunite, reconcile or redeem the whole (cf. Murray 1953). This has been exploited by the West in acquiring for itself the privileged, powerful and dominant position in terms of dramas of encounter and contact.

New Alexandrina, new cosmopolitanisms

In many senses, then, one can see contemporary revivalism too as a microcosm of different and often contested 'cosmopolitics' and potential 'clashes'. Abaddi, for example, made it clear that the process of 'Egyptianization' is not without its potential traumas. In interview he outlined what is perhaps the most significant aspect of contemporary revivalism: that it marks a 'return' to the country's Greco-Roman, hellenistic and cosmopolitan pasts, heritages which have been largely rejected from political national discourse since the 1950s. Abaddi described how the search for national identity which followed the 1952 Revolution (in which Egypt gained its independence) focused upon securing a unity with the Arab-Islamic world while explicitly breaking off engagements with the West: he stated how "the Greco-Roman period was abandoned as part of this shift" due to its "association with the West and with what was then judged as an ancient force of Western colonialism". Ironically then, the Alexandrina is Egypt's 'lost object' too.

Crucially, however, in contrast to the Egyptian state's official line of detachment, Abaddi stated how "The Greco-Roman past has been a line of resistance for Egyptian intellectuals". Abaddi thus saw revivalism as a source of continuity, arguing too that contemporary Egypt's re-attachments with its 'lost' heritage were illustrative of the country reaching a "more stable state of mind" and acquiring "the confidence and ability to acknowledge a more complex multiplicity of heritages both ancient and modern". It was clear that this process of 'Egyptianization', like that of its historical and still dominant 'Westernization', valued the Alexandrina and cosmopolitical paradigms as offering still resonant templates by which dramas of origins, separation and re-attachment could be enacted and worked through. Significantly, this new context illustrates the ways in which Alexandria's ancient past is being re-presented as a 'resource' for memory work – and more specifically as a template not only to re-engage with 'lost' histories but to work through traumas and separations of the recent past.

Modern memory-work

Taking forward the earlier assertion that contemporary revivalism, like contemporary cosmopolitical framings, offers a 'radical destabilization' of "traditional Western moorings" (Clifford 1998: 363; see also Anderson 1998: 272), revivalism is also increasingly bound up in defining a host of 'new cosmopolitanisms' among which have been the "retrieval and circulation of non-Western formulations of cosmopolitics" (Anderson 1998: 274). For example, Abaddi saw revivalism as an opportunity to highlight the presence of the Eastern and Arab-Islamic influences and contributions to Alexandria's cosmopolitan cultures ancient and modern.

Moreover, as this 'destabilization' is occurring further disturbances are being made to Alexandria's myth and memory – as archaeologists (cosmopolitan teams of both foreign and Egyptian missions) are returning objects from the depths of the Mediterranean to the city previously noted for its lack of ancient culture. They have witnessed the return of key artefacts – traditionally regarded as the 'West's' 'lost objects'. Of particular note are underwater excavations made at Fort Qait-Bey, which have located artefacts from the ancient city and massive blocks believed to relate to Pharos; while in Alexandria's eastern harbour, archaeologists have located 'Cleopatra's' palace site (the Ptolemies', now sunken royal quarter) (Empereur 1998; Goddio 1998). These objects are currently providing testimony to a more hybrid culture than previously thought, thus destabilizing traditional characterizations further.

Diplomatic domains – state sovereignty and 'universal' heritage

Abaddi described how he and his colleagues at Alexandria University "played the cosmopolitan card" to secure a "new phase" of the project's development: its re-inscription at national level "under the auspices of President Hosni Mubarak" and in the international arena "under the auspices of the United Nations and Unesco" (GOAL 1990: 12). A key moment in this process came with the Aswan Inaugural Meeting of February 1990, an occasion at which greater depth was given to the process of 'Egyptianization', this time within the diplomatic domain.

This high profile international meeting saw Egypt's President Mubarak and Unesco's then Director-General, Frederico Mayor, officially launch the 'Bibliotecha Alexandrina' scheme in the presence of an international grouping of politicians, diplomats and royalty. They included Queen Noor of Jordan, Queen Sophia of Spain, Princess Caroline of Monaco, Melina Mecouri, François Mitterrand and Sheikh Al-Nahyan of UEA, who acted as representatives of the international community and supporters and authenticators of the project (GOAL 1990: 12). The location of the meeting in Aswan, near to the 'Nubian Monuments', was strategic in that it allowed all participants to re-work their commitment to 'universal' heritage, as Mubarak (GOAL 1990: 17) commented in his speech:

> In supporting the library, you are upholding a great institution which is considered the landmark of Egyptian civilization. Your support recalls what you did in the past when you sponsored the rescue campaign for saving the Nubian Monuments. The international community could not stand back and see the Aswan High Dam's water

destroy those great monuments ... Abu Simbel stands as testimony to the Egyptian civilization, to the international community's awareness and dedication, as well as to the profound feelings of solidarity and unity in the face of challenges.

The commanding presence of the Egyptian Presidency illustrated the potency of both the event and the wider Bibliotecha scheme in terms of Egypt's nation-building. Mubarak used his speeches to formally re-attach Egypt's political national imaginary to the, formerly abandoned, Greco-Roman/hellenistic pasts and to give positive affirmation too to Egypt's pharaonic pasts. His speech married these concerns with demands that the international community recognize Egypt's national sovereignty and its own responsibilities towards the 'universal' heritage. Here Mubarak (GOAL 1990: 17) asserts:

> Egypt, one of the most ancient civilizations, that has nurtured one of the most sublime cultures, has safeguarded great religions, and received great prophets, is aware of the duties imposed on it by its geographical background and cultural heritage ... We consider the Revival of the Library of Alexandria a global cultural event, not exclusive to Egypt alone ... your participation becomes primarily an act for all humanity.

In supportive mode, Mayor (GOAL 1990: 26) used his Aswan address to express Unesco's (cf. the international community's) stake in the Alexandrina's cosmopolitics:

> [The Bibliotecha Alexandrina] goes to the very heart of UNESCO's mission. Our task is, in essence, to promote the sharing of knowledge – knowledge for its own sake, knowledge for development and knowledge for mutual understanding. Sharing implies diversity and thus, by extension, the promotion of those cultural identities that constitute the harmonic richness of the concert of nations; by the same token, it presupposes the protection of the cultural heritage in which our national and supranational identities are rooted.[5]

Thus, in a celebratory re-working of the ancient Alexandrina paradigm, Mubarak and Mayor, keenly followed by other participants, were able to create a new 'cosmopolitical' dynamic which was capable of fusing together a number of potentially antithetical values, such as that of the concerns of nation-state sovereignty and 'universalism', in order to recast them in a mediating role in the cultural politics that mark the global arena. The Aswan meeting was also strategic in consciously re-working Alexandria's ancient role as the 'meeting point' of East and West to affirm old links and to draw out new political and diplomatic directions. For example, official rhetoric states how "Alexandria was predestined for this role: in ancient times a meeting place of civilisations, it is today at the cross-roads between the West and the Middle East" (GOAL 1990: 53).

In an interesting endnote to the Aswan meeting, these speeches were accompanied by the first dramatic images (Figure 15:1 col. pl.) of the Alexandrina's radical new design, allowing participants to anticipate the next stage of development: the emergence of the Bibliotecha as architectural object.

Emergent object: new Alexandrina's architectural languages

The Bibliotecha's architects state that they have "... succeeded in creating a lyrical and uniquely fitting monument" (Snohetta, quoted in Anon. 2000: 117). In interview,

Moshen Zahran, formerly a Professor of Engineering at Alexandria University and the Director of the Bibliotecha Project during its construction phase, took his time to wax lyrical about the design:

> An amazing, truly inspirational building is being constructed which will be a beacon of hope to all the world and to future generations. It will speak an international language by fusing together Egyptian motifs with those of universal culture; ancient symbols with those of modern worlds and even futuristic designs. The central form is an Egyptian sun and moon disk, the roof structure of the library is constructed to look like a microchip, while the exterior walls are decorated with the scripts and alphabets of every language and are ridged to give a sense of the 'layers of time'. Inside – we have revived the main aspects of the ancient institution. We shall have a wonderful library space of both 'real' and 'digital' texts. We shall have museum spaces [museums of science, calligraphy and archaeology], restoration laboratories, a planetarium and, to honor our ancestors, we have the 'Ptolemaic Space' where we shall display busts of the scholars of the ancient Alexandrina.

For many within the international media the 'emergent' Alexandrina has become an object of intense speculation too, with initial attention focused upon the contemporary project's potential to 'revive' and 'redeem' the modern city, a dynamic which echoes the Alexandrina's paradigm's traditional utopianism and more specifically its traditional 'redemptive qualities'. As Mitchell (1998: 22) comments:

> On a promontory jutting from the endless Corniche were arc lights and the shadowy forms of huge cranes. And so it is, for, day and night, they are working on a project almost Pharaonic in its proportions. Designed to awaken the city from its long slumber and carry it triumphantly into the coming millennium, the new Great Library of Alexandria now under construction aspires to become a Wonder of the Modern World.

Comparisons with other cultural regeneration projects also surfaced: *The Economist*, for example, speculated: "Bilbao has its Guggenheim Museum; Paris its Centre Pompidou. Soon, Egypt's long-neglected second city will once again have its Bibliotecha Alexandrina. Like other recent attempts at urban shock-therapy, this daintily named but bluntly modernist revival of the Alexandrina's famed ancient library sets out to provoke controversy" (Anon. 2000: 117).

Increasingly, however, it was this dynamic of 'controversy' which critics explored further. Many picked up on what they saw as the incongruous nature of the Alexandrina's architectural form in relation to the local landscape. More specifically, the Alexandrina's 'futuristic' design saw the media cast the institution as an 'alien' object: *The Economist* (Anon. 2000: 117) dubbed it "... a flying saucer crashed on the shores of Africa", *The New York Times* as "a UFO" (MacFaruhar 2001: 20) and one travel journalist as "a stranded spaceship from another aeon" (Mitchell 1998: 11). It was clear too, from interviews with local informants, that the Bibliotecha's incongruity mirrored a co-existent popular detachment and alienation from the project.

There was some admission by Zahran that the project suffered a form of 'detachment' with Alexandria's urban city landscape. He made it clear that, apart from an 'educated minority' in Alexandria, there was "little education about Alexandria's Golden-Age". He did, however, see both revivalism's and GOAL's own mission as that of nurturing and mediating popular re-attachments: a process which was dubbed

Figure 15:2   The Bibliotecha Alexandrina's construction at the time of its often contested 'melt-down' into the local environment (© Beverley Butler).

by Unesco officials as the project's "meltdown into environment" (Figures 15:2, 15:3), while Zahran, in grander style, preferred to communicate the point by quoting Winston Churchill's dictum: "We shape buildings and afterwards they shape us."

Melt-down

Certain fault-lines, however, re-emerged during the early stages of the 'melt-down' process. Concerns once again centred upon the gaps and gulfs between 'local' and the 'official' (increasingly synonymous with the 'foreign') purchases on revivalism: these illustrated the project's propensity to become bound up in the more distopic 'Clash of Civilizations' thesis. For example, anxieties arose after an initial survey carried out by Unesco, which illustrated that many Alexandrians considered revivalism to be intimately associated with 'a Greek past' and more specifically that this was a 'Western phenomenon' at odds with 'Islamic culture'.

Some local Alexandrians also expressed fears that revivalism would bring an influx of foreign 'experts' to Alexandria which would preclude the involvement of local heritage professionals. It was clear too that the project's association with the Egyptian presidency was regarded as a threat to local autonomy, especially as the scheme brought with it a centralizing culture of Caireen bureaucrats who were regarded as a 'foreign' force in Alexandria. The project's 'top-down' qualities were summed up by one interviewee in the following way: "Cheops built the pyramids, Nasser built the Aswan High Dam and Mubarak built the Alexandrina."

Figure 15:3   Further stages in the Bibliotecha Alexandrina's construction (© Beverley Butler).

Polarizations

This critical discourse which grew up around revivalism made explicit that successful management and mediation of the Bibliotecha's 'Egyptianization' was dependent upon the project's re-attachments with the local landscape and recognition of local needs. The project's 'melt-down' and re-attachments have been, however, synonymous with a number of clashes and polarizations. One of the first concerned an 'outcry' made by 'local' critics (amongst them both Alexandrian elites and foreign archaeological missions) over the damage the Bibliotecha's construction work was doing to the city's ancient archaeological heritage. The Bibliotecha's official literature proudly claims that the new Alexandrina is built on approximately the same area as its ancient self. For local critics this proved a major dilemma. Archaeologists were given only brief access to the site, which is located within the archaeologically-rich Ptolemies' royal quarter, to make assessments. The result was that a few finds were revealed, which gave a "tantalising glimpse of what a full and systematic excavation of the area might have revealed" (Stille 2000: 99). Adding to the anger and frustration was also the "sad irony [that] the new library may actually be built over its earliest forebear, which is known to be located in the same vicinity ... The new library's deep foundations have erased all traces of the past for eternity" (Anon. 2000: 118).

The project has also been haunted by escalating construction costs (which rose from an initial figure of $65 million to over $200 million) with Egypt being "locked into high operating costs in perpetuity" (Stille 2000: 97). These massive financial investments further polarized conflicts over the Bibliotecha's status as what one interviewee described as a "luxury object the city cannot afford". The centring of resources on the Bibliotecha took on a serious edge in terms of planners' response to a lack of car-parking facilities at the site. A decision (which *The New Yorker* (Stille 2000: 97) attributed to Egypt's First Lady Suzanna Mubarak) was made to knock down the building next door in order to provide the necessary space: this was a maternity and children's hospital. Perhaps unsurprisingly, the privileging of the Alexandrina over a hospital proved to be a particularly unpopular act. The details of this particular scandal are still much debated (see Stille 2000: 97).

The need to bring critical, moral and ethical mediation to revivalism's 'melt-down' has been taken even further with respect to the institution's interior library spaces. Critics here have claimed that not only is a library "an unfortunate prioritization in a country where much of the population is illiterate" but have raised concerns over the censorship of texts, currently a sensitive issue in Egypt (Stille 2000: 92). Many here fear that the Alexandrina may become embroiled in Egypt's internal struggles between secularism and militant Islamic extremism – a trajectory which, once again, draws upon the 'Clash of Civilizations' scenario. Others have suggested, not without irony, that there may well be very little for extremists to call to ban, as further scandals have suggested that the contents of the library (or rather the lack of them) are of more major concern. This particular drama relates to the mismanagement of funds, including book-buying monies, which have led to fears of empty shelves in the Alexandrina rather than a reconstructed 'universal' collection (Stille 2000: 97, 99).

Amidst this 'messy politics' a shift did, however, emerge in terms of the sense of ownership of the contemporary revivalist imagination. Attempts by local critics to agitate for new mediation and management of revivalism led to a new, more inclusive, phase of 'melt-down', and to the definition too of a more subtle revivalist thesis between the utopian/distopic positions earlier rehearsed. This new force has placed aside revivalism's dominant 'Egyptianization' and its rhetorics of redemption, in favour of multi-authored attempts to cast revivalism as a more convincing therapeutic force[6] based upon a more subtle and sympathetic 'Alexandrianization'.

'Alexandrianization' and the spectres of cosmopolitics

The disturbances made to both the surface and the depths of the city of Alexandria by recent land and, more especially, underwater excavations have brought even more drama and intrigue to the scene of revivalism. Significantly, these excavations have destabilized the traditional Western 'myth of return' (as premised upon an absence of archaeological remains) by drawing onto centre stage more potent objects relating to ancient Alexandria's legendary landscapes, thus adding more material 'substance' to revivalism and to the force of 'Alexandrianization'.

As previously mentioned, the first objects to be retrieved were from the Qait-Bey and the Eastern Harbour sites (Figure 15:4), which are associated with the myth-histories of Pharos and Cleopatra respectively. The more recent discovery of the 'lost' city and port of Heracleion (which predates Alexandria itself) reveals a space bound up in more myth and which "according to legend was visited by Paris and Helen of Troy" (Kennedy 2001: 27). Furthermore, the search for the final resting place of Alexander the Great has met with increased interest and is currently seducing

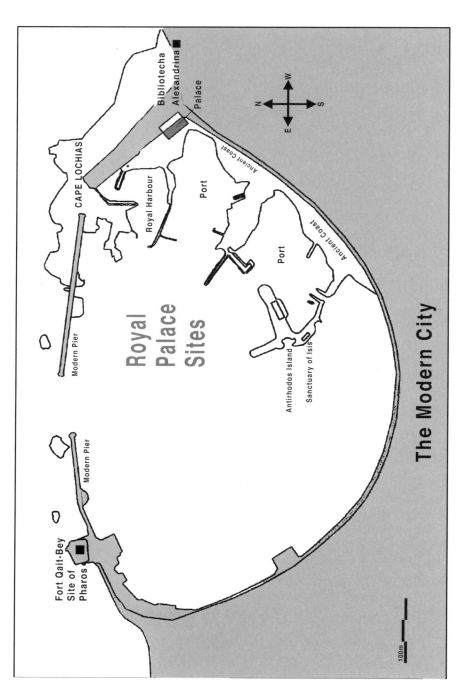

Figure 15:4 Alexandria's eastern harbour, showing the location of the two main underwater excavations of Fort Qait-Bey (the site of Pharos) and of the royal palace sites ('Cleopatra's' palace), with the Bibliotecha Alexandrina project further along the cornice.

archaeologists from both north and south. Collectively, this archaeological revivalism has enabled both the newly created 'all-Egyptian' Underwater Archaeology Department and Alexandria-based 'foreign missions' and their supporters within the Alexandrian elites to agitate for archaeology to be used as a resource to pursue a series of 're-attachments'.

Alexandria as 'Gap'

In interview, French archaeologist Jean-Yves Empereur, Director of the Centre for Alexandrian Studies, outlined the importance of these finds. He began by stating how "Alexandria is typically ignored by mainstream archaeology. It is of no particular interest to Egyptologists while most Classicists tend to focus on sites in Greece". He added how:

> Within Egypt too Alexandria's patrimony has suffered de-attachment. The Greco-Roman period is regarded as somehow 'foreign' or 'outside' of Egyptian history. Alexandria often gets missed out or becomes the 'gap' between the Pharaonic and the Islamic periods. I do, however, think that the new discoveries will address this gap and put Alexandria back into Egyptian history and also allow it to be re-valued at international level.

Empereur, and other Alexandria-based archaeologists, are currently enacting this drama of re-attachment by providing, for the first time, 'new' knowledge of the ancient city. Most dramatically, the return of massive archaeological finds – including sphinxes, capitals and columns – has demonstrated that Alexandria's ancient cosmopolitan culture was much more 'hybrid' in architectural terms than previously believed. Traditional ('Western') archaeological accounts had imagined a 'Greek' city. However, this new thesis asserts that the motif of 'Egyptianizing' architecture was first pioneered in the ancient period. The 'Egyptian' appearance of ancient Alexandria, therefore, as Empereur and others illustrate, was due to the Ptolemies' policy of cultural fusion which saw political, religious and economic domains, as well as architectural motifs, based upon a synthesis of traditions. Most significantly, the city was subject to pharaonic influences. As Empereur further commented, the presence of pharaonic archaeological finds in recent revivalism has been dramatic. These are the result of the movement of objects from Heliopolis (a site situated close to Cairo, which was home to an academy far older than the Alexandrina, associated with the sun-cult) to Alexandria during the Ptolemaic period in order to decorate the city (see also Empereur 1998).

This surfacing of evidence of Alexandria's hybrid cultural contacts has had other, more modern expressions. Finds relating to the more modern colonialisms of the 'West' and of their concomitant violences have resurfaced to complicate the scene of revivalism further. Recent excavations have recovered wreckage from the French flagship 'The Orion', which was sunk off the coast at Aboukir during the Battle of the Nile in 1798 (Goddio 1998: 67). The renewed interest in the Qait-Bey site has also focused attention on the preservation of the 14th century Mameluk citadel located here, which in turn has revealed damage made to the building (by cannon fire) during the 1882 bombardment of Alexandria. The event, which brought much violence to the city, also saw the British enforce their power and presence in Egypt (GOAL 1997).

Moreover, archaeological revivalism has revealed more of the unexpected; pitching even further into the modern age, revivalism has witnessed the discovery of a World War II Royal Air Force bomber, believed to have been involved in the El-Alamein campaigns, lying on top of the palace site (GOAL 1997).

Unbidden return

The Bibliotecha scheme and the dramatic retrieval of the city's archaeological heritage has been accompanied by what another interviewee referred to as "the contemporary desire to return to Alexandria's romantic image as both the 'Capital of Memory' [cf. Durrell] and as a city haunted by the ghosts of its own past". This has had a number of different expressions. First, as a popular cultural dynamic both local and, more particularly, international media commentaries have picked up on the motif of the newly disturbed 'ghosts' of Alexander the Great, Cleopatra, Antony and Julius Caesar haunting the waves and walking the streets of the city (see Nicholl 1996). Other commentators, taking a more serious stance, have employed the metaphor of the city's ghostings to draw out the ways in which recent disturbances have also borne witness to the re-emergence of the spectres of a more problematic modern period of cosmopolitanism, an era intimately bound up in colonialism: as Mitchell (1998: 107), referring back to the Bibliotecha project, states:

> But what of the city in which they are implanting this millennial megalith? Its once richly cosmopolitan community of Jews, Greeks and other Europeans may largely have disappeared – dispersed by the 1952 revolution – but the ghost of a Mediterranean urbanity lingers beneath the Egyptian exuberance.

Significantly, ghosts in cultural-psychoanalytic literature are characterized as the ultimate cosmopolitans, with their power and potency bound up in their capacity to agitate for painful and problematic events and memories to be addressed in order to prevent the return of trauma, and ultimately to define a "more stable and less haunting past" (Feuchtwang 2000a: 75). As one theorist comments: "Ghost stories seem to be telling us about a line of repression such that what might have been silenced in the past returns" (Feuchtwang 2000b: 5).[7] Increasingly, revivalism too has been embroiled in this need to address the silences, repressed memory and traumatic events which mark both the city's modern experience of cosmopolitanism/ colonialism and also the 'history of departures' which followed independence in the 1950s. Such themes are powerfully echoed in similar fears and anxieties which mark academic discourse's 'excavation' of the painful and traumatic modern cosmopolitan colonial contexts: "Why dredge up this tainted and problematic world [of cosmopolitanism]? ... the most defensible answer [is] ... dredge it up so we know, our hands are dirty anyway" (Anderson 1998: 285).

Intellectual returns

Many Alexandrian intellectuals have seized upon the opportunity to reach down deeper into this 'messy politics' and to relate revivalism to alternative 'excavations' of Alexandria's modern cosmopolitan era. There are two different but inextricably linked trajectories. The first maps the intellectual and operational engagements of two key players in contemporary revivalism: Mohammed Awad, an architect and founder of the Society for the Protection of Alexandrian Patrimony of 1880–1920, and Adel Abu Zahra, Professor of Human Sciences at Alexandria University and founder of the Friends of the Environment Association. As Awad makes explicit, both men are "products of the city's old multi-cultural society" and as such are both 'Alexandrians' and 'Egyptian cosmopolitans': Awad shares Egyptian and Greek ancestry, and Zahra, both Egyptian and French lineage. Awad and Zahra are amongst those who are using revivalism as a resource to recover not only the repressed intellectual heritage of cosmopolitanism (of which Abaddi spoke earlier) but also to agitate for the preservation of architectural survivals of the city's still largely neglected and increasingly threatened modern cosmopolitan heritage.

The other dynamic relates to the traumatic separation or departure during the 1950s of 'foreign' Alexandrians – known as 'Khwaga'. This painful history of exile has also re-emerged alongside revivalism in an interview made with archaeologist and writer Harry Tzalas (who was born in Alexandria, to a Greek father and an Italian mother). Tzalas left the city with other 'Greek Alexandrians' in 1956 but has made his own return to Alexandria in order to be part of contemporary revivalism. He is currently Director of the Hellenic Institute of Ancient and Medieval Alexandrian Studies.

1952 revolution

These cosmopolitans have agitated for revivalism to give proper recognition to a more subtle excavation of the ancient and modern cosmopolitan-colonial periods at both an intellectual and operational pitch. Moreover, all three interviewees' accounts of revivalism took as their shared point of departure the key event of the revolution of 1952. Significantly too, all three spoke positively about the very necessary 'act of social justice', as Tzalas put it, upon which Egypt's independence was premised. The complex nature of political support was, however, perhaps best summed up by Tzalas, who commented:

> At that time I was pro-Nasser and took part in anti-British demonstrations ... It has to be said, and said quite clearly, that most of the foreigner's privilege was based on the oppression of the people of that place. The events of 1952 gave me personally a sense of social justice which has never left me ... I was truly happy to see that Alexandria was returned back to the people who really own it.

Awad, however, was able to show the more oppressive features at play:

> In the post-revolution period there was much distortion and hiding of history ... The modern cosmopolitan part of our history was now *mal vieux*, as the French would say, and therefore to be seen as violently colonial and elitist. [There was a subsequent] search for non-European identities which was undertaken to suit Nasser's ideology of Arab nationalism.

While Awad, like others interviewed, suggested that Nasser's political use of the pharaonic past was ambivalent and pragmatic, he emphasized that:

> In such an autocracy there was no space to feature the Greco-Roman and ancient cosmopolitan past which was associated with Mediterranean influences and with the

'foreigners' Egypt had just exiled. [He also insisted that while Alexandria's modern cosmopolitan era was "contaminated with colonialism", it "cannot simply be reduced to this".]

Moreover, both Awad and Zahra, like other Alexandrian intellectuals, also went on to argue that despite this de-attachment, Alexandria's 'cosmopolitan spirit' survived into the present.

Cosmopolitan spirit

Zahra was also keen to defend a more subtle return to Alexandria's modern cosmopolitan era and to prioritize what he argued was its still resonant intellectual qualities. Zahra couched this specifically in terms of what he described as a "cosmopolitan vision of a tolerant humanistic world". Locating his comments in Alexandria's historical experience of cosmopolitanism, he, like Awad, addressed the colonial influences and power at play: "In this historical relationship between the two cultures – the European and the Oriental – the European took the dominant, stronger position." He added that what needed to be salvaged from an understanding of this context was "a whole host of cultural influences which once flourished in Alexandria". Zahra illustrated with an autobiographical vignette:

> My grandfather was a Sheikh [local Islamic holy man] who married a French woman. They used to listen to opera and classical music while reading not only Jean-Jacques Rousseau, Voltaire and Balzac but the Koran and Egyptian authors like Shawqui. They discussed everything with my mother, who later became a professor of French literature ... To find something like that now is impossible: to laugh, joke, attend opera and to listen to Chopin while reading the Koran now would be seen as a contradiction.

He argued that post-1950s, "Egypt lost both her cosmopolitan culture and her cosmopolitan attitude of tolerance", and he stated that this resulted in a still prevalent attitude in which "foreign or Western culture is held in suspicion" and in particular, "that occidental culture in Alexandria is now regarded as dangerous".

Oriental and occidental

Zahra also revived a familiar critical line which pitched cosmopolitanism as a resource capable of resisting this desire to locate both East and West in hermetically sealed worldings. While recognizing the still unequal power relationship between the 'West' and Egypt on the global stage, he ultimately refused to reduce these relationships to a 'Clash of Civilizations' scenario. Zahra was more concerned to describe how, within Egypt itself, Alexandria's "cosmopolitan spirit" is needed "more than ever". Zahra saw this as a means to challenge not only the separatisms and violences of what he described as the "naive nationalism" which emerged post-1950s, but also "the current demands of religious extremists who wish to turn Egypt into an exclusively Islamic society". The latter he saw as a significant force in contemporary Egypt, and he referenced this too to both recent extremists' calls to destroy Egypt's 'pagan' heritage (the physical remains of Egypt's ancient pasts) and to the terrorist attacks on tourists, particularly that of the 1997 Luxor tragedy. Again he stated, "If we want to flourish we [Egyptians] should accept a tolerant relationship with Europeans and other foreigners and not believe that every influence from 'outside' is a plot against us or against Islam".

Awad and Zahra's identities as 'Egyptian cosmopolitans' and therefore as intimates, witnesses and survivors of Alexandria's modern cosmopolitan experience found a deep empathy in revivalism. As Awad has commented (in Stille 2000: 99), "In trying to save this cosmopolitan world, I am trying to save myself". Taking up the 'other side' of the story is Tzalas. Interestingly Tzalas, with some humour, described his hybrid roots as affording him the accolade of 'Citizen of the World'. His autobiographical experience includes both exile from Alexandria and his recent return. Tzalas described the events which saw the departure of 'foreign' Alexandrians – the 'Khwaga' – from the city as "very painful and complex", and he stressed that "the events and aftermath of this departure harmed both the people who departed and it harmed those who stayed ... The balance of communities was broken". This traumatic experience of separation, he reiterated, "affected, in different ways, the whole of the city", a sentiment echoed by many Egyptian interviewees.

Dream of return

Tzalas rejected what he termed the "dreadful nostalgias" which have led to "Westerners weeping at the loss of Alexandria", adding, "the period following a revolution is difficult for all nations. The most positive thing is that it gave Egyptians a sense a pride which was always at risk when the 'Khwaga' were in a powerful position". Looking back to the actual "time of exile and departure [Tzalas left in 1956] ... a certain amount is still left unexplained ... it seems to me that many of us left without reason". He further explained how he, like many other 'Khwagas', were committed to ensuring that shifts in power took place which would support Egyptian self-determination, but he considered the mass departures of 'foreign' communities to be an extreme and unnecessary option. Tzalas outlined the specific reasons why, after the 1956 Suez Crisis, "fear and potential violence reached British, French and Jewish communities and required them to leave" but adds, "the Greeks had a different relationship with the city and its authorities – the Greek government was at fault – it panicked and called its 'nationals' out. It was a mistake". Tzalas commented that 'repatriation' placed him in an "absurd position" in which he was made to 'return' to Greece – "a place I had never been to", and which was also "just recovering from a traumatic civil war".

Tzalas chose to spend time in South America before returning to the Mediterranean. He, like many others, harboured a "dream of a return" to Alexandria, but, he stated, "I didn't want to return as a tourist – after all I *am* an Alexandrian". Tzalas' return was subsequently and effectively mediated via his participation in contemporary archaeology revivalism which he saw as giving him a "useful contributory role in Alexandria while allowing me to re-explore this very real, welcoming and heart-warming city". Furthermore, Tzalas' contribution to Alexandria's literary imagination has resulted in the publication of a volume of short stories (1999) which narrate his childhood and early adulthood in the city.

Global, democratic futures

What was reflected in these particular interviews was a sense in which revivalism's 'Egyptianizing' impulse could be used as a resource to create what Awad described as "an entente with recent history", which echoes the psychoanalytic desire for a "more stable and less haunting past" (Feuchtwang 2000b: 3). On this same theme Zahra too commented, "This contemporary turn towards Alexandria's cosmopolitan pasts is allowing us Egyptians to begin talking with more openness about Egypt's ancient and modern history and crucially too, about the country's future in terms of diversity, multi-culturalism and also human rights". Awad saw this as intimately bound up in the retrieval of the Alexandrina's international cosmopolitan framing, and he argued, "I see a correspondence between the acknowledgement of a plurality of ancient pasts – and of Egypt's commitment to carve out its future roles in the 'global arena'", a process he saw as synonymous with "the construction of a brighter, democratic future for Egypt". Taking this another step further, both Awad and Tzalas stated that, to avoid revivalism being hijacked by top-down political and diplomatic forces, 'real goals' needed to be met in terms of Egypt's internal politics, in particular, the struggle to create a cosmopolitics of 'contemporary civil society'.

Urban revivalism's 'worlds of mixture'

The operational expression of the intellectual's desire to meet 'real goals' has become manifest in attempts to align the force of cultural revivalism with the basic development needs of the modern, urban city. Much of the initial force of this urban revivalism was organized by the Alexandria Governorate and financed by local companies through tax relief incentives: to date it has led to renovations and improvements being made to Alexandria's central areas and along the city's Corniche. Under the influence and direction of Alexandria's intelligentsia, however, attempts have also been made to twin these improvements with strategies to regenerate less salubrious areas of the city. Significantly, commentators have seized upon the potential for this strategy to be used in other contexts. *The Middle Eastern Times* (Schemm 2000: 3), for example, headlined with: "Can Alexandria's facelift be a model for other troubled Egyptian cities?" before hailing revivalism's wider potential as a model for 'Third World' city regeneration. These commentaries investigated such dynamics as: "Is there something unique about Alexandria – are her commercial and bureaucratic strata unusual in that they can forge this kind of alliance?" (Schemm 2000: 3).

Leonardo and Cleo

It is clear too, from a number of projects that have appeared on the scene, that the regeneration of the city has become increasingly bound up in aspirations to reinvent Alexandria as an international tourist destination. Plans are already underway to create an underwater museum at Qait-Bey, with rumours too of a scheme to reconstruct Pharos as a floating laser light show in the eastern harbour. The erection of a series of sculptures and mosaics which feature 'Greco-Roman' motifs also accompanied revivalism's 'return' to origins. The Greek community in Alexandria similarly has taken the opportunity to 'gift' a newly designed statue of Alexander the Great to the city. This is happening at the same time as the Alexandrian authorities are restituting statues of dignitaries from the modern cosmopolitan period – previously kept 'in storage' – to the city's public squares. These old and new architectural additions also provided the backdrop for more *vox pop* interviews. It was here that the capacity of popular culture, in particular, to mix and mingle icons from north and south, ancient and modern worlds, was most tangible.

A new mosaic (Figure 15:5 col. pl.) narrates the founding of the city by Alexander the Great and depicts not only Alexander, but Cleopatra and a host of other ancient icons too. Significantly, these icons are currently more 'foreign' to Alexandria's youth than the contemporary 'Western' icons presently preoccupying them, such as Leonardo di Caprio, Madonna, and McDonald's. However, interviews showed that the ancient icons and new mosaics are undergoing domestication as they become increasingly synonymous with the future aspirations of Alexandria's youth, who are beginning to see revivalism as a medium of re-engagement with the 'outside world'. This re-engagement was anticipated not only as the source of jobs and money (as generated by tourism) but was synonymous with participation in a world of shared, global (popular) cultural exchange. Another vignette which, in its own way, challenged the motif of the 'Clash of Civilizations' relates to a scene in down-town Alexandria in which a poster vendor proudly displayed photographs of Mecca and of the Spice Girls side by side (Figure 15:6 col. pl.): testimony to a real 'world of mixture' (cf. Said 2001).

'Writing to return'

New interventions have been made into Alexandria's traditional motif of 'writing to return'. This form of literary retrievalism, which was used historically by the 'West' in order to redeem Alexandria's 'lost objects' and 'landscapes', has been turned around by more contemporary literary aesthetics and concerns. Interviews with Alexandria's 'Arab Writers Club' revealed a further shift in the contemporary context: as one member commented: "Unlike Mahfouz and the earlier generation of Egyptian writers we do not feel that we have to reclaim Egypt or Alexandria from the colonial powers or from internal authorities. What you do find here is that young Egyptian writers' concerns have turned to the themes which dominate other Arab writers in the Middle East ... much contemporary writing is preoccupied with the subject of Palestine." What is represented here is a significant and strategic centring of a potent contemporary 'lost landscape' which is itself bound up in dramas of traumatic loss, exile and aspirations of return and re-attachment.

Marginalized memory

One further cosmopolitan context which illustrates both the limits and challenges of the revivalist project's 'Egyptianizing' thesis is that of minority communities within the contemporary Alexandrian landscape. These include groups that rarely feature in post-1950s characterizations of Egyptian national identity, which posit a 'homogenized' concept of nation, expressed in terms of the majority Arab-Muslim population. For example, Greek, Italian and Armenian groups stayed in Alexandria after Independence, as did Jewish, Nubian, Sudanese and Coptic Christian communities. These are groups whose identities (in varying degrees) are still relatively 'hidden' and bound up in the 'silences' which continue to exacerbate feelings of marginalization. Perhaps the most convincing testimony for the need for revivalism to extend the inscription of memory, both within the city and outside, came from one Armenian informant who insisted, "Everyone's history is woven together, we each explain the other ... we all need to be given a voice in terms of the future of the city".

Conclusions – new transmissions and translations

In a recent presentation on the Bibliotecha Alexandrina, the institution's newly appointed Director-General (Serageldin 2001) fielded a question regarding anxieties over the future success of the institution which opened in October 2002:

> I don't think there is any guarantee we can give in terms of the Alexandria library's success ... we have tried to assemble together as many possibilities for success as we could ... In fact I am asked regularly 'How can you guarantee that the institution won't be attacked by Muslim fundamentalists?'. I believe that the only way to make the project succeed and the only defence open is if people both within Egypt and in the wider international community are willing to fight and defend it ... This is how movements are created and defended and I believe that the idea of defending a space of freedom and rationality which unites East, West, North and South is worthy of being defended against xenophobias. Only then can we defend dialogue over confrontation; defend the acceptance of others over the rejection of others ... I believe that there is richness in diversity; in fact, seduced by this idea I left my job [at the World Bank] and returned to Egypt. So there are no guarantees but a challenge which I believe is worth taking up.

Interestingly, Serageldin (himself a cosmopolitan, being an Egyptian national, educated both in Egypt and in the US, and formerly the Deputy-Director of the World Bank) made an appeal for those within Egypt and in the global community to support the institution. With more resonance too his comments formed part of his recasting of the Alexandrina scheme as a 'challenge' to the 'Clash of Civilizations' thesis which violently re-emerged following the events of 11 September 2001.

Although it remains unanswerable – whether the Alexandrina in its historical and more recent translations has been more complicit in the polarization of conflict and terror, or in creating cosmopolitical movements of resistance – this sense of ambivalence and 'mixed feelings' echoes theorists' scepticisms concerning both the 'dangers' which 'attend new elaborations of cosmopolitanism' and their propensity to repeat 'old' cosmopolitical violences and clashes.[8] There are, however, recent interventions which have collected around contemporary revivalism and which illustrate the more 'emancipatory' potential of new translations and transmissions.

Mirror to the West

Some critics have 'reversed' the flow of translation of revivalism by suggesting that it is the 'West', and more specifically the contemporary European context, that could best 'learn lessons' in a more tolerant understanding of cosmopolitanism from a re-worked Alexandria paradigm, at a time of increasingly exclusionary and dehumanizing policy on immigration and asylum. As Ilbert (1997: 15) comments,

> As a meeting place and a city of interaction, Alexandria had its shady side, its tensions, its crises. The important thing, however, is to grasp this multitude of threads that made the fabric of the town. For, if not a model then at least it can serve as a reference point in the debate that runs in Europe today over the position of 'foreign' communities and their integration or otherwise. From both sides and according to the angle of approach, Alexandria can well serve as a mirror.

Mirror to the East

In terms of revivalism as a 'mirror' to the East, and as an emancipatory force within Egypt itself, perhaps *the* dominant feature to emerge is the sense in which attempts are being made to position revivalism as a resource to effect an *entente* with the recent past and that psychoanalytic 'stable future'. Through revivalism this process has begun by encouraging a more subtle history of Egypt's encounters with the 'other'; a shift which resists the distopic desires of 'both sides' – East and West – to return to the 'Clash of Civilizations' motif. As Hassan (forthcoming) comments,

> It is a mistake to utilize the 'West' as the determinant of the fate of non-western nations, privileging the West with a far greater influence than it probably has, and overlooking and trivializing the role of local cultures. The attitude of pitting the 'West' against the 'Others' also overlooks the intricacies of cultural interactions, mutual interchanges, assimilation, metamorphosis, and re-formation.

I argue that contemporary revivalism as a 'moral-ethical' force, and as a medium of intellectual-operational re-engagement and translation, must be made subject to 'guarantees' both in terms of its local impacts and with reference to a contemporary politics of inclusion which reaches both within and outside Egypt. This means taking into account the many voices bound up in the process of 'Egyptianization' and is a strategy and a sentiment which echoes the words of the Alexandrian Armenian interviewee: "We all need to be given a voice in terms of the future of our city."

Notes

1   For more information see the Bibliotecha Alexandrina/New Alexandrina website: www.bibalex.gov.eg.

2   The hellenistic age is traditionally characterized as the three centuries from Alexander the Great's death in 323 BC until the battle of Actium in 31 BC (cf. the fall of Egypt to the advancing Roman Empire). Although these dates are subject to "some spill-over" (Ferguson 1973: 6), this period in traditional accounts is considered to be 'seminal'; it is the age in which "the achievement of classical Greece was diffused and transmitted throughout the known world" and the time of "expanding horizons and the emergence of cosmopolitan capitals", in which the forward movement of Greece brought the eastern Mediterranean into the western worldview. Alexandria, as the 'largest' cosmopolis, has been described as "the symbol of the age" (Ferguson 1973: 6).

3   Although recent scholarship has contested traditional interpretations. Authors have
     attempted to ascertain how much damage was caused to the Mouseion/Library by
     'incomers', whether couched as 'pagan', Christian or Muslim. In terms of 'pagan'
     responsibility most writers agree that Caesar's Wars in 48 BC brought some loss to the
     Mouseion/Library buildings, while Canfora (1989: 192–193) has commented that "the
     burning of books was part of the advent and imposition of Christianity". Parsons,
     however, contradicts this account by arguing that "neither the Romans nor the Christians
     accounted for more that a fraction of the total loss" (Parsons 1952: 169). He points the
     finger at the Muslim 'invaders'. Most recent opinion favours the notion of initial damage
     wrought by Caesar's Wars, followed by a severe wounding by Christian culture (in
     particular in the Emperor Theodosius' attempts to destroy pagan places of worship/
     learning). The conquest of Egypt by the Caliph Omar is presumed, by some, to have finally
     put an end to the ancient institution, while others argue that nothing would have been left
     standing (Flower 1999: 23–24).

4   "When the first Muslims erupted from the Arabian peninsula in the seventh century and
     reached Alexandria, they sent a message to the caliph asking for instructions regarding the
     famous central library. 'If the books are in accordance with the Quran, they are
     unnecessary and may be destroyed: if they contradict the Quran, they are dangerous and
     should certainly be destroyed', replied the caliph." Ahmed (1992: 94–95) has observed
     how this myth of a clash of Islam versus West over the ancient Mouseion/Library has been
     used to negatively stereotype Muslims in contemporary contexts as book burners and to
     characterize Islam as an intolerant, chauvinistic and violent force.

5   At the Aswan meeting, Mayor re-worked the traditional characterization of the
     Alexandrina as the epitome of the heritage/conservation paradigm. The ancient
     institution, as a 'paradise lost', is seen to stand in testimony of the need to safeguard,
     conserve and preserve 'universal' world heritage: objectives which obviously lie at the
     heart of Unesco's own 'philosophy' and 'mission' (Mayor quoted in GOAL 1990: 26).
     Mayor, and other participants, also argued the need for revivalism to extend its brief to
     make commitments to issues of development, peace, discourses of human rights and to an
     ethics of pluralism, dialogue and diversity (Mayor quoted in GOAL 1990: 26).
          Writ larger, Unesco's 'birth' on the 'ashes of Second World War' and within the wider
     UN's post-war redemptive vision of reconstruction and peace (see Lacoste 1994) has also
     been responsible for binding the organization up in what Cheah (1998a) – in critical mode
     – has defined as the "cosmopolitan rhetorics" of such supranational, global agencies and
     their intimacy in terms of a Kantian universalist, 'world philosophy'.
          While some critics, such as Spivak (1998), have highlighted the oppressive, neo-colonial
     violences of this kind of discourse, others have drawn out the means by which such
     organizations – through their own or others' strategic use of such 'cosmopolitical'
     dynamics – have been able to creatively manage the tensions between nation state
     sovereignty and 'universalizing' visions (Anderson 1998).

6   The shift from the 'traditional' framing of cosmopolitanism as a Grand Narrative
     'redemptive formula' to its more subtle reformulations as a transformative therapeutic
     force is critically rehearsed by Honig (1998). This takes in a comparative discussion of
     Kristeva's and Ahmed's theses of cosmopolitanism's material forms as both "fetishes of
     nation" and as transitional, therapeutic objects.

7   Feuchtwang (2000b: 21–27) has written of the 'ghost's' cosmopolitan qualities: the liminal
     space they occupy between psychic and physical landscapes and between "personal,
     sovereign and cosmological authorities". With particular resonance for contemporary
     Alexandrian revivalism Feuchtwang has investigated the dramas of the 'return of the
     ghost' as part of a context in which "The historical myth of ghosts would be a myth of the
     return of those who until now were forgotten or rather neglected by historians ..."
     (Feuchtwang 2000b: 23). With even more resonance for the Bibliotecha Alexandrina as a
     particularly potent site of archival memory-work (both historically and in the
     contemporary context), Feuchtwang connects the presence of the ghost to demands for the
     retrieval of 'erased archives' and 'lost memory' and with the desire for the 'recognition' of
     past grief and grievance (Feuchtwang 2000b: 6–8). He further draws out the therapeutics
     of this process in terms of the recovery and 'working through' of repressed and traumatic
     memory. He emphasizes too how this process is based upon a call for 'justice' articulated
     "from a place and a time which is cosmological" (Feuchtwang 2000b: 24). The construction
     of a 'new' or 'revised' and therefore more 'just' archive is the final act of "'closure' which
     Feuchtwang argues is necessary in order to secure a "more stable and less haunting past"
     (Feuchtwang 2000a: 75).

8   Most significantly, theorists have warned how the 'Clash of Civilizations' thesis has
     assumed new life and adherents in both north and south in its newly re-labelled
     contemporary guise as 'Jihad versus McWorld' (Robbins 1998: 18).

References

Note: references to chapters and books in the *Encounters with Ancient Egypt* series are denoted in bold type.

Abaddi, M. 1990, *Life and Fate of the Library of Alexandria*. Paris: Unesco

Abel, R. 1994, *The Ciné Goes to Town: French Cinema 1896–1914*. Berkeley: University of California Press

Ackermann, G. A. 2000, *Jean-Léon Gérôme. Monographie revisée. Catalogue raisonné mis à jour*. Paris: Editions ACR

Ahmed, A. S. 1992, *Postmodernism and Islam: Predicament and Promise*. London: Routledge

Alain 1931, *Vingt leçons sur les Beaux-Arts*. Paris: Gallimard

Aldred, C. 1973, *Akhenaten and Nefertiti*. New York: Viking

Alex, R. and H-D. Kluge 1994, *Gärten um Wörlitz*. Leipzig: E. A. Seamann

Alexander, R. 1958, The Public Memorial and Godefroy's Battle Monument. *Journal of the Society of Architectural Historians* 17, 19–24

Alexeieva, A. V., I. V. Alexeieva, Y. V. Korolev, E. D. Nesterova, N. I. Stadnichuk, A. A. Vassilieva and N. M. Verchinina 1993, *Pavlovsk. The Collections*. Paris: A. de Gourcuff

Allen, H. 1978, My Egypt. *Exposure, The Journal of the Society for Photographic Education* 16, 16–27

Allen, J. P. 2003, The Egyptian Concept of the World, in D. O'Connor and S. Quirke (eds), *Mysterious Lands*, 23–31. London: UCL Press

Altick, R. 1978, *The Shows of London*. Cambridge, Mass: Harvard UP

D'Alviella, E. G. 1894, *The Migration of Symbols*. London

Anderson, A. 1998, Cosmopolitanism, Universality, and the Divided Legacies of Modernity, in P. Cheah and B. Robbins (eds), *Cosmopolitics: Thinking and Feeling Beyond Nations*, 265–290. Minneapolis: Minnesota Press

Andrews, C. 1990, *Ancient Egyptian Jewellery*. New York: Harry N. Abrams

Anon. 1824, *Guida al Giardino Torrigiani*. Florence

Anon. 1825, *Exhibition, 47 Leicester Square, Zodiac of Dendera*. London: J. Haddon

Anon. 1861, Mrs Belzoni on Freemasonry in Egypt. *Freemason's Magazine and Masonic Mirror*, 7 March, 186

Anon. 1880, *Consécration du nouveau temple de la Loge les Amis Philanthropes, rue du Persil n° 4*. Brussels: Baertsoen

Anon. 1884, Le Temple maçonnique de la rue du Persil à Bruxelles

Anon. 1922, Louxor, palais du cinéma, in *La Construction Moderne*, 26 March, 204

Anon. 1933, New Hoover Factory Opened. *Middlesex County Times*, 6 May

Anon. 1968, *Visionary Architects*. Exhibition Catalogue. Houston: University of St Thomas

Anon. 1977, *Jardins en France, 1760–1820*. Exhibition Catalogue. Paris: Caisse Nationale des Monuments Historiques

Anon. 1985, Le Projet Grand Louvre, supplement to *Lettre d'Information* 163, 7 January, 2

Anon. 1986, *Alexandre Brongniart, 1739–1813, architecture et décor*. Exhibition Catalogue. Paris: Les Musées de la Ville de Paris

Anon. 1992, 1992 Historic Preservation Merit Awards. *South of the Mountains. The Historical Society of Rockland County* 36, 5–7

Anon. 1993, Building Study: New Lease of Life for Hoover Factory. *Architects Journal*, 27 January, 37–46

Anon. 2000, Runes on the Ruins. *The Economist*, 8 April, 117–118

Apperly, R., R. Irving and P. Reynolds 1994, *A Pictorial Guide to Identifying Australian Architecture. Styles and Terms from 1788 to the Present*. Sydney and London: Angus and Robertson

Archaeological Journal 1844, 1, The Mummy, 281–289

D'Archimbaud, N. 1997, *Louvre: Portrait of a Museum*. New York: Stewart, Tabori and Chang

Arnold, D. 1991, *Building in Egypt: Pharaonic Stone Masonry*. Oxford: OUP

Assmann, J. 1997, *Moses the Egyptian. The Memory of Egypt in Western Monotheism*. Cambridge, Mass: Harvard UP

Bakos, M. M. 1998, Three Moments of Egyptology in Brazil, in C. J. Eyre (ed.), *Proceedings of the Seventh International Congress of Egyptologists*, 87–91. Leuven: Peeters

Bakos, M. M. 2001, Um Olhar Sobre o Antigo Egito no Novo Mundo: A Biblioteca Pública do Estado do Rio Grande do Sul, 1922. *Estudos Ibero-Americano PUCRS* 27, 153–172

Baltrusaitis, J. 1957, *Aberrations. Quatre essais sur la légende des formes*. Paris: O. Perrin

Baltrusaitis, J. 1967, *La Quête d'Isis*. Paris: O. Perrin

Baltrusaitis, J. 1985, *La Ricerca di Iside. Saggio Sulla Leggenda di un Mito*. Milan: Adelphi

Bancroft, H. H. 1893, *The Book of the Fair*. Chicago and San Francisco: The Bancroft Company

Bandiera, J. D. 1983, The City of the Dead: French Eighteenth-Century Designs for Funerary Complexes. *Gazette des Beaux-Arts* 1,368, 25–32

Bardowskaja, L. W. and N. A. Schwarina 1982, *Schloss- und Parkansichten der Stadt Puschkin bei Leningrad 18 bis 20 Jahrhundert*. Exhibition Catalogue. Dresden: Staatliche Kunstsammlungen

Barrington, R. 1906, *The Life, Letters and Work of Frederic Leighton. II*. London: George Allen

Barry, R. 1847, *An Introductory Lecture on Architecture, Sculpture, and Painting*. Melbourne

Beevers, D. 1983, The Egyptian Style in Architecture, in P. Conner (ed.), *The Inspiration of Egypt, its Influence on British Artists, Travellers and Designers, 1700–1900*. Brighton: Brighton Borough Council

Bely, A. 1912a, Yegipet. Iz puteshestviya. *Sovremennik* May, 190–214

Bely, A. 1912b, Yegipet. Iz puteshestviya. *Sovremennik* June, 176–208

Bely, A. 1912c, Yegipet. Iz puteshestviya. *Sovremennik* July, 270–288

Bely, A. 1913–1914, *Petersburg*. St Petersburg: Sirin

Belzoni, G. B. 1821, *Narrative of the Operations and Recent Discoveries Within the Pyramids, Temples, Tombs and Excavations in Egypt and Nubia, and of a Journey to the Red Sea, in Search of the Ancient Berenice, and Another to the Oasis of Jupiter Ammon*. London: John Murray

Belzoni, G. B. 1880, The Belzoni Masonic. *The Masonic Magazine* 7, 497–501

Bergeron, L. 1990, *France Under Napoleon*. Princeton: Princeton UP

Berlev, O. D. 1991, *Drevniegipetskie Pamiatniki iz Mouzeev SSSR*. Exhibition Catalogue. Moscow: VRIB

Berlev, O. D. and S. Hodjash 1998, *Catalogue of the Monuments of Ancient Egypt from the Museum of the Russian Federation Ukraine, Bielorussia, Caucasus, Middle Asia and the Baltic States*. Freiburg: Universitätsverlag

Bevan, A. 2003, Reconstructing the Role of Egyptian Culture in the Value Regimes of the Bronze Age Aegean: Stone Vessels and Their Social Contexts, in R. Matthews and C. Roemer (eds), *Ancient Perspectives on Egypt*, 57–74. London: UCL Press

Bierbrier, M. L. 2003, Art and Antiquities for Government's Sake, in D. Jeffreys (ed), *Views of Ancient Egypt since Napoleon Bonaparte: imperialism, colonialism and modern appropriations*, 69–76. London: UCL Press

Bigelow, J. 1840, *The Useful Arts Considered in Connection with the Application of Science*. Boston: Marsh, Capen, Lyon and Webb

Birch, S. 1857, An Introduction to the Study of the Egyptian Hieroglyphs, in J. G. Wilkinson (ed.), *The Egyptians in the Time of the Pharaohs*. London: Bradbury and Evans

Blavatsky, H. P. 1878, *Isis Unveiled: A Master Key to the Mysteries of Ancient and Modern Science and Theology*. New York: J. W. Bouton

Boime, A. 1990, *Art in an Age of Bonapartism 1800–1815*. Chicago: University of Chicago Press

Borgogni, M. 1992, Le Architetture di Agostino Fantastici e il Vocabolario di Architettura, in C. Cresti (ed.), *Agostino Fantastici*, 53–64. Torino: U. Allemandi

Bossuet, J-B. 1681, *Discours sur l'Histoire Universelle*. Paris: Texte imprimé par J-B. Bossuet

Bourrut-Lacouture, A. 1990, Égyptomanie fin de siècle. Le typhonium, demeure des peintres Adrien Demont et Virginie Demont-Breton. *Bulletin de la Société de l'histoire de l'art Français*, 277–296

Brancaglion, A. 2001, Introdução, in E. Delange, *Egito Faraônico. Terra dos Deuses*, 20–27. Rio de Janeiro: Fundação Casa França-Brasil

Brand, M. 1988, *Het Warme Bad*. Botrivier: Magdaleen Brand

Bresc-Bautier, G. 1989, La Sculpture de l'attique du Louvre par l'atelier de Jean Goujon. *Revue du Louvre et des Musées de France* 2, 97–111

Bridgeman, S. 1739, *A General Plan of the Woods, Parks and Gardens of Stowe*. London

Brier, B. 1993, Egyptomania. Surveying the Age-Old Fascination with Ancient Egypt. *KMT* 4, 40–51

Brown, C. 1967, *The Prose of Osip Mandelstam*. Princeton: Princeton UP

Brown, K. and H. Taieb 1996, Alexandria in Egypt. *Mediterranean* 8 (9), 7–9

Brugsch, H. 1894, *Mein Leben und Mein Wandern*. Berlin: Allgemeiner Verein für Deutsche Litteratur

Budge, W. 1897, *Chapter of Coming Forth By Day*. London: Kegan Paul, Trench, Trübner and Co

Bullock, W. 1816, *A Companion to Mr Bullock's London Museum and Pantherion, Containing a Brief Description of Upwards of Fifteen Thousand National and Foreign Antiquities and Products of Fine Arts, Now Open for Public Inspection in the Egyptian Temple, Piccadilly, London*. London: Bullock

Burollet, T. 1998, Le Monument aux Morts de Bartholomé, in C. Healy, K. Bowie and A. Bo (eds), *Père-Lachaise*, 138–144. Paris: Délégation à l'Action Artistique

Busby, C. A. 1808, *A Series of Designs for Villas and Country Houses*. London: J. Taylor

Butler, B. 2001, Return to Alexandria: Conflict and Contradiction in Discourses of Origins and Heritage Revivalism in Alexandria, Egypt, in R. Layton and J. Thomas (eds), *The Destruction and Conservation of Cultural Property*, 55–75. London: Routledge

Butler, G. and C. McConville 1991, *Camberwell Conservation Study, Vol. 4*. Alphington, Victoria: McConville and Butler Associates

Caillet, M. 1959, Un Rite maçonnique inédit à Toulouse et à Auch en 1806. *Bulletin de la Société Archéologique, Historique, Littéraire et Scientifique du Gers*, 27–57

Calderai, F. and G. Mazzoni 1992, Agostino Fantastici Disegnatore di Mobilia, in C. Cresti (ed.), *Agostino Fantastici*, 73–80. Torino: U. Allemandi

Calvi, F. and S. Ghigino 1999, *Villa Pallavicini at Pegli, Michele Canzio's Romantic Work of Art*. Genoa: Sagep

Campbell, M. J. 1992, *John Martin: Visionary Printmaker*. York: Campbell Fine Art

Canfora, L. 1989, *The Vanished Library: A Wonder of the Ancient World*. London: Vintage

Carliss, R. 1988, Two Shrines to the Silver Screen. *Time* 39 (26 September), 46–47

Carmontelle: *see* Carrogis

Carolin, P. 1988, Editorial. *Architects Journal*, 8 June, 5

Carreras, J. J. 1976, The Black Cat Story. Public Relations Department, Carreras Rothman's Ltd, leaflet, 9 March

Carrogis, L. (known as Carmontelle) 1779, *Jardin de Monceau*. Paris: Delafosse

Carrott, R. G. 1978, *The Egyptian Revival: Its Sources, Monuments, and Meaning, 1808–1858*. Berkeley: University of California Press

Cassas, L. F. 1798, *Voyage pittoresque de la Syrie, de la Phénicie, de la Palestine et de la basse Égypte*. Paris: Imprimerie de la République

Castanho, C. 1987, *Obras de Arte em Logradouros Públicos de São Paulo*. São Paulo: Secretaria Municipal de Cultura

Cayeux, J. 1964, Introduction au catalogue critique des *Griffonis* de Saint-Non. *Bulletin de la Société de l'Histoire de l'Art Français*, 297–384

Cei, M. 1994, *Il Parco di Celle a Pistoia. Araba Fenice del Giardino*. Florence: Edifir

Çelik, Z. 1992, *Displaying the Orient*. Berkeley: University of California Press

Celis, M. M. 1984, De Egyptiserende Maçonnieke Tempels van de Brusselse Loges 'Les Amis Philanthropes' en Les Vrais Amis de l'Union et du Progrès. *Monumenten en Landschappen*, May/June

Centennial 1875, Egypt to be Presented at the Exhibition. *The Centennial* May, 2

Chailly, J. 1972, *The Magic Flute, Masonic Opera. An Interpretation of the Libretto and Music*. London: Gollancz

Champion, T. C. 2003, Beyond Egyptology: Egypt in 19th and 20th Century Archaeology and Anthropology, in P. J. Ucko and T. C. Champion (eds), *The Wisdom of Egypt: changing visions through the ages*, 161–186. London: UCL Press

Champollion, J-F. 1835–1845, *Monuments de l'Égypte et de la Nubie*. Paris: Firmin Didot

Charpentier, J. 1980, *La France des lieux et des demeures alchémiques*. Paris: Retz

Chauprade, A. 1996, *Histoires d'Égypte* (textes réunis). Paris: Sortilèges

Cheah, P. 1998a, The Cosmopolitical – Today, in P. Cheah and B. Robbins (eds), *Cosmopolitics: Thinking and Feeling Beyond Nations*, 20–45. Minneapolis: Minnesota Press

Cheah, P. 1998b, Given Culture: Rethinking Cosmopolitical Freedom in Transnationalism, in P. Cheah and B. Robbins (eds), *Cosmopolitics: Thinking and Feeling Beyond Nations*, 290–328. Minneapolis: Minnesota Press

Cheah, P. and B. Robbins (eds) 1998, *Cosmopolitics: Thinking and Feeling Beyond Nations*. Minneapolis: Minnesota Press

Chenevière, A. 1988, *Russian Furniture: The Golden Age 1780–1840*. London: Weidenfeld and Nicolson

Chevallier, B. 2001, *Malmaison: Visitor's Guide*. Paris: Artlys

Chicago Tribune 1980, The International Competition for a New Administration Building for the *Chicago Tribune* MCMXXII, Containing all the Designs Submitted in Response to *The Chicago Tribune*'s $100,000 Offer Commemorating its Seventy-Fifth Anniversary, June 10, 1922. New York: Rizzoli

Chiostri, F. 1989, *Parchi della Toscana*. La Spezia: Fratelli Melita

Christ, Y. 1970, *Paris des utopies*. Paris: A. Balland

Cini, D. 1997, *Giardini & Giardini. Il Verde Storico nel Centro di Firenze*. Milan: Electa

Circus Circus Enterprises 1994, *The Making of Luxor*. Video about the Luxor Hotel/Casino

Claassen, J-M. 1987, Functional and Symbolic Use of Domes and Arches in Some Examples of South African Religious Architecture. *South African Journal of Culture, Art and History* 1, 110–120

Clayton, P. 1982, *The Rediscovery of Ancient Egypt: Artists and Travellers in the Nineteenth Century*. London: Thames and Hudson

Clerehan, N. 1982, Three Tombs. *Historic Environment* 2 (4), 23–29

Clifford, J. 1997, *Routes: Travel and Translation in the Late Twentieth Century.* Cambridge, Mass: Harvard UP

Clifford, J. 1998, Mixed Feelings, in P. Cheah and B. Robbins (eds), *Cosmopolitics: Thinking and Feeling Beyond Nations,* 362–371. Minneapolis: Minnesota Press

Coli, J. 2001, A Pintura e o Olhar Sobre si: Victor Meirelles e la Invenção de uma História Visual no Século XIX Brasileiro, in M. C. Freitas (ed.), *Historiografia Brasileira em Perspectiva,* 375–404. São Paulo: Contexto

Conner, P. 1983, *The Inspiration of Egypt. Its Influence on British Artists, Travellers and Designers, 1700–1900.* Brighton: Brighton Borough Council

Conner, P. 1985, 'Archaeology Wedded to Art': Poynter's *Israel in Egypt,* in S. Macready and F. H. Thompson (eds), *Influences in Victorian Art and Architecture,* 112–120. London: Society of Antiquaries

Connor, P. 1978, *Roman Art in the National Gallery of Victoria.* Melbourne: National Gallery of Victoria

Coombs, R. E. 1983, *Before Endeavours Fade, a Guide to the Battlefields of the First World War.* London: Battle of Britain Prints International

Coon, S. F. 1985, Giovanni Battista Belzoni: an Extraordinary and Mysterious Freemason. *Ars Quartuor Coronatorum* 2,076, 1–12

Cooper, A. A. 1986, *The Freemasons of South Africa.* Cape Town: Human and Rousseau

Cox, L. B. 1970, *The National Gallery of Victoria 1861–1968: A Search for a Collection.* Melbourne: National Gallery of Victoria

Cresti, C. 1989, Architetti e Ingegneri Massoni nella Toscana del Settecento e Ottocento, in C. Cresti (ed.), *Massoneria e Architettura. Convegno di Firenze 1988,* 137–142. Foggia: Bastogi

Cresti, C. 1992, Agostino Fantastici: o del Come Ripensare al Secolo dei 'Lumi' per Ritrovare il Senso del Progetto e del Fare Architettura, in C. Cresti (ed.), *Agostino Fantastici,* 9–18. Torino: U. Allemandi e C

Croad, S. 1996, Changing Perceptions – A Temple to Tobacco in Camden Town. *Transactions of the Ancient Monument Society* 40, 1–15

Culbertson, J. and T. Randall 2000, *Permanent Parisians: An Illustrated, Biographical Guide to the Cemeteries of Paris.* London: Robson

Cullican, W. 1973/4, Acquisitions from Egypt and Syria. *Art Bulletin of Victoria* 15, 20–26

Curl, J. S. 1982, *The Egyptian Revival: an Introductory Study of a Recurring Theme in the History of Taste.* London: Allen and Unwin

Curl, J. S. 1986, Legends of the Craft. The Architecture of Masonic Halls. *Country Life,* 21 August, 581–583

Curl, J. S. 1991a, Aspects of the Egyptian Revival in Architectural Design in the Nineteenth Century: Themes and Motifs, in C. Morigi Govi, S. Curto and S. Pernigotti (eds), *L'Egitto Fuori dell'Egitto. Dalla Riscoperta all'Egittologia,* 89–96. Bologna: CLUEB

Curl, J. S. 1991b, *The Art and Architecture of Freemasonry: An Introductory Study.* London: B.T. Batsford

Curl, J. S. 1994, *Egyptomania. The Egyptian Revival: A Recurring Theme in the History of Taste.* Manchester: Manchester UP

Curl, J. S. 2000, *The Victorian Celebration of Death.* Stroud: Sutton

Curl, J. S. 2001, *Kensal Green Cemetery.* Chichester: Phillimore

Curran, B. 2003, The Renaissance Afterlife of Ancient Egypt (1400–1650), in P. J. Ucko and T. C. Champion (eds), *The Wisdom of Egypt: changing visions through the ages,* 101–132. London: UCL Press

Dalziel, E. and G. Dalziel 1880, *Dalziels' Bible Gallery.* London: Dalziel Brothers

DaMatta, R. 1990, *Carnavais, Malandros e Heróis.* Rio de Janeiro: Guanabara

David, E. 1994, *Mariette Pacha (1821–1881)*. Paris: Pygmalion/Gérard Watelet

Davison, G. 1996, The Culture of the International Exhibitions, in D. Dunstan (ed.), *Victorian Icon: the Royal Exhibition Building Melbourne*, 11–18. Melbourne: Exhibition Trustees in Association with Australian Scholarly Publishing

Dawson, W. R. and E. P. Uphill 1995, *Who Was Who in Egyptology*. 3rd edition, revised M. Bierbrier, London: Egypt Exploration Society

De Kock, A. J. 1983, Die Gimnasium in die Paarl, 1858–1908: 'n Historiese Studie, unpublished doctoral thesis, University of Stellenbosch

De Meulenaere, H., P. Berko and V. Berko 1992, *L'Égypte ancienne dans la peinture du XIXᵉ siècle*. Knokke-Zoute: Berko

De Villiers, J. M. W. 1874, *Van der Lingen. Herinnering aan het Leven en de Werkzaamheden van den Wel-eerw. Zeer gel. Heer Goth. Wilh. Ant. van der Lingen, in Leven, Herder en Leeraar der Nederd. Geref. Gemeente aan de Paarl door eene Lidmate dier Gemeente*. Kaapstad: Smuts and Hofmeijr

Del Francia, P. R. 2000, Stibbert: l'Acqua e il Tempietto Egizio. *Museo Stibbert Firenze* 3, 33–41

Del Rosso, G. 1787, *Ricerche sull'Architettura Egizia e su Ciò che i Greci Pare Abbiano Preso da Quella Nazione*. Florence: Giuseppe Tofani

Delille, J. 1782, *Les Jardins, ou l'art d'embellir les paysages*. Paris: P-D. Pierres

Denon, V. 1802 [1990], *Voyage dans la basse et la haute Égypte: pendant les campagnes du Général Bonaparte*. Cairo: Institut Français d'Archéologie Orientale

Description 1809–1828, *Description de l'Égypte, ou Recueil des observations et des recherches qui ont été faites en Égypte pendant l'expédition de l'Armée française*. Paris: Imprimerie Impériale

Dewachter, M. 1993, Champollion et la Russie. *Cahiers du Musée Champollion, histoire et archéologie* 2, 31–43

Dezzi Bardeschi, M. 1984, Sulla 'Maniera Simbolica' di Giuseppe Manetti, in L. Zangheri (ed.), *Alla Scoperta della Toscana Lorenese. Architettura e Bonifiche*, 113–117. Florence: Edam

Dezzi Bardeschi, M. 1986, Le Macchine Desideranti, in A. Vezzosi (ed.), *Il Giardino Romantico*, 29–45. Florence: Alinea

Dezzi Bardeschi, M. 1989, Il Linguaggio Segreto: Architettura e Massoneria a Firenze, 1803–1845, in C. Cresti (ed.), *Massoneria e Architettura. Convegno di Firenze 1988*, 165–170. Foggia: Bastogi

Dmochowski, Z. 1956, *The Architecture of Poland*. London: Polish Research Centre

Dolmetsch, H. 1889, *Der Ornamentenschatz: Ein Musterbuch Stilvoller Ornamente aus Allen Kunstepochen. 85 Tafeln mit 1200 meist Farbigen Abbildungen Erläuterndem*. Stuttgart: Julius Hoffmann

Dominici, L. and D. Negri 1992, *La Villa e il Parco Puccini di Scornio*. Pistoia: Cassa di Risparmio di Pistoia e Pescia

Doré, G. 1866, *La Sainte Bible selon la Vulgate*. Tours: Mame et Fils

Draper, C. n. d., *Islington's Cinemas and Film Studios*. London: Islington Libraries

Dream City 1893, *The Dream City: A Portfolio of Photographic Views of the World's Columbian Exposition with an Introduction by Halsey C. Ives*. Saint Louis, MO: N. D. Thompson Co

Drower, M. S. 1982, The Early Years, in T. G. H. James (ed.), *The Egypt Exploration Society 1882–1982*, 9–36. London: British Museum Publications

Drumont, E. 1879, *Les Fêtes nationales à Paris*. Paris: L. Baschet

Dugdale, M. 1932, Ornamentia Praecox. *Architectural Review,* July, 40

Dunstan, D. and E. Graham 1996, Unrolling a Mummy, in D. Dunstan (ed.), *Victorian Icon: the Royal Exhibition Building Melbourne*, 247–249. Melbourne: Exhibition Trustees in Association with Australian Scholarly Publishing

Durant, W. and A. Durant 1975, *The Age of Napoleon*. New York: Simon and Schuster

Durliat, M. 1974, Alexandre Du Mège ou les mythes archéologiques à Toulouse dans le premier tiers du XIXᵉ siècle. *Revue de l'Art* 23, 30–41

Dutton, T. 1800, *The Dramatic Censor; or, Weekly Theatrical Report*, Vol. 1. London: J. Roach and C. Chapple

Early, P. 2000, *Super Casino. Inside the 'New' Las Vegas*. New York: Bantam

Ebers, G. with S. Birch 1887, *Egypt: Descriptive, Historical, and Picturesque* (trans. C. Bell). London: Cassell

Eckels, C. W. 1950, The Egyptian Revival in America. *Archaeology* 3, 164–169

Edgeworth, M. 1812, The Absentee, in *Tales of Fashionable Life*. London: J. Johnston

Edmond, C. 1867, *L'Égypte à l'Exposition Universelle de 1867*. Paris: Dentu

El Daly, O. 2003a, What do Tourists Learn of Egypt?, in S. MacDonald and M. Rice (eds), *Consuming Ancient Egypt*, 139–150. London: UCL Press

El Daly, O. 2003b, Ancient Egypt in Medieval Arabic Writings, in P. J. Ucko and T. C. Champion (eds), *The Wisdom of Egypt: changing visions through the ages*, 39–64. London: UCL Press

Eliovson, S. 1956, *Johannesburg: The Fabulous City*. Cape Town: Howard Timmins

Elsworth, J. D. 1983, *Andrey Bely. A Critical Study of the Novels*. Cambridge: CUP

Elwall, R. n. d., The Dream Lands of Julian Leathart. *Picture House Magazine*, copy in Kensington Central Library

Empereur, J-Y. 1998, *Alexandria Rediscovered*. London: British Museum Press

Epigraphic Survey 1930, *Medinet Habu. I, Earlier Historical Records of Ramesses III*. Oriental Institute Publications VIII. Chicago: University of Chicago

Erlande-Brandenburg, A. 1976, *L'Église abbatiale de Saint-Denis*. Paris: Editions de la Tourelle

Errera, E. 1997, The Dream of Alexander and the Literary Myth, in R. Ilbert and I. Yannakakis with J. Hassoun (eds), *Alexandria 1860–1960: The Brief Life of a Cosmopolitan Community*, 128–144. Alexandria: Harpocrates

Ettlinger, L. 1945, A German Architect's Visit to England in 1826. *Architectural Review* 97, 131–134

Evans, B. 1993, *Bygone East Ham*. London: Phillimore

Evening Tribune 1924, 1 July, 7

Faulkner, T. 1813, *An Historical and Topographical Account of Fulham, Including the Hamlet of Hammersmith*. Chelsea: J. Tilling

Fazzini, R. with M. McKercher 1996, L'Égyptomanie dans l'architecture américaine (trans. J. Bouniort), in J-M. Humbert (ed.), *L'Égyptomanie à l'épreuve de l'archéologie. Actes du colloque international organisé au Musée du Louvre par le service culturel les 8 et 9 avril 1994*, 227–278. Paris and Brussels: Musée du Louvre and Gram

Feaver, W. 1974, *The Art of John Martin*. Oxford: Clarendon

Ferguson, J. 1973, *The Heritage of Hellenism*. London: Thames and Hudson

Feuchtwang, S. 2000a, Reinscriptions: Commemorations, Restoration and the Interpersonal Transmission of Histories and Memories under Modern States in Asia and Europe, in S. Radstone (ed.), *Memory and Methodology*, 59–78. Oxford: Berg

Feuchtwang, S. 2000b, The Avenging Ghost: Paradigm of a Shameful Past, in *Anthropology II: Beliefs and Everyday Life*, 1–29. Third International Conference on Sinology. London: Academica Sinica

Finch, G. and A. Forman 2001, *Greater London House – Carreras Building*. London: Finch and Forman

Fine Art Society 1978, *Eastern Encounters. Orientalist Painters of the Nineteenth Century*. London: Fine Art Society

Fine Art Society 1980, *Travellers Beyond the Grand Tour*. London: Fine Art Society

Firth, R. 1973, *Symbols: Public and Private*. Ithaca: Cornell UP

Fischer von Erlach, J-B. 1721, *Entwurff einer Historischen Architektur*. Vienna

Fischer, H. G. 1986, *L'Écriture et l'art de l'Égypte ancienne: quatre leçons sur la paléographie et l'epigraphie pharaoniques*. Paris: Presses Universitaires de France

Fischer, H. G. 1992, Review of Humbert's 'L'Egyptomanie dans L'art occidental'. *Journal of the American Research Center in Egypt* 29, 226

Fleming, J. and H. Honour 1989, *The Penguin Dictionary of the Decorative Arts*. Harmondsworth: Penguin

Flit, M. A., A. N. Guzanov, L. V. Koval and Y. V. Mudrov 1993, *Pavlovsk. The Palace and the Park*. Paris: A. de Gourcuff

Flower, D. 1999, *The Shores of Wisdom*. London: Pharos

Fontani, F. 1808, *Viaggio nel Basso e nell'Alto Egitto Illustrato Dietro alle Tracce e ai Disegni del Sig. Denon*. Florence: Giuseppe Tofani

Foster, M. E. and E. H. Sykes 1998, *An Explanation of the Decorations of the Egyptian Room Petersham*. Petersham: United Supreme Grand Chapter of Mark and Royal Arch Masons of New South Wales and the Australian Capital Territory

Foucart, G. 1897, *Histoire de l'ordre lotiforme: étude d'archéologie égyptienne*. Paris: Ernest Leroux

Fougasse and McCullough 1935, *You Have Been Warned: a Complete Guide to the Road*. London: Methuen

Fox, C. (ed.) 1992, *London – World City, 1800–1840*. New Haven and London: Yale UP and Museum of London

Fox, P. 1988, The State Library of Victoria: Science and Civilisation. *Transition* 26, 14–26

Fox, W. L. 1996, How the Sphinx Came to Washington. *Scottish Rite Journal*, May, 19–27

Franco, M. E. 1996, As Pirâmides Triangulares de Mestre Valentim. *Suplemento Literário, O Estado de São Paulo*, 10 December

Fransen, H. and M. A. Cook 1980, *The Old Buildings of the Cape: a Survey and Description of Old Buildings in the Western Province Extending from Cape Town to Calvinia in the North and to Graaff-Reinet, Colesberg and Uitenhage in the East*. Cape Town: Balkema

Frayling, C. 1992, *The Face of Tutankhamun*. London: Faber and Faber

Freeland, J. M. 1970, *Architecture in Australia, a History*. Melbourne: F. W. Cheshire

Fry, E. M. 1928, The New Carreras Building. *Architects Journal*, 21 November, 736–740

Fuller, D. Q. 2003, Pharaonic or Sudanic? Models for Meroitic Society and Change, in D. O'Connor and A. Reid (eds), *Ancient Egypt in Africa*, 169–184. London: UCL Press

Galbally, A. 1995, *Redmond Barry*. Melbourne: University of Melbourne Press

Gallier, J. 1836, On the Rise, Progress and Present State of Architecture in North America. *North American Review* 43, 356–384

Garraud, J-R. 1887, *Un Artiste dijonnais, Joseph Garraud, statuaire, directeur et inspecteur des Beaux-Arts, 1807–1880*. Dijon: Imprimerie de Darantière

Gebbie and Barry 1876, *The Masterpieces of the Centennial International Exhibition*. Philadelphia: Gebbie and Barry

Gebhard, D. and R. Winter 1977, *A Guide to Architecture in Los Angeles & Southern California*. Santa Barbara: Peregrine Smith

Gentleman's Magazine 1833, Egyptian Antiquities. March, 256–257

Gilet, A. 1989, Louis-François Cassas und der Orient, in G. Sievernich and H. Budde (eds), *Europa und der Orient 800–1900*, 279–287. Exhibition Catalogue. Martin Gropius Bau Berlin. Berlin: Bertelsmann

Gladkova, E. S., L. V. Emina and V. Lemus 1961, *Gorod Pushkin*. Leningrad

Glenn, C. *et al.* 1977, *Egypt in LA.* Long Beach: Art Galleries, California State University

Gliddon, G. R. 1843, *Ancient Egypt: a Series of Chapters on Early Egyptian History, Archaeology, and Other Subjects Connected with Hieroglyphical Literature.* New York: J. Winchester

Goad, P. 1999, *Melbourne Architecture.* Sydney: Watermark

GOAL 1990, *Bibliotecha Alexandrina: Record of the Inaugural Meeting of the International Commission for the Revival of the Ancient Library of Alexandria,* Aswan, 11–12 February 1990. Paris: Unesco

GOAL 1997, Pharos Condition Report, in *Proceedings of the International Workshop on Submarine Archaeology and Coastal Management,* held in Alexandria, 7–11 April 1997. Paris: Unesco

Goddio, F. 1998, *Alexandria: The Submerged Royal Quarters.* Paris: Periplus

Gombrich, E. H. 1989, Signs of the Time. The Dream of Reason: Symbolism of the French Revolution. *FMR International Edition* 39, 1–24

Gordon, E. and J. Nerenberg 1979–1980, Chicago's Colourful Terra Cotta Façades. *Chicago History,* Winter, 224–233

Gordon, L. D. with J. Ross and S. Searight 1983, *Letters from Egypt.* London: Virago

Gormon, T. 1993, High Stakes Style. *New York Times Magazine,* 13 December, 14

Gosden, C. and Y. Marshall 1999, The Cultural Biography of Objects. *World Archaeology* 31, 169–178

Gray, A (ed.) 1997, *Eyewitness Travel Guides: Paris.* London: Dorling Kindersley

Gray-Durant, D. and I. Robertson 1998, *Paris and Versailles Blue Guide.* London: A & C Black

Gregory, E. 1997, *ḥ.d and Hellenism.* Cambridge: CUP

Greig, D. 1971, *A Guide to Architecture in South Africa.* Cape Town: Howard Timmins

Grifoni, T. and D. Negri 1998, Il Giardino Romantico e l'Opera di Luigi de Cambray Digny, in G. Pettena, P. Pietrogrande and M. Pozzana (eds), *Giardini Parchi Paesaggi. L'Avventura delle Idee in Toscana dall'Ottocento a Oggi,* 99–106. Florence: Le Lettere

Grimm, G. G. 1963, *Arkhitektor Voronikhin.* Leningrad: Gos. Izdatel'stvo Literatury po Stroitelstvu, Arkhitekture i Stroitelnym Materialam

Guiterman, H. and B. Llewellyn 1986, *David Roberts.* Exhibition Catalogue. Barbican Art Gallery. London: Phaidon

Gurrieri, F. 1974, Prima Nota per l'Architettura Neoclassica nel Territorio Pistoiese. *Antichità Viva* 13, 42–54

Gutheim, F. 1951, Who Designed the Washington Monument? *Journal of the American Institute of Architects* 15, 136–142

Haikal, F. 2003, Egypt's Past Regenerated by its Own People, in S. MacDonald and M. Rice (eds), *Consuming Ancient Egypt,* 123–138. London: UCL Press

Hale, C. R., S. H. Jones and H. Morton 1859, *Report of the Committee Appointed by the Philomathean Society of the University of Pennsylvania for the Translation of the Rosetta Stone.* Philadelphia

Hamer, M. 2001, The Myth of Cleopatra Since the Renaissance, in S. Walker and P. Higgs (eds), *Cleopatra of Egypt: From History to Myth,* 302–311. London: British Museum Press

Harkins, J. 1982, *Metropolis of the American Nile: Memphis and Shelby County.* Woodland Hills, Cal: Windsor Publications

Harper's Weekly 1876, 8 January, 31

Harradine, M. 1991, More About our Pyramid. *Looking Back: Journal of the Historical Society of Port Elizabeth,* March, 24

Harris, J. G. 1991, *O. Mandelstam. The Collected Critical Prose and Letters.* London: Collins Harvill

Harrison, T. 2003, Upside Down and Back to Front: Herodotus and the Greek Encounter with Egypt, in R. Matthews and C. Roemer (eds), *Ancient Perspectives on Egypt,* 145–156. London: UCL Press

Harrods 2000, *Stairway to Heaven: A New Central Elevator.* London: Harrods

Harrods 2002, *Harrods: Store Guide.* London: Harrods

Hassan, F. 2003a, Imperialist Appropriations of Egyptian Obelisks, in D. Jeffreys (ed.), *Views of Ancient Egypt since Napoleon Bonaparte: imperialism, colonialism and modern appropriations,* **19–68. London: UCL Press**

Hassan, F. 2003b, Selling Egypt: Encounters at Khan el-Khalili, in S. MacDonald and M. Rice (eds), *Consuming Ancient Egypt,* **111–122. London: UCL Press**

Hassan, F. A. forthcoming, Terror at the Temple, unpublished manuscript

Hawthorne, N. 1870, *Passages from the English Note-books.* London: Strahan

Haycock, D. B. 2003, Ancient Egypt in 17th and 18th Century England, in P. J. Ucko and T. C. Champion (eds), *The Wisdom of Egypt: changing visions through the ages,* **133–160. London: UCL Press**

Henry, A. [1852], *Le Père Lachaise.* Leaflet, Paris

Herman, M. 1970, *The Early Australian Architects and their Work.* 2nd revised edition, London and Sydney: Angus and Robertson

Hitchmough, W. 1992, *Hoover Factory: Wallis, Gilbert and Partners.* London: Phaidon

Hobbs-Halmay, H. M. 1992, The Development of Egyptian Revival Architecture in San Diego County. *Journal of San Diego History* 38, 93–111

Hölscher, U. 1934, *The Excavation of Medinet Habu. I, General Plans and Views.* Oriental Institute Publications XXI, Chicago: University of Chicago

Honig, B. 1998, Ruth, the Model Émigré: Mourning and the Symbolic Politics of Immigration, in P. Cheah and B. Robbins (eds), *Cosmopolitics: Thinking and Feeling Beyond Nations,* 192–216. Minneapolis: Minnesota Press

Honour, H. 1955, The Egyptian Taste. *The Connoisseur* 135

Hope, C. A. 1983a, A Note on the Collection of Egyptian Antiquities in the National Gallery of Victoria, Melbourne. *Göttinger Miszellen* 65, 45–50

Hope, C. A. 1983b, A Head of Nefertiti and a Figure of Ptah-Soaker-Osiris in the National Gallery of Victoria. *Art Bulletin of Victoria* 24, 47–62

Hope, C. A. 1984, Tby the Elder from Sheikh Farag Tomb 5105. *Abr-Nahrain* 22, 7–28

Hope, C. A. 1988, *Gold of the Pharaohs.* Melbourne: Museum of Victoria

Hope, C. A. 1997, Egyptian Antiquities in the National Gallery of Victoria, Melbourne. *Egyptian Archaeology* 10, 38–39

Hope, C. A. and R. Miller 1984, *Life and Death in Ancient Egypt. Tjeby: An Egyptian Mummy in the Museum of Victoria.* Melbourne: Museum of Victoria

Hope, T. 1807, *Household Furniture and Interior Decoration.* London: Longman, Hurst, Rees and Orme

Hopkins, H. C. 1978, *Kakamas – uit die Wildernis 'n Lushof.* Kaapstad: Nasionale Boekdrukkery

Hornung, E. (ed.) 1994, Zum Bild Ägyptens im Mittelalter und in der Renaissance (OBO 95). Freiburg: Universitätsverlag

Hornung, E. 1997, Hermetische Weisheit: Umrisse einer Ägyptosophie, in E. Staehelin and B. Jaeger (eds), *Ägypten-Bilder. Akten des 'Symposions zur Ägypten-Rezeption', Augst bei Basel, vom 9–11 September 1993,* 333–342. Freiburg: Universitätsverlag

Hornung, E. 1999, *The Ancient Egyptian Books of the Afterlife.* Ithaca: Cornell UP

Hubert, G. (ed.) 1969, *Napoléon.* Exhibition catalogue. Paris: Réunion des Musées Nationaux

Humbert, J-M. 1974, Les Obélisques de Paris: projets et réalisations. *Revue de l'Art* 23, 9–29

Humbert, J-M. 1987, *L'Égyptomanie: sources, thèmes et symboles,* doctoral thesis, Paris; microfilm, Lille University

Humbert, J-M. 1989, *L'Égyptomanie dans l'art occidental.* Paris: Editions ACR

Humbert, J-M. 1994, Egyptomania: A Current Concept from the Renaissance to Postmodernism, in J-M. Humbert, M. Pantazzi and C. Ziegler (eds), *Egyptomania. Egypt in Western Art, 1730–1930*, 21–26. Paris and Ottawa: Réunion des Musées Nationaux/National Gallery of Canada

Humbert, J-M. (ed.) 1996a, *L'Égyptomanie à l'épreuve de l'archéologie*. Paris and Brussels: Musée du Louvre and Gram

Humbert, J-M. 1996b, Postérité du sphinx antique: la sphinxomanie et ses sources, in J-M. Humbert (ed.), *L'Égyptomanie à l'épreuve de l'archéologie*, 97–138. Paris and Brussels: Musée du Louvre and Gram

Humbert, J-M. 1997a, Le Metamorfosi di Iside tra il XVI e il XIX Secolo, in *Iside*, Exhibition Catalogue. Milan: Electra

Humbert, J-M. 1997b, La Folie des pyramides, des Lumières au Grand Louvre. *L'Histoire* 216, 32–33

Humbert, J-M. 1998a, *L'Égypte à Paris*. Paris: Action Artistique de la Ville de Paris

Humbert, J-M. 1998b, *Rêve d'Égypte, l'architecture égyptisante vue par trois photographes*. Paris: Mona Bismarck Foundation

Humbert, J-M. 1998c, Entre mythe et archéologie: la fortune statuaire égyptisante de Desaix et Kléber, in J. Pigeaud and J-P. Barbe (eds), *Le Culte des grands hommes au XVIIIᵉ siècle*, 219–232. Nantes: Université de Nantes

Humbert, J-M. (ed.) 1998d, *France-Égypte: dialogues de deux cultures*. Paris: Musées de la Ville de Paris

Humbert, J-M. 1999, Desaix, héros de l'Égypte, in G. Bresc-Bautier and X. Dectot (eds), *Art ou politique? Arcs, statues et colonnes de Paris*. Paris: Action Artistique de la Ville de Paris

Humbert, J-M. 2001, Les Fabriques égyptisantes entre exotisme et ésotérisme, in J. Pigeaud and J-P. Barbe (eds), *Histoire de jardins. Lieux et imaginaire*, 181–195. Paris: Puf-Perspectives Littéraires

Humbert, J-M. 2002, Les Expositions Universelles de 1867 et 1878 et la création d'*Aïda*: l'image de l'Égypte transmise par Auguste Mariette, dans les actes du colloque la France et l'Égypte à l'époque des vice-rois (IREMAN, Aix-en-Provence, 1998). *Cahier des Annales Islamologiques* 22, 289–309. Cairo: Institute Français d'Archéologie Orientale

Humbert, J-M. 2003, How to Stage *Aida*, in S. MacDonald and M. Rice (eds), *Consuming Ancient Egypt*, 47–62. London: UCL Press

Humbert, J-M., M. Pantazzi and C. Ziegler (eds) 1994, *Egyptomania. Egypt in Western Art, 1730–1930; Égyptomanie. L'Égypte dans l'art occidental, 1730–1930*. Paris and Ottawa: Réunion des Musées Nationaux/National Gallery of Canada

Hyde, R. 1988, *Panoramania! The Art and Entertainment of the 'All-Embracing' View*. London: Trefoil and Barbican Art Gallery

Hyden, W. 1931, *Pavlova: The Genius of Dance*. London: Constable

Ilbert, R. 1997, International Waters, in R. Ilbert and I. Yannakakis with J. Hassoun (eds), *Alexandria 1860–1960: the Brief Life of a Cosmopolitan Community*, 10–15. Alexandria: Harpocrates

Illustrated London News 1854, 22 July

Ilyin, M. A. and A. A. Aleksandrov 1975, *Moskva Pamiatniki Arkhitektury, XVIII-Pervoi Treti XIX Veka*. Moscow: Iskusstvo

Inglis, K. S. assisted by J. Brazier 1998, *Sacred Places: War Memorials in the Australian Landscape*. Melbourne: Melbourne UP

Irwin, J. 1980, *American Hieroglyphics. The Symbol of the Egyptian Hieroglyphics in the American Renaissance*. New Haven and London: Yale UP

Issartel, T. 1990, Les Projets pour le tombeau de Napoléon, in J-M. Humbert (ed.) *Napoléon aux Invalides, 1840, le retour des cendres*. Thonon-les-Bains and Paris: L'Albaron and Musée de l'Armée

Ivanov, V. I. 1911, *Cor Ardens*. Moscow: Skorpion

Iversen, E. 1972, *Obelisks in Exile, II. The Obelisks of Istanbul and England.* Copenhagen: Gad

Iversen, E. 1993 [1961], *The Myth of Egypt and its Hieroglyphs in European Tradition.* Princeton: Princeton UP

Jaeger, B. 1995, La Reviviscenza dell'Egitto Antico nell'Arte Italiana dal Rinascimento ai Giorni Nostri. *Studi di Egittologia e di Antichità Puniche* 14, 33–49

Jeffreys, D. 2003, Introduction – 200 Years of Ancient Egypt: Modern History and Ancient Archaeology, in D. Jeffreys (ed.), *Views of Ancient Egypt since Napoleon Bonaparte: imperialism, colonialism and modern appropriations,* 1–18. London: UCL Press

Jekyll, G. and C. Hussey 1927, *Garden Ornaments.* London: Charles Scribner's Sons

Jencks, C. 1991, *Post Modern Triumphs in London.* London: Academy Editions

Jones, O. 1856, *The Grammar of Ornament.* London: Day and Son

Jones, O. and J. Bonomi 1854, *Description of the Egyptian Court Erected in the Crystal Palace.* London: Bradbury and Evans

Jones, S., C. Newall, L. Ormond, R. Ormond and B. Read 1996, *Frederic Leighton 1830–1896.* Exhibition Catalogue, Royal Academy of Arts, London. New York: Abrams

Jullian, P. 1977, *Les Orientalistes.* Fribourg: Office du Livre

Kaelin, O. 1999, *Ein Assyrisches Bildexperiment nach Ägyptischem Vorbild.* Münster: Alter Orient und Altes Testament

Katsnelson, I. S. 1976, Vstretcha Rossii s Egiptom (Pervaya tret XIX v.), in I. E. Danilova and I. S. Katsnelson, *Tutankhamon i Ego Vremya,* 189–209. Moscow: Nauka

Kelly, A. 1990, *Mrs Coade's Stone.* Upton-upon-Severn: Self Publishing Association

Kennedy, M. 2001, Great Lost City of Ancient Egypt Revealed. 'Sensational' Recovery of Inscribed Slab Identifies Site as Port of Heracleion. *The Guardian,* 8 June, 27

Kérisel, J. 1991, *La Pyramide à travers les âges, art et religion.* Paris: Presses de l'École Nationale des Ponts et Chaussées

Khlebnikov, V. 1968, *Sobranie Sochinenii.* Munich: Wilhelm Fink

Khlebnikov, V. 1985, in C. Douglas (ed.), *The King of Time. Selected Writings of the Russian Futurian,* 85–104. Cambridge, Mass: Harvard UP

Kinsilia, E. B. 1917, *Modern Theater Construction.* New York: The Moving Picture World

Kitchen, K. and M. Beltrão 1990, *Catalogue of the Egyptian Collection in The National Museum.* Warminster: Aris & Phillips

Kitshoff, M. C. 1972, Gottlieb Wilhelm Antony van der Lingen. Kaapse Predikant uit die Negentiende eeu, unpublished dissertation, Vrije Universiteit Amsterdam

Knight, J. G. 1865, *The Australasian Colonies at the International Exhibition, London, 1862.* Melbourne: John Ferres

Kwiatowski, M. 1986, *Lazienki and Belweder.* Warsaw: Arkady

Laborde, A. de 1808, *Description des nouveaux jardins de la France et de ses anciens châteaux.* Paris: Delance

Lacoste, M. C. 1994, *The Story of a Grand Design: UNESCO 1946–1993. Paris:* Unesco

Landy, J. 1970, *The Architecture of Minard Lafever.* New York and London: Columbia UP

Langlois, G-A. 1998, *Folies, tivolis et attractions: les premiers parcs de loisirs parisiens.* Paris: Action Artistique de la Ville de Paris

Lant, A. 1992, The Curse of the Pharaoh, or How Cinema contracted Egyptomania. *October* 59, 86–112

Layton, R. and P. Ucko 1999, Introduction: Gazing on the Landscape and Encountering the Environment, in P. Ucko and R. Layton (eds), *The Archaeology and Anthropology of Landscape. Shaping your Landscape*, 1–20. London: Routledge

Leclant, J. 1985, *De l'égyptophilie à l'égyptologie: érudits, voyageurs, collectionneurs et mécènes*, lecture given during the annual public session, 22 November, CRAI Institute, 4th fascicule, 630–647

Lehner, M. 1997, *The Complete Pyramids*. London: Thames and Hudson

Leigh Hunt, W. 1861, *A Saunter Through the West End*. London, from *The Atlas* newspaper

Lemus, V. V. 1984, *Pushkin, Palaces and Parks*. Leningrad: Aurora

Lenoir, A. 1807 [1814], *La Franche-maçonnerie rendue à sa véritable origine*. Paris: Fournier

Lepsius, K. R. 1849–1859, *Denkmäler aus Aegypten und Aethiopien*. Berlin: Nicholaische Buchhandlung

Lepsius, K. R. 1853, *Letters from Egypt, Ethiopia, and the Peninsula of Sinai* (trans. L. and J. Horner). London: H. G. Bohn

Lepsius, R. 1870, *Koenigliche Museen. Abtheilung der aegyptischen Alterthümer. Die Wandgemaelde der verschiedenen Raeume, 37 Tafeln nebst Erklaerung*. 2nd edition, Berlin: Staatliche Museen

Lewis, M. 1978, *John Frederick Lewis R. A. 1805–1876*. Leigh-on-Sea: F. Lewis

Lewis, P. and G. Darley (eds) 1986, *Dictionary of Ornament*. London: Cameron

Linden-Ward, B. 1989, *Silent City on a Hill: Landscapes of Memory and Boston's Mount Auburn Cemetery*. Columbus, Ohio: Ohio State UP

Llewelyn, B. 1985, The Islamic Inspiration. John Frederick Lewis: Painter of Islamic Egypt, in S. Macready and F. H. Thompson (eds), *Influences in Victorian Art and Architecture*, 121–138, Society of Antiquaries Occasional Paper, New Series 7, London: Society of Antiquaries

Lloyd, L. 1929, The De-Luxe Picture Palace. *New Republic* 58, 175–176

Lo Gatto, E. 1943, *Gli Artisti Italiani in Russia, Vol. III, Gli Architetti del Secolo XIX*. Milan: Libri Scheiwiller

Lo Gatto, E. 1993, *Gli Artisti Italiani in Russia, Vol. II, Gli Architetti del Secolo XVIII a Pietroburgo e Nelle Tenute Imperiali*. Milan: Libri Scheiwiller

Lupton, C. 2003, 'Mummymania' for the Masses – is Egyptology Cursed by the Mummy's Curse?, in S. MacDonald and M. Rice (eds), *Consuming Ancient Egypt*, 23–46. London: UCL Press

MacDonald, R. 1982, *David Syme*. North Blackburn: Vantage House

MacDonald, S. and M. Rice (eds) 2003, *Consuming Ancient Egypt*. London: UCL Press

MacFaruhar, R. 2001, Shadow of a Library. *New York Times*, 11 May, 20

MacKenzie, J. 1995, *Orientalism. History, Theory and the Arts*. Manchester: Manchester UP

MacLeod, R. 2001, *The Library of Alexandria – Centre of Learning in the Ancient World*. London: Tavis and Co

Maehler, H. 2003, Roman Poets on Egypt, in R. Matthews and C. Roemer (eds), *Ancient Perspectives on Egypt*, 203–216. London: UCL Press

Mallett, L. 1988, Deconstruction Hits Homebase. *Building Design* 892, 1

Maresca, M. P. 1986, Da Osiride al Torrino (Il Giardino Torrigiani), in A.Vezzosi (ed.), *Il Giardino Romantico*, 56–60. Florence: Alinea

Maresca, M. P. 1989, Architetti e Committenti Massoni nella Toscana del XIX Secolo: I Giardini Come "Iter" Simbolico e Iniziatico, in C. Cresti (ed.), *Massoneria e Architettura. Convegno di Firenze 1988*, 171–173. Foggia: Bastogi

Maresca, M. P. 1993, Il Giardino Torrigiani a Firenze. L'Invenzione Romantica di un Parco Tra Natura e Allegoria. *Arte dei Giardini* 2, 55–77

Mariette, A. 1867, *Exposition Universelle de 1867, description du parc Égyptien*. Paris: Dentu

Marks, R. 1978, For Los Angeles, This is Really 'Tut II'. *Los Angeles Magazine,* January, 105, 192

Marquet, A. 1983, *La Cathédrale du Mans.* Le Mans

Martellacci, R. 1989, Stilemi Egizi e Massoneria: Le Scenografie di Schinkel per il "Flauto Magico" di Mozart, in C. Cresti (ed.), *Massoneria e Architettura. Convegno di Firenze 1988*, 95–103. Foggia: Bastogi

Martellacci, R. 1992, Disegni di Architettura. Catalogo, in C. Cresti (ed.), *Agostino Fantastici*, 135–189. Torino: U. Allemandi e C

Martin, H. 1945, *Le Style Empire.* Paris: Flammarion

Martin, J. 1997, *Les Glacières Françaises.* Paris: Editions Errance

Martin, M. 1987, An Architecture for the Masses. The Movie Palaces of the 1930s. *Architecture SA,* May/June, 22–25

Massie, S. 1990, *Pavlovsk: The Life of a Russian Palace.* London: Little, Brown

Matthews, R. and C. Roemer 2003, Introduction: the Worlds of Ancient Egypt – Aspects, Sources, Interactions, in R. Matthews and C. Roemer (eds), *Ancient Perspectives on Egypt,* **1–20. London: UCL Press**

McCabe, J. D. 1876, *The Illustrated History of the Centennial Exhibition.* Cincinnati, Ohio: Jones Brothers

McCall, H. 1998, Rediscovery and Aftermath, in S. Dalley (ed.), *The Legacy of Mesopotamia*, 183–213. Oxford: OUP

McKay, J. 1998, 'A Good Show': Colonial Queensland at International Exhibitions. *Memoire of the Queensland Museum: Cultural Heritage Series* 1 (2), 175–343

McKay, J. 2001, 'Only a Gilded Show': Australian Gold at International Exhibitions 1851–1901, in K. Cordell and C. Cumming (eds), *A World Turned Upside Down: Cultural Change on Australia's Goldfields 1851–2001*, 147–163. Canberra: Australian National University

Medina-González, I. 2003, 'Trans-Atlantic Pyramidology', Orientalism, and Empire: Ancient Egypt and the 19th Century Archaeological Experience of Mesoamerica, in D. Jeffreys (ed.), *Views of Ancient Egypt since Napoleon Bonaparte: imperialism, colonialism and modern appropriations,* **107–126. London: UCL Press**

Meijer, R. (ed.) 1999, *Cosmopolitanism, Identity and Authenticity in the Middle East.* London: Curzon

Merrillees, R. S. 1990, *Living with Egypt's Past in Australia.* Melbourne: Museum of Victoria

Merrillees, R. S. 1995, Egyptomania in Australia. *Bulletin of the Australian Centre for Egyptology* 6, 77–87

Merrillees, R. S. 1998, Israel in Egypt Down Under: The First Synagogues in Australia. *Australian Jewish Historical Journal* 14 (2), 260–283

Merrington, P. 1995, Pageantry and Primitivism: Dorothea Fairbridge and the 'Aesthetics of Union'. *Journal of South African Studies* 21 (4), 643–656

Merrington, P. 2001, A Staggered Orientalism: The Cape-to-Cairo Imaginary. *Poetics Today* 22 (2), 323–364

Mirsky, S. 1975, *Der Orient im Werk Velimir Chlebnikovs.* Munich: Sagner

Mitchell, C. 1998, The Renaissance of Alexandria: A New Great Library Revives Hopes for a Return to Alexandria's Intellectual Golden Age. *Highlife,* January, 106–113

Money, K. 1982, *Anna Pavlova, Her Life and Art.* London: Alfred A. Knopf

Monteiro de Carvalho, A. M. F. 1999, *Mestre Valentim.* Rio de Janeiro: Cosac & Naify

Montfaucon, B. de 1719, *L'Antiquité expliquée et représentée en figures.* Paris: F. Delaulne

Montgailhard, G. de 1906, *Lecomte du Noüy.* Paris: A. Lahure

Montserrat, D. 2000, *Akhenaten: History, Fantasy and Ancient Egypt.* London: Routledge

Monumenten en Landschappen 1988, no. 2, March/April, 13–71

Monumenti del Giardino Puccini 1845. Pistoia: Tipografia Cino

Morenz, S. 1968, *Die Begegnung Europas mit Ägypten*. Berlin: Akademie

Morton, S. G. 1844, *Crania Aegyptiaca: or, Observations on Egyptian Ethnography, Derived from Anatomy, History and the Monuments*. Philadelphia: John Penington

Mosser, M. 1990, Le Architetture Paradossali Ovvero Piccolo Trattato sulle "Fabriques", in M. Mosser and G. Teyssot (eds), *L'Architettura dei Giardini d'Occidente dal Rinascimento al Novecento*, 259–276. Milan: Electa

Murray, G. 1953, *Hellenism and the Modern World*. London: Allen and Unwin

Museum of Fine Arts 1876, *Proceedings at the Opening of the Museum of Fine Arts: With the Reports for 1876, a List of Donations, the Act of Incorporation, By-laws etc.* Boston: Alfred Mudge and Son

Nachman, R. G. 1977, Positivism, Modernization, and Middle Class in Brazil. *Hispanic American Historical Research* 57, 1–23

Nasaw, D. 1993, *Going Out: The Rise and Fall of Public Amusements*. New York: Basic Books

Naville, E. 1891, *Bubastis*. London: Kegan Paul, Trench, Trübner and Co

Neve, A. 1984, Paul Bonduelle 1877–1955, unpublished mémoire de fin d'études de l'Institut Supérieure d'Architecture de l'État, La Cambre

New York Times 1876a, 19 January, 2

New York Times 1876b, Denmark and Egypt, 8 May, 5

Nicholl, C. 1996, Lingering Ghosts that Haunt Cleopatra's City. *Mail on Sunday,* 14 August, 67–68

Nivat, G. 1967, Le 'Jeu Cérébral', Étude sur 'Pétersbourg'. Postscript to A. Biély. Lausanne: L'Age d'Homme

O'Bell, L. 1984, *Pushkin's 'Egyptian Nights': The Biography of a Work*. Ann Arbor: Ardis

Oberholster, J. J. 1972, *The Historical Monuments of South Africa*. Cape Town: Rembrandt van Rijn Foundation for Culture

Old Humphrey (pseud. G. Mogridge) 1843, *Walks in London and its Neighbourhood*. London: Religious Tract Society

Overell, R. 1991, The Melbourne Public Library and the Guillaumes: the Relation between a Colonial Library and its London Book Supplier 1854–1865, in F. Upward and J. P. Whyte (eds), *Peopling a Profession: Papers from the Fourth Forum on Australian Library History, Monash University, 25 and 26 September 1989*, 33–63. Melbourne: Ancora

Overell, R. 1997, *Early Book Purchases in the Melbourne Public Library: Redmond Barry's Instructions to the Agent-General December 3rd 1853*. Melbourne: Ancora

Pagler, M. M. 1997, *Theme Restaurant Design, Entertainment & Fun Dining*. New York: McGraw Hill

Pagni, M. 2002, Stibbert – l'Acqua – il Tempietto Egizio, in *L'Egitto e Alessandria in Italia e nelle Marche. Egittofilomania da Augusto ai Nostri Giorni, in Memoria di Evaristo Breccia*, 71–73. Offagna: Accademia della Crescia

Pantazzi, M. 1994a, The "Egyptian Room" in Thomas Hope's House, Duchess Street, London, in J-M. Humbert, M. Pantazzi and C. Ziegler (eds), *Egyptomania. Egypt in Western Art, 1730–1930*, 186–188. Paris and Ottawa: Réunion des Musées Nationaux/National Gallery of Canada

Pantazzi, M. 1994b, "Pendule" in Thomas Hope's House, Duchess Street, London, in J-M. Humbert, M. Pantazzi and C. Ziegler (eds), *Egyptomania. Egypt in Western Art, 1730–1930*, 192–193. Paris and Ottawa: Réunion des Musées Nationaux/National Gallery of Canada

Pantazzi, M. 1994c, The "Boudoir" in Thomas Hope's House, Duchess Street, London, in J-M. Humbert, M. Pantazzi and C. Ziegler (eds), *Egyptomania. Egypt in Western Art, 1730–1930*, 196–197. Paris and Ottawa: Réunion des Musées Nationaux/National Gallery of Canada

Pantazzi, M. 1994d, The Seventh Plague of Egypt, in J-M. Humbert, M. Pantazzi and C. Ziegler (eds), *Egyptomania. Egypt in Western Art, 1730–1930*, 372–373. Paris and Ottawa: Réunion des Musées Nationaux/National Gallery of Canada

Pantazzi, M. 1994e, Three Designs for the Suspension Bridge on the Neva at St Petersburg, in J-M. Humbert, M. Pantazzi and C. Ziegler (eds), *Egyptomania. Egypt in Western Art, 1730–1930*, 322–393. Paris and Ottawa: Réunion des Musées Nationaux/National Gallery of Canada

Parent, C. 1985, La Pyramide à l'envers. *Le Monde*, 14–15 April, 2

Parigi, E. 1998, Idea di Giardino Moderno, in G. Pettena, P. Pietrogrande and M. Pozzana (eds), *Giardini Parchi Paesaggi. L'Avventura delle Idee in Toscana dall'Ottocento a Oggi*, 106–109. Florence: Le Lettere

Parry, E. C. 1988, *The Art of Thomas Cole: Ambition and Imagination*. Newark: University of Delaware Press

Parsons, A. L. 1952, *The Alexandrian Library*. New York: Elsevier

Partington, C. F. 1835, *National History and Views of London and its Environs*. London: Black and Armstrong

Patetta, L. 1991, *L'Architettura dell' Eclettismo. Fonti, Teorie, Modelli, 1750–1900*. Milan: Città Studi

Paul, C. 2000, *Making a Prince's Museum*. Los Angeles: Getty Research Institute

Pearce, S. 2000, Giovanni Battista Belzoni's Exhibition of the Reconstructed Tomb of Pharaoh Seti I in 1821. *Journal of the History of Collections* 12, 109–125

Penny Magazine 1838, New Egyptian Room, British Museum. 10 November, 436–438

Percier, C. and P. F. L. Fontaine 1812, *Recueil de décorations intérieures*. Paris: Percier and Fontaine

Petri, S. 1981, Miguel Dutra: O poliédrico artista paulista, in P. M. Bardi, *Miguel Dutra: O Poliédrico Artista Paulista*, 2–7. São Paulo: Museu de Arte Paulista

Petrov, A. N. and G. N. Bulgakov 1976, *Architectural Monuments of Leningrad*. Leningrad: Stroiizdat

Petrov, A. N., E. A. Borisova and A. P. Naumenko 1969, *Pamyatniki Arkhitektury Leningrada*. Leningrad: Stroiizdat

Pevsner, N. 1968, *Studies in Art, Architecture and Design. Volume I. From Mannerism to Romanticism.* London: Thames and Hudson

Pevsner, N. and S. Lang 1968, The Egyptian Revival, in N. Pevsner (ed.), *Studies in Art, Architecture and Design. Volume I: From Mannerism to Romanticism*, 232. London: Thames and Hudson

Phillips, H. 1986, La Filosofia del Giardino-Parco Inglese del '700, in A. Vezzosi (ed.), *Il Giardino Romantico*, 90–91. Florence: Alinea

Phillips, S. 1854, *Guide to the Crystal Palace and Park*. London: Crystal Palace Library

Picton-Seymour, D. 1977, *Victorian Buildings in South Africa, Including Edwardian and Transvaal Republican Styles, 1850–1910: A Survey of Houses, Churches, Schools, Public and Commercial Buildings with Notes on the Materials used, the Architects Concerned, the use of Prefabricated Ironmongery and the Influence of European Styles*. Cape Town: Balkema

Picture of London 1805, *The Picture of London, for 1805 Being a Correct Guide to all the Curiosities, Amusements, Exhibitions, Public Establishments, and Remarkable Objects, in and near London*. London: R. Phillips

Pierce, P. D. 1980, Deciphering Egypt: Four Studies in the American Sublime, unpublished PhD dissertation, Yale University

Pike, D. (ed.) 1967, *Australian Dictionary of Biography, Vol. 2: 1788–1850 I–Z*. Melbourne: Melbourne UP

Pingeot, A. 1989, Le Décor extérieur du Louvre sur la cour Carrée et la rue de Rivoli (1851–1936). *Revue du Louvre et des Musées de France* 2, 97–111

Piotrovsky, B., N. B. Landa and I. A. Lapis 1974, *Egyptian Antiquities in the Hermitage*. Leningrad: Aurora Art Publishers

Piranesi, G. B. 1769, *An Apologetical Essay in Defence of the Egyptian and Etruscan Architecture. With Diverse Maniere d'Adornare i Cammini*. Rome: Salomoni

Pococke, R. 1743–1745, *A Description of the East and Some Other Countries*. London: W. Bowyer

Poggi, G. 1909, *Ricordi della Vita e Documenti d'Arte*. Florence: R. Bemporad

Pohlmann, U. 1997, Alma-Tadema and Photography, in E. Becker, E. Morris, E. Prettejohn and J. Treuherz (eds), *Sir Lawrence Alma-Tadema*. Exhibition Catalogue, 111–114, Walker Art Gallery, Liverpool, and Van Gogh Museum, Amsterdam. New York: Rizzoli

Polenov, F. D. 1982, *Polenovo: The Vasily Polenov Museum Estate*. Moscow: 'Sovietsaya Rossiia'

Polyzoides, S., R. Sherwood and J. Tice 1992, *Courtyard Housing in Los Angeles: A Typological Analysis*. 2nd edition, Princeton: Princeton Architectural Press

Pomarède, V. 1998, *La Mort de Sardanapale*, Collection solo 9. Paris: Musée du Louvre

Porter, B. and R. L. B. Moss 1972, *Topographical Bibliography of Ancient Egyptian Hieroglyphic Texts, Reliefs, and Paintings. Vol II, Theban Temples*. Oxford: Griffith Institute

Potts, T., M. Legge and A. Dunsmore 1997, Antiquities in Australia: New Antiquities Galleries at the National Gallery of Victoria, Melbourne. *Minerva* 8, 35–39

Pozzana, M. 1996, Giuseppe Poggi Architetto di Giardini, in P. F. Bagatti Valsecchi and A. Kipar (eds), *Il Giardino Paesaggistico tra Settecento e Ottocento in Italia e in Germania. Villa Vigoni e l'Opera di Giuseppe Balzaretto*, 109–118. Milan: Guerini e Associati

Prisse d'Avennes, A-C. T-E. 1878, *Atlas de l'histoire de l'art Égyptien, d'après les monuments, depuis les temps les plus reculés jusqu'à la domination Romaine* II. Paris: A. Bertrand

Pugin, A. W. B. 1843, *An Apology for the Revival of Christian Architecture in England*. Oxford: St Barnabas

Quer, C. S. 1996, De la Vallée des Rois à la "Valle de los Caídos", in J-M. Humbert (ed.), *L'Égyptomanie à l'épreuve de l'archéologie*, 305–341. Paris and Brussels: Musée du Louvre and Gram

Quick, R. 1970, *The Life and Works of Edwin Long, R. A.* 2nd edition, Bournemouth: Art Gallery and Museums

Raaven, M. 1980, Alma Tadema als Amateur-Egyptoloog. *Bulletin van het Rijksmuseum* 28, 103–117

Randall, J. 1806, *Architectural Designs for Mansions, Villas, Lodges and Cottages*. London: J. Taylor

Rapoport, V., A. A. Aleksandrov and E. I. Steinert 1984, *Arkhangelskoye: A Country Estate of the 18th and 19th Centuries*. Leningrad: Aurora

Rebold, E. 1851, *Histoire générale de la franc-maçonnerie*. Paris: A. Franck

Reeves, N. and R. Wilkinson 1996, *The Complete Valley of the Kings*. London: Thames and Hudson

Reilly, R. 1989, *Wedgwood*. London: Macmillan

Reinhardt, H. 1989, L'Influence de la franc-maçonnerie dans les jardins du XVIIIe siècle, in C. Cresti (ed.), *Massoneria e Architettura. Convegno di Firenze 1988*, 87–94. Foggia: Bastogi

Renouvier, J. 1863, *Histoire de l'art pendant la révolution*. Paris: Vve J. Renouard

Repository of Arts, Literature, Commerce, Manufactures, Fashions and Politics, 1809. London: R. Ackermann

Rice, M. and S. MacDonald 2003, Introduction – Tea with a Mummy: The Consumer's View of Egypt's Immemorial Appeal, in S. MacDonald and M. Rice (eds), *Consuming Ancient Egypt*, 1–22. London: UCL Press

Rich, P. and D. Merchant 2001, The Egyptian Influence on Nineteenth-Century Freemasonry. *Heredom, The Transactions of the Scottish Rite Research Society* 9, 33–51

Richards, E. G. 1998, *Mapping Time. The Calendar and its History*. Oxford: OUP

Robbins, B. 1998, Actually Existing Cosmopolitanism, in P. Cheah and B. Robbins (eds), *Cosmopolitics: Thinking and Feeling Beyond Nations*, 1–20. Minneapolis: Minnesota Press

Roberts, D. and W. Brockedon 1846–1849, *Egypt and Nubia from Drawings Made on the Spot by David Roberts R. A., with Historical Descriptions by William Brockedon*. London: F. G. Moon

Romi 1969, Le Calendrier de la Gloire, ou comment Bonaparte a fait Napoléon. *Le Crapouillot* 8, 29–59

Roos, F. Jr 1940, The Egyptian Style: Notes on Early American Taste. *Magazine of Art* 33 (4), 218–223

Rosellini, I. B. 1832–1844, *I Monumenti dell'Egitto e della Nubia*. Pisa: Niccolo Capurro

Rosenblum R. and H. W. Janson 1984, *19th-Century Art*. New York: Harry N. Abrams

Roullet, A. 1972, *The Egyptian and Egyptianizing Monuments of Imperial Rome*. Leiden: Brill

Said, E. 2001, Clash of Definitions, in E. Said (ed.), *Reflections on Exile and Other Literary and Cultural Essays*, 569–593. London: Granta

Salt, H. 1825, *Essay on Dr. Young's and M. Champollion's Phonetic System of Hieroglyphics: With Some Additional Discoveries, by which it may be Applied to Decipher the Names of Ancient Kings of Egypt and Ethiopia*. London: Longman

Sarian, M. S. 1976, *Fragments de ma vie*. Moscow: Editions du Progrès

Saunders, D. 1966, *Historic Buildings of Victoria*. Melbourne: Jacaranda

Sayers, C. E. 1965, *David Syme, A Life*. Melbourne, Canberra, Marrickville: Cheshire Pty Ltd

Schadla-Hall, T. and G. Morris 2003, Ancient Egypt on the Small Screen – From Fact to Faction in the UK, in S. MacDonald and M. Rice (eds), *Consuming Ancient Egypt*, 195–216. London: UCL Press

Schemm, P. 2000, Alexandria's Rebirth. *Middle Eastern Times*, 24 May, 1–3

Schmidt, E. 1986, *Ägypten und Ägyptische Mythologie. Bilder der Transition im Werk Andrej Belyjs*. Munich: Sagner

Schnitzler, B. 2003, Hijacked Images: Ancient Egypt in French Commercial Advertising, in S. MacDonald and M. Rice (eds), *Consuming Ancient Egypt*, 165–174. London: UCL Press

Scott, G. D. III 1992, *Temple, Tomb and Dwelling: Egyptian Antiquities from the Harer Family Trust Collection*. San Bernardino: University Art Gallery, California State University

Seal, M. 1990, The Last Temptation of Isaac Tigrett. *American Way*, 1 November, 71–76, 142–146

Searle, P. 1992, Syme Memorial – 1908 Boroondara General Cemetery, Kew, Victoria, unpublished thesis, Department of Architectural Technology, Royal Melbourne Institute of Technology

Seipel, W. (ed.) 1998, *Mumien aus dem Alten Ägypten. Zur Mumienforschung im Kunsthistorischen Museum*. Milan: Skira

Semionova, I. 1981, *Ostankino: Eighteenth-Century Country Estate*. Leningrad: Aurora

Serafy, S. 2003, Egypt in Hollywood: Pharaohs of the Fifties, in S. MacDonald and M. Rice (eds), *Consuming Ancient Egypt*, 77–86. London: UCL Press

Serageldin, I. 2001, The Revival of the Bibliotecha Alexandrina. Talk given at the Egyptian Cultural Centre, Piccadilly, London, December

Serle, P. 1949, *Dictionary of Australian Biography, Vol. 1*. Sydney and London: Angus and Robertson

Shand, P. M. 1930, *Modern Theatres and Cinemas*. London: Batsford

Siliotti, A. (ed.) 2001, *Belzoni's Travels. Narrative of the Operations and Research Discoveries in Egypt and Nubia*. London: British Museum Press

Skinner, J. S. 1997, *Form and Fancy: Factories and Factory Buildings of Wallis, Gilbert and Partners, 1916–1939*. Liverpool: Liverpool UP

Sky, A. and M. Stone 1983, *Unbuilt America: Forgotten Architecture in the United States from Thomas Jefferson to the Space Age*. New York: McGraw Hill

Smith, F. W. 1900, *National Galleries of History and Art: The Aggrandizement of Washington*, Parts I–III. US Senate, 56th Congress, 1st Session, Document No. 209

Smith, G. 1808, *A Collection of Designs for Household Furniture and Interior Decoration*. London: J. Taylor

Smith, S. 1807, Review of Hope's 'Household Furniture and Interior Decoration'. *Edinburgh Review*, July, 478–486

Smyth, C. P. 1867, *Life and Work at the Great Pyramid During the Months of January, February, March and April, AD 1865: With a Discussion of the Facts Ascertained*. Edinburgh: Edmonston and Douglas

Sokolova, T. and K. Orlova 1973, *Russian Furniture in the Collection of the Hermitage*. Leningrad: Khudozhnik Russian Socialist Federal Soviet Republic

Solé, R. 1997, *L'Égypte, passion française*. Paris: Seuil

Sotheby and Co. 1972, *Costumes and Curtains from the Diaghilev and the Basil Ballets*. London: Sotheby Parke-Bernet

Southey, R. 1807, *Letters from England*. 1951 edition ed. J. Simmons. London: Cresset

Sparks, R. T. 2003, Egyptian Stone Vessels and the Politics of Exchange (2617–1070 BC), in R. Matthews and C. Roemer (eds), *Ancient Perspectives on Egypt*, 39–56. London: UCL Press

Spivak, G. C. 1998, Cultural Talks in the Hot Peace: Revisiting the "Global Village", in P. Cheah and B. Robbins (eds), *Cosmopolitics: Thinking and Feeling Beyond Nations*, 329–351. Minneapolis: Minnesota Press

Sponenburgh, M. 1956, Egyptian Influence in the Sculpture of the United States. *Bulletin de l'Institut d'Égypte* 37, 2, Session 1954–1955, 153–167, figs. I–VII

Staehelin, E. 1990, Zum Motiv der Pyramiden als Prüfungs- und Einweihungsstätten, in S. Israelit-Groll (ed.), *Studies in Egyptology Presented to Miriam Lichtheim*, II, 889–932. Jerusalem: Magness Press, Hebrew University

Staehelin, E. and B. Jaeger (eds) 1997, *Ägypten-Bilder. Akten des ‚Symposions zur Ägypten-Rezeption', Augst bei Basel, vom 9–11 September 1993*. Freiburg: Universitätsverlag

Stanton, J. 1998, Coney Island – Thompson and Dundy, unpublished paper, http://naid.sppsr.ucla.edu/coneyisland/articles/thompson&dundy.htm

Stayton, K. 1990, Revivalism and the Egyptian Movement, in B. Bloeminck, K. Stayton, B. Sigler and L. Hilgemann, *The Sphinx and the Lotus: The Egyptian Movement in American Decorative Arts, 1865–1935*, 5–10. New York: Hudson River Museum

Stern, R., G. Gilmartin and T. Mellins 1987, *New York, 1930, Architecture and Urbanism Between the Two World Wars*. New York: Rizzoli

Stille, A. 2000, Resurrecting Alexandria – Can Rebuilding the Great Library also Redeem the City? *The New Yorker*, 18 May, 90–99

Streidt, G. and K. Frahm 1996, *Potsdam*. Cologne: Konemann

Survey of London 1960, 29, The Parish of St James Westminster, South of Piccadilly, 266–270

Swanson, V. 1977, *Sir Lawrence Alma-Tadema: The Painter of the Victorian Vision of the Ancient World*. London: Ash and Grant

Swanson, V. 1990, *The Biography and Catalogue Raisonné of the Paintings of Sir Lawrence Alma-Tadema*. London: Garton and Co

Sweet, J. 1996, Empire, Emigration and the Decorative Arts: Australian Representation at International Exhibitions 1862–1886, in H. C. Collinson (ed.), *Victorian. The Style of Empire*, 103–120. Toronto: Royal Ontario Museum

Sweet, J. 2001, The Gold Pyramid, in C. T. Stannage (ed.), *Gold and Civilisation*, 90–91. Sydney: Beagle

Tagliolini, A. 1994, *Storia del Giardino Italiano*. Florence: Ponte alle Grazie

Tanner, J. 2003, Finding the Egyptian in Early Greek Art, in R. Matthews and C. Roemer (eds), *Ancient Perspectives on Egypt*, 115–144. London UCL Press

Terrasson, J. 1731, *Sethos, histoire ou vie tirée des monuments et anecdotes de l'ancienne Égypte*. Paris: J. Guérin

Theatre of the Fraternity 1896–1929, Frederick R. Weisman Art Museum, University of Minnesota. Minnesota: University Press of Mississippi

Thornton, L. 1994, *Women As Portrayed in Orientalist Painting*. Paris: Editions ACR

Thornton, P. and D. Watkin 1987, New Light on the Hope Mansion in Duchess Street. *Apollo* 126, 307

Thory, C. A. 1815, *Chronologie de l'histoire de la franche-maçonnerie Française et étrangère, II*. Paris: P-E. Dufort

Tikhomirov, N. Y. 1955, *Arkhitektura podmoskovnykh usadeb*. Moscow: Gosizdatel'stvu Literatury po Stroitelstvu i Arkhitekture

Timbs, J. 1867, *Curiosities of London Exhibiting the Most Rare and Remarkable Objects of Interest in the Metropolis*. London: Virtue and Company

Times of Philadelphia 1876, Centennial, April 27

Trigger, B. G. 1995, Egyptology, Ancient Egypt, and the American Imagination, in N. Thomas (ed.), *The American Discovery of Ancient Egypt*, 21–35. Los Angeles: Los Angeles County Museum of Art

Trotta, G. 1990, *Villa Strozzi al Boschetto*. Florence: Messaggerie Toscane

Tudesq, A-J. 1965, *L'Élection présidentielle de Louis-Napoléon Bonaparte*. Paris: Librairie Armand Colin

Turner, J. (ed.) 1996, *The Dictionary of Art*, Vol. 3. London: Macmillan

Tzalas, H. 1999, *Farewell to Alexandria*. Egypt: American University in Cairo Press

Ucko, P. J. 2001, Unprovenanced Material Culture and Freud's Collection of Antiquities. *Journal of Material Culture* 6, 269–322

Ucko, P. J. and T. C. Champion (eds) 2003, *The Wisdom of Egypt: changing visions through the ages*. London: UCL Press

United States Customs Service 1876, Notebook of the Egyptian Commission. Unpublished Records of the National Archives, Mid Atlantic Region, Philadelphia

Van Bart, M. 1993, Stabilisering van ou Boumateriaal dalk groot Deurbraak. *Bylae Die Burger*, 20 March, 4

Van Daele, P. and R. Lumby 1997, *A Spirit of Progress. Art Déco Architecture in Australia*. Sydney: Craftesman

Van Schoor, M. C. E. 1993, *Die Nasionale Vrouemonument*. Bloemfontein: Oorlogsmuseum

Van Zanten, D. 1987, *Designing Paris: The Architecture of Duban, Labrouste, Duc, and Vaudoyer*. Cambridge, Mass: MIT Press

Vanished City 1893, *The Vanished City, The World's Columbian Exposition in Pen and Picture*. Chicago, New York, London, Paris, Berlin: The Werner Company

Venturi, R. 1977, *Complexity and Contradiction in Architecture*. London: Architectural Press

Vercoutter, J. 1992, *The Search for Ancient Egypt*. London: Thames and Hudson

Vityazeva, V. A. and B. M. Kirikov 1986, *Leningrad: Putevoditel'*. Leningrad: Lenizdat

Vyse, H. 1841, *Operations Carried on at the Pyramids of Gizeh in 1837, Vol. 2*. London: Fraser

Vyse, H. 1842, *Operations Carried out at the Pyramids of Gizeh in 1837, Vol. 3*. London: Fraser

Wagner, A. 1997, Outrages: Sculpture and Kingship in France after 1789, in A. Bermingham and J. Brewer (eds), *The Consumption of Culture 1600–1800*, 294–318. London: Routledge

Walker S. 2003, Carry-on at Canopus: the Nilotic Mosaic from Palestrina and Roman Attitudes to Egypt, in R. Matthews and C. Roemer (eds), *Ancient Perspectives on Egypt*, 191–202. London: UCL Press

Wallis, T. 1933a, Factories I. *Journal of the Royal Institute of British Architects*, 25 February, 301–312

Wallis, T. 1933b, Factories II. *Journal of the Royal Institute of British Architects*, 11 March, 367–368

Warren, J. C. 1823, Description of an Egyptian Mummy, Presented to the Massachusetts General Hospital: With an Account of the Operation of Embalming, in Ancient and Modern Times. *Boston Journal of Philosophy and the Arts* 164–179, 269–287

Washington, P. 1993, *Madame Blavatsky's Baboon. Theosophy and the Emergence of the Western Guru*. London: Secker and Warburg

Watkin, D. 1968, *Thomas Hope, 1769–1831, and the Neo-Classical Idea*. London: John Murray

Watkin, D. 1974, *The Life and Work of C. R. Cockerell*. London: Zwemmer

Watkin, D. 1996, *Sir John Soane: Enlightenment Thought and the Royal Academy Lectures*. Cambridge: CUP

Waugh, D. C. 1977, Azbuka Znakami Lits: Egyptian Hieroglyphs in the Privy Chancellery Archive. *Oxford Slavonic Papers* 10, 46–50

Weber, B. 1988, Tut, Tut. *New York Times Magazine*, 18 December, 102

Weisse, J. A. 1880, *The Obelisk and Freemasonry according to the discoveries of Belzoni and Commander Gorringe*. New York: J. W. Boston

West, D. M. 1980, *Mandelstam: The Egyptian Stamp*. Birmingham: University of Birmingham

Westmacott, C. M. 1834, *British Galleries of Painting and Sculpture, Comprising a General Historical and Critical Catalogue, with Separate Notices of Every Work of Fine Art in the Principal Collections*. London: Sherwood, Jones and Co

Whitehouse, H. 1995, Egypt in European Thought, in J. M. Sasson (ed.), *Civilizations of the Ancient Near East*, 15–31. New York: Charles Scribner's Sons

Whitehouse, H. 1996, L'Égypte sous la neige, in J-M. Humbert, *L'Égyptomanie à l'épreuve de l'archéologie*, 161–186. Paris and Brussels: Musée du Louvre and Gram

Whiteley, J. 2001, Jean-Léon Gérôme: View of the Nile at Luxor. *The Ashmolean* 41, 18

Wildung, D. 2003, Looking Back into the Future: The Middle Kingdom as a Bridge to the Past, in J. Tait (ed.), '*Never had the like occurred': Egypt's view of its past*, 61–78. London: UCL Press

Wilkinson, J. G. 1837, *The Manners and Customs of the Ancient Egyptians*. London: J. Murray

Wille, J-G. 1857, *Mémoires et journal*. Paris: Vve J. Renouard

Willms, J. 1997, *Paris: Capital of Europe From the Revolution to the Belle Epoque*. New York: Holmes and Meier

Wilson, E. 1877–1878, *Cleopatra's Needle, with Notes on Egypt and Egyptian Obelisks*. London: Brain and Co

Wilson, M. J. 1984, *William Kent, Designer, Painter, Gardener*. Boston, Melbourne: Routledge and Kegan Paul

Wischermann, H. 1997, *Paris: An Architectural Guide*. Paris: Arsenale Editrice

Wischnitzer, R. 1975, The Egyptian Revival in Synagogue Architecture, in J. Gutman (ed.), *The Synagogue: Studies in Origins, Archaeology and Architecture*, 334–350. New York: Ktav

Woldman, D. 1983, Des Architectes pour les usines du XXe siècle. *Monuments Historiques* 128, 72

Woronzoff, A. 1990, The Hieroglyph in Andrej Belyj's Peterburg: A Reading of Sisnarfné/ Enfransis. *Slavic and East European Journal* 34, 30–39

Yerasimos, S. 1999, Cosmopolitanism: Assumed Alienation, in R. Meijer (ed.), *Cosmopolitanism, Identity and Authenticity in the Middle East*, 35–43. London: Curzon

Young, J. Z. 1973, Chairman's Introduction, in Professor Lord Zuckerman (ed.), *The Concepts of Human Evolution*, 167–168. London: Academic Press

Yoyotte, J. 1959, in G. Posener, *Dictionnaire de la civilisation égyptienne*. Paris: Hazan

Zangheri, L. 1984, Alle Origini dell'Architettura Moderna. L'Opera di Giuseppe e Alessandro Manetti, e di Carlo Reishammer, in L. Zangheri (ed.), *Alla Scoperta della Toscana Lorenese. Architettura e Bonifiche*, 15–30. Florence: Edam

Zoo d'Anvers 1988, no. 4, April, 1–53

Zubaida, S. 1999, Cosmopolitanism and the Middle East, in R. Meijer (ed.), *Cosmopolitanism, Identity and Authenticity in the Middle East*, 15–35. London: Curzon

Zukowsky, J. 1976, Monumental American Obelisks: Centennial Vistas. *The Art Bulletin* 58, 574–581

Index

Note: figure numbers are denoted in bold type.